Unrepentant Leftist

Unrepentant Leftist

A Lawyer's Memoir

Victor Rabinowitz

University of Illinois Press

Urbana and Chicago

© 1996 by the Board of Trustees of the University of Illinois
Manufactured in the United States of America
C   5   4   3   2   1

This book is printed on acid-free paper.

Library of Congress Cataloging-in-Publication Data
Rabinowitz, Victor.
Unrepentant leftist : a lawyer's memoir / Victor Rabinowitz.
p.   cm.
Includes index.
ISBN 0-252-02253-X (cloth)
1. Rabinowitz, Victor. 2. Lawyers—United States—Biography.
3. Civil rights movements—United States—History—20th century.
4. Peace movements—United States—History—20th century.
5. Socialism—United States—History—20th century. I. Title.
KF373.R23A3   1996
340'.092—dc20
[B]   95-50239
                                                                CIP

To Joanne, Joni, Peter, and Mark

Contents

Preface

This is a memoir of my professional and political life over a period of six decades. Those years have seen United States involvement in three shooting wars and one cold war, the rise (and fall) of a militant trade union movement, a socialist revolution in Cuba, the civil rights movement of the early sixties, the antiwar movement of the later sixties and seventies, the free speech movement of the seventies, and the collapse of the Soviet Union and the Eastern European bloc of socialist nations. Each of these events has impinged on my politics, my legal practice, and my life. From the time I walked into the offices of Boudin, Cohn, and Glickstein in 1938, to the day before yesterday, things have been happening, and the impulse to tell about them all is nearly irresistible.

But that impulse had to be resisted, or this manuscript would never have been finished. And so I have had to make a lot of hard choices. Several arguments in the United States Supreme Court have been omitted altogether. Much of my work in the trade union movement in the forties and fifties and again in the eighties has also been omitted or given short shrift. There's much about Cuba in this volume, but I've left out as much as I've included. The same is true about the American Labor party and the Communist party. Despite the urge to write more and more, wiser heads have advised me that more is not necessarily better.

Eric Hobsbawm, in *The Age of Extremes,* an excellent history of the "Short Twentieth Century" from 1914 to 1991, wisely observes that the dichotomy "capitalist/socialist" is political, rather than analytical, and it is in the political sense that I use those terms. The varieties of capitalism and socialism are many, and some are "better" than others. To avoid misunderstanding, let me set forth my credo from the outset.

I've been a Marxist and a socialist virtually all of my adult life. My goal is an egalitarian, compassionate, peaceful, and democratic society, marked by an economic system that provides enough food, clothing, and shelter for everyone, the opportunity for gainful employment, and protection against disastrous illness or disability. I am not sure whether those goals can ever be reached, but I am sure they're not attainable under an economic and social system built on the private ownership of the means of production, the driving force of which is to accumulate more and more capital. Further, I believe that the continued existence of human civilization as we know it will not be possible under a highly competitive capitalist economic regime.

And so I seek a solution in an economic system built on the collective ownership of property, in which production is not for profit but for use. The failure of the attempt to establish such a state up to this time merely means that we need to try again. Until we get there, there are many intermediate causes to be fought for—that's what I've tried to do.

I recognize that I'm a lawyer and not a professional revolutionary, but I found early that the law can be used to advance the cause of social justice. That knowledge does not come automatically with a law school diploma. After a few years as a very junior lawyer to whom were assigned routine corporate and patent law cases, I came to the conclusion that I wasn't using my legal talents, such as they were, to bring about the better world I dreamed of. Furthermore, I was bored and found that it didn't matter much to me whether my clients won or lost—many of them didn't deserve to win anyhow. By a stroke of luck, I had a chance for a job with a firm representing trade unions. I grabbed at that chance, and the broad outlines of my legal career and my life were set. Trade unions, free speech, the Cuban revolution, civil rights, resistance to the Vietnam War—these were the causes that occupied me and my late law partner, Leonard Boudin, for the ensuing years. I doubt I brought socialism any closer, but I've done my best and, at least in retrospect, I've enjoyed all of it.

This volume is my story.

∎

The reader of this book will, I assume, understand that there are many lawyers not mentioned in this memoir who have been associated with our firm, most of whom shared our perspective and all of whom worked diligently in the service of our clients. Some have gone into academia; some into public service; many into private practice. Some have quit the law and a few have died.

There are many such colleagues and I'll try to list them all. I hope I haven't forgotten anyone. If I have, I apologize up front: Gloria Agrin, Mark Barenberg, Emily M. Bass, Linda Bosniak, Dorian Bowman, Mary Ellen Burns, Edward Copeland, Susan Davis, Laurie Edelstein, Thomas Fox, Sheila Ginsberg, Kristin Booth Glen, Joan Goldberg, David Goldstein, David Golove, Terry Gross, Laurence Helfer, Cheryl R. Howard, Gordon L. Johnson, Herbert Jordan, Sanford Katz, Mary M. Kaufman, Judith Levin, Jules Lobel, Michael Ludwig, Beth Margolis, Louise Melling, Nicolas E. Poser, Hillary Richard, Margarita Rosa, David Rosenberg, Caroline Rule, Arthur Schutzer, Katherine Stone, Elizabeth St. Clair, Susan D. Susman, Simon Taylor, Thomas C. Viles, K. Randlett Walster, Henry Winestine, Adrian Wing, and Ellen J. Winner.

■

Joan Whitman read the whole manuscript for this book in its earliest stages and made many valuable suggestions, not only as to content but also as to structure. Professor Eric Foner took time off from his work at Cambridge University to write an extensive critique of the book at a later stage. Moses Foner also read the manuscript and supplied much encouragement. Professor Jules Lobel likewise sent his comments along, with special emphasis and thought on the Cuba section. Judy Crichton read and made valuable suggestions as to the first half of the book. My son Peter contributed helpful advice. John Simon has been available at all times to supply information and to argue disputed points of theory and history. Mike Standard has contributed his thoughts as well, as did Sally Belfrage shortly before her sad death.

Other specialists read parts of the manuscript at various times: my sister, Lucille, on our childhood and parents; Ernest Goodman, Ann Ginger, and Doris Walker on the National Lawyers Guild; and my daughter Joni on her chapter. They didn't all agree with my interpretation of events or even with my memory, but they expressed their opinions nevertheless. Michael Neville, Marney Kliever, and Knoll Lowrey contributed valuable research services. In the final days of writing, Susan Braudy asked many questions, provided many answers, and helped a great deal with the photographs.

Several years ago, I dictated an oral history for the Oral History Research Office of Columbia University, with the help of Lenore Hogan and Professor Norman Silber of Hofstra University Law School. That extended interview was of great help in the writing of this book.

I need not add that my wife, Joanne, has supplied her stamp of approval or frown of disapproval on virtually every word. She's a tough editor.

To this I append the customary notice that I alone am responsible for what appears herein, despite all the sage advice given. To the Taminent Institute, my thanks; for anyone who writes on political topics or on historical subjects touching on labor or political events, its library is an invaluable resource.

Finally, my deepest appreciation goes to my secretary, Kezia Gleckman Hayman, who was able to get my thoughts from inside my head to this piece of paper with unexcelled skill and good humor.

Prologue

One day early in October 1955 I stepped into a crowded elevator in the Statler Hotel in Buffalo, where I was representing a number of trade unionists who had been subpoenaed to appear before the House Committee on Un-American Activities (HUAC). Richard Arens boarded the elevator on the next floor. He had been, at various times, counsel to HUAC and to the Sub-Committee on Internal Security of the Senate Judiciary Committee (SISS), and he worked full time in attempting to destroy the lives of friends of mine—both political and personal. Consequently he and I had tangled many times at hearings of one or the other of those committees since 1951. As the committees traveled around the country and clients of mine were subpoenaed, I also traveled and generally found Arens there. This happened in Memphis; it happened in Gary, Indiana; in Philadelphia; in Washington; in New York; and this time in Buffalo. The very first time we met, in 1951, he had served a subpoena on me personally, and on a later occasion he had come close to assaulting me. I despised him, and I suppose he didn't care much for me either.

Nevertheless, when I met him in the hotel elevator, he suggested that I join him at breakfast before the hearing. I accepted after a brief hesitation. That, I guess, is the style between lawyers—like the time Joe McCarthy threw his arms around me in an affectionate bear hug in front of fifty astonished spectators. The breakfast with Arens started off with the usual small talk: the weather, a visit to Niagara Falls ("better view from the un-American side," I suggested), how long will the hearings last, how many more witnesses are there, and so on.

Then, Arens said, "Do you have a family?" "Yes." "Do you have any children?" "Yes." "How old are they?" "A girl aged twelve and a boy aged ten." Then, said Arens, "And do they believe in God?" I was surprised; he seemed a bit rude, on our first social contact, but I answered that I didn't really know, because I hadn't asked them recently. It was his turn to be shocked. "Didn't you raise them to believe in God?" I said, perhaps disingenuously, that I hadn't tried to influence them in one way or the other, and I had told them, when they raised the question, that they would have to decide for themselves. Arens followed up: "If you aren't raising them to believe in God, you're making a terrible mistake." I asked him why he thought so. "People can be saved from acting in a wrongful and sinful fashion only through a belief in God. How can they be trusted to act properly otherwise?"

I told him that I thought my children were well brought up. I had taught them as well as I could to accept certain moral principles, which had nothing to do with God. "Like what?" "To treat all other humans with respect; to refrain, so far as possible, from inflicting pain or distress upon anyone; to have concern and compassion for others less fortunate than they were." I was embarrassed that I would have to utter such platitudes to a grown man, but I didn't think it likely that I could convince him that I was right.

"That's all very well," said my companion, "but no one will obey these fine precepts unless they fear eternal punishment for wrongful conduct. Unless people believe that they will burn in hell for their sins, they will not refrain from sinning." I had, of course, heard such doctrine before, but never over a breakfast table. I understood that he was really advising me, and not my children.

I still haven't asked my children whether they believe in God. Probably they don't. If Arens's cosmology is true (and who can say for sure?), my whole family will probably burn in everlasting fire.

1

Where I Came From

On the way to visit Grandpa, Mom and I took the St. John's Place trolley to the end of the line, where we transferred to the New Lots trolley—very exciting, because the transfer point was at a terminal of the line and there were many trolleys moving in and out of barns. The ride on the New Lots trolley ran through the open fields of Brooklyn, allowing an occasional view of a live chicken or horse, quite different from the corner of Eastern Parkway and Howard Avenue, where we lived. We got off the trolley after a while—Snediker Avenue or Van Siclen or something like that—and walked a block or two to Grandpa's house on Schenck Avenue. Probably my sister, Lucille, two and a half years younger than I, was with us, and maybe my father, too, since he was very fond of Grandpa, but I only remember Mom, for sure.

I remember Grandpa, too. He seemed very old. He was in fact seventy-four years old, and I was only five or six. Every grownup, especially a man with a beard, seemed truly ancient. Like many Jewish male immigrants, especially the Orthodox ones, Grandpa had a full white beard. However, he was far from Orthodox. Some years later I decided from pictures of him around the house that he looked like Karl Marx, but in 1916 I suppose I had not yet heard of Marx. Grandpa, my mother's father, was very kind. He took me on his lap and he smelled of sweet tobacco. We didn't communicate much—in fact, we didn't communicate at all, since I spoke no Yiddish and, so far as I knew, he spoke no English. However he did give me JuJubes, a popular sweet of the day.

I was only one of several grandchildren. My mother and her sisters had seven children among them, but there were always other people around Grandpa's house—people I didn't really know. One of them was Mom's stepmother, and there were some stepsisters, too, and maybe a few stepcousins. Being familiar with the story of Cinderella, I assume that

Mom's stepmother and her stepsisters were very cruel, and Lucille thinks so, too, but I have no hard information on that subject.

Grandpa had another name, which I did not learn until much later. He was named Jacob Netter, and he was quite an important man in his circle. He was the author of several books in Yiddish and wrote for and sometimes edited several Yiddish anarchist newspapers, *Die Frei Arbeiter Stimme* and *Zsukunst*. Around him were gathered many other anarchists, including Emma Goldman and Alexander Berkman. Goldman made occasional references to the Netter family in her autobiography, giving it credit for supplying political support as well as groceries from Netter's store. Berkman inscribed on the flyleaf of a copy of his excellent book, *Memoirs of a Prison Anarchist,* a notation, addressed to my mother: "To my little friend, my former prison correspondent, Rose Rabinowitz, in memory of my Pennsylvania nightmare." Berkman had spent fourteen years in prison as a result of an unsuccessful attempt to assassinate Henry Clay Frick, chairman of the board of the Carnegie Steel Company, during a bitter strike at the Homestead Mills in Pittsburgh.

Netter's radicalism rubbed off on his children. The oldest of my mother's sisters, Annie, had married Michael A. Cohn, a very successful physician practicing in Brownsville, then a Jewish working-class section of Brooklyn. They were both part of the Goldman-Berkman set. Annie was active in street political work, and Michael, whose name in our family was simply "Uncle," was a frequent speaker at radical meetings in Brownsville, a hotbed of socialist/anarchist activity. I barely remember Aunt Annie. She died of cancer when I was nine and she had been ill for some time. But Uncle I knew very well. He was, of course, the family doctor. He was quite prosperous by the time I came along. He owned the house we lived in on Eastern Parkway and another house on President Street, near my home but considerably upscale economically and socially. He also owned a house in Seagate, which was very far up the social scale from Brownsville. He owned a Pierce Arrow, too, and employed a uniformed chauffeur, who was something of a neighborhood sensation when he picked me and my family up at our home for the drive to Seagate. That trip, like the one on the New Lots trolley, gave me a chance to see cows and goats grazing in Flatbush and Coney Island.

Shortly before Uncle died in 1939, or perhaps in his will, he gave me a copy of Trotsky's *History of the Russian Revolution,* which I have from time to time read together with the Stalinist version of the same events. He also left me a leather-bound multivolume set of the works of Tolstoy, a limited and numbered edition with volume 1 missing. I never read very much of that, and after my son Peter had grown up I gave the set to him. He still has it and may even occasionally read in it. It is a very impressive set of books, but I have never been a great Tolstoy fan.

Aunt Esther, another of Mom's sisters, was also a radical, ground down by poverty by the time I knew her. She was married to a man Mom often described to me as a socialist, but I barely knew him, except as a shadowy figure coughing his life away on a bed as he died of consumption. On the wall in their tiny dark apartment was a picture, framed in black, of the Haymarket Martyrs, four anarchists who were executed in Chicago in 1887. The men were convicted of murder, as a consequence of the bombing of a trade union meeting in Chicago the previous year. There is little doubt that none of the executed men were in fact guilty, and the labor movement of the time regarded them as heroes. Years later, Illinois's governor, John Peter Altgeld, declared the 1886 trial to have been unfair and pardoned several others who had been sentenced to long prison terms.

Mom, whose name was Rose, was the youngest of the siblings and the only one to live beyond the age of fifty. Pictures of her taken in her early womanhood show her to have been very beautiful, and I remember her as such. She was very quiet in manner. Her political views were like the others expressed in the Netter household, but she was completely overshadowed by my father, an energetic, ambitious, and capable man, whose life resembled that of a Horatio Alger hero.

Pop (first name Louis) came to this country from Rossein, a small village in Lithuania, at the age of sixteen, shortly after the death of his father, who had been rabbi of the village. He had received a rigid Orthodox Jewish education, which he repudiated with energy as soon as he got away from home. He was not only an atheist but a militant one. Charles Darwin was one of his great heroes, and he told of how, after he came to this country, he sat in the library at Cooper Union trying to teach himself English by reading simultaneously a copy of *The Descent of Man* and a dictionary. After some weeks of this, a kindly librarian told him that there were other, and easier, ways of learning English, namely to substitute *The Adventures of Huckleberry Finn* for Darwin. Pop eventually spoke English quite well, but always with a heavy accent.

Somehow he fell into the Netter circle as a very young man and was soon deeply involved in debates over anarchist theory. Family tradition has it that he was courting one of the other girls in the Netter household—I suppose one of my mother's cruel stepsisters—when, on the trolley en route to Netter's house, he met my mother, bound for the same destination. They were married in 1910.

Pop was very fond of Jacob Netter. Many years later, perhaps in 1951 or 1952, in the course of a family dinner at which my parents, my wife, Marcia, and I were present, together with Lucille and her husband, Sam, Mom produced an old clipping from the *Jewish Daily Forward* that she'd come across while doing some housecleaning. The *Forward* was a well-established Yiddish socialist paper that had, on the occasion of Netter's death, printed a laudatory obituary. My mother gave the clipping to my father, who read it aloud at the dinner table, translating from the original Yiddish into English as he went along. As he read, tears rolled down his face.

Pop spoke often of the theory of anarchism and urged me to read the principal modern proponent of anarchist theory, Peter Kropotkin, and perhaps I will do so someday. He also seemed to be on speaking terms with other nineteenth-century thinkers—Marx and Hegel and John Stuart Mill. The family library had a copy of Mill's *Political Economy* in two volumes and Hegel's *Philosophy of History,* although it may very well be that both were in mint condition when I inherited them from my father. The Hegel is still in my library, still in mint condition. I did read some of the Mill in connection with college courses in economics.

Pop was not only well read; he was also a self-taught and highly skilled machinist who in 1914 started his own business, on capital supplied in large part by Uncle, his fellow anarchist. Pop had invented a complex sewing machine for making hook-and-eye tape; the business turned out to be quite successful.

Years later, in about 1953, Pop spoke at a meeting of the newly formed Emergency Civil Liberties Committee. It was shortly after the Communist party trials in New York at which the party had vainly sought to defend itself by arguing that its advocacy of revolution as set forth by Marx, Engels, and Lenin was merely a theoretical concept and far from a call for action. In defending the right of free speech, Pop recalled speeches made from streetcorner platforms on the lower East Side in the first decade of the century. "When the speakers then urged the overthrow of the government," he said, "they weren't talking about a distant political event. They were calling for the violent overthrow of the government that same evening." Pop's anarchism, I fear, was not much more than talk, but it was good talk, and it was part of the environment in which I was brought up.

I recall vividly one incident from the early days. When I was nine or ten years old, the assigned reading in class was "The Man without a Country," a short story by Edward Everett Hale. At its climax, there appeared a poem by Sir Walter Scott, which we were obliged to memorize. I can still recite it:

> Breathes there the man with soul so dead,
> Who never to himself hath said,
>   'This is my own, my native land!'
> Whose heart hath ne'er within him burn'd
> As home his footsteps he hath turn'd
>   From wandering on a foreign strand?
> If such there breathe, go, mark him well;
> For him no minstrel raptures swell;
> High though his titles, proud his name,
> Boundless his wealth as wish can claim;
> Despite those titles, power, and pelf,
> The wretch, concentred all in self,
> Living, shall forfeit fair renown,
> And, doubly dying, shall go down
> To the vile dust from whence he sprung,
> Unwept, unhonour'd, and unsung.

This poem troubled me a great deal. My father never intended to return to his native land. I didn't know exactly what a "dead soul" was, but it certainly was a bad thing, and I was sure my father didn't have one. The last two lines were even worse. It was there stated that my father was to go down into the vile dust from which he sprung. A bit unclear if taken literally, but terrifying nonetheless.

The poem never caused me to think less of my father, whom I loved and respected, but I quickly grew to despise and, in a sense, fear the thought advanced by the poet. What was all this nonsense about a "native land"? Why was it any better than any other land? Why was a man's worth tied to any land? And why should we have to memorize such a nasty verse?

So I pondered at the age of ten.

When I was about twelve, Pop told me about Darwin and the theory of evolution, pointing out its inconsistency with the Old Testament's version of creation. I remember thinking, "This is startling news. When it gets around, there will be no more belief in God, no more need for churches, no more need for religion, and all of us will live in a more sensible society in which our energies can be devoted to more constructive purposes."

So my home environment was radical/rational, and the names that I heard at home were Marx, Mill, Darwin, Goldman, Berkman, Lenin, Eugene Debs, Morris Hillquit, and Meyer London, all of whom, somewhat jumbled together in my young mind, had pride of place over Washington, Jefferson, and Lincoln. I gloried in the fact that Debs ran for president in 1920 while he was in jail and got almost a million votes. (Teddy Roosevelt rated well, too, not because of his politics but because he traveled and hunted elephants and lions in Africa. Some of his books about those expeditions were around the house, and I read them avidly. They were very exciting books, and they had exciting pictures, too. Regrettably, like my Babe Ruth baseball cards, they have long since disappeared.)

I cannot remember a time when I did not believe that trade unions were a good thing. My neighbors and the parents of my schoolmates were all poor people, and they were employed by bosses who were rich people, and it seemed to me self-evident that poor people would do better if they would join forces to get higher wages from rich people. There were picket lines sometimes to be seen on Pitkin Avenue, the retail center of Brownsville, and it never occurred to me or to my parents that one might cross such a line to enter a shop whose workers were on strike. No one had to teach me any of this; I knew it from the very beginning.

Similarly, I was a socialist long before I knew what socialism was. I found out much later that there were serious doctrinal differences between the socialist Debs and the anarchists Netter and Goldman, but those differences didn't concern me for a long time. Getting rid of capitalism, of war, and the extremes of wealth and poverty—that was the goal, and it couldn't be achieved so long as the banks and factories and railroads were privately owned. That's what I believed as far back as I can remember thinking about such things, and that's what I still believe.

I was interested in the politics of the day at an early age. A big event in 1924 was the Democratic National Convention, held at Madison Square Garden. The contest for the presidential nomination was between Al Smith, who was governor of New York, and William Gibbs McAdoo, who was the son-in-law of former President Wilson. McAdoo had a slim majority of the delegates, but the Democratic party then required a two-thirds vote for the nomination, and Smith together with a gaggle of favorite sons had enough support to block him. I was only thirteen at the time and can't now understand why I was interested in that convention. The Yankees were doing fairly well that year. They finished in second place; Babe Ruth was hitting a lot of home runs, and it is now a wonder to me that I should have let politics deflect me from my usual consuming interest in baseball.

It was the first national convention to be broadcast. There were 103 roll calls of the delegates on the nomination of a presidential candidate, and I listened to most of them over the state-of-the-art receiver my father had bought. Alabama was the first state to be called, and each time the chairman called for the vote of Alabama, the spokesman for that state answered in deep tones, "Alabama casts twenty-four votes for Oscar W. Underwood." That announcement, repeated over a hundred times on my radio, was for the next few years good for a laugh at countless performances by standup comedians.

Pop was a Smith supporter. It was a bad time for progressive politics. The country seemed to be bathing in prosperity, and the possibility that the incumbent Republican president, Calvin Coolidge, could be defeated was remote. Pop thought Smith the best of the lot, and I thought so, too, out of family loyalty. The convention finally nominated John W. Davis as a compromise candidate. He was a prominent Wall Street lawyer, but the Democratic party pretended he was from Virginia, because he had been born there long before. I lost all interest in the election. The Yankees almost won the American League pennant that year and that was the October contest of significance, not the one between Davis and Coolidge.

The first residence I recall was in a mixed working-class and lower middle-class neighborhood, close to the terrible slum in which Aunt Esther lived, her household supported in large part by Pop and Uncle. My playmates were, in economic terms, a mixed bag. I went to elementary school at P.S. 156, which produced not only me, but many of the Jewish gangsters of the 1940s. In fact, I've taken a bit of pride in the fact that Abie Reles, one of the most violent of that mob, may well have been a classmate of mine, but I've never checked it for fear that it may not be true. After a while, we moved about six blocks away to Crown Heights, a slightly better neighborhood, and I transferred to P.S. 167 and then moved on to Boys' High School. No one ever told me that I was expected to get good grades, but my parents were obviously displeased when I rated only a B+ or (horrors!) a B on a report card.

Both neighborhoods in which we lived were predominantly—almost exclusively—Jewish, and so were the schools my sister and I attended. Because we were strict nonbelievers, Lucille and I both went to school on the Jewish holy days. Mom said anything else would be dishonest. Sometimes we were the only students in our schools to show up. We were looked upon as peculiar by our teachers and classmates, but I don't recall any overt reactions.

Every Friday night, when our neighbors were at synagogue, we went to the theater, seeing many memorable plays in an era when the New York theater was at the height of its glory. Among those Lucille and I recall are W. C. Fields in *Poppy*, Walter Hampden in *Cyrano de Bergerac*, Ethel Barrymore in *The Second Mrs. Tanqueray*, Gertrude Lawrence and Bea Lillie in *Charlot's Revue*, Spencer Tracy in *The Last Mile*, and Ed Wynn in *The Perfect Fool*. There were many others, a substantial number of which we didn't understand. We came home by taxi, riding when our religious neighbors could only walk. Lucille and I looked forward to these Friday night trips into Manhattan; not only were the plays themselves enjoyable but we were being treated as adults, and that was great.

In the course of my preuniversity schooling, I skipped several grades. This was a phenomenon much valued by the community in which I was brought up. It meant that when I finished grade 6A it was not necessary for me to take grade 6B, but I could move directly into 7A. An incidental result of that was that it took me a long time to find out what happened in the Civil War, which I was to have studied in 6B. A more serious effect of this skipping business, however, arose some time later. I skipped four times, making up two years. The result was that I entered college at the age of sixteen. This did not affect me much in terms of intellectual competition, but it was a major problem socially. Everyone else in my class was eighteen years old and much more sophisticated than I. They knew more about girls than I did; they had even dated girls, something that I never did, and occasionally they would brew a kind of alcoholic beverage which they called beer—all of this was during Prohibition—and though I joined them, I thought it tasted terrible.

There was no concept of violence in our house. That one of my parents should have touched me in anger is inconceivable. I was a very well-behaved child—perhaps too well behaved. The only occasion I recall on which my father raised his voice in reprimand was when he found me whipping my dog in an effort to teach him not to chase automobiles. Physical cruelty was not tolerated. "You can't teach a dog, or anyone else, to do anything by hitting him," my father said. The incident was very upsetting. I still remember where I was standing when the conversation took place and how close I came to breaking into tears at this unprecedented scolding.

As a child growing up in this sort of middle-class intellectual atmosphere, I read a lot of books, beginning with the *Bobbsey Twins* and the *Boy Allies at Gallipoli* and running on through Jack London's *White Fang* and *John Barleycorn* and even, by the time I was fifteen or sixteen, *War and Peace.* I went to a summer camp, which was terrible. It was fiercely competitive, which I was not. It was a typical jock camp of that era, while my greatest strength was at chess. I returned to that camp year after year, partly because I thought my father had made a financial sacrifice in sending me and I didn't want to appear ungrateful. In my first year of camp I learned to ride a horse, and that was great fun—better than competitive athletic activities.

In the meantime, the family prospered. We moved to a rather affluent section of Flatbush, built a house, and acquired a car plus a chauffeur. That wasn't uncommon in our economic class but Pop, always a few steps ahead of his crowd, also bought a horse. Although I had learned to ride at camp, I remember being rather surprised that Pop could ride, too. None of my friends had fathers who owned horses, but Pop did, and he, Lucille, and I spent many Sundays riding in Prospect Park.

In 1927 I entered the University of Michigan, where I took both my undergraduate and law degrees. I majored in political science. I remember doing for my political science professor a state-by-state analysis of the Smith-Hoover presidential campaign in 1928, in which I predicted a close vote. It was the first, but not the last, time my electoral predictions were spectacularly wrong.

In law school, I was on the staff of the *Law Review,* a Moot Court finalist, and all that stuff. I graduated in 1934, still two years in age behind the rest of my class.

On reflection, perhaps the most important thing I learned at the university was how to speak in public in an advocacy role. For my last four years there I was a member of the university debating team, and I enjoyed every minute of it. The debates were very formal and governed by all sorts of ritual, but membership on the team required the ability to research a highly controversial subject; the preparation of a public speech addressed to either side of the subject; delivery of the speech in an effective and convincing manner; and the ability to meet the arguments of the opposition. I was able to master all of those skills with considerable facility—skills that turned out to be relevant to the rest of my life.

Signing off on a complex brief on which I have been working for a few months still provides a moment of high exhilaration. I am never more comfortable than when I can speak to a more or less captive audience, whether it be a single judge or a meeting of two thousand people. I am frequently embarrassed or ill at ease or bored in gatherings at which I am supposed to engage in small talk or casual gossip, but I am never uncomfortable when I'm speaking as an advocate. The greatest thrills I have ever experienced in the practice of law have been in arguing cases before any court, the more judges the better; the more complex the issues, the better.

I also had a brief experience in college relating to something analogous to independent political action. In my junior year, a group of us nonfraternity students organized an "independent" slate of candidates for the student council. There weren't any real issues, but we were interested in challenging the fraternity population, which controlled most student activities. It was a spirited campaign, in the course of which the only issue was whether students who were not members of fraternities could be elected to the student council. We were soundly trounced. Most students didn't care, and few voted. Another learning experience: I learned how to run for office on an antiestablishment ticket and lose.

Today, my contemporaries, when asked about what event in their early lives had the greatest influence on their political thinking, almost automatically say "the Great Depression of 1929." That wasn't true in my case. Pop, like most men in his economic class, took a beating in the stock market crash, and for a short time he was concerned about his economic survival and the survival of his growing business, but he never discussed it with me, and I never raised it with him. I had a feeling, and sometimes I still do have the feeling, that Pop will be standing by to save me from disaster. I didn't spend much money, and he was quite generous, so I made out without undue economic hardship. I wasn't wealthy, but I got along without worrying about where the next dollar would come from while I was at the university—it would come from Pop.

I was vitally interested in the economic situation, but intellectually, not emotionally. I had been taught, in my second year at Michigan, that depressions couldn't happen in a capitalist system, because the economic structure had many self-correcting mechanisms. I didn't believe a word of it, and I took a perverse satisfaction in observing in 1930 and 1931 that everything I heard in Economics 52 was nonsense. I was shocked and distressed to see the lines of homeless men and women selling apples on Times Square when I returned to New York. And, of course, I read about protests by the unemployed throughout the country. There was in my mind a connection between these events and Kropotkin, Debs, and Lenin, but I cannot truthfully say that I was deeply concerned about the domestic situation in 1929 and the very early thirties.

The events that in my twenties contributed most to my political thinking were not the Depression but the rise of fascism in Germany in 1932 and 1933; the burning of the Reichstag; Dmitrov's courageous speech to a German court, attacking Hitler and calling on the world to resist him; the establishment of a dictatorship by Hitler; and, above all, the Spanish civil war in 1936. Even Pop couldn't protect me from those threats.

I graduated from law school in 1934 and married Marcia Goldberg a year later. Our courtship was a long one, having been conducted mostly by correspondence during my attendance at law school. She came from an Orthodox religious family—my father attended our Orthodox wedding only under strong protest—but Marcia had long since ceased any religious observance except when necessary to please her parents. Politically, too, we thought alike. In due course we had two children, Joan (sometime later changed to Joni), born in 1941, and Peter, in 1944. That marriage broke up in 1963 and ended in divorce in 1967, when I married Joanne Grant. Our son Mark was born in 1969 and our daughter Abby in 1971. Abby was born with Down syndrome.

I was hired right out of law school as a clerk at Hays, Podell, and Shulman, a small New York law firm with a big practice, consisting mostly of stockholder actions. The work was dull and the pay was little, but jobs were hard to come by, and I got this one only because my father was a client of the firm. I was assigned to do research work, which I did with a reasonable amount of skill but little enthusiasm.

But something good did come out of the association. Ben Algase, a junior partner, one day gave me a copy of a magazine called *New Masses*. In it was a story by Albert Maltz, called "Man on a Road." It was a poignant tale of a man of about thirty-five or forty who should have been at the height of his earning capacity, but who had contracted silicosis as a coal miner and whose ability to earn a living was over. I found the magazine impressive and asked Ben a few questions about it. He urged me to subscribe to it, which I did. It was a Communist political and literary weekly, with a long and honorable history—its direct predecessor, *The Masses*, had been barred from the mails in 1917 because of its opposition to World War I, giving rise to an important free speech controversy. It published a great deal of fine writing in the thirties and forties, and I read it regularly until it ceased publication.

Ben, who was some variety of left-winger and saw a good prospect in me, questioned me thoroughly on my political and social views and finally said that a young lawyer with my political outlook could help in the progressive movement, which needed lawyers badly. He referred me to Al Hirsch, who worked for the Hotel Workers Union Local 6 of the Restaurant Workers International Union. Al, in turn, urged me to get into an organization I had never heard of before, the International Labor

Defense (ILD). I was enthusiastically welcomed by the ILD. It was a Communist-created defense organization that supplied lawyers, money, publicity, and other forms of support for the scores of radicals who throughout the country were being jailed, beaten, and sometimes lynched. I was totally inexperienced in this kind of activity. In my employment up to that time, I had never been in a courtroom, except once, to deliver a parcel. But the ILD did get me into night court once or twice to see Sam Neuburger, Joe Brodsky, Manny Bloch, and other ILD lawyers defend an assorted group of clients, ranging from vagrants to pickets to radicals accused of more serious crimes. About ten years later, Sam became my law partner.

The ILD had a list of causes—political legal cases—it had undertaken to support. "Political cases" included a variety of things—political charges, such as sedition and throwing bombs at capitalist enterprises (the cases of Tom Mooney, Warren Billings, Jim McNamara, and others), and victims of racial persecution, notably the Scottsboro boys, who had no political views of their own but whose judicial lynching was a matter of nationwide interest in the 1930s. Then, of course, there were some like Angelo Herndon, who was a victim of both racism and political repression; he was a black who was charged with sedition for soliciting membership in the Communist party. He was convicted in Georgia and sentenced to a term of eighteen years; through the efforts of the ILD and other similar organizations, his conviction was reversed by the Supreme Court, in 1937.

The ILD collected money for these cases. On some clement evenings, I stood on busy streetcorners with a collection can, collecting nickels and dimes for Angelo Herndon. (Not much use for my legal skills here.) Sometimes, someone dropped a quarter, or once, a half dollar, in the can. That was lot of money in 1935. I have a clear recollection that my sister, Lucille, was involved in this activity too, but she denies it. She does remember having been recruited into the ILD by me, but most of her activity was as a research assistant for the organization rather than in a courtroom or in streetcorner fund-raising. Together we attended many meetings of the ILD, to discuss the political climate that called for our activity and to learn what we could do to help those whose cases we supported. All of the ILD cases were, in one way or another, relevant to the class struggle—all of our "clients" were oppressed by the capitalist system. That oppression was violent, and it was shocking to me.

This was my first contact with a Communist front organization. In 1936 Vito Marcantonio (Marc) became president of the ILD. He was the idol of East Harlem, having been elected to Congress in 1934 on the Republican ticket, at the age of thirty-two, representing the Twentieth Congressional District. In a short period of time, by virtue of his industry, his eloquence, and his outspoken advocacy of a program close to that of the radical Left in the United States, Marc had developed a position of great influence in Congress. It is doubtful whether any freshman member of Congress in recent years has had such a strong impact on the House of Representatives. He was a small and vibrant man, whose arm-waving and foot-stomping oratory could and did move his audience to enthusiastic cheers and energetic action. He was the only radical in the twentieth century to serve in Congress for more than a single term, until the election of Bella Abzug in 1972. In his first term in Congress in 1935 and 1936, he had led the fight for expansion of the New Deal program and had been from the very beginning a leader in the movement for the formation of a national Farmer-Labor party. In the 1936 election he was again nominated on the Republican ticket but was defeated in the Roosevelt landslide of that year. He was elected once more in 1938 on the American Labor party ticket, with Republican endorsement, and was reelected every two years after that until 1950. He was in later years one of my good friends.

Marc never was a member of the Communist party; neither was Lucille nor I (at that time) a member. Marc and Lucille and I were all working to support a cause we accepted. The work we were trying to do (Marc on the top level; Lucille and I at the bottom) was made possible only because of the existence of an organization that the Party had created and supported.

The years from June 1935 through June 1938 were momentous times that decisively affected the rest of my life. Sometime during this period I started to read radical literature, and I read incessantly. I don't remember what it was that started me off—perhaps Ben Algase, or "Man on a Road," or Al Hirsch, or the ILD, but I read everything in sight: lots of Marx and Engels: the *Communist Manifesto; The Civil War in France; Theses on Feuerbach; Value, Price and Profit; Anti-Duhring*, and dozens of similar pamphlets. I tried *Capital*, but my economics is limited, and I was much more interested in the political and methodological aspects of Marxism than in the economic, although I recognized that all of these strands were closely interrelated. Lenin and Stalin came next: Lenin's *Imperialism, State and Revolution* and *What Is to Be Done* and Stalin's *Foundations of Leninism*. Marxist pamphlets filled my bookshelves and my mind.

Equally important were the more contemporary works: Strachey's *Coming Struggle for Power* and Dutt's *Fascism and Social Revolution*. And there were many less portentous books—novels and memoirs like Steinbeck's *Grapes of Wrath* and *In Dubious Battle;* Wright's *Native Son;* Dreiser's *American Tragedy;* Sassoon's *Memoirs of a Fox Hunting Man;* Graves's *Good-Bye to All That;* Barbusse's *Under Fire;* Remarque's *All Quiet on the Western Front;* and scores of others that made a lasting impression on my mind. I also read, regularly, a weekly (or was it monthly?) publication called *International Press Correspondence* (*Inprecor*), which carried news of Communist party activity all over the world.

All of this reading reinforced my view that capitalism can't work (a conclusion easily reached in view of what was happening all around me), that socialism was a workable alternative form of social and economic structure, and that the problem was to get from here to there. I perceived that, as Henry Adams remarked in a different context, civilization was poised between a dead world and a world struggling to be born. This view affected—in fact determined—the rest of my political and professional life. I could not then and cannot now draw a blueprint of the socialist society I wanted. Sidney and Beatrice Webb in their monumental and seriously flawed work on *Soviet Communism* provided such a blueprint long ago, but that was for another and different country, and even as I read it it seemed too slick and too mechanical to be real even for the Soviet Union. All of these problems would have to be worked out in the new world in the process of coming to life.

My reading of history as well as the daily newspaper also taught that the transfer of wealth from the private owner to public ownership was unlikely if attempted in a peaceful fashion, and any effort to accomplish it by orderly, democratic process, such as by the vote, would probably result in forcible resistance from the capital-owning class and hence result in a violent revolutionary struggle.

In that 1936–38 period came the Spanish civil war, a textbook example of the theories promulgated by Marx, Strachey, and Dutt. In February 1936, a coalition of left-wing parties denominated the United Front won an election in Spain and undertook a program designed to accomplish a peaceful transition to a socialist economic system. Within five months a large portion of the army, under the leadership of General Francisco Franco, mounted a counterrevolution under the banner of anticommunism. This was the very struggle between socialism and fascism of which Strachey and Dutt had written.

Nothing in my life up to that time and few things since have affected me as much emotionally as that conflict. This was as clear a struggle between good and evil as one is likely to meet in this world. To be sure, there were many sharp differences among the forces on the left—the government had been a coalition of uneasy partners from the beginning—but they were all antifascist, and there was no trouble in defining the Franco forces as absolute evil.

The civil war became an international conflict almost at once. German and Italian intervention on the side of Franco and the subsequent Soviet support of the loyalist Spanish government raised the level of the conflict to where it looked like a preview for a second world war, as indeed it was. The Roosevelt administration, like the governments of England and France, took a position of neutrality and refused to sell arms to the government of Spain, while the Franco forces were fully armed by Hitler and Mussolini. This was a crime of the highest order and colored my attitude toward my own government.

Over the next two years, about forty thousand antifascist young men and women, from all over Europe, Canada, and the United States, joined the Spanish government forces, to make up the International Brigades. Thirty-three hundred came from the United States (in violation of the neutrality laws) and formed the Abraham Lincoln Battalion. Casualties in the brigades were heavy; about half of the U.S. volunteers were killed, including several of my acquaintances. I sometimes thought of volunteering, but I could not imagine myself shooting a gun and I stayed home nursing a residue of guilt.

The reports of the *New York Times* on the progress of the civil war—on the course of each battle and each campaign—were the most important news every day. Some place names in Spain became as familiar to me as the names of the stores on Avenue J, where I lived. The battles for Toledo and Barcelona, the bombing of Guernica, the massacre in the bull ring at Seville, and above all the siege of Madrid were stories that unfolded before my eyes over a three-year period. Recollections of that struggle even now have the power to move me, and I cannot hear the great Spanish loyalist songs of the time without a catch in my throat. I picked up a recording of such songs in the Jefferson Book Shop and played it until it was worn out. Paul Robeson singing "Freiheit" and "Die Moorsoldaten" or Pete Seeger singing "Viva la Quince Brigada" were and still are great musical and political experiences. I was deeply depressed when Madrid fell and the war was over. Fascism had won a great victory.

In the years following World War II, the situation in Spain changed a great deal. Many friends, including persons with whom I was politically allied, and some who had fought in the civil war, visited Spain on vacations, and all came back with stories of how it now had a democratic government and how beautiful Spain was, but I never considered a visit. The very idea of going there was disturbing. Many years later, in about 1963, I had to make a professional trip to Spain. I was then an experienced air traveler, and I was feeling fine on the trip over, but as the plane landed at the airport in Madrid, I became ill and vomited. The signposts all over the area near the airport in Madrid—Barcelona, Toledo, Teruel, Seville—were emotionally disturbing and brought back memories of this terrible war that had so affected me many years before.

■

In the 1935–38 period also, the American Labor party (ALP) and the National Lawyers Guild (NLG) were both organized, one an alternative political party and the other an alternative bar association. I was to devote a major part of my time, energy, and devotion to both in the years to come.

And finally, I left my job at Hays, Podell, and Shulman in mid-1938. Algase told me he was leaving the firm to join Louis Boudin's firm, which was engaged almost entirely in the practice of labor law, and he suggested that I might come along with him. I jumped at the idea. The Hays, Podell firm was reasonably progressive politically. David Podell was an eminent Roosevelt supporter, and Morty Hays was, a few years later, president of the New York City chapter of the National Lawyers Guild. No one complained when I took a few hours off now and then to do work for the ILD or the American Labor party. But the practice of law at that firm was unutterably dull. I never got into court and wasn't interested in the kind of cases I was working on. Labor law was much more romantic and exciting.

There was a downside to the change also. I took a pay cut from sixty dollars to fifty dollars a week. My father warned me that I would never make much money at labor law, and that I was automatically setting a top limit to potential earnings—a top limit that was pretty low. I knew he was right, but I didn't hesitate very long. Marcia was working, and Pop was willing to help out a bit with a few bucks. Although he disapproved of my move, he would never put any pressure on me. The cost of living was not very high in 1938, and Marcia and I were able to make out. At the last minute, Ben Algase decided not to leave his job, so I went uptown alone to the Boudin firm.

2

The Boudin Office

Ben Gold had a great collection of stories. One was about a Russian lord who was entertaining some of the neighboring nobility at his estate. Ben described in graphic detail the food served at the feast and the pigs under the table eating the scraps. After a few, or more than a few, drinks of vodka (straight), each of the guests began to boast of what his favorite Jew could do. "My Jew," said one of them, "is a wonderful cook. He can bake bread and pies out of cornhusks. He can roast a horse so that it is as tender as veal." Another boasted, "My Jew is a great tailor. He can make coats of cotton that are as warm as the warmest fur."

After a while, the host, not to be outdone by his guests, said, "Do you see that pig? My Jew can teach that pig to fly." The others scoffed, and so the host called in his oldest and wisest Jew and, pointing to a pig rooting under the table, commanded, "Jew, teach that pig to fly."

"But, my lord," said the Jew, "how can I teach a pig to fly?" "That's your problem," said the lord. "If you don't, I'll chop your head off." "All right," said the Jew, "but I'll need a year." To this reasonable request, the lord agreed. When the Jew reported this event to his wife, she started to weep. "How can you teach a pig to fly?" "Stop crying," said the Jew, "we've got a whole year. Maybe the lord will die. Maybe I'll die. Maybe the pig will fly."

The other story is of two men sitting side by side in a railroad train alongside an open window. This was long ago, when train windows could open. The man on the aisle seat turned to the passenger sitting next to the window and said, "Would you mind closing the window; it's cold outside." His neighbor made no response. Two or three minutes later, the first man turned again to his neighbor. "Would you please close the window; it's cold outside." Again, no response.

The third time, the man in the aisle seat leaned over his neighbor in anger and slammed the window shut. The man at the window looked at his impatient seatmate and said, "So, now is it warm outside?"

These punch lines became a part of my vocabulary. "Maybe the pig will fly" became a justification for trying to delay any unpleasant event, even if inevitable, in the hope that a miracle might occur. "Now is it warm outside?" became the response to many irrelevant arguments.

Ben was one of the exciting men I met at the office of Boudin, Cohn, and Glickstein (in those days, alas, almost no women). Dynamic and charismatic, he was president of the International Fur and Leather Workers Union and highly placed in the Communist party. He evidently considered me a good prospect for something and took a sort of fatherly interest in me, but there were many others with whom I associated on a daily basis at the Boudin office.

The practice of law in that office bore no resemblance to the practice of law I had experienced in the few years since my graduation. Furthermore, the chance to represent the militant, progressive unions of the day was exhilarating. I dreamed of one big movement that someday—maybe in ten years, maybe in one hundred—might lead to a socialist society on earth. I was only twenty-seven years old and was permitted such fantasies.

Louis Boudin, the senior partner, was a brilliant lawyer and an innovative legal scholar. He was a longtime radical and had been a member of the left wing of the Socialist party in 1917, when he was outspoken in opposition to our entry into the Great War. I don't believe he was ever a member of the Communist party, but he was trusted by the trade union members of the party and had represented many of them for years before. He was also a prolific writer, both on Marxist theory and American legal history.

Sidney Cohn and Hy Glickstein were the other partners; they seemed to me to be much older than I but they really weren't, except in experience and in their understanding of the trade union movement. When I came into the office I was in awe of both of them, but not for very long. Hy was a good trial lawyer and a man after my own heart in terms of politics. He left the practice of the law a few years later for a commercial enterprise in Puerto Rico that made him very prosperous. Sidney was a warm, gregarious fellow and a good politician who knew how to get clients and keep them happy. He had the lawyer's equivalent of a good bedside manner but almost never walked into a courtroom except as an observer.

And he was sophisticated, too. At the end of my first week on the job, Sidney told me to go to a National Labor Relations Board (NLRB) hearing on the next Monday. The case involved charges by the American Communications Association (ACA) that Western Union was maintaining a company union in violation of the National Labor Relations Act (the Wagner Act). I was to attend the hearing as a representative of ACA, a union of communications workers, but I was to keep my mouth shut, because the charges were being presented to a hearing officer by Will Maslow, the lawyer for the NLRB, and I knew nothing of the facts in the case. But Marvin Rathborn, then president of ACA, was to testify, and, said Sidney, "On cross-examination, Kimball, the lawyer for Western Union, will ask Rathborn: 'Are you a member of the Communist party?' At that point, you will object. The trial examiner will uphold your objection, and after a decent interval, you can come back to the office and go on with your work."

I was pretty naive. "Why doesn't Maslow make the objection?" I asked. "The board lawyers don't like to object to that question," Sidney said. "But suppose the trial examiner overrules the objection?" I asked. "Don't worry," said Sidney, "he won't."

The scenario was played out as Sidney had predicted.

Most of the other young lawyers at the office had been there for a year or so when I came in. Leonard Boudin, Louis's nephew, was one of them. He became—and was for the next half century—a close friend and, for almost all of that time, my law partner.

The trade union movement was, beginning in 1933, an important and dynamic element in the national political and economic scene, and progressives and radicals of all varieties were swept up in it, much as, twenty-five years later, the progressive community was caught up in the civil rights movement. "Solidarity Forever" was its theme song, as "We Shall Overcome" was the anthem of the sixties.

Trade unions, though legal, had long functioned in the shadow of a disapproving government and hostile courts. But in 1933 Congress passed, and President Franklin Delano Roosevelt signed, the National Industrial Recovery Act, which declared that employees had the right to organize and to bargain collectively through representatives of their own choosing. The next year, the National Labor Relations Act supplied the necessary machinery for the enforcement of those rights. It provided that a union which could demonstrate, by way of an election held by the NLRB, that it represented a majority of the nonmanagement employees of an employer would be certified by the board as the collective bargaining representative of such employees. The employer was required by law to bargain with such representative as to the terms and conditions of employment. This was, to the trade union movement, a truly revolutionary development and the Wagner Act was generally referred to as the "Magna Carta of Labor." Almost overnight, hundreds of new unions appeared and millions of workers joined them and sought NLRB certification.

There were a few faint voices of doubt heard among some of my ultraradical friends. This setup, they said, would lead to government control of the trade union movement. Certification was the equivalent of a license. If certification could be granted, it could also be denied, and denial could destroy a union. Paraphrasing the Trojan prophet Laocoön, they warned, "Beware of the capitalist system, even when it comes bearing gifts." But as contemporaries of Laocoön paid no attention to him, his modern counterparts ignored their warnings—until the passage of the Taft-Hartley Act in 1947.

I was one of those who heard the warnings, and I was troubled by them. Why should capitalism be serving up these goodies? This did not look much like the class conflict Marx and Lenin had described. But millions of workers were joining unions. The Magna Carta of Labor couldn't be so bad.

The influx of new members in unprecedented numbers forced major changes in the structure of the American Federation of Labor (AFL), with which most of the unions of the day were affiliated and which had for years been small, ineffective, right wing, and corrupt. And with a few exceptions, where radicals had infiltrated some of its local unions, it had shown little interest in organizing new members.

In 1935, six AFL unions formed the Committee for Industrial Organization, which under the leadership of John L. Lewis, president of the United Mine Workers of America, demanded that the AFL engage in a concerted campaign to organize the masses of workers in large industries, who were still outside the trade union movement. Lewis was a forceful and dynamic leader who would not tolerate Communists in his union but was quite willing to work with them in other organizations where they posed no threat to him. Unique among trade union leaders, he was a great orator, in style, if not in content, comparable to the Bible-thumpers of the fundamentalist churches. His thunderous speeches were loaded with phrases taken from the Old Testament, or at least, when John L. delivered them, they had a biblical sound.

After about a year of unsuccessful effort to involve the AFL leadership in this project, the unions that had formed the committee withdrew from the AFL and organized the Congress of Industrial Organizations (CIO). As president of the new CIO, Lewis spurred major organizing drives in almost all segments of heavy industry in the country, staffed in large part by members of the Communist party hired and encouraged by him. The six original unions were joined by many others in the next months and years. The dramatic organization of the workers in the automobile, steel, rubber, mining, shipping, electrical manufacturing, and other industries followed. None of this happened easily. The workers occupied the plants of the automobile companies before they could get the recognition the law mandated. There was a great deal of violence, particularly in the steel and mining industries, which had a long history of violence in labor disputes. Major strikes characterized the industrial scene for several years. But by 1941, the membership of the trade union movement was close to ten million, as compared to less than four million a few years before, and the new CIO was heavily influenced by young and militant members of the Communist party.

New York City had no heavy industry, but it was nevertheless a "union town." By the outbreak of World War II, a large proportion of its working population was organized. The restaurants and hotels, the subways and taxis, the department stores and most of the retail chain stores, the warehouses, the building trades, the teamsters, the garment manufacturers, the longshoremen, the communications companies, the printing trades, the theaters, the teachers, the police and fire departments—all were organized, some into AFL unions, some into CIO unions, and some into independent unions. Of the principal industries in New York City, only the financial community held out, and even here, many insurance agents had become union members.*

By the time I came into the Boudin office, the big organizing drives had been completed, but there was plenty to be done and I joined with exhilaration. No doubt I (like all my associates) romanticized the trade union movement and everything connected with it, but there was romance enough to go around. And so there was lots of enjoyable work and, after work, all the trappings of a popular crusade—picket lines, songs, parades, slogans—all spiced by resistance, some of it violent, from the representatives of industrial capitalism, those called "the economic royalists" by our sometime friend, President Roosevelt.

*The hospital workers in the city were likewise unorganized until after the war. At the time of this writing, however, they are organized into Local 1199, what well may be the strongest union in the city and certainly the largest.

Most of the leadership of the unions the Boudin office represented was probably Communist. At the core of the office practice were the food workers unions, all left-wing AFL affiliates. With the help of Tom Dewey, district attorney of New York County, they had just broken the grip of the racketeers who had controlled the unions until the mid-thirties. We represented five or six of these unions, which were busily engaged in organizing and bargaining for waiters, cooks, cafeteria workers, hotel workers, and bakers, and in cleaning up the remnants of the racketeering influence in the industry. There were similar situations in other unions: in the Painters Union, the Sheet Metal Workers Union, and others, rank-and-file insurgents were struggling against corrupt and racketeering leadership.

Added to these were a number of smaller CIO unions formed to organize workers in industries where trade unionism was very weak or virtually unknown: ACA; the United Office and Professional Workers (UOPWA); the Federation of Architects, Engineers, Chemists, and Technicians (FAECT); the Department Store Employees; the Furniture Workers; and others. Some of these unions had existed in an ineffective form in the AFL but now pulled out and joined the CIO.

These unions, old-line AFL and new CIO, were clients of the Boudin office, and their officers and organizers spent much of their time in our office. I represented many of them in court, at labor board hearings, at arbitrations, and in collective bargaining. To my mind then and now, they were true heroes who were devoting their lives to the trade union movement, sometimes at great personal sacrifice, and who were bringing significant benefits to the people they represented. Many had decades of experience in the movement. Ben Gold, Sam Kramberg, Harry Reich, Bill Albertson, Louis Weinstock, Frank Dutto, Jay Rubin, Irving Potash, and others came in and out of our office and in and out of my room on a daily basis. All of these men were assumed by me to be members of the Communist party. Gold and Potash were openly so. Albertson became a Party functionary shortly after, and most of the others made no secret of their political orientation.* A few solicited me for membership in the Party, but I was not ready for such a commitment.

*Potash, like Gold, was an officer of the International Fur and Leather Workers Union and was a high-ranking, public member of the Party. Kramberg was president of the Cafeteria Workers Union; Reich, the president of the Cooks Union; Albertson was an organizer for the Waiters Union; and Rubin was chairman of the Hotel Trades Council. Weinstock was an insurgent rank-and-file leader of the Painters Union; Dutto was organizer for the Bakery and Cafeteria Workers.

The CIO leaders who frequented the Boudin office—Lew Merrill, Leon Berney, Joe Selly, John Stanley, Joe Kehoe, Bill Bender, Peter Hawley— were also a militant, friendly, and politically sympathetic lot, much younger than the AFL crowd but equally dynamic and equally committed to the trade union movement. More than likely, most were Communists.*

I was in heaven. The class struggle had come out of my books, onto the streets, and into my office.

Work in the Boudin office was stimulating, and I learned how to prepare and try cases, how to deal with trade unions, and how to work as a member of a team of lawyers. But above all, I learned about politics. The "old line" radical AFL leaders were, with one or two exceptions, garrulous, and proud of their political beliefs and their experiences. Jay Rubin was dour and remote, but the others regaled us young folks with their views as to the desirability of a socialist economic structure and with many stories of their own heroism and that of their comrades. The younger fellows in the new CIO unions talked more about the future. But all would talk politics endlessly. The firm took on more employees and moved to larger quarters.

I was usually at the National Labor Relations Board or the State Labor Relations Board two or three times a week. The state board was patterned after the NLRB and performed the same functions as to employers not engaged in interstate commerce, such as restaurants, retail stores, and the like.† I knew, by first name, all of the personnel of both boards, from the file clerks to the directors. I knew the rules and how to use them. I knew the law and how to apply it. I read every new decision by the local board, the state or national board, and the courts. I was among the first to hear all of the gossip, and sometimes I created it. I did a good job for my clients.

A major part of my duties involved attending night court, which was in session from about 8:00 P.M. to 2:00 or 3:00 A.M. Its function was to arraign persons arrested too late to be arraigned in the daytime court session. Strikes were many and militant in those days. Picket line arrests were frequent, and my job was to get the pickets released on bail or, if

*Selly and Bender were officers of ACA. They were both Party members. Merrill was president of the UOPWA and was also a Party member. Kehoe was an ACA officer; Stanley, Berney, and Hawley were officers of the UOPWA.

†As we shall see, the UOPWA filed charges against the Metropolitan Life Insurance Company before the state board to avoid a contention by the company that it was not engaged in interstate commerce and hence not within the jurisdiction of the NLRB. Such an argument by an insurance company would today be regarded as absurd, but the meaning of "interstate commerce" was not so clear, as a matter of law, in 1938.

the sitting magistrate was friendly, to try the case. Frequently I would have to wait three or four hours before my cases were called. That was bad enough. The courtroom was hot in the summer and freezing in the winter and filthy all the time, and the lighting was not good enough to permit me to read a book while waiting. But worst of all was the arraignment of vagrants.

We were still in a deep economic depression, and the streets were full of the homeless. Every night at about eleven o'clock, the twenty or thirty vagrants arrested that evening would be herded into the courtroom. The stench was overpowering, and many of the waiting lawyers walked out into the hall until this feature of the court session was over. The men (and an occasional woman) were all regulars; many of them were brought in two or three times every week, and the judges and court clerks knew them well. They were all derelicts, many of them drunk, many of them mentally disturbed. Some of them seemed quite young, under the grime and dirt covering them, but most were probably over fifty. Many could not remember their names, or when they had last worked, or whether they had a family. Some judges sadistically mimicked them and tried to get laughs out of the courtroom audience at their expense. Others were deeply concerned.

But no one knew what to do about them. In clement weather, they were held overnight and released the next morning, only to be picked up again a day or two later. In the winter, they were sentenced to five, ten, or twenty days, depending on the whim of the court. Some judges let them set their own sentences.

The picture of these human wrecks, shuffling into court every night and shuffling out again after the law had gone through its meaningless ritual, has stayed with me all my life. I haven't been to night court for many years and am not anxious to return.

Early in my stay at the Boudin office, I was assigned to represent Local 30 of the UOPWA in a proceeding against the Metropolitan Life Insurance Company before the State Labor Relations Board. The union had filed charges with the board contending that Met Life had maintained an illegal company union and had fired about forty industrial insurance agents for their union activity. Lengthy hearings were held before the board, at which Eugene Cotton and David Scribner, both then in their twenties and later prominent and able trade union lawyers, represented the general counsel of the board, and Paul Herzog, chairman of the board, presided. I represented the union. Met Life was represented by Samuel Seabury. Seabury was at that time about sixty-eight years old.

He had been a Democratic candidate for governor in 1916 and then a judge of the New York Court of Appeals. In 1932 he had been counsel for a legislative committee set up to investigate corruption in New York City and had been responsible for the removal of Mayor Jimmy Walker and the institution of a reform city government. Of all the eminent lawyers in New York, he was the most eminent. He was a direct descendant of the first Protestant Episcopal bishop in America. He was the very essence of honor, rectitude—and conservatism. The idea of collective bargaining was to him hard to conceive. He was outraged by the growth of the New Deal under Roosevelt and took much of it personally. He had no trace of a sense of humor—a good representative for Met Life.

Seabury was a very good, even a great lawyer, with both feet firmly planted in 1932, but he was totally out of place in 1939, when a gaggle of young lawyers alternated in challenging his old-fashioned views of the law and confronting him with a philosophy of labor relations he could not understand. Every Monday, Wednesday, and Friday for over a year, the hearing went on before Herzog. I must have attended eighty days of hearing. It was my first extensive courtroom experience, and I learned a great deal.

It was also great fun. Seabury had a good research staff—the kind of staff that had ousted Tammany Hall from City Hall a few years before, and it supplied material for his vigorous cross-examination of the union's witnesses.

"Mr. Rudick," said Seabury, drawing himself up to his full 6'5" height and advancing on Bill Rudick, holding a sheaf of papers as one would a weapon. "I show you an application for employment with Metropolitan Life dated June 1, 1920. Will you please tell me if that is your handwriting and what information you gave to the company as to your place of birth."

Rudick, a portly fifty-year-old agent who had been fired for his union activity, looked at the paper and replied, "Yes, sir, that is my handwriting. I stated my place of birth as Dublin."

Seabury showed Rudick a record of his voter registration in 1928. It showed his place of birth as Germany. A third document was an application for a driver's license in 1930. It gave Rudick's birthplace as Russia. A record of jury duty showed his place of birth as Latvia. Each document had been signed by Rudick.

Now came the devastating final question, trumpeted triumphantly by Seabury: "Can you tell us, Mr. Rudick, which three of these four answers are falsehoods?"

Wonderful stuff, I said to myself with admiration and some uneasiness. No one had prepared Rudick for this line of examination. But Rudick had probably been waiting for a moment like this all his life.

"Judge," he said, "I have always been confused as to my place of birth. You see," he went on, teaching Seabury a lesson in European history, "I was born on a German flagship en route from Riga, where my parents had lived, to Dublin. Over the past forty years, Riga has sometimes been in Latvia and sometimes in Russia. So I've never been quite sure of my legal birthplace. I'm sorry if I misled you."

End of cross-examination.

Ultimately, the union won before the board and the court, and a good collective bargaining contract was entered into.

I also did a great deal of work for the various food workers unions, the Bakery Workers Union, the other locals of the UOPWA, Local 140 of the Furniture Workers Union, and many others, but after the first eighteen months and for years after, most of my work was for the American Communications Association.

After four years with Boudin, Cohn, and Glickstein, I became a bit restless. I liked the work, but I suppose I wanted to be my own boss. I wasn't quite happy about the money I was making, either. Sam Neuburger, a friend dating from the ILD days, suggested that I might be interested in joining him and Sam Shapiro in a small law firm that, like the Boudin office, had a practice almost entirely in the field of labor law. Joe Selly, then president of ACA and potentially my most important client, thought it was a swell idea—he didn't like Sidney Cohn much. I was interested but only if Leonard Boudin was willing to come along.

Leonard and I had become very close friends over the preceding years. We saw each other almost daily and often played chess while lunching at our desks. (He almost always won.) Nearly every major case either of us handled was the subject of extensive consultation between us. Socially, too, our relationship was a close one, and our families visited each other occasionally.

Sam Neuburger didn't know Leonard, except by reputation, but he was a very good-natured and easy-going fellow and readily agreed to include Leonard in the firm. Leonard accepted at first but after much waffling decided not to leave the Boudin office. After waffling on my part, I decided to go without him.

I joined the two Sams on January 1, 1944, and we practiced under the name of Neuburger, Shapiro, and Rabinowitz. Neuburger and Shapiro represented the unions at Macy's, Gimbel's, Bloomingdale's, Hearn's,

Stern's, and other large department stores in the city, and their practice was a very active and important one. I brought with me the American Communications Association, Local 140 of the Furniture Workers Union, and perhaps one or two smaller locals. After a year or so, I broached the subject to Leonard again, and again he agreed and once again backed out, this time after announcement cards and new stationery had been printed. This, of course, irritated Neuburger no end. But he cooled down, and in the fall of 1947, Leonard finally joined up, the new firm being styled Neuburger, Shapiro, Rabinowitz, and Boudin. Leonard brought with him the United Office and Professional Workers Union and all of its locals in New York, and again, a few smaller unions.

The enterprises that occupied most of my time and energy were the American Labor party and the Communist party, which I joined in 1942, and representation of ACA.

Other changes took place in the same period of time. Belle Seligman (a.k.a. Belle Harper) joined us in 1947. Also in that same year, the Wholesale and Warehouse Workers Union, District 65, then one of the largest and most militant local unions in the city, retained us. The result was that by the end of that year, we were a strong labor law firm—large (as left-wing offices went in those days), and with a top-notch reputation. And we had a great deal to do.

3

The American Communications Association

The American Communications Association (ACA) was a wonderful union and a wonderful client. In 1940 it was young, and so was I. It was a CIO union with jurisdiction over employees in the telephone, telegraph, and radio broadcast industries and was battling some of the largest corporations of the United States, an enterprise of which I fully approved. Its political stance was left wing. Its leaders were enthusiastic and highly principled, and they were personally and temperamentally attractive. What more could I want? My relationship with ACA rapidly developed into much more than a professional one, and from the time I joined the Communist party in about 1942 until 1949 when the Party branch at ACA disbanded, I was a member of that branch and met regularly with it.

The president of the union after 1942 was Joe Selly. He had been an architecture student at Cornell but left school with the rise of the CIO to apply for a job with John L. Lewis, as an organizer. Joe was a member of the Communist party and was very highly regarded in Party circles, as one of the brightest and most competent of the young trade unionists in the country. He and I spent a great deal of our time together throughout the forties and fifties, much of it in Washington, on the West Coast, and at places in between. He was well read and a good conversationalist, a good poker player but an indifferent chess player.

Joe Kehoe was ACA's director of organization. He was a black Irishman in the tradition of the antichurch Irish revolutionaries of 1917. He had, as a child, been taught to spit when he passed a Catholic church. He had a great voice and would sing Irish ballads at the slightest provocation, and often without provocation. Sometime in the forties, I heard my first concert performance of the Berlioz *Requiem* with him, from the top balcony of Carnegie Hall. His death in 1960 left a gap in my personal life that has not been filled. I have known few people like him.

Bill Bender was in charge of organizing in the broadcast industry. In 1949 he married Gerry Shandross, the union's legislative representative. Other members of the ACA staff were equally close to me. Together they made up as radical a group of trade union leaders as could be found in the eastern part of the United States. Their spouses were equally attractive and compatible, and Marcia and I formed strong social and political bonds with many of the staff.

In the years after 1942, representation of ACA probably took half of my lawyering time. There was big litigation, and there were little grievances. There were union meetings and Communist party meetings. I was almost as well known to the union members as were the union officers. I spoke at union meetings; I attended union executive board meetings and union conventions; I accompanied Joe Selly to CIO conventions. There was hardly a week in the next decade in which I did not spend some time on ACA-related activities.

The Federal Communications Commission

Much of the work for the union was in Washington, wherein dwelt the Federal Communications Commission (FCC), which, like most government regulatory agencies, was ideologically the captive of the industry it was supposed to be regulating—in this case the telephone and telegraph industries. I was in and out of hearings before the FCC constantly from 1942 to 1946. The National Labor Relations Board and the War Labor Board were also based in Washington. Perhaps 10 percent or 15 percent of my practice during the war years required my presence in the capital. Aside from the fact that the substance of these proceedings was interesting, the ambiance in which I lived was stimulating. Social life after work was pleasant and not too strenuous. I often stayed at Gerry Shandross's apartment in Washington, hotel accommodations being hard to come by during the war. Vito Marcantonio came over now and then to discuss and decide the fate of the world, until the small hours of the morning. The inequities of the Washington establishment and the glory of Thomas Jefferson were favorite subjects. Marc was a frequent dinner companion, too, and the only time in my life I really got drunk—I mean sick drunk—was at the Mayflower Hotel in a vain effort to keep up with Marc.

I was called up for the draft in April 1944. I passed my physical exam and was assigned to the navy. ACA applied for an occupational deferment for me on the ground that the work I was doing in the communications industry was important to the war effort, and a year's deferment was granted. When the year was up, the war was winding down and the selective service system was no longer drafting men in my age group.

When I came to the Boudin office, ACA had a nationwide collective bargaining agreement with one of the two existing domestic telegraph companies, Postal Telegraph-Cable Company (about fourteen thousand employees), and contracts with several international communications companies, the largest of which was RCA Communications. ACA was engaged in organizing the employees of Western Union, the larger of the domestic telegraph carriers, and early in 1942 it won an NLRB election among the employees of that company in the Metropolitan Division, consisting of New York City and its environs. Shortly after, it signed a contract covering the employees of Western Union in that geographical area.*

In 1943 Congress passed a law permitting the merger of Western Union and Postal Telegraph upon a finding by the FCC that the merger was in the public interest. The carriers presented a merger plan to the FCC in May, and hearings were held intermittently between July 7 and September 23, 1943. I represented ACA at those hearings. The commission had for years been in favor of merger; the administration supported merger; the armed services had been whipped into line; the financial community favored it; and there was expected to be little, if any, opposition.

---

*A nationwide telegraph system was an essential part of the communications system of the United States in 1940. It provided the only rapid method of record communications for commercial transactions at a time when long distance mail was slow and uncertain as to time of delivery. The financial community depended on stock tickers operated by the telegraph companies for the speedy transmission of financial news. The press depended on telegraph circuits for all but local news. Almost all international traffic utilized telegraph circuits to get to the point of connection with the international cables at New York and San Francisco. Long distance telephone service was expensive, unreliable, and slow, with frequent interruption of service. Further, in 1940, only 40 percent of the households in the United States had telephone lines, as compared with well over 90 percent today. Answering machines were not yet in use, and it wasn't until the late 1980s that facsimile transmission became generally available to the public. Telegraphic greetings for weddings, birthdays, and similar occasions were part of American life, and while such services may seem trivial, the image of the Western Union messenger delivering flowers or a congratulatory telegram was a familiar feature of our culture. In modern times, facsimile mail and teleprinter services supplied by the telephone companies have almost completely replaced the telegraph companies.

But there was opposition, and it all came from ACA. We recognized that we could not defeat the merger, but we saw our job as protecting the public interest and getting as much protection as possible for members of the union and other employees of the carriers. Merger meant a diminution of telegraph circuitry—the carriers called it the elimination of duplicate circuits—whereas we contended that the war effort required an expansion, rather than a contraction, of available telegraph capacity. And there were many respects in which merger might adversely affect the workers in the industry. Certainly the commission would not effectively protect the public interest; it was much too intent on the consummation of the merger to do that. Nor did the commission give a damn about the rights of the workers in the industry.

I cannot honestly claim that ACA's opposition to the merger was motivated only by its regard for the public interest. A merged carrier would have about sixty thousand employees of which, at the time of the hearing, ACA represented no more than twenty thousand, the remainder being represented by several AFL unions. In a companywide NLRB election, likely to follow within a year or two after a merger, ACA would be in danger of being wiped out.

The FCC hearing opened with presentation of the plan and formal testimony by the FCC staff. Then, after two or three days of testimony by the company officials, it became my turn to cross-examine.

A proper prayer of a lawyer about to cross-examine a witness is: "Wouldst that mine adversary had written a book." In this instance, my adversaries had indeed written a book. They had testified not only at the FCC hearing, but at the congressional committee hearings on proposed merger bills over a period of years. All of that testimony was full of internal inconsistencies and inexact formulations. Congressional testimony is never meant to be the subject of cross-examination, but it now was.

I cross-examined for three or four days, equipped with an elaborate analysis of the testimony the company officials had given on several occasions in the past. I still remember standing at the lectern with a sheaf of papers in my hand, confronting Ed Chinlund, of Postal Telegraph, and A. N. Williams of Western Union, with testimony they had given at the congressional hearings—testimony not easy to reconcile with the testimony they had just given at the FCC hearings. Chinlund and Williams were about twice my age and came out of the dignified WASP environment that supplied high-level industrial executives in the forties. They were not accustomed to the irreverent treatment to which they were subjected nor the style, which was lively and less formal than proceedings at a board meeting of a large commercial or industrial corporation. Their lawyers, too, came from the same board rooms and golf clubs.

It was my first experience in big-time corporate litigation. Labor board stuff was trivial compared to this, and I gloried in it. My clients were ecstatic. Joe Kehoe wrote a letter to Marcia, signed by the Sellys and Gerry Shandross, on the evening following the conclusion of my cross-examination. It not only provides the flavor of the hearing; it does much to present a picture of the clients with whom I was working. Here it is.

Friday nite—10:00 P.M.

Dear Marcia,

We passed a motion today, unanimously and by acclamation, to frame Vic, put him in cotton wool, in a glass cage, and later on lend him to the Smithsonian Institute (but in the meantime to provide a body guard of strong minded and strong fisted goons to provide him safe conduct to his wife and daughter) for the terrific job he has done on the million dollar a year Wall Street big shots who from now on out will tremble at the sight, sound or mention of the name of "RABINOWITZ."

He really was sensational. Even the modest, retiring and generous Sidney Cohn was falling all over himself praising Vic (I could see the gleam of a raise in his eye) and as for the ACA delegates, they're almost ready to kiss him every time he smiles sweetly at the bastards opposing him, while he is legally and morally cutting their throats.

This is much too good for you to miss, and the International Office, one and all, hereby pass another unanimous motion instructing, urging and insisting, that you come back to Washington with him to be in on the kill.

So this guy from Buffalo says to me: "Why didn't you tell me this guy Rabinowitz was so terrific?" I've seen him in negotiations but I never saw him like this. Jesus Christ he blitzed them!"

So-o-o-o-o- Chinlund who gets $75 grand a year from Macy's and god knows how much graft from Postal and Lehman Bros and J P Morgan was on the stand. So Victor goes to work on him. He was pretty cocky, but he took out that silk handkerchief and started mopping his brow before long. And Williams, who gets 85 grand from Western Union was a piece of putty in the hands of your husband who played with him like a cat with a mouse. Well, a one-sided contest is never too interesting to guys who are used to close pitcher's battles, so it was pretty bad for the company guys. It was moider, really! We give Victor the croy de gair, the distinguised soivice cross, and the ACA spashul extra oak leaf cluster. For why? Because, for years we've listened to these guys with their Wall Street layers, I mean lawyers, and they've pushed everybody around like a leaf in a hot wind, and here comes a guy with all the stuff against him, and a lost case, and three men on base with two and three on the batter and Babe Ruth at bat and what do you think? Does he walk him? Does he quail? Does he Falter? Does he hesitate? Does he compromise? No! A thousand times no! He lays it on the line across the middle and strikes the opposition out! And so that's the story. Class always tells. And that's why we give Victor a *Lone Ranger medal.*

In the meantime what we really mean is Happy Birthday to Joanie from all of us. We know you would enjoy seeing Vic in action, as we did, and hope you can make it.

It is a large imposing room. The Commission sits on a dais in red leather chairs that lean a—way back. Around the tables in front of the dais are the counsel, attorneys, stooges, assistants, pratt boys, etc., of the companies.

In these hallowed halls have woiked the smartest operators from Jay Gould to Sosthenes Behn. The history of capitalism, red with the blood and sweat of the workers is ensconced in these halls, if the walls could talk! But, in charges ACA with VR in the van, brandishing lances and swords and the edifice falls. Mighty emperors of industry quail before the scalpel of the inquisitor VR. Like Torquina da of the old spanish set-up VR drives them into a corner and then burns them to a crisp on the stake of cross-examination. Lady, Joanie will be a Portia, sure as god if she takes after paw.

With warmest fraternal greetings,

Joe Kehoe
Joe Selly
Gilda Selly
Gerry Shandross

One of the major issues during the hearing pertained to speed of service and extent of coverage by Western Union. The company had stated that all messages sent by Western Union could be delivered within two or three hours—if necessary, by telephone or by special messenger when local branch offices were closed. This of course was far from the truth; many such messages—even those of an emergency nature—were often delayed for half a day and sometimes longer when sent to an addressee in a rural area. William Dean Embree, the pompous and dignified lawyer for Western Union, took it upon himself to offer personal anecdotal evidence that the company did indeed go to extremes to deliver messages promptly. "At my ranch in Laramie, Wyoming," he suavely stated, "it often happens that the Western Union office asks us to help deliver an emergency message to an outlying address. I've authorized the foreman of the ranch to accept such messages by phone and to deliver them to the addressee, by horseback if necessary."

We worked up a ploy to counter this. We advised half a dozen union members living in rural areas that we would send urgent-sounding telegrams from Washington to them, to test how many would be delivered and when. We sent such "emergency" messages ("Aunt Mary very ill. Call at once.") to addresses in Keene, New Hampshire (near where I spent summers as a boy); in Anniston, Alabama (near the home of FCC Commissioner Clifford Durr); in Laramie, Wyoming (to test Embree's boast); and to three other locations. The messages were all filed at 5:00 as of the time of the addressee's offices, which virtually guaranteed non-delivery, since all of those offices closed at 5:00 or 5:30.

Not one of the messages was delivered on the day it was sent, and one or two were delivered several days thereafter by mail.

The commission approved the merger, with Commissioner Durr dissenting. Durr held that the merger was not in the public interest because it provided no guarantee that telegraph service would be improved or that the resulting carrier would be financially sound enough to take advantage of the technological advances waiting in the wings. He commented on the contention of Western Union that delivery of all messages was assured even when the local office was closed, saying, "This contention, however, collapsed in the face of specific examples given of unsuccessful attempts to send urgent messages after the closing hours of the office in the community to which the messages were addressed."

Durr was the one progressive voice on the commission and one of the few progressives left in Washington in 1943. In the early days of the New Deal, he had been appointed as counsel to the Reconstruction Finance Corporation and later to the Federal Communications Commission. He served on the commission for a number of years, representing what passed for the left wing of the commission, which by that time had turned quite conservative. He resigned from the commission in 1948 and became president of the National Lawyers Guild in that year. He lived in Montgomery, Alabama, where for many years he was the only white lawyer who regularly represented blacks who were the subject of racial oppression in that state. He and his wife, Virginia, were famous throughout the South as outspoken supporters of full civil rights for blacks, and the home of the Durrs in Montgomery was a stopping place for members of the Student Nonviolent Coordinating Committee (SNCC) or others who, two decades later, were coming down from the North to work in the South. I stopped over at their home once or twice in the mid-sixties.

The Western Union Strike

The headline in the *New York Times* on January 9, 1946, proclaimed, "Wire Strike Slows Business in City; Only 15% of Messages Go Through." Seven thousand Western Union workers in New York City had walked out, crippling operations at 60 Hudson Street, the telegraph center of the nation, and closing the company's branch offices all over the city. The result of the strike was a blackout of a large portion of the city's communications network. Every bank in New York was affected by the strike; newspapers had difficulty in getting copy from out-of-town sources; commercial transactions, long dependent on telegraphic confirmation, could not be completed in the usual course of business; the stock and commodity exchanges could not keep transactions current; international communications traffic from all over the country was halted.

The events leading to the strike were themselves stormy. To avoid labor disputes during the war and to check inflationary wage increases, a tripartite War Labor Board had been established, consisting of representatives of management, labor, and the public. Regional offices of the board were established to hear management-labor disputes, with appeals to the national board in Washington. The board could not force the parties to a dispute to accept its "directives," but its findings had great effect on the courts, other governmental agencies, and public opinion. But now the war was over and strike was in the air. The wartime processes, designed to prevent or slow down wage increases, were no longer acceptable to most unions, and strikes occurred or were threatened in coal mining, telephone, oil, longshore, auto, tug boats, lumber, and many other industries throughout the country.

Negotiations for a contract between ACA and Western Union began in September 1945. Settlement was reached on a few fringe matters, but wages were a hot issue, and the parties were never even close to agreement. A three-man panel of the Regional War Labor Board was set up to hear the wage issue.

We had a good case. Wages in the telegraph industry had never been high, and they had lagged far behind the increase in the cost of living during the war. One-third of the employees in the metropolitan division earned less than fifty-five cents an hour; half earned less than sixty-five cents an hour.

We won a complete victory after about two weeks of hearings before the regional board. Most of the employees were to get raises of between fifteen cents and twenty-five cents an hour (a great deal in those days), with many raises running to thirty cents and beyond. On the night of the decision, about three thousand union members crowded the auditorium at Manhattan Center to get the news, and enthusiasm ran high. Joe Selly made the principal speech. I spoke for forty minutes, analyzing the decision in detail. The response of the members was what might have been expected. They had been waiting for a wage increase for a long time, and the decision represented a great victory for them and for their union.

An appeal by the company to the national board was inevitable, and we all feared that it would be hard to make the decision stick. The next few weeks were spent in efforts to get Western Union to accept the award, or, alternatively, to prevent the national board from reversing the regional board's decision.

The day after the decision, the union demanded that the company put the increases into effect. The company refused. The union sponsored a series of "spontaneous" job actions, which increased in intensity from day to day. Union sanction of these actions was covert, but a nod or a wink was enough to set off a stoppage, which might last for an hour or a day. A strike vote was taken, and a strike was supported by a vote of about 5,300 to 470. If we exclude the messengers, many of whom were casual short-term workers, substantially all of the employees in the metropolitan division participated.

The company, as was to have been expected, claimed it was unable to pay the increases. The situation was complicated by the fact that the Western Union employees outside of New York, represented by AFL unions, had received an award from a regional board, in a sum of less than half the increases granted to the New York workers. Reconciliation of the two awards was difficult and no one had the standing even to address the problem. The matter was of great importance to both unions, which were competing for the allegiance of all the employees of the company, since a nationwide representation election was foreseen in the not-too-distant future.

Argument before the national board took place in Washington. It was quite an event. Joe believed in the value of visible and active rank-and-file support and so about five hundred Western Union workers came from New York to attend the hearing.

Ralph Kimball, the lawyer for Western Union, addressed the board for about an hour and forty-five minutes, insofar as he could be heard over the jeering and booing of the audience. Joe spoke for about twenty minutes, giving an overall picture of the situation, and I followed with an argument that took an hour and forty minutes. Notes I made after the argument state that I thought that it was the best argument I had ever made and that I was helped a great deal by the crowd behind me, cheering every word I said. It would have been hard not to be eloquent under the circumstances. Even the board seemed impressed.

Tension increased over the next few days. The board was due to go out of existence on December 31; on December 28, the decision was handed down. We lost on almost everything, the vote being eight to four, with the labor members dissenting on substantially every issue. All those great wage increases were gone.

The few days after the decision saw frantic efforts to avoid a strike, with a few new characters intervening in the situation. For one thing, on January 1, Bill O'Dwyer became mayor of New York, and the situation was dumped into his lap. O'Dwyer had been elected to office with an American Labor party endorsement, and we all felt that he owed a great deal to labor. As a leader of the ALP in Brooklyn, I had met with him, his brother Paul, and his law partner, Oscar Bernstien, frequently during the mayoralty campaign and had come away from those meetings with the feeling that he had some sympathetic understanding of the trade union movement, although I understood full well that like all candidates for public office, he was promising more than he would be able to deliver. Anyhow, I was now calling on him to meet his promises—inferential, but unmistakable.

Another new actor in the drama was Arthur Meyer. Arthur had, two years before, acted as arbitrator in two contract disputes between ACA and both Western Union and Postal Telegraph and had handed down decisions highly favorable to ACA in both cases. He was a former chairman of the New York State Mediation Board and was the most respected and most experienced of the labor arbitration professionals in New York State. He had become a close friend of Selly's and mine, and we spent a good deal of time in the next several weeks consulting with him on strategy connected with the strike. Another person appearing on the scene for the first time was Joseph L. Egan, newly elected president of Western Union.

On Sunday, January 5, Joe Selly and I met at Bernstien's house with the mayor, Arthur Meyer, Sidney Cohn, and Bernstien. We were told that Meyer and O'Dwyer had conferred all afternoon with Egan and Kimball, and that Egan, under considerable pressure, had uttered some vague words about a possible arbitration. He said that there could be no arbitration unless it was agreed that any increase in wages would not exceed an aggregate of $300,000; further, the board of directors of the company would have to agree to arbitrate the dispute.

As O'Dwyer and Meyer reported their conversation with Egan, I thought he had not agreed to anything but was merely attempting to defuse the mayor's pressure. He must have known that the $300,000 cap would not be acceptable to the union. Further, Egan could always get the board of directors to disapprove. As reported to us, Egan had been quite arrogant. He didn't think that the union could strike effectively for more than five days in view of the cold weather and the fact that the union was small and not prepared to pay significant strike benefits.

Arthur Meyer, a very clever man, shared my doubts that Egan had actually agreed to arbitrate, but he urged us to treat Egan's conversation with him and the mayor as though it were a bona fide offer. Joe found the $300,000 cap unacceptable, but after about two hours of discussion, he accepted Egan's "offer" to arbitrate, believing that Egan would renege. Nothing was said about the person who was to act as arbitrator, an important—even critical—consideration.

At 11:30 P.M., the mayor called Egan, who announced that the company would not arbitrate the dispute. This was regarded by O'Dwyer as a repudiation of an "agreement" reached earlier that day, and he became quite angry. He gave the company until 2:00 the next afternoon to reconsider and warned Egan that Western Union would not get any breaks from the city if Egan did not come through. The company never called the mayor, so far as I know. O'Dwyer thereupon issued a statement for the press with the mayor's conclusion that the union had agreed to arbitrate and the company had refused. The press and the radio featured the story; the press was quite favorable to the union throughout the strike that followed.

The workers went out on strike at 7:00 on the morning of January 9. A picket line formed very quickly and grew rapidly until 9:00, when there were over three thousand on the line at 60 Hudson Street, the company headquarters, including officers of many of the most important and powerful unions in the city. There were a few brushes with the police for the first few hours, but no arrests were made, and the company was shut down almost completely. Substantially no telegraph traffic moved, and only a handful of scabs went into work.

The effect of the strike was everything that had been hoped for. Not only were the newspapers, the banks, the stock exchanges, and other commercial establishments seriously affected; international traffic was likewise affected, since most traffic originating outside New York and destined for foreign points had to pass through 60 Hudson Street in order to be transferred to the international telegraph companies. The police acted with great restraint, and except for one demonstration at the Times Square branch office, when ten people were arrested (including Joe Selly), no more than three or four arrests were made during the first two weeks of the strike.

Most of the time the picket line presented a festive appearance. Marcia took Joan and Peter down to the line on the third or fourth day. Peter was less than two years old and picketed in a stroller, showing little understanding of the issues in the strike. It was Joan's first (but not last) picket line experience, and she loved it, especially the cops and horses. There was a great deal of singing, mostly of a song consisting of the line, "We're gonna roll the union on," and variations thereof.

There was much support for the strike from the labor community, and collections were taken up for strike relief at community groups throughout the city. By and large, the strike was going well, but it had to settle sometime, and communication with the company was at a minimum. On the union side, we looked for arbitration of the dispute as a solution. But could we get a good arbitrator?

The first and only real trouble on the picket line was on January 25, when the line was particularly large and the police felt impelled to act. Even then, there were only thirteen arrests, for assault and disorderly conduct. However, it gave the company an opening to take the offensive. Late on that afternoon, Joe was served with a set of injunction papers to enjoin the picketing, returnable the next Tuesday. Injunctions in labor disputes had been very difficult to get under New York law for the past decade, and the application wouldn't have bothered us much except that the judge scheduled to hear the case was Aaron J. Levy, something of a notorious figure, and very well known to my family.

I had been hearing Levy's name around the family dinner table for years. My mother and father knew him well and considered him malevolent, crooked, and a liar, not to be trusted in any situation. Levy was not antilabor, my father explained, because he had no principles at all and would rule in favor of anyone who paid enough. Pop warned me not to rely on anything he said. Pop's opinion reflected the general opinion of the bar—Levy was widely distrusted as dishonest and readily available to be bought. His entire career was marked by one scandal after another.

On the return date of the motion, I made a request for an adjournment. Levy granted my request, but only after he denounced "mass picketing" and he "directed" the police to keep the lines open to permit scabs to enter and leave the premises. The press referred to his remarks as a temporary restraining order, though such an order was not permissible under New York law. Neither the pickets nor the police paid any attention to Levy's direction.

In the meantime, the CIO unions in New York were frantic about the possibility of a labor injunction in a major strike in New York, and the New York Industrial Union Council threatened a citywide protest stoppage. The court hearing on Thursday opened in an atmosphere of high tension. The courtroom was packed to capacity, including eight or ten lawyers representing other unions, who sought to intervene in some unarticulated capacity. Levy was angry and ordered all of them to shut up, threatening to have them thrown out of the courtroom. I had a bad case of laryngitis and was unable to talk loudly enough for my voice to reach the bench, and Sam Neuburger took over the proceedings for the union. He moved for a further adjournment—motion denied. He moved that the case be sent to another judge for hearing, the normal procedure at the time—motion denied. He then asked that the judge disqualify himself on the ground that his remarks two days before showed that he had prejudged the case.

Levy, a short, stout man with a shock of white hair, and wearing pince-nez glasses, almost fell off the bench in rage. He screamed at Sam and directed him to appear before the court at the end of the court day, to be held in contempt. The other lawyers present also started to shout, and the courtroom broke out into a riot. I was probably the only one in the room who couldn't yell.

Levy called a recess, and a hearing on Western Union's application for the injunction started late in the morning. After the court day was over, Levy and Sam met and made up. The hearing continued for several days; by the second day I had recovered my voice sufficiently to do my job. The hearing closed on the afternoon of February 6.

Levy then called Kimball into chambers alone and, a half hour later, Selly and I joined them. After some pointless talk, Kimball left, and Levy saw us alone.

He started by telling us how much he loved my mother and father, particularly "Rosie." He repeated that Kimball was concerned mostly with the reaction of the AFL if the company were to settle on the union's terms. Levy said that Kimball thought that he could handle it with the AFL if an arbitrator were appointed who would, by prearrangement, decide in favor of ACA. Kimball therefore agreed to arbitrate, with Max Meyer (no relation to Arthur) as arbitrator, subject, however, to the approval of the company's board of directors. At least that was the message Levy conveyed.

This sounded preposterous to me. Several years earlier, Max Meyer had decided an important arbitration case against Western Union, and only two days before, during the course of the hearing, Kimball had called Max a crook and said he'd never arbitrate a case before him. I didn't know whether Levy or Kimball was trying to set us up—probably both—but I saw no reason to argue with Levy at that point, and I was willing to let the game play out. I told Levy we would arbitrate if Max were the arbitrator. There was no more talk of a fixed arbitration— I knew Max would have none of that, but I also knew the union would do well on the merits.

Levy asked me to stay for a few minutes after Joe left. He pulled a piece of paper off his desk and read to me what he said was a part of the decision he had been about to issue. It was a decision in favor of ACA, and I'm not sure even now why he found it necessary to show it to me, except that he loved to talk, and I suppose he was indicating to me how much he loved the son of Rosie.

The next afternoon we were advised that the board of directors of Western Union had agreed to the proposal to arbitrate, except that the company would not accept Max Meyer as arbitrator.

The company's rejection of Max was the rejection of the idea of arbitration, unless someone else could be found whom the union could trust to view the issues as the regional board had viewed them. We certainly would not give Levy power to chose an arbitrator. I told Levy that the company had rejected Max. He answered that Max wasn't the only arbitrator in the country and that there must be others acceptable to the union. I agreed. That night, I drew a list of about eight arbitrators who would be acceptable to us. The next morning, Joe and I met with Levy for about three hours. He suggested that Judge Sears or Judge Close could act as arbitrator. Both had been judges of appellate courts in New York. Both were very conservative men, completely out of sympathy with the concept of trade unionism, and I rejected them out of hand. I submitted my list. Levy pointed out that they were all Jewish (not true). He suggested that we settle with the company and that he would name as arbitrator anyone that Joe and I would suggest, provided that it was a reasonable suggestion. With him, I reviewed the list of names I had compiled, and finally we all agreed on Abe Pomerantz. I was still apprehensive, keeping in mind the repeated warnings my father had given me, but we seemed to be making progress.

Pomerantz was a successful corporate lawyer. He was well respected in the legal community. I knew of him but had never met him. He was a member of the National Lawyers Guild and an enrolled member of the American Labor party. I assured Joe that he would be as good an arbitrator as we were likely to get.

We met with the company two hours later and drafted a settlement agreement calling for arbitration by an arbitrator to be named by Levy. The company and the union representatives then met in Levy's chambers, where we formally signed a settlement stipulation with the name of the arbitrator left blank. There followed some more discussion as to the arbitrator to be named—discussion that made me very nervous since Levy had privately agreed that very morning to name Pomerantz. In a casual sort of way, Levy tossed out once again the names of Judges Close and Sears, adding Judge Knox, who was, if possible, worse than the others.

The company representatives left, but Joe and I stayed on. I asked Levy why he was talking about Close, Sears, and Knox, as we had agreed on Pomerantz. He pointed out that he could now name anyone he wanted, because the signed copy of the settlement agreement was in his hands, and he could fill in the blank with any name he wished. Joe told him he was wrong—the settlement agreement was, by its terms, subject to approval at a membership meeting to be held the next afternoon (Saturday), and there would be no approval unless a satisfactory arbitrator was named in advance of the meeting. Joe said we wouldn't leave chambers until Levy had filled in Pomerantz's name. Levy said, "What's the matter, Joe? Don't you trust me?" Joe answered, "No." Levy filled in the blank with Pomerantz's name.

For the next two hours we lounged around in Levy's chambers and drank his liquor. Levy got quite drunk and told endless and mostly pointless stories, many of which were apocryphal and featured Rosie. At one point he called me aside and again showed me the opinion he had intended to hand down—but this time it was a decision *against* the union. We finally got away at about nine o'clock.

The proposed settlement was unanimously approved at an overflow meeting of the local at Manhattan Center on Saturday. Joe announced that Abe Pomerantz had been named as arbitrator, and while probably no one in the audience had ever heard of Abe Pomerantz, the members accepted Joe's assurance that he was an honest arbitrator and that we'd get a fair shake. The workers returned to work on Monday.

I relaxed a bit over the weekend. On Monday, I had a conversation with Abe Unger, a leading member of the Lawyers Guild, at the guild office. Abe knew Pomerantz, and he told me that Levy was trying to get Pomerantz to quit, on the ground that he was a Jew, that this was a highly controversial matter, and that Jews shouldn't get mixed up in such things. This was, to say the least, disturbing. Later that day, at a session with the arbitrator, Kimball asked Pomerantz to disqualify himself, on the ground that he was enrolled in the ALP and had been a candidate on that ticket for judge in 1945. (Pomerantz had, in fact, run on both the Democratic and ALP tickets in that year, in Westchester County, where only Republicans were ever elected.) Kimball pointed out that Sam Neuburger, Joe Kehoe, and I were also ALP enrollees. Pomerantz refused to quit. An arbitration session was set for the next Monday.

On the adjourned date, Kimball asked for a further adjournment, claiming that he wasn't ready. On Pomerantz's pressing, he said that he would be ready to go ahead on the following Thursday.

When I got to my office the next day, I found an order seeking the removal of Pomerantz as arbitrator, on the ground that he was enrolled in the ALP and had evinced prolabor views in connection with two strikes in Westchester County in the preceding year. The motion was returnable before Judge Hecht, a jurist whose principal claim to distinction was that he was a Republican on a bench composed almost completely of Democrats. He was justly famous for his mediocrity, a man whose instinct would be to avoid making a decision.

We appeared before Judge Hecht two days later. On Kimball's motion, Hecht referred the case to Levy, as we had expected and feared.

The next night, Marcia and I had dinner with my mother and father, in accordance with a long-established Friday night tradition. By this time, Pop had become emotionally involved in the situation, largely because of Levy's role in it. He urged us to confront Levy, directly and physically—to do everything but beat him up. (Pop was nonviolent, but he endorsed yelling at Levy in these circumstances).

At 8:00 on Monday morning, Joe and I met in Levy's chambers with the company lawyers. Levy went through two hours of play-acting. He claimed he was embarrassed by the motion; Pomerantz was really a very fine man; why doesn't the company let Hecht handle the motion; he was very fond of me, my mother and father (this last, to me alone); Levy had to do his duty, no matter how unpleasant it was; "I won't stultify myself"; he loves Rosie, and so on. Finally, he said he would hear argument in open court.

Argument was held and decision was reserved. Joe and I then met with Unger and Paulson, who told us another disturbing story.

It seemed that Levy had spoken with Pomerantz several times in the past few days. He did his best to get him to withdraw, finally stating that the company had to get a favorable decision. He said that Judge Martin, presiding judge of the Appellate Division, was a close friend of Egan's and that Martin had spoken to Levy about the case, saying that the company would go bankrupt if the union won. Levy, in his conversation with Pomerantz, had predicted, accurately, that the company would make the motion to disqualify him.

All this was pretty bad. Joe and I agreed that Pop's advice was good, namely, that we ought to try to scare Levy. We intended to confront him with the story about his meetings with Pomerantz and see whether we could threaten him—almost threaten him physically—to get him to throw the matter back to Hecht. However, we had to find him first. We called his house and left urgent messages for him but were told he was not there. We parked outside the house, which was dark, calling the house every half hour from a nearby bar, until 11:45. No answer. I called Levy at home at 8:15 the next morning and was told he had left for court. At the court I was told that he hadn't arrived yet. At 10:30, a clerk came out and told us that Levy didn't want to see anyone. At 3:00 Levy signed an order removing Pomerantz and appointing Samuel Seabury as arbitrator.

As I've already said, Seabury and I knew each other very well. He had represented Metropolitan Life in proceedings before the State Labor Relations Board a few years before—a case in which I had represented the Insurance Agents Union. A more conservative man would be hard to find.

Of course, we took an immediate appeal from Levy's order. We had a good case, but I knew that there wasn't much chance that we would win. The feeling in legal circles was that the issue was not so much one between ACA and Western Union as it was between Pomerantz and Seabury, and in that kind of a fight, it was difficult for Pomerantz to win, given Seabury's reputation as being the very essence of honesty and purity. I wasn't concerned much with his honesty and purity but with his conservative and antilabor views.

We lost in the Appellate Division by a vote of five to one. The Court of Appeals affirmed by a vote of six to one. By this time the disappointment had worn off. It was five months after the end of the strike, and we were mostly reconciled to the result.

A week later, I visited Seabury and asked him to withdraw. I told him that the membership had no faith in him and had grave doubts as to his ability to hand down an impartial decision. I said that in ratifying the settlement, the membership had done so with the understanding that Pomerantz was to be the arbitrator; that the personality of the arbitrator was a critical feature of the whole settlement; and that the membership would not have approved the settlement if Seabury had been named as arbitrator in the first instance.

As I expected, Seabury refused, although he was very polite indeed. He said that he wouldn't run away from a responsibility, and that he had a duty to the court and to the public. It was, superficially, a friendly chat, but produced nothing.

Seabury decided the case the next January, and we lost. I confess I didn't feel upset by the result. This was a battle that had been fought and lost months before; the effect of the loss had worn off, and I had accepted it when Seabury was first appointed as arbitrator.

ACA v. Douds

The trade union movement emerged from World War II stronger and more militant than ever. The CIO had organized most large industry, and even the more conservative AFL unions showed an unprecedented degree of activity. The end of the war released a great deal of pent-up energy arising from the fact that during the war there was a virtual ban on strikes, and strict limitations on wage increases. The result was more organizing and more industrial disputes, culminating in many major strikes in 1945 and 1946.

Reaction was not slow in coming. The Republicans won an overwhelming victory in the 1946 election and controlled both House and Senate in 1947. Legislation to curb the growing labor movement was high on the agenda. Simultaneously, but not coincidentally, the cold war against communism was developing. A result was the Taft-Hartley Act.

The Taft-Hartley Act imposed many limits on trade union activity. Many varieties of secondary boycotts were banned; it became more difficult to collect dues; new legal restrictions were placed on trade union activities. Most important to this story was section 9(h) of the law, which provided that a union could not be certified as the representative of any employees for purposes of collective bargaining, nor could it file charges against an employer for violation of the National Labor Relations Act unless each of its officers had filed with the NLRB an affidavit stating that he or she was not a member of or affiliated with the Communist party, and that "he does not believe in and is not a member of or supports any organization that believes in or teaches" the overthrow of the government.

On its face, section 9(h) was a violation of First Amendment rights, and the CIO trade unions had lobbied vigorously against its passage, as did civil liberties groups generally. The CIO had sponsored a large parade in New York protesting the bill; the press reported that one hundred thousand participated, though it seemed more to us. All of this was of no avail. Congress passed the bill by a large margin. President Truman, no great defender of civil liberties, vetoed the bill, but Congress passed the bill over his veto, and it became law on June 23, 1947.

Section 9(h) struck a hard blow at the trade union movement and particularly at the CIO, many of whose unions had officers who were Communist party members or who feared they might be held to be "affiliated with" or "supporters of" the Party. Such vague and ill-defined phrases in the law were capable of casting a net wide enough to include many trade-unionists who were not Party members, and a chill ran through the ranks of the officers of many labor organizations.

Together with a handful of other lawyers, I attended numerous meetings in New York and Washington of union leaders who were members of the Party or close enough to be fearful of the effect of section 9(h). Similar meetings were held in other parts of the country. It wasn't only the Communist lawyers and their clients who met to discuss the law. The CIO convention in the fall of 1947 spent much time and spoke many militant words concerning the new law and section 9(h) in particular. Even Phil Murray, president of the CIO and of the Steelworkers Union, one of the largest unions in the country, was firm in his determination not to file the requisite affidavits. I attended the convention with the ACA delegation and heard him say:

> I stated [at a meeting of the CIO Executive Board] I was unwilling to file an affidavit that I wasn't a Communist. That is a matter of principle. I do not know why the Congress of the United States should require me to do that, as a citizen. I think the Congress is very presumptuous, because I think if they could do that to me about the question of communism, they could do it with any other citizen about any other kind of question. . . . I shall not attempt to explain the manifold reasons . . . which I attach to that principle.

But Murray, like Lord Byron's heroine—while asserting, "I will ne'er consent"—consented. All his brave sentiments dissolved in the cruel light of reality, and he signed the non-Communist affidavit not long after.

There weren't many options. There was much discussion of the labor movement's taking united action against section 9(h), in the form of a boycott of the NLRB and its processes. The labor movement, a few argued, was strong enough to stand on its own feet and could confront even the largest employer with the use of traditional labor methods, primarily the strike, without the aid of the labor board. If not every union could adopt such a tactic, at least some could. Some unions did, in fact, delay in complying with the affidavit provisions of section 9(h), and the United Mine Workers never did comply, but no other major union was strong enough to survive without the services of the NLRB and the certification it could provide. The concept of boycott of the board assumed a courageous, unified, and honest labor movement, and the movement in the United States was not courageous, unified, or honest.

What was happening was precisely what had been foreseen by a small handful of radicals ten years earlier. The National Labor Relations Act provides for the government licensing (or certification) of trade unions, and licenses can be given or withheld. Unfortunately, in this country, disputes between unions are frequent and often more bitter than struggles between unions and employers, and the union without a license has no chance when competing with a licensed union. Originally, licenses were to be given to unions representing a majority of the workers; section 9(h) provided that licenses were to be given to unions representing a majority of the workers only if they have no Communists or Communist sympathizers among their officers.

An illustration of how section 9(h) operated was close at hand. ACA was the collective bargaining representative of the employees of Press Wireless under a contract expiring in August 1948. In June of that year, the Commercial Telegraphers Union (CTU), a rival AFL union that had filed the required affidavits, filed a petition with the NLRB claiming to represent the employees of Press Wireless. An election was thereupon ordered by the board, but ACA was not given a place on the ballot because it had not filed the 9(h) affidavits. Of course, the CTU won the election and was duly certified by the board, replacing ACA.

This experience was duplicated for almost every CIO union that did not immediately comply with section 9(h). Raids by AFL unions on CIO unions were commonplace and even raids by complying CIO unions on noncomplying CIO unions became the order of the day. Every day saw further losses by the left-wing noncomplying unions.

I was tireless in my efforts to convince my friends in the Party and in the affected unions that a legal attack on section 9(h) should be started at once. I was realistic enough to know that such an action might well be lost, though I saw four sure votes for us on the Supreme Court (Justices Black, Douglas, Rutledge, and Murphy), with a slight chance of picking up Jackson, who had written some very good opinions in the recent past. But I saw no downside to legal action, since it didn't seem likely that the progressive trade unions would be able to fight the law politically or in the field, and litigation was the only other option I saw. Bill Standard, attorney for the National Maritime Union, did bring an action early in 1948 in an effort to challenge the law, but it failed for technical reasons, and the constitutional issues were not reached.

I got ACA to authorize the commencement of a suit to declare section 9(h) unconstitutional, and I filed such an action in June 1948, almost a year after the law became effective. We lost before a three-judge court in the district court, with one judge dissenting, and immediately took an appeal to the Supreme Court. The United Steelworkers brought a similar action, in a case presenting a different and somewhat weaker factual situation; more important, however, the moral position of the steelworkers' union was severely impaired by the fact that that union, before its case was argued in the Supreme Court, had itself amended its constitution to prohibit Communists or Communist supporters from holding office in the union, a fact made much of by the government in its argument to the Supreme Court. It was inconsistent logically, if not legally, for the steelworkers to have taken this position internally while objecting to Congress's right to make a law to the same effect. Murray's support of the ban on Communists in his own union was inconsistent with his speech at the CIO convention a year before, but Murray was a supreme pragmatist and never concerned himself overly much with matters of principle. Besides, by 1948 he was having problems with the Communist party as to internal CIO policy, and consideration of freedom of speech and assembly had to take a back seat.

The 9(h) litigation was profoundly important. Not only did it affect the entire trade union movement and the participation of Party members in that movement, but it was a test of the constitutionality of a statute that, for the first time since Reconstruction days, imposed a political test on the right to enjoy the benefits of an act of Congress. A decision holding such a law to be constitutional would open the doors to any number of similar regulations by federal or local government agencies in all areas of governmental action.

Belle Seligman and I worked for weeks on the Supreme Court brief, which reads well even now, almost half a century later. It provided an historical as well as a legal analysis of the place of free speech and the right of association in our history.

I've always enjoyed writing "big" briefs—that is, briefs addressing a significant and important legal issue. If it involves historical research, so much the better. I've always been an historian manqué, and this brief was full of history—particularly the history of freedom of speech as understood by the Jeffersonians of the late eighteenth century: George Hay, George Nicolas, John Taylor of Caroline, Albert Gallatin, James Madison, and, of course, Thomas Jefferson. I'm not sure about how convincing, for example, an essay by George Hay is to a court of the twentieth century, but the research was great fun. It was not entirely an irrelevant display of learning. Judges, too, like to load their opinions with historical precedents, and Justice Black, in his dissent in this case, did his own historical research into sixteenth-century English law. The writing of the brief, too, was thoroughly enjoyable—enjoyable, that is, in retrospect. In fact, it was characterized by a constant battle between Belle and me. We fought over every word, as we did in a few other briefs on which we collaborated. She was never willing to accept my superior status as her employer. It takes a long time to write a brief in this fashion, but the constant clash of ideas makes for a better result, and besides, I liked it. I don't know whether Belle did.

It was not until April 1949 that the case was scheduled for argument. About two weeks before that date, after all the briefs had been filed, I got a call from Joe Selly, asking me to attend a meeting of union officers that evening. The meeting turned out to be a gathering of many of the Communist leaders of the union, together with Roy Hudson and Dora Lipshitz. Both were high-ranking members of the Party, and I had met with both of them, most often with Hudson, at meetings of the ACA section of the Party. Hudson was a tall, raw-boned seaman who spoke in slogans, as though his thoughts were eternal truths. He was one of the most didactic of the Party leaders—light years away from Ben Gold and Irving Potash. Dora Lipshitz was an even higher ranking member of the Party. I never understood exactly what her formal position was, but everyone spoke of her with awe and respect. She was much older than the rest of us and spoke very quietly, as though she were our grandmother, giving us guidance through this difficult world.

Joe told us that Phil Murray had asked him to postpone the argument in our case until the next term of the court in October. I was astonished. I asked what possible reason there could be for such an adjournment. Every day the strength of ACA and other noncomplying unions was being eroded by the activities of raiding unions. Speed, not delay, was essential. Someone should have mounted such a case a year earlier. The very idea of delay horrified me.

Joe explained, or tried to. Murray had told Joe that Truman had asked

Murray to get the argument postponed, because he (Truman) was going to try to get Congress to repeal the law and that such an attempt would not be possible in the event of a Supreme Court decision holding the law constitutional. If we argued the case in April, a decision by the Court was likely by the end of the term in June, and any action by Congress would be impossible before that date.

I was furious. I didn't believe Truman had any such idea in mind. He hadn't even been able to get a third of the Congress to vote to uphold his veto the year before; how could he expect a majority vote now to repeal the law? I wasn't sure why Murray wanted the delay, but I was sure that he wasn't trying to help ACA. Indeed, ACA, like the other left-wing unions of the CIO, was under constant attack by Murray, and by April 1949, the handwriting was on the wall for all who were able to read. The expulsion of ACA from the CIO was coming, and in fact, such expulsion did take place the next year.

The debate on delay was one of those all-night affairs. There was a great deal of support for my position, but it was clear enough that the Communist party was in favor of yielding to Murray's request. I heard no reasons for delay except that Murray wanted it and that he claimed to be speaking for Truman. I saw no reason that we should yield to the request of either of them. It seemed to me an attempt to appease Murray and that it wouldn't work—as turned out to be the fact.

After we were all talked out, a vote was taken. The decision to delay carried, by a single vote—eight to seven, or eleven to ten, or something like that. The decisive votes had been cast by Hudson and Lipshitz, and I was troubled by the fact that a decision had been made by persons who were not members of the union; I was even more troubled by the fact that the decision was a wrong one. And so the next day, on instructions of my client, I asked the Court to postpone the argument until the next October. The government agreed. The postponement was granted. Needless to say, no effort was made by Truman to get Congress to repeal the law.

I well remember that appalling summer of 1949. It was a succession of depressing events. Justice Murphy died of a heart attack in July. Justice Rutledge had a stroke and died in August. And then, late in September, Justice Douglas had a horseback-riding accident at Goose Creek in Washington and was unable to take his place on the bench when it convened in October.

Three sure votes lost, in two short months.

In August, Attorney General Tom Clark was nominated by Truman to succeed Murphy, and he took his seat on the bench on October 3. Judge Sherman Minton,* judge of the Court of Appeals for the Seventh Circuit, was named by Truman to succeed Rutledge.

When the Court convened to hear argument in the ACA case in October, there were only six judges sitting. Douglas was still recovering from his riding accident; Clark disqualified himself, because he had been attorney general at the time the law was passed and when President Truman vetoed it; and Minton had not yet taken the oath of office. Since a tie vote results in an affirmance of the decision below, we had to get the votes of four of the six sitting justices, a formidable task.

Over the past two years I had seen the onrush of what came to be known as the cold war—the president's loyalty order; the indictment, trial, and conviction of the leaders of the Communist party; the imprisonment of ten prominent Hollywood writers for contempt of Congress for their refusal to answer questions by the House Un-American Activities Committee (HUAC); the passage of section 9(h) of the Taft-Hartley Act. Clearly any radical or even mildly progressive speech or thought seemed to be in for a hard time.

None of these issues had yet reached the Supreme Court, and despite my better judgment I looked to the Court as the ultimate guardian of the First Amendment. Intellectually, I knew my reliance on the Court was ill placed. I recognized that the Court was not about to defy the strong political pressure being exerted. We have an independent judiciary in the United States but not when the political chips are down.

But still I remembered the wonderful language in the Supreme Court decisions of the 1930s by Justices Black, Murphy, and Douglas, and, at an earlier date, those by Holmes and Brandeis. Was it not Justice Jackson who had said in an oft-quoted passage in *West Virginia Board of Education v. Barnett:* "If there is any fixed star in our constitutional constellation, it is that no official, high or petty, can prescribe what shall be orthodox in politics, nationalism, religion or other matters of opinion or force citizens to confess by word or act their faith therein. If there are any circumstances which permit an exception, they do not now occur to us."

The atmosphere at the Court on the day of oral argument made all of those wonderful opinions seem irrelevant. I was not only depressed;

---

*It is rumored that, for some years, the reporters covering the Supreme Court gave annual (but informal) recognition to the most poorly reasoned Supreme Court decision of the year. It was called the Sherman Minton Award.

I was also frightened at what was going to happen to the trade union movement, to the Communist party, and to free thought. It turned out worse than I feared.

American Communications Association v. Douds was the first of many arguments I made before the Supreme Court. The subsequent arguments were sheer ecstasy. A chance to argue with nine justices having different personalities and representing different points of view is stimulating. There is a veneer of dignity and solemnity to the proceedings; all that marble and those attendants saying, "Button your jacket" and "Silence, please"—all that ceremony and protocol—is likely to have an effect even on experienced lawyers, whose natural cynicism is at least for the moment diluted by all the pomp and circumstance. At any given moment, most of the justices are likely to be good lawyers and some of them even brilliant. In all but the dullest cases an advocate can count on at least four or five justices staying awake even in the afternoon, and sometimes all nine listen. Metaphorically speaking, the sun is shining brightly in the courtroom when my case is being argued, and I glory in all of it, especially when I'm speaking.

But not so when I argued *ACA v. Douds* in October 1949. The sun wasn't shining in that courtroom on that morning. The weather was dark and foreboding. There were only six judges sitting up there, and those three empty chairs that should have been filled by the sympathetic figures of Douglas, Rutledge, and Murphy were depressing. The hostility in the courtroom was palpable.

It isn't that I was nervous when it came my time to argue. I had never argued a federal appellate case before and only one or two unimportant state court cases, but Leonard and I had rehearsed my argument the night before and I was well prepared. However jumpy I might be before I get on my feet to address a court, I'm never nervous when I start to speak. It was, rather, that I knew that disaster was inevitable.

The argument was a disappointment. Chief Justice Vinson said almost nothing. His opinion was probably written before the clerk pounded his gavel and announced that the Honorable Court was in session. Black was surly and dispirited, as he might well have been, in view of the absence of his three strongest supporters. I have always had trouble in responding to Black's questions from the bench. He spoke with a deep southern accent and in a very low tone, and sometimes I had to guess what questions he was asking. The few queries he put to me merely called for my agreement. Frankfurter, as always, asked more questions than anyone else on the bench, most of them because he enjoyed baiting lawyers from his position of dominance and authority. Jackson and the others were fairly quiet. I thought I argued well; I had no doubt of the justice of my case—or of the outcome of the case.

Solicitor General Philip Perlman argued for the government. If he was representing a president who wanted the law repealed, he certainly gave no sign of it. His argument wasn't much good, but it didn't have to be. A young lawyer once asked me, at the height of the cold war, about the relative importance of the various elements in presenting a case to an appellate court. He wanted to know how much does the brief count, how much the argument, how much the law, how much the facts. I answered, "The brief counts about four points; the argument, three points; the law, five points; the facts, three points; and representing the government, one hundred points." And so it was.

I walked out of the courtroom exhausted and depressed. Everyone on the bench except Black had been hostile, and there was a note of exhilaration in their hostility, as though they had a personal stake in the result, and that result was not going to be favorable to my client. Black was neither hostile nor friendly; he was just angry and bitter.

The Court held the statute constitutional, and the floodgates for repressive legislation were open. Vinson wrote a long opinion upholding the statute. After all, he pointed out, the law doesn't interfere with the right of the union members to choose whomever they want as an officer; it merely means that the government was withholding from a union the use of government facilities if the members chose to elect subversive persons as officers. The opinion showed either a total ignorance of the way the NLRB operated or, much more likely, a disingenuous and dishonest argument intended to support the law despite its clear unconstitutional underpinnings. Black wrote a typically strong dissent, characterized by the expression of outrage he felt at this rape of the First Amendment.

Separate opinions were written by Frankfurter and Jackson. Both opinions were examples of how a good lawyer can reason his way around fundamental legal principles in order to reach the political conclusion he desires. Both judges were men of great intelligence and learning, and both had boasted of liberal credentials in the past. Frankfurter was regarded as a dangerous radical when he was appointed by Roosevelt in 1939. He had defended the anarchists Sacco and Vanzetti while a professor at Harvard Law School. He was coauthor of an influential prolabor book on the use of injunctions in labor disputes, and he had been an articulate supporter of the New Deal in the early thirties. Once on the bench, he was verbose, arrogant, and reactionary. He could be counted on to vote the wrong way almost every time, and to support his decision with great skill cloaked in liberal verbiage. Jackson was an eloquent writer and speaker. He was a staunch defender of freedom of speech—only so long as it didn't matter much. He was great in cases involving freedom of speech for Jehovah's Witnesses—but not when the Communist party was involved.

The concurring opinions of both Frankfurter and Jackson were shameful. It will be recalled that the act required that an affidavit be filed by each officer of the union "that he is not a member of the Communist Party or affiliated with such party, and that he does not believe in and is not a member of or supports any organization that believes in or teaches the overthrow of the United States government by force or by an illegal or unconstitutional method." Both Frankfurter and Jackson found the statute constitutional insofar as it required an oath regarding nonmembership in the Communist party; both quibbled as to the inclusion in the oath of the words such as "believes in" and "affiliated with," but their quibbles made no difference in the result. Jackson repeated all his fine words as to the great importance of free speech and association but found the speech and association of Communists different and subject to governmental control.

I had been angry at the delay that deprived us of three votes on the Court, but in fact, the Court was on a reactionary track; even with the missing judges, there could have been only four votes on the bench to hold the statute unconstitutional, and the result would probably have been much the same if the case had been argued as originally scheduled. The decision itself was cited as justification for years of reactionary legislation, the evil effects of which are still felt in our society. In his dissent in *Braden v. United States*, in 1960, Black noted that "[f]or at least 11 years, since the decision of this Court in *American Communications Assn. v. Douds*, the forces of destruction have been hard at work."

ACA v. Douds was, in effect, overruled by the Warren court in 1964, in *United States v. Brown*, but it had done its job in helping to destroy a strong and growing trade union movement, by eliminating from its leadership a cadre of competent, honest, and militant men and women.

4

The American Labor Party

In 1942 I ran on the American Labor party (ALP) ticket against Jacob Schwartzwald, the Democratic candidate for County Court Judge of Kings County. Shortly before that election, I had occasion to meet with Irwin Steingut, who was the Democratic leader of the Eighteenth Assembly District of Kings County and one of the two or three most powerful Democrats in the state. After we finished our business, whatever it was, he said, "Why don't you join the Democratic party? We need bright, young, Jewish men like you. You'll never get any place in this labor party. If you work in a Democratic club for two or three years, I can almost guarantee you a judgeship or, maybe, a seat in Congress. This fellow Schwartzwald was nominated by us by default. We don't have too many talented people in the party and would certainly be able to put you to some valuable use."

I was not at all tempted. For one thing, I had just joined the Communist party. I wasn't interested in "boring from within" the Democratic organization. Furthermore, the Democratic party of 1942 was far from a satisfactory home for me. The ALP had been organized only a few years before because neither of the major parties had an acceptable program, and nothing much had changed during the intervening years. And so I politely declined Steingut's invitation.

The ALP was organized in 1936. By the end of the previous year, the New Deal, which had exploded with force when Franklin Delano Roosevelt took office as president in March 1933, was running out of steam. Unemployment was still high, and a third of the nation was, in Roosevelt's words, still "ill-housed, ill-clad and ill-nourished." Clearly much more vigorous remedial action by the government was called for.

One of the obstacles to any such action by Congress was the alliance between the conservative Republican party and the Democratic senators and congress members from the South, an alliance that effectively blocked even the modest measures the Roosevelt administration was prepared to sponsor.

The result was renewed interest in a third party—a party based on the rapidly growing labor movement in the industrial areas of the country and the awakening populist movements in the agricultural Midwest. Such third party movements were not uncommon in the history of the United States. There had been a strong Populist party in the Midwest and the South in the late nineteenth century, and there was still a flourishing Farmer-Labor party in Minnesota that had been successful in electing both a governor and a United States senator. And look at what the Labour party had been able to do in England.

The Communist party pushed hard for such a program and often took the lead. Throughout the country, progressive groups, mostly led by the trade unions, called for the creation of such a third party that could prepare and present programs for health insurance, social security, civil rights, and all the other items on the progressive agenda.

I was an enthusiastic supporter of the idea of a Farmer-Labor party, and Marcia and I, together with Lucille, early in 1936 had formed a community group in the Flatbush section of Brooklyn, operating as "The Flatbush Committee for the Formation of a Farmer-Labor Party," or some such name. I recall no direct Communist party participation in the club, though no doubt many of its forty to fifty members were Party members and most of us were sympathetic to the Party. Similar clubs were being organized throughout the city, and in June, a loosely structured citywide coordinating committee of such clubs was set up.

There were two other forces interested in a third party in New York. One was the needle trades unions, most of whose members were foreign-born Jewish and Italian workers with strong socialist backgrounds. The other was President Roosevelt, who felt his nomination by a newly formed labor party would help to hold the votes of a potentially disaffected segment of the working class in the forthcoming presidential election. And so in June 1936, Jim Farley, chairman of the Democratic National Committee, joined with Sidney Hillman, president of the Amalgamated Clothing Workers of America (Amalgamated); David Dubinsky, president of the International Ladies Garment Workers Union (ILGWU); and Alex Rose, president of the Hat and Millinery Workers Union, to form the American Labor party.

Shortly after, the neighborhood clubs merged into the ALP, and clubs were established in every assembly district in New York City. In this process, our Flatbush Farmer-Labor party club, now affiliated with the ALP, absorbed into its membership many members of the needle trades unions residing in our neighborhood. The same was true of similar clubs throughout the city.

Despite the shortness of time and an inadequate organization, the ALP did very well in the 1936 election. In a campaign financed mostly by the needle trades unions, it polled 239,000 votes in New York City (and 36,000 more upstate, where there was almost no organization). This was 11.6 percent of Roosevelt's vote in New York City. No candidates for local office had been put forward by the ALP.

For the Democratic party, the ALP had performed its function, and had it been in charge, the ALP would have been allowed to fade away. But it wasn't in charge. For the leaders of the needle trades unions, the ALP was a political party with, perhaps, permanent and national possibilities—but a party controlled by its leaders as tightly as they controlled their own unions. To us out in the field it presented the possibility of a genuine Farmer-Labor party with a socialist orientation.

There were many differences between Hillman, Dubinsky, and Rose, but one thing that all three had in common was bitter opposition to the Communist party. This hostility had roots in the severe ideological intraunion struggle between rank-and-file members led by the Communist party and the entrenched leadership of all three unions, waged with ferocity a decade earlier—a struggle characterized by much physical violence. All three men were in favor of democracy within their unions, but not too much.

At the time, I was chairman of the ALP club for the Second Assembly District of Kings County, the largest assembly district in the state. It was part of the Eighth Congressional District, then perhaps the most populous in the country. We were strong in the large Jewish population of Flatbush and Brighton Beach, weak elsewhere. In Brighton Beach particularly, there had long been a strong Communist party club, which helped the ALP organization. The introduction into the ALP club of large numbers of members of the Amalgamated and the ILGWU increased the size and effectiveness of the club but it had another result as well.

We "left-wingers" who had organized the Flatbush club were not needle trades workers or even the sons or daughters of needle trades workers. We were not prepared to accept the leadership of the needle trades union officers, with their record of virulent hostility to the Communist party. We were lawyers, teachers, housewives, students, doctors, printers, office workers, and miscellaneous liberals who were interested in progressive politics. A few were members of the Communist party and most, like me, were prepared to accept Party participation, if not leadership. On the average we were probably twenty years younger than the Amalgamated and ILGWU members who became members of our club. We wanted to pick our own local candidates for local office, with the assistance of, but not interference from, Hillman, Dubinsky, and Rose and their unions. We didn't red-bait, and we became angry when union officials came to our club and attacked the Communist party: "Communist kids from Brooklyn College" was their usual epithet.

There were also many differences in style of work. We wanted a year-round program of community activity on both local and national issues— open forums, petition campaigns, street rallies, and the like; our opposition saw the ALP primarily as an election apparatus. We wanted more democracy in the party; "they" feared that more democracy meant a threat of control by the Communist party and its allies, as it had in their unions.

Our experience in the Second Assembly District club was duplicated almost exactly in every other assembly district in the city.

The legal governing bodies of the ALP—the state committee and the county committees—had been set up by the Hillman-Dubinsky-Rose forces to begin with, and were controlled by them. On the other hand, a significant majority of the active members of the ALP—those who belonged to the neighborhood clubs, who circulated nominating petitions and who voted in primary elections—were strongly influenced by the Communist party.

Except for a twenty-two-month period between August 1939 and June 1941, when the left wing (following the lead of the Communist party) strongly opposed entry into the war in Europe while the right wing bolstered Roosevelt's strong support of the British and French forces, there was little programmatic difference between the left wing and the right wing. But there was virtual warfare over the matter of control of the ALP. Primary fights were inevitable.

Control of the party machinery meant many things. It affected choice of candidate, choice of issues to be emphasized, and the nature of day-to-day political activity. More important, it affected the question of whether Communists were to be welcomed into or excluded from the organization. An exclusionary third party in which anticommunism was a dogma was not acceptable to me or my friends.

The left-wing forces, organized under the name of the Progressive

Committee to Rebuild the American Labor Party, quickly won control of the New York County Committee of the ALP, but the primary fights in Kings County, my base, were more intense.* In 1941, there was a primary fight for members of the county committee, which we lost when the incumbent county officers, officers of the ILGWU, called the organization meeting of the committee at a hall that would accommodate about one-third of the members of the committee, and those who had been elected on the progressive committee slate could not even get into the hall. We started immediately to prepare for the primary elections to be held in two years. In 1942 I won a primary against the right-wing candidate for the office of City Court Judge for Kings County. In April 1943, I became executive secretary of the Progressive Committee of Kings County, with the responsibility of managing the primary campaign of that year.

Both we and the right wing filed full lists of candidates in the 1943 primary. We waged a vigorous campaign, involving thousands of devoted volunteer workers. We elected 1,952 committee members; the right wing, 1,477. But we remembered the 1941 experience, and we still confronted the task of prevailing at the meeting of the county committee. We brought a lawsuit prior to the meeting seeking a court-appointed referee to run the meeting. We were unsuccessful.

The county committee meeting was held on August 30, 1943, at a larger hall than in 1941 but it was still not large enough. We had the support of about 75 to 80 percent of those attending. John Gelo, as incumbent chair, presided at the meeting. We nominated John Crawford of the American Newspaper Guild for chair of the committee. Gelo was also nominated and forthwith declared himself elected on the basis of a voice vote. The meeting was quickly adjourned.

After the meeting, our people stayed for hours to sign affidavits of protest for use in a lawsuit to declare the meeting a nullity. We worked

*A word on the political structure of New York City may be helpful to those who don't live there and perhaps some who do. There are five subdivisions of the city, which for purposes of city government are designated "boroughs" and for purposes of state government are called "counties." The County of Kings is the Borough of Brooklyn; the County of New York is the Borough of Manhattan; the County of Bronx is the Borough of *The* Bronx; the County of Richmond is the Borough of Staten Island; Queens is Queens, whether county or borough. The result is sometimes confusing to out-of-town visitors. Elections are conducted in counties, but we use borough names in ordinary discourse. No one visits "Bronx"; they visit "*the* Bronx." No one ever refers to "Kings," except in a formal legal sense, and our baseball team was the Brooklyn Dodgers.

all night to collect about 1,400 affidavits, and since the total announced attendance at the meeting was only 2,500, our chances in court were quite good. We did in fact win, in a case that went up to New York's highest court, and a new meeting was ordered for October 11, in a larger hall.

The weather was cold on the night of the meeting, and a light drizzle fell throughout the evening. At 5:45 P.M. the doors were opened and the delegates to the meeting were permitted to enter; in a short while the line outside the entrance into the hall had extended all around the block. It was 11:30 before all the delegates were admitted. Numbered credentials had been issued to all elected committee members. The right-wing members got credentials numbered 1 to 1,499; our elected members received credentials numbered 1,500 and over. It was thus easy for the guardians of the doorway to identify our supporters and to delay and discourage them. The doorkeepers insisted on careful and meticulous examination of the credentials of every one of our delegates; those who could not supply identification were denied admission and often had to go home to get some acceptable documentation.

However, the primary campaign had been a very intense one, and we felt that we had been fighting a holy war. Almost all of us stuck it out despite the inconvenience and the inclement weather. This meeting was, in the minds of everyone, the result of a hard-fought campaign for which we had been preparing for two years, and no one was ready to give up at the moment of realization of victory, just because it was raining. I spent most of the evening on the street walking up and down the line of those seeking admission to keep spirits high.

At 11:50 P.M., Gelo called the meeting to order. He spent fifteen minutes in greeting the assembly, appointing a Sargent at Arms and a few more officers to help run the meeting. Then, glancing at his watch, he said, "It is now past midnight on October 12. The court ordered the meeting for October 11, and that is clearly impossible. Moreover, today is a holiday [Columbus Day], and it would be illegal to hold a meeting today. I therefore declare the meeting adjourned." He walked off the platform and out of the hall.

Pandemonium broke loose. Fist fights flared in a few spots. The pro-Gelo forces walked out; our delegates remained. I took the chair, called the meeting to order, and quickly went through the necessary formalities. The meeting proceeded to choose county committee officers. We were finished at about 1:30 A.M., when Vito Marcantonio, who was chairman of the New York County committee and the accepted leader of all of the left-wing forces, who had arrived an hour earlier, made one of his usual rousing speeches. We all went home with the feeling that we had won a great victory, and so we had. The board of elections recognized us as the legitimate county committee, and that decision stuck despite the usual litigation. At last it seemed possible to build a militant and progressive American Labor party without interference from an anti-Communist right wing.

The outbreak of the war between Germany and the Soviet Union and the attack on Pearl Harbor resulted in a significant realignment of forces in the ALP. All of Hillman's energy for the next few years was devoted to the prosecution of the war, and he had no time or desire to carry on a political battle against the Communists and their sympathizers in the ALP. On the contrary, he was prepared to work with persons he knew or thought were Communists to build a strong ALP, demanding only that they not be publicly and officially members of the Communist party. The road wasn't always a smooth one, but it resulted in a greater degree of unity in the party than we had ever known.

Dubinsky and Rose and their respective unions thought otherwise, and their campaign against everyone in the ALP whom they thought was a Red (a class that now included Hillman) was relentless. The 1944 primary for control of the state committee was a victory for the left-wing forces, now supported by Hillman.

Dubinsky and Rose left the ALP and led their members into a newly organized Liberal party, splitting the potential third-party vote. Needless to say, this resulted in much confusion among the electorate. When one of the members of our left-wing Kings Highway Club attempted to rent a meeting hall in a building owned by Mrs. Dubin, a member of Dave Dubinsky's family, he was asked, "Is this David's ALP or Sidney's ALP?" He had to look elsewhere for a meeting hall.

But while all this was going on, we were working to organize and build a political party, to develop a political program, and to present candidates for political office. There were few districts in New York City prior to the mid-1930s in which either of the major political parties carried on a local campaign or raised any significant political issues, since the Democratic party was dominant and the victory of its candidates was a foregone conclusion. It had been, for decades, enough to assure the voters that its candidates were "Honest, Able and Fearless," a slogan that appeared with minor variations on thousands of election placards.

That situation had changed significantly in 1937. From 1937 to 1952, the ALP ran candidates on its own line for substantially every elective office in New York City (I'm not sure about upstate, but it was probably true there too). We ran an independent (i.e., third-party) candidate for president (Henry Wallace in 1948); for governor of New York (Dean Alfange in 1942); and for mayor of New York City (Vito Marcantonio in 1949). In about 35 percent of the elections for Congress and the state legislature held in New York City, we ran our own ALP candidates. Otherwise we endorsed the Democratic candidate and occasionally even the Republican. In my district, we almost always ran an independent candidate. In every case, we raised our own issues. Sometimes we won.

I have turned up a few copies of leaflets I distributed in my 1947 campaign for Congress. They show that I presented several current issues: the increase in the cost of living, lack of adequate housing, proportional representation, repeal of the Taft-Hartley Act, and establishment of a Jewish state in Palestine. None of these issues except the last was addressed by either of the two major parties.

A Jewish state in Palestine was a hot issue in 1947. Prior to World War II, the most radical segment of Jewish thought, which I had assimilated almost by osmosis, was anti-Zionist and opposed a Jewish state in Palestine. Such a state, my father pointed out to me, could not survive in the midst of a much greater and hostile Arab population, which differed from it in religion, culture, and language. All of this changed with the persecution of the Jews by Hitler, and most progressives favored the establishment of a Jewish homeland in Palestine. The issue was certainly of great importance to ALP voters. Today all of the arguments of the anti-Zionists are being repeated, with full force. I rejected the premise of Zionism in 1932 and in 1995, but not in 1947.

Though we ran independent candidates quite often, it was unusual that our candidate expected or even wanted to win. I ran for office three times, and the thought of winning would have horrified me if it had ever crossed my mind. An exception to this rule was Jim King.

The congressional race in our district in 1944 resulted in a serious confrontation with the Communist party. District lines had just been redrawn, and as a result, there was no incumbent in the Fourteenth Congressional District. Furthermore, the district was one of the two or three strongest ALP districts in the state (Marc's district, of course, was always first in ALP strength). I was then the district leader. The district clubs decided early in 1944 to put Jim King forward for Congress. He was a very attractive candidate. He was president of a local of the State, County and Municipal Workers Union, a CIO "left-wing" union. He was personable, an excellent speaker, and very progressive in his political views. He was anxious to run and felt that he could get support both in money and personnel from other CIO unions. He was in every respect an ideal candidate.

We easily collected the necessary signatures and filed them with the board of elections. Under the election law, we had until the next Friday at midnight to withdraw his name, and three days more to substitute another. At 10:00 Friday morning, Jim and I were invited to attend an "important meeting" at the Kings County office of the Communist party, where we met Joe Roberts, who was the Kings County organizer for the Party, and several other Party officials. We were told that Jim was to withdraw as candidate for Congress in favor of Leo Rayfiel, the Democrat who had represented part of the new district. Rayfiel was a nondescript lawyer who had compiled a nondescript record as an assemblyman and a congressman.

Jim and I were stunned, though we had been forewarned. There had been, for a month or two before, a running conflict between the Communist party organization in Brooklyn and the Communist party members in the ALP (such as me). The Party, pursuant to its then-prevailing united front policy, had been attempting to deliver the ALP nominations to a number of Democratic candidates in the county and evidently had made promises to the Democratic party to that effect. We in the ALP local clubs had been resisting this process, resulting in endless ill-tempered meetings. To my mind, the situation in the Fourteenth Congressional District represented the worst aspect of the united front policy. United action by all of us was seen as necessary to win the war, but I could not see how the endorsement of Rayfiel for Congress would have any effect on the war. To me the maintenance of ALP identity was of prime importance and endorsement of a third-rate candidate for Congress had no justification.

At our Friday meeting, I tried, without success, to convince the Party representatives that the ALP was to choose its own candidates through its own apparatus and that Communist party advice would be listened to but that Communist party direction would not be tolerated. Even if there had been a good reason for endorsing Rayfiel (and we saw none), Jim's withdrawal would have had devastating organizational effects, and to me that was of even greater importance than the question of running a candidate. I've long since forgotten the reason put forth for our proposed endorsement of Rayfiel. Among other things, the Party thought King couldn't win, a conclusion I thought not to be decisive.

The meeting broke up at about 6:00, with everyone in a bad mood. Jim and I left the meeting and walked through the streets of Brooklyn for the next few hours. We stopped to have a bite to eat and walked and walked. Neither of us took the views of the Party lightly, but we could not accept this dictation of policy. Twelve o'clock was the deadline for withdrawals, and finally, when midnight approached and passed, a heavy load was lifted from our shoulders. Of course, we still had the matter of running a campaign, and both of us were concerned lest the Party and the state ALP organization might be only lukewarm in supporting Jim's candidacy, but nevertheless we had made our decision.

The campaign was a good one, though we didn't get as much support from either the Communist party or the state organization of the ALP as we thought we were entitled to. For one thing, Marcantonio was running for Congress, and many campaign workers felt that his reelection was of the greatest importance and went up to the east side of Manhattan to help him. (He won the primary elections in all three parties that year.) Jim carried on a swell but losing campaign; sadly he became convinced in the last few weeks of the campaign that he would win. This is a common fantasy of candidates for office—one I never shared.

Henry Wallace had been vice-president during Roosevelt's third term from 1940 to 1944. In 1948 he ran for president on the Progressive party ticket. The ALP was the New York arm of the Progressive party, and those of us who believed in a nationwide third party greeted this campaign with enthusiasm. No one expected Wallace to win, but both Truman and his opponent, Tom Dewey, were unpopular with our constituency. We carried on an active campaign in our congressional district, hoping that a big vote for Wallace might result in the election of a congressman. The Progressive party supplied us with a candidate who had a nationwide reputation: Lee Pressman, who had been general counsel for the CIO and for the steelworkers union for some years. He was as strong a candidate as we could have wished for—he had high-level name recognition, skills as a speaker, and a program that would appeal to the voters in our district. As a matter of fact, he was seen as so much of a threat that the Democratic and Republican parties, for the first time in our district's recent history, both endorsed the incumbent Democrat to prevent a Pressman victory.

But what about his campaign? Well, as mentioned later in these memoirs, I wasn't very fond of Pressman. I managed the campaign as well as I could, but his arrogance came across strongly. He had been accustomed to associating with the most influential figures in the Truman administration and the task of touring the six or eight ALP clubs in the congressional district or addressing anything less than a mass meeting did not appeal to him; he carried out such chores seldom and reluctantly. But a remote campaign, consisting of speeches at Madison Square Garden meetings, did not go over well with the electorate, who were interested in someone they could relate to on a more personal level. As it turned out, Pressman could not have won anyhow, but we missed the chance to record a good showing for the organization.

The Wallace campaign was a failure. The cold war was at that time well underway, and the red-baiting was intense. Philip Murray, president of the CIO, and Hillman were both close to Truman and exerted great pressure on the CIO unions to support him. Furthermore, the progressive part of the electorate, while it may have been attracted by the Wallace program, was truly frightened of Dewey, who represented, in its eyes, the most reactionary forces in the United States. Primitive exit polls in our district indicated that many voters preferred Wallace but were frightened of Dewey and were afraid of splitting the Truman vote.

We never yielded to the idolatry of Truman, who had dropped the atomic bomb on Japan, broken a railroad strike, instituted proceedings against the Communist party leaders, enforced with vigor the Taft-Hartley Act, and initiated the most severe attack on civil liberties in a hundred and fifty years. It is doubtful Dewey could have done worse. His record on civil liberties was better than Truman's and his international policy couldn't be worse, as we saw it. Once again, we saw little difference between the Republican and Democratic parties. But most of our potential voters didn't agree, though the ALP vote in New York City and in our district was not bad—in fact our vote for Wallace was higher than our vote for Roosevelt had been four years before.

In 1949, Marcantonio ran for mayor of New York on the ALP ticket, against the incumbent, O'Dwyer. We waged a good campaign, and Marc himself was tireless, but we really had no chance, though Marc, like most candidates, thought differently. He was attacked by every newspaper in the city as a Communist, and the ALP didn't have the resources to meet that attack. Although the ALP lingered on for a few years more, it could not survive the cold war, and it was formally dissolved after the 1952 election.

I played an active role in all of these ALP campaigns through 1949— those in which I was a candidate as well as all of the others. Rarely could we afford to pay a campaign manager, and so I often undertook that job, with all the administrative work that came with it. I spoke a great deal on streetcorners, sometimes as often as two or three times a night during the election campaigns. I enjoyed that. In the early days of the ALP, certainly until the war, the Christian Front, a Catholic organization, was intent on breaking up our meetings, and many of them were carried on only under police protection. The corner of Kings Highway and East Seventeenth Street was a favorite place to congregate, and often we had a meeting on one corner and the Christian Front had its meeting across the street, with a half dozen police officers between. The members of the Front were vociferous opponents of President Roosevelt and contended that we were a bunch of Communists, a point of view they expressed by throwing rocks and bottles.

As I look back on the scene from fifty years down the road, the devotion of the ALP club members was astonishing. Election campaigns at the grassroots level consist of quite dull work, whether it be a primary or a general election. Long hours are spent in tasks requiring clerical rather than political skills—the preparation of legally required petitions, the preparation of campaign material, the mailing of appeals for money, and more. Much of our campaign was carried on in the streets— meetings, distribution of leaflets, the posting of placards, and most important of all, door-to-door canvassing. We never could afford newspaper or radio ads or telephone or mail campaigns. All campaign work, of course, was done by volunteers. We never had enough money even to pay the printers on time.

I enjoyed all of it, not only in retrospect, but even while it happened. None of us stood to gain anything from the work we were doing. Except in the very rare case, we were not going to elect our candidate to office. No patronage was going to come our way. No storekeeper could come to us to ask that we smooth over a problem with a city licensing department. We couldn't even fix a traffic ticket. There was, of course, the rare case, and that was Marc's district in East Harlem. He provided effective help in dealing with the government at all levels and his constituency loved him as a result and elected him over and over again. But such good fortune was not visited on anyone else.

Much of my life at this time was devoted to a succession of meetings at local, county, and city levels, especially after the formation of the Progressive Committee in 1940. I was chair of the Kings Highway club for much of the time between 1936 and 1945 and executive secretary of the Progressive Committee beginning in April 1943. I was chair of the Kings County committee for part of the time after the 1943 primary. After 1945, most of my activity was at a county rather than a club level. I ran for Congress in 1947 and managed the Pressman campaign in 1948.

All of this was at a time when my work for ACA was at its peak. It wasn't at all unusual for me to catch a train to Washington at 8:00 in the morning for a 2:00 P.M. meeting at the Federal Communications Commission or at the NLRB, to return to New York on the 4:00 train and to attend one or two ALP meetings in the evening. Air travel was impossible during the war and for a year or two after, and it was frequently difficult even to get a seat on the train.

The ALP was a vital force in New York City politics for thirteen years. When, in 1937, almost half a million voters—over a fifth of the electorate—gave the ALP their support, they did so not because of the popularity of its candidates (who also ran on the Republican and Fusion lines) but, we must assume, because they accepted the premise that the ALP was preferable to the Democratic or Republican parties. The ALP corralled over 11 percent of the vote in New York City every year but one from 1937 to 1949, and in many districts the vote was consistently over 20 percent. In my district, we were the second-ranking party much of the time.

Marcantonio, the chairman of the ALP, was elected to Congress seven times. He was the most effective spokesperson for progressive politics in that body. Leo Isaacson was elected to Congress for a single term, on the ALP ticket. Fiorello La Guardia, who was enrolled in the ALP, was elected mayor of the city in 1943. He was probably the most influential mayor in the United States. We elected several members of the state legislature and of the city council. In 1948, in a presidential campaign characterized by intensive red-baiting, 422,000 voters chose Henry Wallace in New York City; in 1949, 356,000 voters supported Marc for mayor.

During all of its existence, the American Labor party promoted a political program far in advance of anything the major political parties espoused. The platform in my 1947 campaign for Congress, described above, was typical—adequate housing, reduction of the cost of living, protection of the trade union movement, peace—and we discussed these issues with the electorate, not only at election time but throughout the year. Neither of the other parties carried on any campaign on a local level. We were the only political voice in opposition to the Korean War, and Marc cast the only vote in Congress against increasing the number of U.S. troops in that conflict.

There is a byproduct of the ALP that has great importance. Like Shakespeare's English soldiers who fought the battle of Agincourt under King Henry V, there is a generation of radicals who remember the battles of their youth—standing in the rain during the 1943 county committee meeting in Brooklyn, or canvassing for Marc in 1949, or shouting down the hecklers on streetcorners. Many of them (or their children) formed the backbone of the anti–nuclear weapons movement of the fifties, of the civil rights movement of the sixties, and of the antiwar movement of the sixties and seventies. Some went into the reform Democratic movement in New York and changed the face of the Democratic party in the city. Most of them have never left the Progressive movement. Their activity may be a bit dulled by age but their political principles are still sharp, and this is no small contribution.

In the late years of the Bush administration, the ideological wasteland of both major political parties once again aroused widespread interest in independent political action, and beginning in 1989 many organizations appeared with overlapping but not identical agendas dedicated to the sponsorship of a new political party. Success has been limited. The question arises as to what, if anything, can be learned from the ALP experience.

The experience of one generation cannot easily be transposed to another, many years later. Fifty years is a long time in our dynamic society, and the political, demographic, and sociological characteristics of the electorate in the mid-1990s differ greatly from those a half century earlier, especially in the large population centers. The ALP could not have lasted beyond its first political campaign had it not been for the trade union movement and the Communist party, and the community clubs that had been created by them even before the ALP existed. The trade union movement in 1995 seems uninterested in political action outside the mainstream; and today there is no effective Communist party.

Furthermore, the nature of political campaigns has changed materially. Television, which now dominates the election process, is expensive beyond the wildest dreams of any third-party movement not backed by a multimillionaire. Street campaigners, the lifeblood of the more successful ALP campaigns, will find it difficult to compete with popular television programs; door-to-door canvassing is not likely to be successful in the inner cities; and in many places, the middle-class liberal intellectuals, an important element of the ALP, have fled from large urban centers to the suburbs, where their political influence is often diverted into the Democratic party.

This said, it is clear that there is once again widespread voter disaffection with the major political parties. Perot, running for president in 1992, polled 19 percent of the vote on a platform totally devoid of substance but backed by millions of dollars. Furthermore, the American voter has never been locked into his or her party affiliation, and vote splitting is a common phenomenon in almost every major election. And so both the need for independent political action and the opportunity are clear. That, however, is not enough.

No new left-wing political party will be able to compensate for its inability to provide expensive media coverage except by creating a mass political organization capable of supplying large numbers of young and enthusiastic campaign workers at election time, and between elections as well. This is not an easy task, and I don't believe it can be done at all by a political party, unless the party appears on the ballot in support of its own candidates and in support of a platform that differs significantly from the platform of the other two parties.

Nor will it be sufficient if electoral contests for public office are confined to contests of slight visibility. An independent party that defines its goal as the election of two members of a thirty-five-person city council or a member of a county board of supervisors will have trouble building a state or national party. The conclusion that a new national or state independent party is needed is based on the premise that in many—perhaps most—electoral contests, neither existing party fields satisfactory candidates.

This does not mean that an independent party must propose an independent candidate for every office in every election. Many candidates of the major parties will have progressive records and should be supported. But I don't believe any kind of organization can be built if the third party does nothing but support the better of the candidates of the Democratic and Republican parties.

The ALP was fortunate in its origin. It sprang fully armed from the unusual coordinated efforts of FDR, the needle trades unions, and the Communist party in 1936, each pursuing a different end result. Even local clubs were, in many districts, already in place when the statewide party was formed. That was sheer luck and will not be easily duplicated.

The ALP was most successful when it was able to arouse its constituency in support of a candidate of its own. Marcantonio was such a candidate; La Guardia was regarded as such a candidate, and those who were chosen by local ALP clubs were similarly seen as "our" candidates. It sometimes happened that support of a Democrat or even a Republican was able to arouse the necessary enthusiasm of ALP workers, but that was the exception and not the rule.

Beyond this, it is difficult to formulate general rules for success. Election laws differ from state to state, and further, no two electoral situations are likely to be identical.

■

The ALP did not formally dissolve until 1953, but I dropped out after the 1949 election. The rising tide of the cold war—which threatened to destroy the radical trade union movement, the Communist party, and my law practice, more or less simultaneously—occupied all of my thoughts and consumed all of my energy, and it seemed certain that the ALP could not survive the coming storm. I do not suppose I analyzed the options then as rationally as I do now, but I could not save the whole world and I let the third-party movement go.

Moreover, I moved out of Brooklyn to New Rochelle, in Westchester County, in 1950, and by that time the ALP club in New Rochelle was all but invisible.

But a third party—a left-wing third party—is needed now as much as it ever was, if not more. Now, as then, most people in the United States are not represented by any party, and that representation is increasingly needed.

I listen carefully for a trumpet call to action, but I hear it only faintly.

5

The Struggle for Socialism

It was sometime late in 1942 that I joined the Communist party. It was ✓ not a Big Event in my life. There was no soundtrack playing either triumphant or ominous music. The only remarkable thing about it was that I hadn't joined sooner. Since 1938, I had been surrounded by members of the Party, most of whom I admired, and many of whom seemed intent on recruiting me. It was one of the union crowd at ACA who finally signed me up and gave me one of those cards that congressional committees talked about a few years later.

Everything I saw around me confirmed my understanding of the principles of Marxism. Capitalism had resulted in successive periods of severe economic depression and two worldwide wars in my lifetime. Fascism was an imminent threat. A new order of things was called for, and the only credible alternative in sight was socialism.

The attraction of socialism wasn't merely negative. It promised an egalitarian and compassionate organization of society. Not so the promise of capitalism. A capitalist economy requires the accumulation of great wealth by some, and Adam Smith, the high priest of capitalism, had prophetically stated, "Wherever there is great property, there is great inequality. For one very rich man, there must be at least 500 poor and the affluence of the rich presupposes the indigence of the many." This goal of the capitalist system has easily been reached. It is reported that in the United States there are 93 billionaires and about 27 million persons living below the poverty level. The promise of socialism may perhaps be illusory, but the objective of capitalism is misery for many. Why opt for the latter?

Socialism in the United States was a far-off goal, but there were many intermediate goals: honest and militant trade unionism; racial equality; universal health care; the alleviation and ultimate eradication of poverty; and the extension of democracy. None of this could be accomplished without organization and there weren't many organizations available that looked to socialism as the ultimate goal. I had met Norman Thomas, the leader of the Socialist party, and had heard him speak many times. He was too charming, too gentle, too "churchy" to lead a revolution. The Socialist Workers party, the Socialist Labor party, and other splinter groups seemed didactic and powerless. The Communist party was the only game in town. It led the campaign for the rights of blacks, particularly in the South and in the trade unions; it was the most dynamic voice against fascism. It gave leadership to the most militant trade unions. Its agenda was my agenda.

And then of course there was the Soviet Union, which was carrying the red flag of socialism and offering leadership to the oppressed of all the world. I had identified with the Soviet Union almost from the time I began to read the newspaper. Its form of socialism was working as well as could be expected, given the many obstacles it had to overcome. I knew that socialism in the United States would have to find its own shape, but the U.S.S.R. provided a model, imperfect as it was. The role of the Soviet Union in the Spanish civil war had served to increase my enthusiasm for it. It was the strongest antifascist force in the world.

The Communist Party of the United States of America (CPUSA) was the local representative of the ruling Communist Party of the Soviet Union. This was true in more than a rhetorical sense. From the very beginning the CPUSA had been affiliated with Communist International (the Comintern), which consisted of most of the Communist parties of the world—all those accepting the leadership of the Soviet Union. In 1940, the CPUSA disaffiliated from the Comintern, but only nominally, I suspect. In any event, the Comintern itself dissolved in 1943, its leaders stating that national differences made centralized leadership of the world Communist movement no longer appropriate. This was undoubtedly a step calculated to help relationships between the Soviet Union and Roosevelt and Churchill, and I viewed it as an unpleasant necessity.

I regarded cooperation among the world Communist parties as perfectly reasonable. The ideological goal of all was the same—though as time passed, the differences among those parties grew. The ultimate goal of the Communist movement was socialism for all the industrialized world. This was not necessarily to be effected through violent revolution. Indeed, Marx had expressed the optimistic hope that in the most advanced industrial countries, namely the United States and Great Britain, a peaceful transition to socialism might be possible. But certainly close cooperation among the Communist parties of all the world was called for, and in that community of Communist parties was the Communist Party of the United States.

To all of this was added a skillful public relations campaign by the Soviet Union supported in every way possible by the Party in the United States and by all of us, Party members and fellow travelers alike. Excellent Soviet films, ballet, music, books, and dramatic presentations flooded the country—or at least they flooded New York and other metropolitan centers. The World's Fair of 1939, held in New York, featured a sensational Soviet exhibit housed in a massive building made of red marble and surmounted by the then familiar logo of the idealized Soviet man and woman striding confidently into the bright future, unaware that just ahead was the most terrible war in history.

Much has recently been made of the "discovery" that money from the Soviet Union—or, to be more accurate, from the Comintern—had supported the CPUSA. The charge was an old one indeed. I had heard it long before I joined the Party. I had no personal knowledge of the facts, but I had always assumed that it was true. Recent disclosures indicate that such funds were used to establish a bookstore and to support the Party newspaper.

It has also been revealed that the Comintern and perhaps the Soviet Union had espionage agents in the United States and that some of them were members of, and indeed had been recruited by top leaders of, the CPUSA. Every large nation, including the United States, has always employed spies, and I would suppose they are recruited from many sources. But espionage is, by definition, a secret matter, and certainly none of the rank and file or secondary leadership of the Party could have known about such activities, nor did they affect the aims and activities of ordinary Party members. There has been no suggestion that any Party members so recruited were motivated by anything other than ideological considerations, and it is not surprising that in the context of 1935–45, many Party members would have felt a deep sense of loyalty to the idea of socialism as then embodied in the Soviet Union.

The escutcheon of the Soviet Union was, I recognized from the outset, not unblemished. The Trotskyist trials of the mid-thirties gave me pause, but not much. I read the transcripts of the trials and they puzzled me. I did not at that time realize the extent of those purges, but it wouldn't have made any difference. One does not renounce a cause in which one believes because crimes are committed in its name. Practicing Catholics remain in the church with full knowledge of the horrors of the Inquisition, and one does not forswear the United States because it slaughtered hundreds of thousands of Native Americans to steal their land. I knew that internal and bloody battles within the forces of a successful revolution are commonplace (see for example the French Revolution) and I accepted the trials of the thirties as a more or less normal aftermath of the Russian Revolution and the civil war that followed. It is too bad that a socialist revolution was so bloody, but the purges in the Soviet Union in 1934–38 happened, and we cannot undo them, nor let them stand in the way of progress.

The nonaggression pact between Hitler's Germany and Stalin's Soviet Union was another problem. It was followed by Hitler's invasion of Poland and war between Germany, and England and France. The war spread rapidly throughout Western Europe. The pact and its consequences sent a profound shock through the ranks of Party members and Party sympathizers. One of my Party friends quipped, "All of the non-Party members are tearing up their non-Party cards." Clever, but many Party members tore up their Party cards, too, and many turned into lifelong anti-Communists. The defection was particularly severe among intellectuals, both Party members and sympathizers. The rank and file, both in the street branches and in the trade unions, were not so seriously affected, though membership did fall off even in this category. The effect on me, as on others, was traumatic. Clearly I had to abandon my Manichean view of the world—all elements in it were not wholly good or evil.

However, it took me little time to adapt to this change in circumstances. Worldwide fascism was clearly on the march. Hitler had taken over Austria and a good part of Czechoslovakia. His surrogates, Mussolini and Franco, had conquered Ethiopia and Spain. Only a fool could believe that the Nazis would rest on their laurels. The only question was the direction in which they would strike.

It was clear that the Western powers had no love for the Soviet Union and that many in the United States, England, and France saw Nazi Germany as a bulwark against communism. If Hitler struck toward the east, England, France, and the United States could be counted on to maintain the same hands-off "neutrality" they had observed in the case of the earlier depredations of fascism in Ethiopia, Czechoslovakia, and Spain, and the destruction of the Soviet Union and the ultimate victory of Hitler might well be the result. And so the pact; it was an evil, but in this world of great power intrigue, a necessary evil. This was *Realpolitik;*

ideology had to give way in this crisis. Such was the conclusion I reached at the time, and nothing has happened since to change my view.

In the twenty-two months between the nonaggression pact and the German invasion of the Soviet Union, the line of the Communist party in the United States was one of militant neutrality, and that line appealed to a streak of pacifism in my nature. My friends and I went to antiwar meetings, sang antiwar songs, and joined hands with some of the most reactionary forces in the country in an effort to keep the United States out of "the imperialist war." I followed the line faithfully but I was more than a bit uneasy. All of the combatants were capitalist, imperialist powers, but to say that there was no difference between German imperialism and British imperialism defied reason. However, I was a disciplined non–Party member and went along, even though it was not quite clear why the Nazi-Soviet Pact required United States neutrality in England's war against Hitler. In retrospect, the policy of the Party can be seen to have been wrong-headed and self-destructive, and I take no pride in having supported it.

When, in June 1941, Germany attacked the Soviet Union, the Party line changed again and, from that point on, supported the war. By the time I joined the Party, in 1942, things had straightened out. The Moscow trials and the pact were far in the past, perhaps not chronologically, but in my mind. The war was now that singular anomaly, a "good war." The Soviet Union was finally lined up with the United States in fighting fascism.

And so I joined the Party.

I hadn't fully anticipated the effect Party membership would have on my life. After all, for years I had accepted Party leadership and Party ✓ policy. In the jargon of the day, I was the prototype of the "fellow traveler." But membership did make a great deal of difference. The Party was influential in all of my activities—the ALP, the trade union movement, the National Lawyers Guild, my legal practice, and even my social life. Everything I did was part of a whole system. Just as the knee bone is connected to the thigh bone, so the ALP was connected to the NLG; both were connected to the trade union movement, and the Party was the connective tissue. Today the Party is gone, and so is the connective tissue. I look for it often in these days, but I can find no connections to anything except a few other comrades who, like me, are seeking a structure long gone.

We were living in a time when ideology was central to our existence. Until the end of the war, the world was engaged in a vital struggle between democracy and fascism, and it was by no means certain that democracy would win. After the shooting war, the cold war started, without more than a moment's pause, and the world was abruptly divided into two competing economic systems. Just as there were few neutrals in the democracy-fascism struggle, so there were few neutrals in the conflict between capitalism and socialism. On the domestic front, the class struggle continued and preservation and extension of a militant Communist party were essential if we were to change the world. Our goal was exactly that—to change the world—and we were serious about it. So there was a lot to think and talk about and a lot to do.

I was a member of a branch of the leadership of ACA. We were scheduled to meet every two weeks, but we were all much too busy for that and probably averaged about one branch meeting a month. The branch was regarded by the Party as particularly important; after all, ACA was a CIO International union. We were visited now and then by members high up in the Party hierarchy, but they brought no orders or directives, only advice. Generally, we made our own agendas and reached our own conclusions. Some of the discussion at these meetings was intensely practical (How can we best organize the telephone workers on the West Coast in the face of AFL red-baiting?) and some was theoretical (Did the transformation of the Communist Party into the Communist Political Association in 1944 indicate the Party's abandonment of socialism as a goal for the United States?). Of course, some of the meetings were dull, but most were not, and in some the debate was lively and helpful.

The ACA branch disbanded after the Taft-Hartley Act was declared constitutional. I joined a lawyer's group, also scheduled to meet, I think, every two weeks, but it too met erratically. We were concerned mostly with the legal problems confronting the Party, and the organizational problems confronting the National Lawyers Guild, and there were many.

It wasn't only the branch meetings that took time. There were endless meetings, mostly in the ALP, between active ALP members such as myself and the Communist party hierarchy, to discuss policy and tactics on the electoral front. In effect the CP members in the ALP functioned as a caucus that influenced, but did not always govern, the left wing of the ALP. There was a great deal of tension in this relationship. The Party often made electoral decisions based on its view of proper policy, without consultation with the membership of the ALP. Party members like me resented and often refused to accept these decisions, which, we held, were within the jurisdiction of the local ALP clubs. The same kinds of tensions arose from time to time in the trade unions.

Finally, the Party made frequent calls on me in my professional ca- ⌄
pacity. For example, when I was asked to represent Steve Nelson, a Party organizer, I felt this to be a Party obligation. The same was true when,
after the Supreme Court affirmed the conviction of eleven members of
the national leadership of the Party under the Smith Act, four of those
leaders failed to surrender and forfeited their bail, which had been posted
by the Bail Fund of the Civil Rights Congress of New York. When the
government sought the names of those who had contributed to the bail
fund, I represented Dashiell Hammett and Fred Field, in legal proceedings that sent both to prison. (I discuss the Nelson and bail fund cases
later in this book.) Such litigations were not trivial. Some lasted for a
number of years and required a tremendous amount of time, frequently
for no compensation and never for adequate compensation. I didn't do
any of this begrudgingly. I could afford to undertake the cases, because
my office was reasonably prosperous and my partners were cooperative.
The cases were interesting—even enjoyable—in themselves, and I felt
that I was making some contribution to the good society.

A major political weakness of the Party was the fact that it was, at least
in large part, an underground organization. In England, France, Italy, and
other countries that had no Bill of Rights, no First Amendment protecting freedom of speech and assembly, the Communist party was legal and
open. There were trade union leaders, government officials, and members
of parliament throughout Europe who were avowed Party members, and
in some of those countries, the Communist party was the second- or third-
ranking party—in France it was, for a time, the first party in popular votes.

But not in the United States. The Party was a legal one, and it appeared on the ballot in many local and national elections. The governing bodies of the Party were publicly known, but the membership in large
part was secret. This had been true ever since the Party was organized
in 1919. United States public opinion has never been kind to radicals,
and our history is replete with persecution—even lynchings, murders,
and executions—of anarchists, members of the IWW, Communists, and
other militant dissenters, extending back to the days when Catholics were
mobbed, when Mormons were lynched, when abolitionists were murdered, when trade unionists were slaughtered in the mines of Colorado
and in the steel mills of Pennsylvania, throughout the nineteenth century and the first half of the twentieth. The Communist party was created on the heels of the Palmer raids, a period of severe repression against
all perceived "subversive" activity. So a large degree of secrecy as to Party
membership was probably seen as a necessity from the beginning.

True, many persons belonging to neighborhood branches of the Party were openly members. That was also true in a handful of unions. Those members sold copies of the Party newspaper; they circulated Communist party nominating petitions, they collected money for Party causes, and in their organizations they openly represented the Party. But these were people who were willing to make great personal sacrifices for the privilege of being a public member of the Party, or people whose economic situation was such that Party membership would not adversely affect them. They were a minority of the membership. Open membership was not the rule for most rank-and-file trade union members and their leaders, and for most professionals or government employees. It certainly was not the rule for lawyers.

Many other Party members knew I was also a member, but generally speaking, other friends and acquaintances did not. I suppose that many persons who knew me, particularly in the American Labor party, in ACA, and among lawyers who were familiar with my practice, assumed that I was in the Party, but no one (aside from congressional committees) ever asked, and I never had occasion to proclaim my membership or, for that matter, to deny it.

I was never seriously concerned that security might be breached and my Party membership publicly disclosed. Conceivably, my status as a lawyer might have been in jeopardy, but I never feared that I might be disbarred solely because of membership; I had committed no crime nor had I violated the code of ethics. I knew that some applicants for admission to the bar had been challenged on grounds of alleged Party membership, at least one lawyer was disbarred for membership in the Party in Maryland, and disbarment proceedings had been started against another in Florida and successfully resisted. But I didn't worry much about it. Disclosure of my membership certainly wouldn't have had any effect on my practice. To the extent to which my clients cared at all, Party membership would be as much an asset as a liability. Reasonably or not, I had a personal sense of security.

Nevertheless, the secrecy surrounding the Party and its membership was a serious obstacle to organization. People engaged in lawful political or trade union work found it distasteful to have to conceal their membership. Recruitment of new members was difficult and, particularly after 1945, concealment of Party membership carried with it an aura of disloyalty to the United States or even espionage. The "underground" Communists weren't disloyal or spies; they were just trying to keep their livelihoods or their social standing. But in the political climate of the time, secrecy seemed unavoidable for most.

Further, this secrecy had a serious effect on any hope of democracy in the making of Party policy. At the crux of the Party structure was a concept of "democratic centralism." As in most political organizations, members of the Party were, in theory, to elect members of their county, state, and national committees. Such committees and an occasional convention were to make policy for the Party. Unlike most other organizations, all Party members were expected to conform to that policy and to abstain from public disagreement with or criticism of it. Change of policy was to be sought only within the organization. For example, I thought the Party's advocacy, in the early fifties, of a separate "black nation," made up of those portions of the deep South in which blacks constituted a majority of the population, was nonsense, but I expressed that view only within the Party apparatus. (That idea surfaced again in 1968, in the National Lawyers Guild, discussed more fully below.) Similarly, I thought that the flight in 1951 of four convicted members of the Party's national executive committee was a dreadful error, but I confined my criticism to discussion within the Party organization, and even tried to defend the flight, albeit without conviction, in discussions with nonmembers.

Democratic centralism turned out to be all centralism and no democracy, and it is hard to see how it could have been different. Any democratic process assumes free and open discussion prior to the making of policy, and that was virtually impossible with a membership most of which could not openly participate in the process.

In fact, changes in fundamental policy came with disconcerting frequency and with little or no effective membership participation. For a while in the late 1930s, the policy of the Party was one of close collaboration with the capitalist establishment—a policy characterized as the Popular Front—required, it was argued, because of the rise of fascism in Europe. This policy changed abruptly in August 1939, when the Nazi-Soviet Pact was signed, but changed back in 1941, when the Party went all out for the war effort, even before the United States was attacked at Pearl Harbor. There is no one more ardent than the converted, and the hierarchy of the Party seemed to forget almost everything it stood for—certainly the word "socialism" wasn't often mentioned, even as a postwar goal. A no-strike pledge for the duration of the war was high on its agenda, and while the pledge was generally accepted as a wartime necessity, it was not without a great deal of grumbling. I was one of the doubters, as were several of the Party members in my ACA branch, although in the end we all agreed on the policy—but only, we said, while the war continued.

This was not the end of the Party's accommodation of its program to the war effort. Early in 1944, Earl Browder, then the chief executive officer of the Party, announced that the Party was dissolving, and a new organization to be called the Communist Political Association would take its place. Browder seemed to call for the adoption of a program of postwar collaboration with capitalism and the abandonment of the most fundamental tenets of Marxism. What had happened to the class struggle? Would the war produce a "good capitalism," free of all the defects we had experienced before the war? I was upset at this proposal, which certainly had not been discussed in advance at the Party branches. Nor did I know to what extent it had been a decision of the national committee of the Party. I know now that the change had been decided upon by the committee, but the rank and file of the Party knew nothing of it until after it had been announced. The change was discussed in some detail in my ACA branch, but only for a week or two. We had many practical things on our minds. The union was deeply involved in important organizing tasks and some of the members of the branch were impatient with a discussion about what would happen when the war was over. Indeed, I don't think there was a lot of discussion in most branches. There were other issues more critical to all of us at the time, as the war was drawing to a climax, and the opening of the second front in Europe was expected momentarily. Moreover, in terms of the day-to-day operation of the Party, I could see very little difference. But I was deeply disturbed. This wasn't the organization I had joined.

In the summer of 1945, all of this was changed, when as a result of a highly critical article written by Jacques Duclos of the French Communist Party, the Party was reconstituted and the top leadership was substantially altered—Browder was replaced by Eugene Dennis as general secretary, and William Z. Foster became leader of the Party, in fact if not in name. Many of Browder's associates were removed from the governing bodies of the Party. This was the only time in my experience in which there was a great deal of discussion of party policy within the Party ranks. I attended one meeting of the national convention and several county meetings devoted exclusively to a discussion of the issues raised in the Browder-Duclos controversy. The Party press was filled with letters and articles on the subject. Probably every Party branch spent much time discussing this issue—I know ours did. All of this was very intense and, I thought at the time, very healthy. I welcomed the result.

Much nonsense has been written and spoken about the place of discipline in the Communist party. Innumerable movies and testimony by ex-Communists before congressional committees have presented lurid pictures of sinister Party leaders who have compelled members to engage in activities contrary to their principles or disloyal to their unions, their organizations, or even their country. I had positions of some responsibility in the American Labor party, in several trade unions, and in the National Lawyers Guild during my fifteen years in the Party, but I was never called on to do anything I thought was unprincipled, with a single exception. A day or two after the flight of the four Smith Act defendants, a member of the Party approached me and made a suggestion that astonished me. At the time I was living in New Rochelle in a rather large house. It included an attic that was fairly complete in terms of living accommodations. The proposal was made that I might, for a week or two, house one of the fugitives in that attic while a more permanent hiding place could be found. It was pointed out that the household facilities were sufficient to enable him to live in the rooms in the attic without ever leaving the house—there was running water, a somewhat rudimentary kitchen, and bathroom facilities.

I was shocked at the idea. As I've said, I disapproved of the flight of the Party leaders in the first place. Further, it involved the commission of a rather serious felony and, aside from any moral considerations, if it were ever revealed I would be promptly disbarred. And it seemed to me that it would quickly become public. I had two small children and the presence of a stranger living in the attic would not likely be kept secret from their playmates. I rejected the suggestion as being absurd and heard no more about it.

Otherwise, the only demands made on me were that I would pay dues; that I would go to meetings of my branch when I could; that I would not openly criticize the Party or its policies outside the Party; and that I would carry out Party policy to the best of my ability. I found none of these requirements burdensome.

Once, while I held a position of some importance in the American Labor party, I was strongly urged by Party officials to take action contrary to the wishes of the ALP unit I represented. This story has been told above in my discussion of the American Labor party. I refused, and nothing happened to me, except perhaps that Pete Cacchione (the Party leader in Brooklyn) and Joe Roberts thought I was a naughty Party member. Another time, Party officers not members of ACA directly influenced the union to take action that I thought inadvisable. This story has also been told above. I thought that this activity was improper, and I said so. Again, nothing happened to me. Once the Party urged me to hire a lawyer as an associate. I did so and received the praise of Party officials. A year later, I fired him and was severely scolded by the Party. Aside from these instances, I do not recall that the Party ever interfered or sought to interfere with my legal practice or my political work, and I do not believe that my differences of opinion with the Party in these cases affected my standing in the Party.

This is not to say that discipline was not important. We were dedicated to a serious purpose and took our responsibilities seriously. Many members had given up their freedom or even their lives in pursuit of that purpose, but that was because they were so moved, not because they were so directed. Most of the discipline influencing Party members was self-imposed, not externally applied.

It is true that members were disciplined by the Party from time to time. Such discipline usually took the form of expulsion from the Party, and that happened with some frequency, mostly on a top leadership level, beginning with the early days of the organization, years before I came along, and continuing throughout the period of my membership and, I think, even today. Such action, when it is the result of sharp differences of basic theory, is probably inevitable. The Communist party was not analogous to the Republican or Democratic party, ready to embrace anyone who would vote the ticket. It was dedicated to fundamental change in the economic system in the United States, and only persons who agreed with the principles of the Party could be expected to become and remain members. There is, of course, the problem of distinguishing between factionalism (a bad thing, resulting in expulsion) and dissent (a good thing)—a distinction too often in the eye of the beholder.

But none of this bothered me too much. I was more interested in works than in faith, and so, I believe, were most of the rank-and-file Party members. Doctrinal differences might be interesting to argue about, but most of the time they didn't really matter. What did matter was: how close are we getting to our goal, whether it be a good social security system, organizing the unorganized, or, maybe, socialism? For example, the sharp disagreement between the Soviet Union and Yugoslavia in 1948 was of interest to us because it weakened the Communist movement in general, but we never thought much about the differences in theory leading to the break. It was worth ten minutes of discussion at a branch meeting, but we devoted most of our attention in that time to the Taft-Hartley Act and the effect it would have on the Party in the United States.

It must be kept in mind that the Party consisted not only of doctrine but also of people. A distorted view of the Party results when we permit disagreements over Party policy and the changes in its direction to obscure the wishes, sentiments, and activities of those who made up its membership. The accomplishments of the Party were many. The unemployed councils of the Great Depression; the social advances of the Roosevelt New Deal; the growth of a militant trade union movement; the resistance to fascism, both domestic and international; the fight against a nuclear war; the movement for racial equality and justice—all were spurred on by the Communist Party of the United States. There was hardly a progressive movement in the period between 1930 and 1955 that did not bear the Party's mark and that did not benefit from the energy and devotion of its members. The arts too—the theater, the movies, literature, graphic art—felt its presence, and the academic world at all levels, from kindergarten to university, reflected the influence of the Party. And this was true throughout this period, whatever the "line" of the Party may have been.

More than that, the Party provided a center through which progressives in varied spheres of activity could communicate with each other and exchange ideas, as well as provide support for each other, and to me this was of prime importance. The ultimate goal of the Party was to establish socialism. It was a single aim, which involved black men and women seeking freedom in the South, farmers protesting foreclosure of their farms in Kansas, steelworkers organizing unions in Indiana, and women striking for peace in New York. The Party connected all of these struggles.

Or it sought to do so. Many of its goals—perhaps most of them—were never realized. Party members, both its leaders and its rank and file, were humans with their full share of human imperfections. The bureaucracy of the Party was often arbitrary, arrogant, and stupid, and those characteristics, common to all bureaucracies, were particularly galling because our goal was socialism, which was not supposed to be arbitrary, arrogant, or stupid. But the men and women I worked with were, with very few exceptions, honest, and they were hard workers. Our faults were many, but insincerity and laziness were not among them. By and large we formed a true band of brothers and sisters who felt a high degree of loyalty to each other and to the cause of socialism, and, until we got to socialism, to all of those intermediate goals to which I referred above.

And then there was another loyalty, too, and that was the loyalty—often blind—to the Soviet Union. The importance of the Soviet Union to the Communist Party of the United States can hardly be overestimated. With all of its imperfections the U.S.S.R. represented, to me and all those I worked with, Socialism Triumphant. Its proclaimed goals were our goals; its hopes were our hopes. After the unfortunate 1939–41 period of the

Stalin-Hitler pact had been endured, the Soviet army was the dominant force in the war against Hitler. Its victory at Stalingrad was the decisive battle of the war, and the siege of Leningrad was one of the most dramatic stories of all time. And before 1939, and again after 1945, the international policies of the Soviet Union stressed nuclear disarmament and world peace.

But along with all of this, and frequently overshadowing it, were those imperfections. The Soviet invasion of Hungary was no great problem, at least to me; fascism in Hungary ran deep, and I did not see Soviet intervention as an assault on democracy or inconsistent with the development of socialism. The invasion of Czechoslovakia was quite another matter. It seemed that, in that country, a democratic socialism was in the process of formation. And, of course, above all, the terrible record of Stalin with respect to civil liberties was difficult to accept. But accept it we did. At least, we accepted part of that record. The other part we denied.

The CPUSA drew great strength from its closeness to the Soviet Union, and I doubt whether it could have exerted its very substantial influence from 1932 to the 1950s without that connection. Certainly none of the other political organizations in the United States that professed to hold socialism as a goal had any similar success. We claimed vicarious credit for all the great accomplishments of the Soviet Union, but along with that came vicarious blame for all its faults. The Party perceived itself as required to defend the Soviet Union in all circumstances, a task that became more and more difficult in the postwar period. The result was that it became easier and easier to attack the Party as the willing tool of the Soviet Union and to denigrate its many accomplishments as Soviet inspired and therefore evil.

This is not the place for a treatise on the history of the Party or its relationship to the Communist Party of the Soviet Union. It is true that in the 1939–41 period, and again after 1948, the leadership of the Party could have, in many instances, withheld its unconditional support of the policy of the Soviet Union, although it would require a detailed history of postwar politics to expand on this thesis. In fact the Communist parties of Italy and France, and other European Communist parties of non-socialist countries, did develop some degree of independence from, though not hostility to, the Soviet Union, but I cannot recall any instance in which the Communist Party of the United States took a stance even mildly critical of the Soviet Union.

By the mid-fifties, the cold war had frightened off all but the most hardy of the Party members in the United States. Then, early in 1956, Nikita Khrushchev, at the Twentieth Congress of the Communist Party of the Soviet Union, described in terrible detail the crimes of the Stalin regime. His speech traumatized those of us who had weathered the domestic red-hunt; the effects were felt perhaps even more severely in the highest levels of the Party structure. The result was a bitter factional struggle within the Party leadership, while membership in the Party declined precipitously. The Party had claimed seventy-five thousand members in 1945 but fewer than five thousand in 1958. The leadership proved quite incapable of coping with the objective situation. Perhaps no leadership could have done better.

However, the result was that the Party no longer performed any useful function so far as I could see. Internally it spent its time in leadership disputes; externally it had turned into a civil liberties organization devoted to saving itself through appeals to the constitutional rights of free speech and assembly. Little mention was made of socialism.

I don't know whether the Party could have survived the cold war in any event, but certainly its blind adherence to the Soviet Union's position on all issues, and the revelations of the Khrushchev speech, made its demise as a significant entity inevitable.

I date the end of my membership in the Party at sometime in 1960 or 1961. There was no formal act marking the end of the relationship. I just stopped going to meetings and paying dues and considered myself a nonmember, and I suppose the Party came to the same conclusion, though I continued to meet with Party members to discuss both political and legal matters for many years after.

Why, then, did I stay in the Party as long as I did? I suppose I was influenced by loyalty to persons I considered my comrades and to an institution that had served me well and that was under unremitting attack. I had been comfortable in the Party. That is where most of my friends were; it was where I could discuss the politics of the day in terms mutually understood. It had had a helpful and beneficial effect on almost all aspects of my life. One does not lightly leave such an organization.

At substantially all times in my adult life I have, in both private and public discussion, sought to defend the Soviet Union, even when, viewed objectively, its policy was but barely defensible. During all of this time the Soviet Union was viewed with bitter hostility by the Establishment in the United States; even during the war, such hostility was present although somewhat muted. I found it emotionally and politically impossible to join those who hungered for the destruction of the Soviet Union and who gloried in its every fault. For me, it was representing socialism— a flawed socialism perhaps, but still the best we had.

The flaws in the socialism of the Soviet Union, as revealed by Khrushchev in his 1956 speech to the Twentieth Congress, bothered me a great deal, but they did nothing to diminish my advocacy of socialism. Socialism is an economic system, to be administered by human beings, who may be good or evil, intelligent or stupid, principled or greedy. Those humans do not define the economic system.

And so felt many of my comrades in the United States. We were disoriented by the effective loss of the Party and upset by the description of the Stalin era given in Khrushchev's speech, but few of us saw it as the death of socialism. The immediate goals were the same: the ultimate goal of a socialist society hadn't changed, but it was going to be a bit harder to accomplish.*

So stood the state of affairs at the end of 1958.

On the first day of 1959, the revolutionary army led by Fidel Castro entered Havana, and a new socialist government was aborning. It takes time for a new economic and social system to take shape, and the socialist shape of the new Cuban government was not immediately apparent, but I recognized it almost at once. At the very least this was a *de facto* U.S. colony proclaiming its independence of U.S. capitalism, and such a situation seemed to me to bear the seeds of socialism. Perhaps there was a large element of wish fulfillment in my thinking. In the event, the seeds germinated and grew rapidly in Cuba's fertile soil. Here was a new socialism, and a more congenial one. To this socialism I devoted much of my time and energy for the following thirty-five years.

Along with the Cuban revolution came the U.S. economic blockade, and along with the blockade came the close alliance between Cuba and the Soviet Union. As a consequence, my regard for and support of the Soviet Union continued, not so much because it was an exemplar of modern socialism (Cuba was that) but because once the United States imposed its embargo, the Soviet Union was a lifeline for Cuba, to which I felt a much closer bond than I had felt for the Soviet Union for many years.

Elsewhere in this memoir I discuss a trip I took to Cuba in February

---

*The perceptive reader will note that I have barely mentioned the other great socialist power on this earth—China. The truth is I don't know much about China and haven't been able to follow or understand the events there since about 1950. Further, I don't see that events in China have had much influence on the subject of this volume—my life. And I don't believe the Chinese Communist experience has much to teach us. The same goes for North Korea, Vietnam, and Laos.

1960. While I was there, Anastos Mikoyan, foreign minister of the Soviet Union, was visiting, and he and Fidel Castro announced an economic agreement between Cuba and the Soviet Union whereby substantial aid would be given to the former. In the years that followed, the Soviet Union gave enormous amounts of aid to Cuba. Not only my professional life but my emotional life was closely tied to Cuba, and the aid given to it by the Soviet Union was more than enough to counterbalance many of the less praiseworthy acts of the Soviet Union before and after 1960.

Although I traveled outside the United States with some frequency after 1960, I never visited the Soviet Union. I had a fear, never expressed aloud and probably not often admitted to myself, that I would be disappointed with the society that I would find. Not so with Cuba. I found that society joyful and full of hope.

The sudden collapse of the Soviet Union and the rest of the European Communist bloc in 1989 was a much more serious blow to the idea of socialism than all the atrocities committed in the name of socialism over the years. Much has been written to explain this startling event, and doubtlessly it will be the subject of speculation and thought for decades to come. I have no desire to join in that speculation, but the event can hardly be ignored.

It is clear that the material benefits derived from socialism were substantial and provided an example of some of the services a government can provide for its people. Although conditions varied from one nation to another, the Eastern European socialist countries had no unemployment, no homeless poor, no starvation. Health care was available to all, without cost. Education was likewise available to all, and illiteracy was substantially eliminated. Rent was very low and seldom required a significant portion of one's income. Even the wealthiest of the capitalist countries could not boast such features. It is true that people cannot live by bread alone, but bread is necessary for life, and socialism supplied that.

Nevertheless, the system failed in Eastern Europe. Many are the reasons for that failure: the overcentralization of the economic structure, caused in part by the lack of a satisfactory method to govern the market, especially for consumer goods; the growth of a powerful and corrupt bureaucracy; the failure of the Soviet Union to keep abreast of modern technology; the distortion of the economy caused by the perceived necessity for the production and maintenance of a large defense establishment, with the consequent failure to produce consumer goods in adequate quantity and quality; the failure to solve "the national question." No doubt all of these and more played their share. And we must not forget that an entire generation of young men was wiped out by the war, so that as the leadership grew older, there were no younger men and women to challenge and replace them.

Most important was the failure of Soviet socialism to create an open society, in which new ideas, new technology, new concepts can be debated freely. In Stalin's time and even after, scientists were imprisoned or exiled because their ideas on genetics or nuclear power ran counter to the official view. A society that resists the changes in thinking so characteristic of the twentieth century cannot thrive.

I must admit, with some shame, that I saw all of this dimly but failed to recognize its full significance. But the question remains as to how much of this is an essential characteristic of socialism.

I can see no inherent reason why a socialist society cannot be as open and "democratic" as any other—indeed more so than most societies on this planet. Like most concepts of this sort, "democracy" is an elastic term, having almost as many definitions as there are those who attempt to define it. The very concept of democracy doesn't have a good track record—there aren't more than five or six nations on the earth that can boast a continuous democratic government, however defined, for as long as half a century. Let us not be too sanctimonious in judging the governmental systems of others—our own falls far short of perfection.

It is, however, reasonable to require that a government, to be acceptable, permit the free and open discussion of new ideas and concepts, and provide opportunity to have those ideas accepted as well as a system of rights and privileges determined by some rules that are, in general terms, acceptable to most of the people. I would expect that every government—socialist, capitalist, or even tribal—has the right to protect itself; a government that will tolerate effective sedition is almost beyond one's imagination. But within those limits, a "good" government must permit and even encourage open discussion of new ideas, and provide a fair opportunity for their adoption.

Utopian? Probably. But I can see nothing in the idea of socialism that prohibits an approach to such utopia. I had always assumed that socialism in the United States need not repeat the troubles encountered by less industrialized countries. In the meantime, in the capitalist world, the rich get richer and the poor get poorer, and the class struggle continues.

6

Years of Growth

My admission to the bar, my marriage, the American Labor party, the many ACA matters, and my legal practice—all these personal and political factors—enveloped me completely, and I did my best to pay attention to all of them. It sounds impossible that I should have been able to juggle so many balls at the same time, and perhaps I dropped one or two now and then, but I had the energy of a thirty-year-old, a state of affairs I look back on with disbelief fifty-five years later.

It may be that of all of these elements, the family got the least attention, but I think it thrived nevertheless, at least for about thirty years. Marcia and I had a typical middle-class nuclear family. We lived in a well-to-do Jewish neighborhood in Flatbush, just a few doors away from the residence of my parents. I was an often absent father who worked on many nights and in many places throughout the country. Marcia also worked when she wasn't interrupted by the creation and care of the children.

In 1950, we moved from Brooklyn to New Rochelle, in accordance with the well-established practice of middle-class families moving out of the city to the suburbs. This was all something like the life of the Bobbsey Twins, except in political outlook. I don't know whether the Bobbsey Twins had any political outlook, but in our family, politics was pretty important. Marcia carried on her political work in the community in Brooklyn and later in New Rochelle. She spent whatever time she could on the racial problems of New Rochelle, centering on the important school desegregation campaign then pending—a campaign that ultimately resulted in one of the first court orders in the northern part of the country directing that an all-black school be integrated.

As in the case of many Jewish families, we frequently gathered at my parents' house on Fridays for dinner. Those present included my sister,

Lucille, and after she married Sam Perlman and after he got out of the army, he was also present. The meal was typical, standard, and very good: chicken soup, roast chicken, and delicious apple pie. There was an almost invariable sequel to those gatherings: an angry, bitter, and intense argument, mostly between Pop and me, although Lucille and Marcia joined in when they could break into the loud discussion carried on by the male members of the family.

We argued about almost everything, mostly politics, but also art, law, ethics, science, philosophy, or anything else we could think of. Mom was much troubled by this contentiousness. She took it much more seriously than was justified and occasionally would ask me please not to have an argument that night or to go easy because, she said, Pop wasn't feeling well. But I don't think that her concern was justified; I believe Pop was feeling quite well during all the discussions. In fact, many were provoked by him, and while the arguments were ill-tempered and violent, and although we all felt very strongly on the issues, it never interfered in the slightest in the personal relations between Pop and the rest of us.

Many of the disputes were set off by some event of the time. One of the early arguments arose out of a strike by a hospital workers' union involving the employees of Brooklyn Jewish Hospital in 1937. Pop was a director of that hospital, and we urged him as strongly as we could to use his influence to settle the strike. He agreed in principle with unionization, but he wasn't so sure about this particular case. "How can hospital workers strike? The patients, who are not parties to the dispute, will suffer, and they are the ones who have the least power and the most to lose from a strike." Lucille and I pointed out, with energy, that his position was inconsistent with the fundamental right to organize, that hospital workers were badly underpaid, and that the result was that the workers made an involuntary contribution of their labor to the hospital—a contribution they could not afford. We got nowhere.

The strike was a very bitter one. It was characterized by a great deal of violence, both by the police and by the strikers. After awhile Pop agreed that he would do what he could to settle the strike, but he either could or would do nothing. The union was wiped out, to be resurrected some years later as Local 1199, at this writing the largest and perhaps the most militant union in the city.

Another source of considerable contention around the dinner table was the question of employment of blacks. By the mid-forties Pop's factory employed perhaps thirty to forty people, all of them white. We chided him for this and urged him to employ an integrated workforce. He was completely in favor of equal treatment for blacks, but he said it wasn't practical in his shop because, he explained, "I can't afford to install separate toilets." That infuriated us younger folk. In later years Pop hired blacks, and he discovered that separate toilets weren't necessary. As a matter of fact, he was highly principled on the employment of blacks in other establishments (just as he was in favor of unions except in his hospital), and in 1944 he resigned (or threatened to resign) from the board of directors of the Brooklyn Jewish Hospital because a black doctor was refused a promotion.

On national and international topics, we had many, many discussions, and heated ones, about the Soviet Union, Hitler, the Nazi-Soviet Pact, and all of the related events that swirled about us between 1936 and 1950. Pop was wedded to the Roosevelt position on most matters. He cheered for the Loyalists in Spain but supported Roosevelt's position on the arms embargo. He disagreed vehemently and totally with the position of the Communist party between the time of the Nazi-Soviet Pact in August 1939 and Hitler's invasion of the Soviet Union in June 1941. We younger folks disagreed loudly all through this period of time, generally taking the position of the Communist party, whatever it happened to be at the moment.

Another subject of dispute was the American Labor party. Pop was opposed to the creation of the party, certainly after the first year or two, because he saw no reason for it, believing that the Democratic party, or at least the left wing of the Democratic party, could accomplish everything that the ALP could. Lucille, Marcia, and I felt otherwise. Again, many evenings were taken up in discussing the role of the ALP and what it was possibly able to accomplish. Although Pop opposed the party, he always made contributions, which I considered too modest, to my campaign fund when I ran for office, and he helped in whatever way he could with my political work, as long as it didn't involve actual assistance to the Communist party. When I did run for office, which was quite often, we gave fund-raising parties at his home, and he never raised any objection. There was a bit of a conflict in his mind in 1948, when Henry Wallace ran for president on the ALP/Progressive party line. He was a good friend of Wallace's and admired him a great deal. I think he made some contribution to Wallace—though not through me—and he was quite enthusiastic about the campaign and correspondingly disappointed at the result.

I never told him that I had joined the Communist party, and of course he never asked me, since that would have been an unthinkable violation of my privacy. I cannot imagine, however, that he did not know, and my guess is that he dated my entry into the Party years before I actually joined.

These arguments, loud and bitter though they were, were really intellectual exercises, although Mom never understood that fully. We usually ended the evening with a game or two of chess.

In the midst of all this activity, normal family life continued. Both of our kids were wonderful, and I'm sorry I didn't see more of them, between trips to Washington, San Francisco, and elsewhere. We made no conscious effort to interfere with their political views, but just as Lucille and I grew up in a political atmosphere created by our parents, so Joni and Peter grew up in a political atmosphere created by Marcia and me.

When Joni was about six or seven, she asked me whether I believed in God. I told her I didn't, but that she could make up her own mind. She addressed the same question to Marcia and got the same answer. A few days later, Joni reported on a bit of sociological research. "Do you know," she said, "that everyone on this block believes in God except Grandma and us?" I asked her how she knew that, and she said that she had made a house-to-house survey.

While I'm telling anecdotes, I might as well add another about Joni. In the first or second grade of school, Joni ran into a serious disciplinary problem. The reading for the day was a popular book of the time, named *Little Black Sambo*. Joni objected to the book. "Why talk about Sambo's color?" she asked her teacher. "No one calls me Little White Joan or even Little Pink Joan," she is supposed to have said. Her teacher was upset about it and sent a note home complaining about Joni's impudence and disruptive attitude in the class.

To the extent possible, we integrated the kids into our lives, including our political lives. There were lots of exciting things around. There were picket lines in those days, and Joni, Peter, Marcia, and I picketed during the Western Union strike in 1946, and during a strike at the Times Square Stores a few years later. We also participated in the exciting, colorful May Day parades that were annual features of New York life in the late thirties and forties. Those parades brought together large segments of the radical population in militant, joyful, and colorful demonstrations. Unfortunately those events are things of the past, and their renewal in the foreseeable future seems unlikely. Not that the May Day parades were totally peaceful. On one occasion Joni asked me why the people who were watching the parade from the sidewalk were throwing tomatoes at her. I told her that they didn't like us, but did not attempt any more detailed explanation.

■

All of the unions that the firm of Neuburger, Shapiro, Rabinowitz, and Boudin represented were active and generated a great deal of legal work. At the end of 1947 we may have had the largest trade union practice in the city. Our firm was a fine one. Sam Neuburger was a good salesman. He was not Leonard Boudin's kind of lawyer nor my kind but he was very effective in the magistrate's court and did well in the rough and tumble of criminal cases, where most of the time law didn't matter very much. In the average misdemeanor or minor felony cases, the principal talent required of a lawyer is the ability to plea bargain, to reduce a sentence, or in some way to get his client off as a result of manipulation rather than by extensive legal argument, and at this Sam was very good. There was a considerable amount of antagonism between Leonard and Sam; Leonard had total contempt for Sam's legal ability, and Sam thought that Leonard was too intellectual and not sufficiently practical. I suppose they were both right, and things got along reasonably well unless their paths crossed, which happened only once or twice in the course of our practice. Leonard was a great lawyer, with a keen analytical mind. And he had another characteristic, which I envied, and that was the ability to identify personally with his clients, all of whom loved him.

There were, of course, the usual financial problems involved in getting an office established and in running it on the kind of fees trade unions paid. As a result of the additions to the firm and our retainer with District 65 of the Wholesale and Warehouse Workers Union, we had to get a larger space, and that of course meant greater expense. Our representation of District 65 improved our standing at the labor bar immeasurably, but it didn't help our financial situation much. The retainer called for six thousand dollars a year, which even at the preinflation rates of 1947 was preposterous.

An interesting and, in retrospect, amusing episode occurred at about this time that seemed to offer a chance for a financial windfall. The Wage and Hour Law provides that time worked in excess of forty hours a week is to be paid for at time-and-a-half the regular hourly rate. In *Anderson v. Mt. Clemens Pottery*, the Supreme Court held that for purposes of the application of the law, hours were to be calculated "from portal to portal"—i.e., from the time a worker entered the plant gate to the time he or she left. Universal industrial practice was to pay workers from the time they clocked in to the time they clocked out. The difference may seem trivial, and perhaps it was in most shops, but it turned out to be extraordinarily important in many.

To illustrate: We represented a union whose members worked for Squibb and other shops dealing with chemicals. The workers normally entered the plant about fifteen minutes before clocking in, to change into acid-resistant work clothes. They picked up their tools and then clocked in. At the end of the day, after clocking out, they put their tools away and showered and changed back into street clothes, taking perhaps another thirty minutes. They worked forty hours a week, clock-in to clock-out, but forty-three hours and forty-five minutes portal to portal. Assuming fifty weeks a year, that added up to 187.5 hours a year of overtime work to be paid for at time-and-a-half. Assuming an hourly rate of $.70 ($1.05 overtime), that totaled $196.87 a year per employee, quite a large sum in 1946. In a shop of 100 employees, that came to $19,687 a year. If each worker sued, that would be $19,687 for each of six years (the limitations period in New York) or $118,122 of unanticipated wages. The Wage and Hour Law also provided liquidated damages in an equal amount and counsel fees to be awarded by the court. Thus, in a fairly small shop, the total bill to the employer could easily amount to a quarter of a million dollars of unbudgeted expense. This, at a time when the subway fare in New York was five cents.

In a large automobile or steel plant employing thousands of workers, where there was a fifteen-minute walk from the plant gate to the time clock, and another fifteen minutes from the time clock to the plant gate, the recovery could run into many millions.

All over the country, including in our office, lawyers for unions started to organize such lawsuits. There was an intense flurry of activity in signing up individual workers, an easy task, under the circumstances, and one undertaken with enthusiasm by union organizers who were in a position to offer to their members a substantial gift. The resulting legal action would be a simple one and would present merely an accounting problem. We started several such actions, in at least one of which we were suing on behalf of over one hundred workers. It was a solution to our financial problems—and at the expense not of the workers or the unions but of the employers.

Needless to say, it didn't happen that way. The situation became a matter of serious concern to Congress, and a congressional committee reported that, in the seven months between July 1, 1946, and January 31, 1947, almost two thousand such suits had been started in the federal courts. The amount claimed was well in excess of six *billion* dollars; there were also hundreds of state court actions pending. As was inevitable, Congress and the courts came to the rescue, and Congress quickly passed the Portal-to-Portal Act, changing the rule of the *Mt. Clemens* case. It decreed that industrial practice was the proper measure of hours worked and provided that the new act was to be retroactive.

The Supreme Court held the law constitutional. I always thought the new law was unconstitutional, as it affected pay for hours worked before the law was passed, but the consequences of the *Mt. Clemens* decision were too enormous to expect the courts to make any other decision. I doubt whether the Court, when it decided *Mt. Clemens*, had any idea of what its result would be. After all, none of the justices had ever worked in a chemical plant.

Throughout this period we tried hard to extend our trade union practice, and now and then small unions retained us, often for a specific occasion such as the negotiation of a contract or the settlement of an important grievance. Most of them didn't need full-time lawyers, and few of these contacts ripened into long-term retainers. Some of the unions I represented worked in obscure trades, and I remember particularly the Egg Candlers Union and the Diamond Cutters Union. The latter used a vocabulary I never understood. The trade had its origin in Amsterdam, Holland, and many of the terms used were of Dutch derivation. I wasn't around long enough to find out what the members of the union were talking about.

Among the larger unions, we were consulted often by left-wing rank-and-file workers battling a conservative and sometimes corrupt national leadership. One intense litigation of that sort involved a struggle within the International Association of Bridge, Structural, and Ornamental Iron Workers Union, in which the international sought to discipline an obstreperous left-wing local led by Lou Secundy, an old-time radical trade unionist whose roots went back to the prewar days. After a bitter courtroom fight the case was settled, as I recall it, on terms favorable to the local, recognizing its autonomy. If my memory serves me correctly, one of the terms of that settlement was that the local would *not* retain me as its lawyer—another of the many cases in which I worked very hard and won but received little reward except satisfaction. To get a settlement, the local had to give up something, and I was the thing.

Another lawsuit on behalf of a left-wing rank-and-file group involved the Hotel and Club Employees Union, Local 6, a union represented by Boudin, Cohn, and Glickstein during my employment there. A change in the political stance of Jay Rubin, long a prominent left-wing leader in the trade union movement (and a man I always thought was a high-ranking Party member), resulted in a bitter internal struggle; in 1950, the left wing, by then in opposition to Rubin, won an election for officers of the local. The international, acting at the instance of Rubin, appointed a trustee over the local and removed the newly elected officers. In the litigation that ensued, Sidney Cohn and Simon Rifkin (a former federal judge and a leader of the New York bar) represented the international, and we were retained by the ousted local officers. They were an attractive group of radicals who had worked in the industry for many years and had participated in the battles of the thirties to drive the racketeers out of the restaurant business. I had represented many of them while I was at Boudin, Cohn, and Glickstein.

The case was assigned to Isadore Wasservogel, a retired Supreme Court judge, to sit as a referee. It was a bitter case, but we lost, and our clients were driven from the union and the industry. The litigation upset me a great deal, not only because of the result, but because Sidney Cohn, my former employer and long a defender of left-wing unions, was representing a reactionary right-wing international union. I found the situation painful.

Another incident arose in connection with the Marine Engineers Benefits Association (MEBA) in which a mixed group of Communists and anti-Communist radicals had formed a somewhat unstable coalition to wrest control from a conservative leadership. They consulted me about a series of legal and organizational problems they faced. I have long since forgotten the details of the controversy but I recall that a major issue was whether the members who consulted me (the left-wingers) were eligible to run for office under somewhat ambiguous provisions of the international constitution. I advised my clients that I thought a reasonable interpretation of the constitution would give them the right to run, and they acted on that advice.

Shortly after, Lee Pressman was also consulted by someone (I don't recall by whom, if I ever knew) on the same question and gave a contrary answer. I was furious. Lee had been told I was working on the matter and should have spoken to me about it. His failure to do so was, I think, part of his personality, which refused to recognize the legitimacy of trade union lawyers other than himself and two or three close friends. Quite aside from the fact that I didn't enjoy being in a direct conflict with Lee, the result of Lee's opinion was the ineligibility of my clients to run for office. Lots of angry words followed, and the rank-and-file movement I represented collapsed.

I never did get along well with Pressman. He was a fine lawyer, but he moved in very select circles. He had been general counsel not only to the CIO but to the Steel Workers Union. Like his boss, Phil Murray, he dealt on the very highest levels of labor politics. As a mutual friend remarked: "After all, he can pick up the phone and talk to President Truman when he wants to. You can't expect him to answer your calls readily."

The Taft-Hartley Act had presented the trade union movement with a host of new and complex legal problems, quite apart from section 9(h). A series of very valuable and informative meetings on the effect of the act were held in Washington at gatherings of the lawyers of the CIO, organized by Pressman, then general counsel to the CIO, and Eugene Cotton, associate general counsel. The meetings contributed a great deal to our understanding of the act and helped to establish CIO policy with respect to litigation that was sure to follow. Some of the CIO meetings were held in conjunction with meetings of the Labor Law Committee of the National Lawyers Guild (there was a lot of overlap in membership).

When, during the meetings, lunchtime came, Lee never had lunch with the "rank-and-filers" such as Leonard and myself who represented small unions like ACA and the UOPWA; his luncheon companions were always John Abt and Nat Witt. I didn't resent this at the time. I didn't think Lee would have been a very pleasant lunch companion in any event, and besides, he had been Witt's law partner before his job with the CIO, and John Abt was a very old friend; it was reasonable that he should have lunch with his old companions. All three had held responsible governmental jobs in the early days of the New Deal, when I was still in law school, and they had moved into the trade union movement when the CIO was organized—Nat as lawyer for the Mine, Mill and Smelter Workers and John as lawyer for the Amalgamated Clothing Workers. Much later, John became the lawyer for the Communist party.

Lee left his job as counsel for the CIO and the Steel Workers Union in 1948 and was succeeded by Arthur Goldberg. In 1950 he testified before the House Committee on Un-American Activities. He stated he had been a member of the Communist party. He named only three other persons as having also been members of the Party; two were his lunch companions, John Abt and Nat Witt.

7

The Cold War and Congress

It was the era of the Great Fear.

Phillip Loeb was a successful television actor who was blacklisted after Lee J. Cobb named him as a Communist party member at a hearing of the House Un-American Activities Committee. Humiliated and fearful of losing his ability to make a living, he committed suicide by swallowing an overdose of sleeping pills.

Harry Dexter White, an unusually dynamic and imaginative public official who was assistant to the secretary of the treasury, was named as a Communist by two witnesses before congressional committees. He voluntarily appeared before HUAC, and three days after an emotional and stormy hearing at which he denied Party membership, he died of a heart attack.

F. O. Matthieson, a Christian Socialist and a professor at Harvard, was named as a Communist by several committee witnesses, resulting in a great deal of unfavorable publicity in the academic community. He committed suicide by leaping from the window of a high-rise apartment.

A series of political trials unprecedented in the history of the United States resulted in the execution of Julius and Ethel Rosenberg, the imprisonment of Alger Hiss, and the conviction of about one hundred leaders of the Communist party, all on evidence that would not have resulted in a single conviction in more tranquil times.

School libraries throughout the country removed from their shelves books such as Mark Twain's *A Connecticut Yankee in King Arthur's Court* and Steinbeck's *Grapes of Wrath*.

Almost four hundred school and college teachers in New York City alone were dismissed because of their "subversive" activities or resigned under pressure. Thousands of others suffered the same fate throughout the country.

During the Truman administration, over 1,200 federal employees were dismissed on charges of "disloyalty" and another 6,000 resigned under pressure. During the Eisenhower administration, 1,500 more were dismissed and an additional 6,000 resigned.

Between 1948 and 1956, 750 members of the armed forces were given less than honorable discharges as a result of charges that they were guilty of "subversive" activities.

From 1949 to 1953 about 300 aliens were arrested for deportation, almost all of whom had been living in the United States for many years and had established families here. Over half of them were actually deported, and most of the others lived in terror of deportation while the slow processes of the law dragged on, sometimes for a decade or more.

More than a score of witnesses before congressional committees and grand juries were convicted of contempt and many served jail time for refusing to inform on friends and associates.

It was the worst of times.

To discuss the period of political repression in the United States after World War II, we must cut the seamless web of history somewhere. The Iron Curtain speech of Winston Churchill at Fulton, Missouri, in March 1946 was to me the opening salvo of international hostilities between East and West that weren't resolved for over forty years. In that speech, Churchill declared war—a cold war, but nevertheless a war—on the Soviet Union and the Eastern European socialist bloc. On the domestic level, the war may be said to have been initiated the following year with Truman's Loyalty Security program, which sought to purge all "subversives" from government employment. The floodgates were opened by Executive Order 9835, only the first in a series of similar orders that drove from federal service thousands of devoted government employees, some on very high levels, whose only offense was that they had once signed a Communist party nominating petition, had joined the National Lawyers Guild, had enrolled in the American Labor party, had been members of some organization deemed to be subversive, or had relatives or friends who had done any of the aforesaid. The twelve years that followed saw a series of indictments of the leadership of the Communist party for conspiracy to advocate the violent overthrow of the government in violation of the 1940 Smith Act. The first of the indictments, against eleven of the national leaders of the Party (the *Dennis* case), was brought in New York in 1948.

Following the Supreme Court decision in June 1951 upholding the conviction of the defendants in the *Dennis* case, indictments against a hundred Party officers were returned in New York and other parts of the country. Convictions resulted in most of these cases under conditions designed to arouse public fear of an imminent threat to the security of the United States. Thus, for example, four hundred police had surrounded the courthouse in New York when the trial opened in the *Dennis* case, although there was no reason to expect disorder. In none of these trials was it ever proved or even alleged that anyone had engaged in any actual conduct that might result in the overthrow of the government. The only conduct charged and proven was speech.

State red-hunters joined in, and "little Smith Act" prosecutions were undertaken in Pennsylvania, Massachusetts, Kentucky, and Florida.

These years also saw extended congressional committee hearings into "un-American activities," the purge of Communists and those "affiliated with" the Communist party from the trade union movement through enforcement of section 9(h) of the Taft-Hartley Act, the deportation of many aliens suspected of radical affiliations, and the denial of passports to many citizens suspected of similar affiliations.

All of this was repeated on a state and local level. There were city and state committees investigating subversives in the school system, in universities, in libraries, and in state employment. And, of course, the private sector joined in the red hunt with enthusiasm by employers seeking to rid themselves of "troublemakers" among their employees.

Covering this was an all-encompassing press campaign, quick to stigmatize as "red" any progressive idea that managed to break through the barrage of repressive propaganda.

It was a terrible and terrifying time. There were, no doubt, many in this country unaffected by the Great Fear, but I met very few of them.

The result cannot even be summarized in a short compass. It became dangerous to utter radical or even progressive thoughts in an audible tone of voice. The motion picture industry was stripped of many of its best writers, and the remainder were frightened into mediocrity. Our schools were left with teachers who did not dare to utter a word critical of United States foreign policy or many aspects of its domestic policy. Ordinary citizens purged their libraries of books that someone might think were anti-American, and public libraries followed suit. Progressive congress members, and many who were not progressive but who would not red-bait, were driven from office and sometimes from public life. Scores of progressive organizations were destroyed although they posed no political threat of any kind. Thousands of people lost their jobs, with little prospect of finding new ones quickly. Families were destroyed and friendships wrecked.

By 1960 the cold war, to some extent, had run its course on the domestic front. For one thing, there weren't many more reds to pick on. For another, a new generation was coming on the scene—a generation that tended to view with some cynicism the ideological battles of the forties and fifties. The word "communism" did not bring such an immediate hostile reaction from the young people who had their own and new battles to fight.

Many excellent books have been written dealing with the subject, and a few plays and motion pictures have been produced. David Caute's book, appropriately titled *The Great Fear,* is especially recommended. All I can do here is to treat the cold war as it affected my practice of law, and even that cannot be done fully without risk of boring the reader who, if he or she is not old enough to remember, will find the story difficult to believe. So I will describe what must be a few bits and pieces of my practice from 1947 to about 1962.

Congressional Investigating Committees

I was meeting with several union members at the office of Local 19, of District 65, in Memphis, Tennessee, at about 7:00 in the evening, when Richard Arens and Donald Connor walked in without knocking. I asked Arens what he wanted. He said he wanted to examine the membership records of the union. I asked whether he had a subpoena, and he answered in the negative. I said that we would not produce the membership records, which were confidential, and asked him to leave.

He and Connor pushed me aside and walked through the office. At that moment Arens seemed to me to be about six feet tall and to weigh about two hundred pounds. Connor seemed even taller and heavier. Actually, neither of these men is quite that big, but I felt very small. In any event, I managed to get between them and the file cabinets and said I would not consent to their looking at the files, and while they were big enough to force their way through, they would have to beat me up first. I was a bit scared, but my adrenalin was working well, and I didn't think they would really hit me. The members of the union, watching this encounter from about thirty feet away, wisely decided to stay out of the conflict. All but one of them were black, and this was in 1951, a decade before the civil rights struggle of the sixties and even before the school desegregation decision of the Supreme Court. They had been brought up in an environment in which blacks do not challenge angry cops. In any event, Arens and Connor left after ten minutes or so of unfriendly conversation, and I went back to meet with my clients, all of us somewhat shaken by the experience.

I had come to Memphis at the request of District 65 to represent several members of the union who had been subpoenaed by the Senate Subcommittee on Internal Security (SISS), and I was interviewing the witnesses when Arens and Connor walked in. I knew Arens well. He was the most experienced of the lawyers for the congressional investigating committees and I had confronted him on several occasions earlier in the year. Connor was a member of the staff of the committee; its chairman was Senator James Eastland of Mississippi, perhaps the most reactionary of the members of the Senate. The thought that blacks could join a trade union horrified him—in his district they weren't even allowed to vote.

Memphis lies just across the Mississippi border, and Eastland's home base was only a few miles away. He walked through Memphis as if he owned it. Every police officer, every court officer, every public official greeted him as a friend, and he responded with the cordiality of a well-established politician. Blacks stayed out of sight to the extent possible when Eastland was strutting through the streets of Memphis.

Even before the visit of Arens and Connor, tension was high at my meeting with the union members. It required much courage for anyone to join a union in Memphis in the early fifties and even more for blacks to do so. We all knew that the proposed hearing involved alleged communism in District 65, and that was an additional disquieting factor.

Ed McCrea was the only white member of the union who had been subpoenaed. He was an experienced organizer and, while apprehensive, provided some leadership for the others. Most of my task with respect to the others was to convince them that no harm could come to them if they kept their heads and testified as I advised.

My advice to the witnesses was much the same as the advice I had been giving to persons in similar situations for some years. I told them that if they denied membership in the Communist party they might find themselves facing perjury charges, since there seemed to be several people in Memphis prepared to testify that they had met the witnesses at meetings of organizations they considered to be Communist. Besides that, any black who belonged to a trade union in Memphis in 1951 was *ipso facto* regarded as a Communist. I doubt whether any of the them were Party members, but if any were and they admitted membership, not only would they be required to inform on other Party members, but they would most certainly lose their jobs and find it impossible to find another in Memphis or anywhere else in the region. The remaining alternative was to refuse to answer the questions on the grounds of either the First or Fifth Amendment to the Constitution, or both. The First Amendment protects freedom of speech and association; the Fifth provides that person could not be compelled to testify against himself. Refusal solely on grounds of the First, as the law stood then, would certainly subject them to a charge of contempt of Congress. Refusal to answer on grounds of the Fifth would provide legal protection. Nothing could be done to save their jobs, except such protection as the union might provide.

There was agreement they would all plead the Fifth, and I assured them that I would be acting as their attorney throughout the hearing and would be permitted to sit alongside them to give legal advice and some moral support.

We went to the hearing the next day at the United States Courthouse. The room was crowded, and every face in it seemed either hostile or scared, except for a number of reporters who anticipated a good show. A witness gave testimony concerning the alleged Communist influence in District 65 and the Memphis local. I was seated in the back of the room when Eastland, whom I had run into before, saw me, called me to the front, and directed me to testify, interrupting the witness on the stand.

I had testified before the committee in the past, and I knew what to expect. The atmosphere in the hearing room, however, was much more tense and hostile than in previous hearings in New York and Washington. Eastland was on his own turf, and I was in a foreign land. My testimony is illustrative of the quaint behavior of United States senators in an era long gone by. But it was not at all amusing when it happened.

After I was sworn in as a witness, the transcript shows, the examination proceeded, Eastland and Arens taking turns in questioning me:

SENATOR EASTLAND. Do you have some clients here, Mr. Rabinowitz?

MR. RABINOWITZ. Yes.

SENATOR EASTLAND. Who are your clients?

MR. RABINOWITZ. I represent the Distributive, Processing, and Office Workers of America. . . .

. . . . . .

SENATOR EASTLAND. Are you a Communist? . . . Are you a member of the Communist Party?

Mr. Rabinowitz. I decline to answer that question on the grounds of my privilege under the fifth amendment. That question has been asked to me by this committee before and I have given the same answer.

Senator Eastland. Yes, sir. What other organizations do you represent? What other unions?

. . . . . .

Mr. Rabinowitz. Well, on general retainer I represent . . . the American Communications Association—

Mr. Arens. The American Communications Association is an organization which was investigated by the Internal Security Committee in the course of the last few months, was it not? . . . And, in the findings of the Internal Security Subcommittee in its report in conjunction with the American Communications Association, the subcommittee found that the leadership of the American Communications Association were all Communists, did it not?

Mr. Rabinowitz. I regret to say, Mr. Arens, that I have never read the report. I should have, but didn't.

Mr. Arens. Who is the president of the American Communications Association?

Mr. Rabinowitz. Joseph P. Selly.

Mr. Arens. And he was identified as a Communist before the Internal Security Subcommittee?

Mr. Rabinowitz. I don't know. I didn't read the report, as I say.

. . . . . .

Mr. Arens. Who is Joseph Kehoe?

Mr. Rabinowitz. He is the international secretary-treasurer of the ACA.

Mr. Arens. You appeared as counsel representing Mr. Selly and Mr. Kehoe, did you not?

Mr. Rabinowitz. Yes; I did.

Mr. Arens. And you advised them not to answer questions—

Senator Eastland. Wait a minute. All of those witnesses refused to answer the questions put to them as to whether or not they were Communist Party members on the ground that it might incriminate them. That is true, is it not?

. . . . . .

Mr. Rabinowitz. I can't say whether all of the witnesses that I have represented before this subcommittee have refused to answer that question.

. . . . . .

Mr. Arens. Are you a member of the National Lawyers Guild?

Mr. Rabinowitz. Yes, I am.

MR. ARENS. The National Lawyers Guild has been cited as a Communist front, has it not?

MR. RABINOWITZ. I don't know. Perhaps it has.

. . . . . .

SENATOR EASTLAND. What is the fifth amendment? I want you to state your reason now.

. . . . . .

MR. RABINOWITZ. Under the terms of the fifth amendment to the Constitution, a person may not be compelled to bear witness against himself. Now, that amendment to the Constitution has been interpreted by court decisions and by authorities in the field of constitutional law to provide that a witness may not be required to answer questions which might either furnish evidence in a prosecution against him for a crime or which might furnish a link in evidence which might connect him with a crime.

SENATOR EASTLAND. And it is being used by Communists, is it not, as a pretext to prevent the legally constituted authority in this country from securing evidence of a villainous conspiracy to overthrow this Government, is it not?

MR. RABINOWITZ. I don't believe so, Senator.

. . . . . .

MR. ARENS. You got into a little difficulty in New York City that time in the ACA hearing, did you not?

MR. RABINOWITZ. No; I never had any difficulty except with Senator Eastland.

MR. ARENS. Did not Senator Smith order you to be removed from certain sessions during the hearings on American Communications in New York City?

MR. RABINOWITZ. He didn't order me. He thought it would be a good idea and I agreed.

. . . . . .

SENATOR EASTLAND. That will be all. You are under the rule, Mr. Rabinowitz. We will excuse you, but hold you under subpoena.

MR. RABINOWITZ. For how long?

SENATOR EASTLAND. Until I decide to release you. I would like him to be separate from other witnesses.

MR. RABINOWITZ. I am free to go about my business, am I not?

SENATOR EASTLAND. You are under subpoena.

MR. RABINOWITZ. I know that, but that doesn't mean I am under arrest.

SENATOR EASTLAND. You can do as you want to at your peril. You are under subpoena to this committee and I am going to enforce it.

Gentlemen, I would like to say that Mr. Rabinowitz is a very able lawyer
who always shows up representing big-time Communists.

For most of the afternoon session, while my clients testified, I was kept
out of the hearing room on the theory that I was a witness under subpoena and was not permitted to talk to other witnesses, but my clients
had been well advised as to how to answer questions and they didn't make
any mistakes, although they were harassed unmercifully by Eastland and
Arens. My subpoena was withdrawn at the end of the session so that I
could meet with my clients in the evening, and I was allowed in the hearing room the next morning when a few more union members testified.
Every time I attempted to say anything, Eastland gaveled me down.

We then recessed for lunch. It was a beautiful day, and I had never seen
the Mississippi River from ground level, and so I decided to sit on a park
bench near the courthouse and watch the river flow majestically by. My
clients, meantime, went to lunch and stopped off at the union office.

After lunch, I returned to the courthouse and was met by McCrea and
the others. They told me that during the lunch recess Arens and Connor had returned to the union office and had forcibly seized the union
membership records. In my absence, no resistance had been offered. I
was furious. When the hearing opened, I stood up to protest in language
as indignant as I was able to manage. I had not said more than one or two
sentences when Eastland shouted, "Throw that damn scum out of here.
Get rid of him."

The printed transcript reads, at this point: "Mr. Rabinowitz was ush-
ered out of the hearing room." What actually happened was that two
court officers even bigger than Arens and Connor, stereotypes of sheriffs in the deep South, physically lifted me out of my seat and put me in
an office in the courthouse where they kept guard over me for the rest
of the day. I got permission to make a telephone call, but I couldn't think
of anyone to call.

In the meantime, my clients testified in my absence. They had enough
presence of mind to rely on their Fifth Amendment rights. After the
hearing a reporter told me he had spoken to Eastland, who said that
"Rabinowitz and Lee Pressman are the best Communist lawyers in the
U.S." The reporter wanted my comment, which I refused to give.

I cannot remember the incident Arens and Eastland referred to concerning my having been removed from a hearing by Senator Smith, and
I have searched through the minutes of earlier hearings at which I have
been present. The first of those hearings was an investigation into ACA

by the committee in May 1951. Senator Willis Smith presided at that hearing, and I represented a number of officers of ACA who were called to testify. Arens was present as counsel to the committee. The first witness was Joe Selly. When I stated that I was representing Selly, Arens asked that I be sworn in. I protested, saying I had not been subpoenaed. Arens promptly made out a subpoena, handed it to me, and I testified.

Arens ran through the litany of questions, asking me what organizations I belonged to, and I relied on my Fifth Amendment privilege. My testimony was relatively short, and he then proceeded to examine Selly and the other witnesses. I took my seat alongside the witnesses. Occasionally the witnesses consulted me, and I whispered my answers to their queries.

After a few minutes, Arens complained that I was telling the witnesses how to answer the questions. I said that wasn't true: I wasn't telling anyone how to answer. I was merely advising them as to their rights, a distinction that, under the circumstances, was not very significant.

My discussions on this subject with Arens and Smith occupy more space in the transcript of the hearings than the testimony of the witnesses. At no point did Smith "order" me out of the hearing, nor did I leave.

At a later hearing before SISS I represented Alex Sirota, an old and dear friend. Senators Eastland and Jenner presided. The printed transcript shows that at one point Alex said he wanted to consult his lawyer and Jenner said, "I understand the attorney was in here, and was excused from the hearing room." I suppose that is a senatorial way of saying that I had been ordered out of the room. Evidently I remained outside the door, and Alex came out of the hearing once or twice to consult me. The same procedure was followed two weeks later when I represented Irving Velson before the same committee, with Eastland presiding. There is nothing in the published transcript of either of those hearings to explain why I wasn't in the hearing room; those transcripts are often edited.

Aside from SISS there were two other congressional committees then entrusted with the task of hunting down reds, parlor pinks, crypto-Communists, fellow travelers, and other subversive elements. The most active of these was the House Committee on Un-American Activities, but the most flamboyant and, for a while, the most terrifying was the McCarthy committee, formally the Senate Committee on Government Operations.

So notorious was its chairman that the period of the domestic cold war is, in popular parlance, often referred to as the McCarthy period, and "McCarthyism" has become a part of our vocabulary as describing virulent, shameless, and mendacious attacks on all varieties of left-wing or even mildly progressive thought. Indeed, "McCarthyism" has become an epithet, a sort of second cousin to "fascism."

Actually, Joe McCarthy didn't appear on the scene as a significant figure until February 1950, when in a famous speech in Wheeling, West Virginia, he claimed that he had documentary proof that there were 205 Communists employed in the State Department. In the spring of 1954, afflicted by a degree of megalomania seldom seen in public life, he decided to take on the most sacred of sacred cows in our nation, the United States Army, and his downfall was as meteoric as his rise.

Off camera, as when drinking at the bar in the Carroll Arms Hotel, across the street from the Senate Office Building, he was a genial, extroverted, and not unpleasant man—a good-natured drunk. His attitude paralleled that of the Earl of Warwick, who, in Bernard Shaw's *Saint Joan*, remarked to the ghost of Joan of Arc: "The burning was purely political. There was no personal feeling against you." But in his self-appointed role as the protector of his country, McCarthy showed not the slightest hint of humanity. He pursued his victims with the cruelty we usually associate only with religious persecutions such as the Inquisition. In tandem with Roy Cohn, counsel to the committee, he played the role of a malicious god, stamping out his victims randomly and thoughtlessly. An instance may be seen in the case of Sylvia Berke—a small incident, perhaps, in the big picture, but significant enough to the witness.

In the latter part of 1953, McCarthy mounted the most sensational of his investigations up to that time, into alleged Communist activity in the United States Army Signal Corps base at Fort Monmouth, New Jersey. Preceded by the usual inflammatory statements emanating from the senator, which built up a high degree of public anticipation of lurid disclosures, the investigation played to SRO crowds for several weeks at the federal courthouse in New York. The usual informers testified, and the press covered the hearings with banner headlines.

Our office had represented the Federation of Architects, Engineers, Chemists, and Technicians, a CIO union, and many of its members, subpoenaed by the committee, looked to us for representation. Leonard and I represented a dozen or so of the witnesses. Late one evening in December, while at the courthouse in New York for one of those hearings, I noticed a young woman obviously in considerable emotional distress. I asked her what the trouble was, and she said she had received a subpoena from the committee to testify that evening. It seemed that at one time she had been employed by the signal corps. Her name was Sylvia

Berke; she had no lawyer, knew nothing about the procedures before the committee, and was frightened. I told her that, in view of the fact the subpoena had been served on her only the day before, I thought there would be no problem adjourning the hearing.

The hearing was adjourned for a few days, and in the next week I had an opportunity to meet with Sylvia. She was divorced and was the sole support of a five-year-old child. She was somewhat fortunate in that she had secured a job as a temporary clerk with the board of education. There is nothing lower in the hierarchy of the board and nothing more poorly paid than the position of temporary clerk, but the job had an important peripheral value. She was permitted to enroll her child in the kindergarten at the school where she worked and was thus saved the expense of a babysitter. While far from affluent, she managed to support herself.

I don't know whether she was or was not a member of the Party, and I didn't ask her, since she was intelligent enough to assess the situation and the danger of a possible perjury indictment should she deny membership. She decided to refuse to answer the inevitable questions as to her membership in the Party by pleading the Fifth Amendment. She knew, and I knew, that she would lose her job with the board of education as a result, since it was then the declared policy of the board to dismiss anyone who "took the Fifth Amendment" before a congressional committee. There was not much I could do for her except attend the hearing with her and provide whatever support I could. However, I did promise to see if I could appeal to McCarthy's sympathy to get her excused from testifying.

The hearing was held a few days later at the courthouse. The eighth floor, on which the hearings were held, was crowded with spectators, not unlike those who, one hundred years earlier, had gathered at Newgate to watch public hangings in London.

I waited in the hall to catch McCarthy as he came up in the elevator, and a few minutes before ten o'clock he stepped out of an elevator car, saw me, and with his usual geniality, which he exhibited only in personal relations, threw his arms around me, shouting, "Hello, Vic! What can I do for you?" There were perhaps fifty people in the hall, and I did not relish the greeting. I told him I wanted to see him about one of the witnesses, and he took me to a room adjacent to the courtroom.

I asked him whether he would excuse Sylvia from testifying. I pointed out that it seemed unnecessarily cruel to this young woman to deprive her of employment in a situation that made it possible for her to work and raise a child, albeit on a very low salary. She was going to take the

Fifth Amendment anyhow, so the committee would get no information from her.

McCarthy's answer was typical: "It's all right with me, but you'd better take it up with Roy."

Roy Cohn was standing ten feet away, and when I put the problem to him, his answer was quick and peremptory. "Nonsense," he said. "We can't withdraw this subpoena. This woman possesses a great deal of information concerning subversive activity at the signal corps. She's one of the most important witnesses in this investigation." I told him that since she was going to plead the Fifth Amendment, the only result of the investigation would be that she would lose her job. It made not the slightest impression on Cohn.

Of all the evil men I've encountered in six decades of law practice, Roy Cohn was the most vicious. His legal career started as an assistant United States attorney in the prosecutions of Julius and Ethel Rosenberg, and William Remington, leading political cases of the early fifties. His rise was rapid, and he was hired as chief counsel to Senator McCarthy and masterminded the inquisitions of the McCarthy committee. McCarthy fell from power when he was censured by the Senate in 1955, but Cohn landed on his feet to establish a very successful law practice in New York. Utterly unprincipled, he was also a very able lawyer. Indicted four times by grand juries in New York, he was never convicted, though he was disbarred in 1986. He died of AIDS at the age of fifty-nine.*

■

By this time every seat in the hearing room had been taken and about twenty-five people were standing in the hall trying to get in. I pushed my way through the crowd only by announcing that I represented a witness, collecting many hostile stares on the way. I couldn't find a seat and stood in the back of the room and watched McCarthy and Cohn put on a typical show. When Sylvia's name was called, she took her seat at the

---

*A parenthetical anecdote: In about 1977 a lawyer, whose name I cannot recall, asked our firm to represent Tony Salerno, a high-ranking Mafia figure, in racketeering charges then pending. He left the file with us and visited a few days later. He offered a generous fee—enough to enable us to represent ten of our usual impecunious clients. But, he said, the fee would be paid in cash. I said I didn't care how the fee was paid, but we would, of course, report the fee to the IRS as income and record the source on our books. Tony's lawyer left. A week later he called: "Sorry, but we can't retain you. Send the file over to Roy Cohn."

witness table and I made my way through the crowded aisle to the front of the room. "Commie lover" and "Go back to Russia" were a few of the milder epithets tossed at me, and one or two of the gentlefolk in the audience spat at me as I passed by.

The questioning of this young temporary clerk at the board of education was vintage McCarthy, as the transcript shows. After she had pleaded the Fifth Amendment as to her Party membership, McCarthy, referring to the policy of the New York Board of Education, said: "Well, if the board of education follows the rule which they have laid down, and I am sure they will, I think they should be complimented for it, you might apply for a job over at Harvard. It seems to be a privileged sanctuary over there for fifth amendment cases. The president of Harvard has announced that he will not discharge fifth amendment cases."

She lost her job at the board of education a day or two later.

It had seemed to me from the very beginning that McCarthy and his committee had no authority to investigate alleged subversive activities. The jurisdiction of the Committee on Government Operations, as set forth in the Senate rules, had nothing to do with espionage, subversion, internal security, foreign affairs, or any related subject. The committee's purpose was to investigate governmental efficiency, and its duty was defined by phrases such as "studying the operation of government activity at all levels with a view to determining its economy and efficiency" and "evaluating the effects of laws enacted to reorganize the legislative and executive branches of the government."

In about 1951, I started two actions, one in the District of Columbia, the other in New York, seeking to get a district court to enjoin hearings by the McCarthy committee. I was unsuccessful because both courts held that until a witness had been asked specific questions, there was no way of knowing whether the subject under inquiry was within the committee's jurisdiction. In addition, there are constitutional problems raised when a court is asked to interfere with a congressional function. The only way to test the jurisdiction of the committee, therefore, was to find a witness who was prepared to refuse to answer questions and who, on his or her subsequent indictment, could raise the issue in a criminal proceeding.

A good opportunity for a test presented itself in December 1953, when Albert Shadowitz was subpoenaed before the McCarthy committee. I represented him at the hearing and in the subsequent court proceedings. At the opening of his hearing, Al made a statement challenging the jurisdiction of the committee and advising it that he would object to any substantive questions put by the committee.

After a few questions relating to his employment, he was asked whether he was a member of the Communist party. He responded:

> In answer to this question, I am going to follow completely the course of action advised by Dr. Albert Einstein, both to every one in general and by personal consultation to me in particular. I refuse to answer this question because it is in violation of the first amendment. I will refuse to answer any question which invades my rights to think as I please or which violates my guaranties of free speech and association. In addition, I specifically wish to object to the jurisdiction of the committee and to deny the right of this committee to ask any questions of me concerning political association.

The hearing proceeded:

> THE CHAIRMAN. In other words, you went to Dr. Einstein and he advised you not to answer the questions? Is that right?
>
> . . . . . .
>
> MR. SHADOWITZ. He advised me not to cooperate with this or any other committee of a similar nature. He said that on any question involving my personal beliefs, my policies, my associations with other people, my reading, my thinking, my writing, I should refuse to answer on the basis that it is a violation of the first amendment, that I should not invoke the fifth amendment, that on questions involving espionage I should refuse to answer this committee on the grounds that they do not have the jurisdiction to ask these questions of me, but should then voluntarily on my own make a statement concerning the very questions asked, and this is the plan I propose to follow.
>
> . . . . . .
>
> THE CHAIRMAN. I would suggest that if you do not want to spend considerable time in jail, that you advise with your lawyer rather than Mr. Einstein. But you have a perfect right to advise with whoever you want to.
>
> MR. SHADOWITZ. I have secured what I believe to be competent legal advice. I feel perfectly secure.

I had, of course, discussed his testimony with Al, though his visit to Dr. Einstein was his own idea. He was the client I'd been waiting for. Shadowitz was courageous and self-confident and was prepared to take the risk involved. He was in time indicted for contempt of Congress, and I made a motion to dismiss the indictment on the ground that the committee had no jurisdiction. Two other witnesses, Corliss Lamont and Abe Unger, a lawyer who frequently represented the Communist party, were called before the same committee at about the same time and joined in the attack on the committee's jurisdiction.

In July 1955, Judge Weinfeld dismissed the indictment, finding it invalid in that it had not sufficiently set forth the subject under inquiry by the committee, or the authority of the committee to hold a hearing on subversive activity. The decision, though a victory for us, was phrased in technical terms, and did not make the substantive statement I was looking for. Fortunately, when the government appealed, the Court of Appeals was more explicit, holding that the subject of "subversive activity" was outside the committee's jurisdiction. By that time, McCarthy had been dethroned.

Between February 1953 and March 1954 alone, the McCarthy committee had carried on over a hundred hearings and examined hundreds of witnesses including high-ranking officers in the United States Army, all of this without any challenge to its jurisdiction. By the time the courts got to the point of finding a lack of jurisdiction, the problem had passed; the McCarthy committee was no longer functioning, McCarthy himself had been censured by the Senate, and his role in the cold war was over. The damage, of course, had been done. For all of the notoriety of the McCarthy committee and the terror it inspired, I do not believe anyone who challenged that committee ever was convicted of contempt. The difficulty was that so few were prepared to challenge it.

The beginning of the end of McCarthy's activities came in March 1954. At that time, I was retained to represent Mr. Gross and Mr. Johnson before the committee (both names are fictitious since disclosure might result in some embarrassment to the witnesses). Gross was a short, excitable, and tense man who was badly frightened, as he had good cause to be. He was employed by a firm working under government contracts, and he knew that if he took refuge in the Fifth Amendment he would be discharged immediately. He was a draftsman; he had a wife and two small children, and all the way down on the train to the hearing in Washington he expressed his concern about how he could possibly make a living at an occupation that would enable him to support his family. He was so upset that I had doubts as to whether he would be able to pull himself together sufficiently to testify coherently on the next day.

Johnson was quite the opposite in temperament. He was a tall, slim salesman selling some product that had nothing to do with government procurement or national security. He had no family and did not think a Fifth Amendment plea by him would affect his earning capacity in the slightest. If worst came to worst he could move out of New York and no one would know or care what his political views were.

The next morning we walked into the hearing room in Washington. The room was crowded, more than usually so, and as soon as we entered,

Roy Cohn approached me and said, "Look, I've got a problem. I've sub-poenaed five witnesses this morning, and I only have time for four. I can't take anybody else this afternoon because we have some very important business to consider which cannot be postponed. I'll be able to take only one of your two witnesses. I don't care which one. We'll have to post-pone the hearing of the other to some time next week." I complained a bit about requiring a witness to come to Washington and then sending him home, but this sort of thing had happened before, and Cohn didn't care about anyone's inconvenience anyway.

I met with my two clients and told them what had happened. Gross's response was, "I want to testify. I haven't slept for the last week, and I know I'm going to lose my job, but I can't stand the worry and anxiety of having this subpoena hanging over my head. I couldn't live through another week waiting to be called down here again." Johnson, on the other hand, said, "I don't care. It doesn't matter to me. I'm perfectly willing to come down again whenever the committee wants me."

Gross testified, "took the Fifth," and lost his job. Johnson was never called back to testify. On the day after Gross's testimony, the army, its patience exhausted by McCarthy's attacks, submitted to the committee and the press a list of forty-four instances of improper conduct, over a period of eight months, by which McCarthy and Cohn sought to get preferential army treatment for David Schine, a former member of Mc-Carthy's staff who had just been inducted into the army. Schine was widely reputed to be Cohn's homosexual partner. The so-called "Army-McCarthy hearings" airing those charges provided the press sensation of the spring and summer of 1954 and ultimately resulted in the cen-sure of McCarthy by the Senate. McCarthy never recovered from the disgrace. Two or three desultory hearings were held by his committee late in 1954, and the McCarthy terror was over.

Of the three investigating committees, HUAC was the most active over the longest period of time—about twelve years. For submission to the Supreme Court, I prepared a partial study of HUAC's activity. From 1949 to 1959, over 28,000 pages of testimony were printed and there were thousands more pages of testimony given in executive session that have never been made public. In the period from 1955 to 1958 alone, 931 wit-nesses were called in open session by the committee, of which 797 were "unfriendly" witnesses, that is, witnesses who refused to answer ques-tions as to their political activity. Of the "friendly" witnesses, 33 were FBI agents, 39 were other government employees, and 46 were former members of the Communist party who provided the committee with the names of other Party members.

It has been estimated that over 5,000 subpoenas were issued by the committee. It had issued two indices containing the names of about 42,000 persons and organizations that were "mentioned" in a HUAC hearing or report up to 1956. The indices are convenient sources of the names of persons who have been accused of being Communists, available to any private organization or government agency that wishes to conduct its own purge.

I don't know how many hearings before these investigating committees I attended in the fifties. I suppose I may have represented as many as 150 witnesses, and Leonard represented perhaps another 75. Hardly any were in a position to pay adequate counsel fees, and we considered ourselves lucky when we were able to get travel expenses for hearings out of New York. I do not believe there was a single instance in which we turned down a witness because of his or her lack of funds.

A great deal of publicity was given to many of these hearings. Even people who did not follow these events closely had heard of the Hollywood Ten and knew that there had been a purge of movie stars, directors, and writers during the late forties and the fifties. But most of the witnesses called by the committee were not VIPs whose names were known to all. Most of them were trade unionists, steelworkers, auto workers, teachers, doctors, city employees, housewives, and other ordinary citizens who suffered severe economic deprivation and occasionally social ostracism from the mere fact that they were called and resisted the demand of the committee that they become informers. It also must be kept in mind that the work of the congressional committees was supplemented by hundreds of state and local agencies that mimicked the congressional committees in their efforts to get rid of alleged subversives.

From the very beginning of the hearings, a serious policy question was raised with respect to the conduct of unfriendly witnesses called before the committees. This problem justifies somewhat extended treatment.

The First and Fifth Amendments

In 1947, Leon Josephson, an avowed member of the Communist party, was called before HUAC, where he was represented by Sam Neuburger. He was asked whether he was or ever had been a member of the Communist party. He refused to answer, claiming a privilege under the First Amendment, in that the question interfered with his freedom of speech and his right of assembly, and further, that the question was not within the jurisdiction of the committee. He was convicted of contempt of Congress, and his conviction was sustained on appeal. Review was denied by the Supreme Court, and he was sentenced to a year in jail. In the same year, ten Hollywood writers and directors made the same claim at hearings before the same committee, when they were asked the same question, with the same result.

In 1948, Patricia Blau and Jane Rogers appeared before a federal grand jury and were asked, in substance, the same question. Blau refused to answer on the grounds that her membership in the Communist party was privileged under the Fifth Amendment in that an answer might tend to incriminate her. She was also tried for contempt and convicted, but the Supreme Court reversed the conviction, holding that her Fifth Amendment plea protected her. Rogers, on the other hand, testified that she was a member of the Party, but refused to name other members, also pleading the Fifth Amendment as a reason. She also was convicted of contempt, but the Supreme Court affirmed the conviction over a strong dissent by Justice Black. The majority of the Court held that she had waived her Fifth Amendment rights, saying: "Where criminal facts have been voluntarily revealed the privilege cannot be invoked to avoid disclosure of the details."

As of the end of 1950, therefore, a witness called before any of the investigating committees or before a grand jury had several options:

1. He (or she) could refuse to answer all questions as to membership in the Party or any related subject, pleading the Fifth Amendment. Such a witness was free from threat of indictment. Whether he (or she) would be fired or blacklisted depended on many other considerations.
2. He could refuse to answer on First Amendment and jurisdictional grounds, risking criminal prosecution and trusting to good luck, a good lawyer, or a sympathetic court to beat the rap. Many witnesses taking this option were never convicted of contempt, or convictions were reversed on appeal, but over a score did jail time.
3. She could deny membership in the Party, thus running the risk of a perjury indictment. There were a dozen or so professional informers around who, truthfully or falsely, named hundreds of persons as having been Party members. Some traveled from city to city with the committees, as if part of a road show. Further, almost every union or other organization coming under the scrutiny of a committee spawned its own informers ad infinitum.
4. He could admit membership, refuse to name others, and face the possibility of indictment and subsequent jail time.

5. He could admit membership and inform on other members; in the usage of the day, he would become a "friendly" witness. None of these were represented by Leonard or me. Their names are remembered in infamy (at least by me) even to this day, some thirty-five years later. Elia Kazan is a great stage director; he not only informed on his comrades but boasted of it. Jerome Robbins is a great choreographer, but he too informed. Some informed with enthusiasm; some with real or pretended reluctance. Some informed only on dead people, or only on people who had been named by others, or only on people who were both dead *and* had been named by others. E. M. Forster once put the hardest case: "If I had to choose between betraying my country and betraying my friend, I hope I should have the guts to betray my country." None of these informers faced Forster's dilemma. Presented with the alternatives of betraying their friends or saving their careers, they chose to betray their friends.

To me, all of the informers are sinners, and I find it difficult to forgive any of them.

Most of the unfriendly witnesses, when confronted with the available options, "took the Fifth" and walked out of the committee room free from the fear of prosecution (and also, in most cases, without a job). No one liked this, neither witness nor lawyer. Although the courts had said over and over again that a plea of Fifth Amendment privilege was not in any way to be understood as an admission of guilt, in the public mind there was something sinister about the plea, an admission of some sort of wrongdoing. Witnesses who in fact had been or were members of the Communist party and who were not ashamed of that fact were asked, "Why plead the Fifth Amendment if you've done nothing wrong?" The answer is clear, if not understood by everyone who asked: "Because if I admit my own Party membership, I'll have to inform on others or risk jail."

It was inevitable that reliance on the privilege against self-incrimination, repeated over a thousand times, by as many witnesses, cast a pall of perceived criminality with respect to the Party and its activities, even among the more liberal members of the community. There was seen to be an implicit confession that the Party was indeed engaged in some kind of a conspiracy to do something wrong.

The witnesses were so many and the possible choices so few that most lawyers representing those witnesses in the early fifties fell into the habit of advising all clients to "take the Fifth." That was certainly true when several members of a trade union or other organization were subpoenaed at one time. While I dutifully explained the available options to my clients, I did it in such a way that their choice was almost automatic. There was a handful of brave souls who challenged the committee directly, by refusing to rely on their self-incrimination privilege. Such were the playwright Arthur Miller; the folksinger Pete Seeger; my close friend and fellow member of the National Lawyers Guild, Martin Popper; and a few others. But they were all risking indictment and they were few in number.

Popular usage of the day quickly divided those who would not inform into two groups: the "First Amendment Communists," and "Fifth Amendment Communists." The committees, the press, many employers, most government agencies, and large sections of the public rapidly adopted that formulation. Both kinds of Communists were usually fired from their employment and blacklisted from their occupations, though a few employers made a distinction, firing only the Fifth Amendment witnesses. Thus some First Amendment witnesses kept their jobs—but were indicted.

If the Communist party had an official policy on the subject, it was never transmitted to me, but it was clear that it had no objection to the widespread and almost automatic use of the Fifth Amendment, despite its destructive effect on the public perception of the Party. The Party functionaries I represented and the others who testified during this time automatically pleaded the Fifth and never raised the possibility of any other course of conduct. The history of the committees might have been different had the Party urged the opposite approach—an approach that would have been tantamount to civil disobedience. I hungered after such a policy and argued for it, but I was regarded, perhaps properly, as a romantic or, even worse, an ultraleftist. It would have entailed great risks (as does most civil disobedience), and I doubt whether the Party had the power to enforce such a policy. But it certainly did not try, and I myself pleaded the Fifth Amendment the first two times I testified. The spectacle of hundreds of witnesses risking indictment to stand on a question of principle would have been politically inspiring, but at the time the Party was engaged in a bitter struggle against the Smith Act indictments, and the thought of encouraging hundreds of rank-and-file members to incur a great risk would have been rejected by the Party leaders, if indeed it had even been seriously considered.

An interesting phenomenon developed as the thousands of subpoenas issued by the three congressional investigating committees flooded the country and as state and local committees joined in the hunt. In time a bond was created among the witnesses who decided not to inform. I rarely asked any client whether in fact he or she had ever been a member of the Party. If the witness was not going to answer questions put by the committee, membership was not important; anyway I preferred not to know. I have no doubt that many of my clients had never been members of the Communist party, although most had been quite close to it. Some of them probably could have denied membership with little real risk of a perjury charge.

But none of them did. I think most felt that a denial of membership under the guns of the committees was a violation of solidarity with those who were or had been members and who were, together with them, suffering the attacks of the witch-hunters. In a sense, denial of membership under those circumstances was copping out, and many of us looked with a slight measure of scorn on those progressives who had joined with Party members in many of their activities but who, when faced by the committee, denied membership. I was upset that Leonard Boudin denied membership when applying for a passport, and his oral history shows that he was himself troubled by his action, but he wanted the passport badly. I never discussed the matter with him, but I felt that he was, in a sense, betraying a principle that many of his own clients had upheld.

In 1957, the legal situation changed. Three years earlier, John Watkins had testified before HUAC. Watkins, an organizer for the United Auto Workers, said that he had never been a member of the Party but had cooperated with it closely between 1942 and 1948, so that many people might think that he was a member. This was clearly intended to head off a perjury indictment. When asked about the membership of other persons, he offered to, and did, answer questions as to those whom he knew to have been members of the Party and whom he believed still were members, but he refused to answer about those who had left the Party. He did not rely specifically on any provision of the Constitution but claimed that the questions he refused to answer were not relevant to the committee's purpose. He was convicted of contempt, and his conviction was reversed in June 1957 by the Supreme Court in a six-to-one vote, in an opinion by Chief Justice Warren, with two justices not voting, and Justice Clark dissenting. This, it will be noted, was ten full years after Josephson and the Hollywood Ten had first challenged the committee's jurisdiction on similar grounds.

The Court reversed on two grounds: (1) "[W]hen First Amendment rights are threatened, the delegation of power to the committee must be clearly revealed in its charter." There was no such clear delegation of power here, the authorizing resolution of Congress being impermissibly vague; and (2) the questions put to Watkins were not pertinent to any subject under inquiry. Justice Frankfurter concurred in the result, finding only that the questions were not pertinent.

The decision was greeted with joy by all of us engaged in daily battle with the committees, and it was discussed at great length and in much detail by the press. The *New York Times* ran a series of editorials on the subject over the next week, the first of them headed "A Day for Freedom" and, on the following Sunday, another entitled "A New Birth of Freedom." Coverage of the decision was nationwide. Although the opinion wasn't as unequivocal as we would have wished, it did seem to rid us of the unpleasant need to rely on a self-incrimination defense. Congressional delegation of power to the committee had been the same for many years, and if it was insufficient for Watkins, it was insufficient for everyone else.

Within days after the *Watkins* decision, a group of lawyers met at the Vanderbilt Hotel in New York, for a meeting that began at about 8:30 in the evening and ran until the early morning hours. Participants included Harry Sacher, Abe Unger, Dave Freedman, Dave Rein, Joe Forer, and myself, and perhaps others. It had been called by Marty Popper. We were all lawyers active in the representation of witnesses before congressional committees, and Sacher, Unger, Rein, and I had ourselves testified before one or more of the investigating committees. The purpose of the meeting was to discuss the implications of the *Watkins* decision. Although we had no power to direct any of our clients as to how they should testify, nor would we have exercised such a power if we had it, many of our clients looked to us for political guidance and leadership.

Unger and Freedman were attorneys for the Party; Sacher had been lead defense counsel in the prosecution of the Communist party leaders under the Smith Act; I was a member of the Party and the others were close to it if not members. We certainly weren't making Party policy, but our views would have some influence on the Party and its members. The issue before us was whether we should encourage clients to refuse to answer on First Amendment and jurisdictional grounds and to abjure reliance on the Fifth, and what kind of reasonable assurance we could give to them that they were not running much risk of indictment.

The discussion was a long one. Marty argued that continued reliance on the Fifth Amendment was causing much damage to the Party and in a sense was legitimatizing the committees. He urged strongly that our clients should be encouraged not to take refuge in the Fifth Amendment privilege but to attack the jurisdiction of the committees on First Amendment grounds. That was just what Josephson and the Hollywood Ten had done, and they had gone to jail, but the *Watkins* case provided at least some hope that continued reliance on the Fifth Amendment could be avoided. Of course, we could not reasonably advise our clients that they were safe in relying only on jurisdiction and the First Amendment, but we could at least point to the downside of continued reliance on a plea of possible self-incrimination and the political advantage in taking the offensive and attacking the committee's right to conduct any investigation into "subversive activities." Continued reliance on the Fifth Amendment, Popper argued, was a tactic perhaps appropriate for most witnesses but not automatically for all. Unger took the same position.

Forer and Rein both disagreed, with their usual energy. They were close friends of ours, and we used their office in handling our Washington litigation, and sometimes their homes when we could not get hotel accommodations. They were wonderful lawyers and wonderful people. They were also very pragmatic—less interested in a political argument of the sort urged by Popper and Unger and more concerned with protecting witnesses with as little complication as possible. "Get the witness on and off the stand as quickly as possible," was their motto. They pointed to the fact that possible changes in the personnel of the Court made reliance on the *Watkins* decision risky. It should be noted that in terms of numbers of client/witnesses, Popper and Unger represented relatively few; Forer and Rein represented very many, probably more than anyone else in the country. Popper's clients were drawn mostly from the entertainment industry; Unger's from the ranks of the Party. Forer and Rein, like Leonard and me, drew clients from the rest of the ranks of radicals—trade unionists, teachers, salesmen, doctors, government employees, and a whole miscellany of persons in the radical community.

Marty was one of the most convincing advocates I've ever known. Clearly, his approach could not be utilized on a wholesale basis. Most witnesses would agree with the Forer-Rein approach—get in and get out. There were a handful, however, who I thought might be attracted by the Popper position. An opportunity to try this out was not long in coming. Both SISS and HUAC were then conducting forays against ACA. In fact, Vinnie Trautman and Sam Testa had already received subpoenas returnable before SISS three days after the *Watkins* decision. At my request, the committee adjourned the hearings for two weeks, to give me an opportunity to analyze the decision. In July or August, Frank Grumman and Bernard Silber were to testify before HUAC. All four were members of ACA, all but Silber being officers.

I appeared for all four witnesses. All relied on a challenge to the committees' jurisdiction and the First Amendment. All specifically disavowed reliance on the Fifth Amendment. There were other ACA members who testified at the same hearings who were also represented by me and who relied on the Fifth. In every case I met individually with the witnesses and carefully explained the options available, the risks involved in refusing to rely on the Fifth Amendment, and the political issues inherent in the situation. Grumman and Silber were later indicted and convicted. They appealed, and the Supreme Court accepted their cases for review. Testa and Trautman were never indicted. All four kept their jobs, in some cases winning in arbitrations brought under their union contract.

A few months after the ACA hearings, I represented Ed Yellin. He was a steelworker, working in Gary, Indiana, and was subpoenaed by HUAC along with several coworkers to a hearing in Gary in February 1958. I met with Ed and most of the others who had been subpoenaed, and Ed and some of his friends agreed that they would rely on the First Amendment, challenge the jurisdiction of the committee, and refrain from reliance on the Fifth.

Four days before the hearing, I sent a telegram to the committee, asking that Ed be examined in executive session because "testimony needed for legislative purposes can be secured in executive session without exposing witnesses to publicity." A day later I received an answer from Arens, as staff director of the committee, denying my request.

The reason for this denial was apparent when the committee held its hearings at the courthouse in Gary. The first four rows of seats in the courtroom, normally available for spectators, were roped off, and shortly before the hearing opened, a few dozen high school students trooped in to occupy those seats. The local newspaper carried banner headlines announcing the coming of the committee—events such as this were not as common in Gary as they were in Washington or New York. The committee was playing to a full house and was seeing to it that the schoolchildren of the area were properly educated. The courtroom was packed with a standing-room–only crowd, which cheered and booed as if on cue.

Ed was the first unfriendly witness. After a few preliminary questions, I interrupted and asked that the chairman read into the record the exchange of telegrams between myself and the committee. Congressman Francis P. Walter, who was presiding, answered, "We will decide whether it will be made a part of the record when the executive session is held. Go ahead."

I again protested, stating that I sent the telegram because I wanted it to appear in the record. Walter replied, "Well, whatever the reason was, whether it has been stated or otherwise, it will be considered in executive session. . . . Do not bother. You know the privileges given you by this committee. You have appeared before it often enough. You know as well as anybody. Go ahead, Mr. Tavenner."

Ed, like eleven other witnesses appearing that day, refused to answer questions as to his Party membership past or present, challenging the jurisdiction of the committee and relying on the First Amendment, but not the Fifth. Ed was promptly indicted. Three others were also indicted, but those latter indictments were dismissed by the government years later, after Ed's case was decided by the Supreme Court.

After Yellin's appearance before the committee, but before his trial for contempt, the Supreme Court decided *Barenblatt v. United States.* In 1954 Lloyd Barenblatt had testified before HUAC and had attacked the jurisdiction of the committee to ask any political questions, relying on the First Amendment and expressly disclaiming reliance on the Fifth. Between the *Watkins* decision and *Barenblatt,* the personnel of the Court had changed. Two new justices (Whittaker and Stewart) had been added, and two others (Frankfurter and Harlan) saw a distinction between the two cases, so that in June 1959 the Court by a five-to-four vote, in an opinion by Harlan, held Barenblatt's attack on the committee insufficient and affirmed his conviction.

Barenblatt had objected to *any* inquiry by the committee as to his associational activities. Watkins, on the other hand, accepted the right of the committee to ask *some* questions. His stance, no doubt, was much closer to Frankfurter's view (and perhaps Harlan's) than Barenblatt's blanket refusal to answer, but it is somewhat difficult, in legal terms, to justify the difference of results in the two cases. Like most Supreme Court cases, and in fact like most cases of any kind, there are extralegal political and philosophical considerations that motivate judges; that was true to an extraordinary extent in the case of Frankfurter. He could identify easily with Watkins, but not with Barenblatt.

Hence, when the *Yellin* case came on for trial in the district court in March 1960, the *Barenblatt* decision had in effect overruled *Watkins,* so far as my attack on the jurisdiction of the committee was concerned. But I found what I thought was a further defense for Ed in the language of the Court in the *Barenblatt* case, where the Court said: "Where First Amendment rights are asserted to bar governmental interrogation, resolution of the issue always involves a balancing by the courts of the competing private and public interests at stake in the particular circumstances shown."

In the *Barenblatt* case, the Court held, the record was barren of any factors to lead to the conclusion that the private interests of Barenblatt outbalanced the interests of the state.

This language was something of a shock to the civil liberties community. We had always argued that First Amendment rights had primacy and that they could not be abrogated merely because such abrogation was deemed to be in the public interest. In fact, the very purpose of the First Amendment was to protect speech and association even when they were *not* in the public interest. Furthermore, the balancing test itself was, in the words of Justice Black, nothing but a "high-sounding slogan."

However, the language of the *Barenblatt* Court did give me an issue on which I might hang my hat. And so, taking the opinion on its face, I proposed to prove that when competing private and public interests are balanced, private interests (i.e., the right to remain silent as to political beliefs) would prevail in Yellin's case—in fact, that there wasn't much public interest at all in getting Yellin's testimony. Hence, I argued, Yellin's private interests were entitled to protection. To prove this conclusion, I offered the expert testimony of Professor Thomas Emerson of the Yale Law School. Emerson had written extensively on political and civil rights, and he offered his analysis of the balance that the *Barenblatt* court seemed to find determinative of the case.

In his proposed testimony, Emerson outlined existing legislation relating to the protection of internal security in the United States. He pointed out that in industry, and most other areas of American life, the Communist party, "the organization against which this Committee has directed most of its activities," had little influence. He also pointed out that the committee had already collected a great deal of information on the subject at hearings held in many cities throughout the country, and that the additional testimony being requested of Yellin could have no significant bearing on the subject the committee was investigating.

Emerson then turned "to the other side of the scales." He discussed the interest of the individual in his right of expression and in his right of silence and the nature of the interest of society in freedom of political expression in a democratic society. He considered the economic and social effect upon a witness called before the committee as well as the effect upon his right of association.

The district court, in holding Yellin guilty of contempt, refused to accept Emerson's testimony, saying: "Expert testimony of this kind is not material in that it is not a question of fact as to what elements go to make up the balance of interests, public and private, but a legal matter, which is within the province of the court to decide; and it is not a subject of expert testimony."

This conclusion makes little sense. If, as *Barenblatt* said, the right to remain silent is to be determined by a balancing of competing private and public interests, there must be some evidence before the court as to what that balance is. Here there was no evidence at all; the district court proceeded under the theory that the judge could take judicial notice of facts not on the record and come to a conclusion as to the balance called for in the *Barenblatt* decision.

That left me with one remaining defense, arising from the denial of my request for an executive session. The district court held against Ed on this ground also.

After his testimony, Ed was awarded a National Science Foundation scholarship as a graduate student in engineering at the University of Illinois. Following his conviction in the district court, the scholarship was withdrawn when members of HUAC undertook an investigation of the award. He was also suspended from his courses, but the suspension was lifted a week or two later when a faculty-student committee, appointed by the dean to consider his case, recommended such action.

The Court of Appeals affirmed the conviction and the Supreme Court agreed to hear the case "since the case presented Constitutional questions of continuing importance." The case was set down for argument in April 1962; the *Grumman* and *Silber* cases were to be argued on the same day.

I argued *Yellin* first. I knew that I could not get the Court, as then constituted, to declare HUAC to be totally without jurisdiction, and I sought to apply the balancing test. It should not be, I argued, a matter for the Court to decide on the basis of what it thought, but a question of fact as to whether the state's interest in finding out about Yellin's political beliefs outweighed Yellin's First Amendment rights of free speech and free association. And those facts were a matter for evidence at the trial—i.e., Emerson's expert testimony.

I thought this a strong point, and so did at least some members of the Court at the time of oral argument. This was an attack on all of the congressional committees whose pretense of being engaged in legislative investigation was a facade to cover Communist-bashing. It was because I had raised this point that the Court accepted the case for review in the first place.

Grumman was argued next, by Dave Rein, restrained, quiet, and, as always, very good. After a lunch break, I returned to argue the *Silber* case. Even before I stood up, I felt that something was wrong. I was completely disoriented and had difficulty in focusing my mind on my argument and my eyes on the court. I had trouble in progressing from one point to the next; I was unable to remember what I had said thirty seconds before; I hesitated and stumbled in a manner quite different from my performance just a few hours earlier in the *Yellin* case. I was in obvious distress, so much so that Justice Brennan stepped in to guide me, leading me gently from one argument to another until my time was up and I sat down, still in a deep fog.

I still don't know what happened to me. I had argued cases before the Court on other occasions and had gone through the *Yellin* argument without difficulty. This time, I could barely find my way out of the courtroom. My lapse had nothing to do with the decision. The issue was the same as in the *Grumman* case, and both were decided the same way.

(The same thing happened to me once again. A year or so later, I was asked by the Harvard International Law Society to debate the issue raised by the case of *Banco Nacional v. Sabbatino*, then pending before the United States Supreme Court, which I had argued a few months before. The debate was with Carlyle Maw, a leading conservative lawyer, who later became legal adviser to the State Department, and Andreas Lowenthal, assistant legal adviser to the State Department. The day before the debate, the Court decided the case in favor of Banco Nacional, and I did not get a copy of the decision until a few hours before the debate. I had only a short time to read a rather lengthy and complex opinion. Again, I found myself talking nonsense during the debate, with no ability to follow a coherent line of argument or even to recall what I had said a moment before. There was no Justice Brennan to guide me through the evening. My confusion lasted through the debate and almost all the way to the airport.)

In June, the Supreme Court reversed the convictions of Grumman and Silber. It found a technical defect in the indictments—namely that the subject under inquiry had not been set forth. This same technical defect had gone unnoticed in many of the preceding cases; the fact was that, by this time, the Court was getting tired of contempt cases arising from congressional committee hearings. The decisions in *Grumman* and *Silber*, however, did not dispose of the *Yellin* case, because the *Yellin* indictment met the requirements of the *Grumman* decision.

A few days later, the Supreme Court ordered reargument of the *Yellin* case. No reason was given. Reargument was heard in December, and the Court, by a five-to-four vote, reversed Yellin's conviction, in an exceedingly technical opinion by Chief Justice Warren.

The Court, in a footnote, explained that the constitutional questions raised by the record, including the First Amendment issue and the question of the availability of expert testimony, need not be passed on, because the case could be decided on another issue, namely the failure of the committee to consider my application for an executive session. The Court held that the committee rules had been violated and that Yellin had a right to refuse to answer.

This was fine for Yellin, who was home free, but a disappointment to me and of no significance at all in the struggle for First Amendment rights. The constitutional issues that were not decided were much more interesting and important than the trivial issue on which the court spent so much time and energy.

Two other cases should be mentioned to complete this story. In 1958, Carl Braden and Frank Wilkinson testified before HUAC at a hearing in Atlanta. They were both full-time activists expending great effort to a movement to abolish HUAC. Both refused to answer questions on First Amendment and jurisdictional grounds; both were indicted and convicted of contempt; and in both cases, their convictions were upheld in the Supreme Court in 1961 by votes of five to four.

Braden was represented by our office; Leonard argued his case at all levels of the proceedings. I helped on the brief and prepared an elaborate appendix analyzing the activities of HUAC, to show that it had no legitimate government purpose. The dissents in the two cases utilized my material, but the majority ignored it.

For myself, I decided that when and if called again, I would put my reliance on the First Amendment and stay away from the Fifth. I didn't have much chance to prove my courage. I was called again before HUAC went out of business. I don't remember the subject of the inquiry, but I do recall that Arens asked me once more whether I was a member of the Communist party. I refused to answer, prepared to rely on the First Amendment alone, but Arens deprived me of my opportunity to be a hero by saying, in effect, "Oh, never mind, you'll plead the Fifth Amendment again," and I was excused.

In 1959, Irving Potash and Hy Lumer were subpoenaed to testify before HUAC. Irving, a friend from the Boudin, Cohn, and Glickstein days, was a member of the national committee of the Communist party and had been convicted in the first Smith Act case. Hy was educational director of the Party and had been convicted on charges that he had engaged in a conspiracy to violate section 9(h) of the Taft-Hartley Act.

I met with both of them on a bright, sunny day on the lawn of my house in New Rochelle. I presented to them all of the arguments in favor of reliance on the First Amendment, rather than on the Fifth Amendment privilege. I pointed out to both men that they were intelligent and articulate. I was sure that they could formulate answers that would give them an opportunity to state what they understood to be the true purposes of the Communist party, an opportunity that was rarely afforded to anyone in those days, while attacking the jurisdiction of the congressional committee on First Amendments grounds.

I finished my pitch and Irving looked at me somewhat sadly and said, "There is a risk that we will be indicted and ultimately go to jail, isn't there?" I answered, "Yes, there is a risk." Irving said:

> I am fifty-one years old, and I've spent about ten or fifteen years of my life in jail. My health is not good, and really I don't think that I am prepared to take the risk of another term in jail, even if it's a short one. I'm not at all sure that the opportunity to present another attack on the jurisdiction of the committee is worth the risk. Everything you say about the evils of pleading the Fifth Amendment is quite true, but so far as I am concerned, I don't want to spend another year in jail. I don't have much longer to live, and I don't want to give up any part of the rest of my life in defending against another criminal prosecution, even if I win in the end.

Hy Lumer answered in much the same way. He too had recently served a considerable term in prison; he had a family whom he had not seen much in the past few years, and he also was doubtful about the value of another case testing the First Amendment position.

Both Potash and Lumer were right, and I didn't argue with them. Both had paid their dues. Both went to Washington with me, testified before HUAC, took the Fifth Amendment, and went home.

It takes only a few pages to describe the court battles over the authority of the congressional investigating committees and only a few minutes to read about them, but it took sixteen long years—between the *Josephson* and Hollywood Ten cases in 1947 and the *Yellin* case in 1963—to play them out. The devastation wrought by the committees during this period was overwhelming, and I have tried to suggest its scope. The courts were of no help whatsoever.

8

The Cold War beyond Congress

The congressional committee investigations got the most publicity over a period of about twelve years but the hunt for "subversives" was by no means confined to Congress. On the contrary, there was hardly a sphere of intellectual or political life in the country that could not boast its own red-hunt. And it must be kept in mind that for every victim of the red hunt whose situation was the subject of litigation, there were hundreds, if not thousands, who suffered greatly in relative anonymity. This chapter presents only a handful of the cases our office handled arising out of the cold war waged outside of Congress. They may be taken as typical.

The Steve Nelson Case

One Sunday evening at the end of June in 1952, I received a telephone call from Steve Nelson, whom I had met once or twice over the past decade. He asked if I could represent him in the Pittsburgh sedition case then pending against him. Specifically, I was asked to undertake the appeal from his conviction a few weeks earlier. More specifically, could I come to Pittsburgh to represent him at a hearing to be held the next day, at which time Nelson's motion for a new trial would be ruled on and, possibly, sentence imposed?

I knew something about Steve Nelson. He was a full-time organizer for the Communist party and when the civil war broke out in Spain, he became one of the officers of the Abraham Lincoln Battalion, a group of United States volunteers who had gone to Spain and joined the Loyalist forces against Franco—action that violated United States neutrality laws. The volunteers were joined by others from England, Italy, France, Germany, and elsewhere to make up the International Brigades that fought in this early struggle against fascism.

Nelson was wounded in the civil war and returned to take his place as an organizer for the Party. In 1950 and for some time before that, he was district secretary of the Party for the western district of Pennsylvania, with offices in Pittsburgh.

That city and its industrial environs had a long history of radicalism, going back to the Homestead Steel strike and the attempt by the anarchist Alexander Berkman to assassinate Henry Clay Frick in 1892. A strong, prounion working class had developed over the years, and with it, an active Communist party in the steel mills and coal mines. The end of the war and the onset of the cold war sparked a strong and violent anti-Communist movement in Pittsburgh. Nelson had a high profile, and he was marked as the primary target of the anti-Communist forces.

Those forces were orchestrated by Michael Musmanno, a colorful and flamboyant lawyer who, riding the tide of anticommunism, had been elected to the court of common pleas of Pittsburgh. Together with several others he had organized a vigilante organization called Americans Battling Communism. In 1950, he doffed his judicial robes for a few hours while he personally led a raid on the Party bookshop in Nelson's office, seizing a load of books, records, and personal papers. The county district attorney submitted the fruits of the raid to a grand jury, which obliged by issuing a multicount indictment, charging Steve and two other Party members, Andy Onda and Jim Dolsen, with violations of Pennsylvania's sedition law. Among the offenses charged was the distribution of books such as *The Communist Manifesto* and *The Foundations of Leninism,* and the commission of other similar acts "with a view to overthrowing and destroying by force and violence and by a show and threat of force the government of this state and of the United States of America."

Hy Schlesinger, a founding member of the National Lawyers Guild, had for years been representing Nelson and other left-wing clients in Pittsburgh before HUAC and in local legal matters, and Musmanno had set out to destroy him. Musmanno had instituted disbarment proceedings against Hy, and while Hy ultimately beat the charges, it occupied much of his energy and time for about ten years and destroyed his practice. The message was clear; the bar was terrified and no one was available to represent Nelson.

So Steve and his codefendants had to look to out-of-town lawyers to represent them, and John McTernan of Los Angeles, Aubrey Grossman of San Francisco, and Basil Pollitt of New York, all NLG members, took over the representation of the defendants.

The trial started in January 1951 and ran on until early May, when Nelson was seriously injured in an automobile accident. The case proceeded against his two codefendants but was severed as to him.

Nelson was again faced with the problem of getting a lawyer when his renewed trial was rescheduled. He wrote to literally hundreds of lawyers in the Pittsburgh area asking them to represent him. The overwhelming majority didn't answer. A few did and pleaded other professional commitments. A handful said that they were willing to represent Steve, but they asked fees so high as to make it clear that they expected to get rich on the case, or really didn't want to take it.

The result was that Steve Nelson represented himself in the second trial. It is somewhat doubtful that anyone could have won this case for the defendant. The judge was Harry Montgomery, who, like Musmanno, had been one of the organizers of Americans Battling Communism. He was hostile from the beginning. As in the first trial, Musmanno testified against Nelson. He had run for judge of the state supreme court in the election just completed and had been elected. In the course of his testimony against Nelson, a recess had to be taken so that he could be sworn into his new position.

The trial was colorful enough to get full-scale media coverage. The spectacle of a judge of the supreme court of Pennsylvania stepping down from the bench to testify as to the dangers the Communist party posed to the governments of the United States and Pennsylvania was quite sensational. Musmanno got bad press throughout the United States as a result, certainly in professional circles, and the Allegheny County Bar Association censured him for his political activities while on the bench. None of this, however, helped Steve much, and he was convicted. He made the usual motion for a new trial, still representing himself. It was at this stage that I was requested to come in to represent Steve—on less than twenty-four hours' notice.

No one ever said anything to me about compensation, either at that time or at any other time during the following four years in which I represented Steve, nor did I ever raise the question. I have always had trouble in asking for fees from clients in political cases. Steve had risked his life fighting the good fight in Spain—in a sense he was fighting for me, along with other antifascists. He had returned to organize workers in heavy industry in the United States, again risking his life and enduring discomforts I could barely imagine. Now he was facing a long term in a Pennsylvania prison for distributing books and advocating socialism. All this time, I was living a middle-class life, playing with my kids, taking occasional vacations, reading the same books Steve was distributing, and advocating the same ideas Steve was advocating. I wouldn't have been much good in Spain or in the coal mines or the steel mills, but I had some skills as a lawyer that might be devoted to helping Steve, and thus balance the scales a bit. Was I motivated, in part at least, by a feeling of guilt? Probably.

I knew that any fees that might be paid would come from the Party and not from Steve personally, but this did not make much difference. A legal fee for defending Steve Nelson seemed almost obscene. Fortunately, the rest of my practice enabled me to live reasonably comfortably, if not in luxury, and I was not confronted with a very hard choice. I was lucky in other respects, too—my partners never resented my spending time on this and other like cases.

However, the summons to appear in Pittsburgh for Steve was not one I could meet on such short notice. And so Steve appeared without counsel before Judge Montgomery, who denied the motion for a new trial. The court agreed to postpone sentencing but revoked bail and remanded Steve to jail. I appeared for Steve at the time of sentencing and made my best pitch, but he was sentenced to twenty years and was fined twenty thousand dollars. I immediately filed a notice of appeal to the superior court of Pennsylvania, and a motion to the same court for his release on bail. Bail was denied there too and Steve remained in jail until February 1953 when the case reached the supreme court of Pennsylvania.

I visited Steve several times at the Allegheny County Prison at Blawnox. The prison was dreadful—it looked just like prisons in dozens of grade B movies I had seen. The entire structure was gloomy and gray; there didn't seem to be a bright light in the place. I watched the prisoners shuffle into the mess hall for a meal. They wore traditional prison garb and carried traditional prison eating equipment, and all had the same gray pallor. In the line was my client. I had difficulty in picking him out, because everyone looked much the same. It wasn't until we got into a dark and dingy conference room that his personality revived and he became a human being separate from the rest of the prison population.

During his stay in prison, he was given a hard time. He was a notorious person, and the guards were quick to discipline him for minor or imaginary violations of prison rules. Steve bore the whole thing quite stoically, but he spent a great deal of his time in solitary confinement and in defending himself against charges of fancied violation of prison rules.

An appeal to the Pennsylvania Superior Court was quickly prepared, and I briefed and argued it in the fall of 1952. The court said not a word.

There was no reason to believe any of the judges heard a thing I said. It quickly affirmed the decision of Judge Montgomery, not even bothering to write an opinion.

I've lost lots of cases in my time, and frequently I have trouble understanding how the court could have ignored the arguments I made. This proceeding was one of the worst. That Montgomery and Musmanno should have disregarded Nelson's rights was understandable; they were part of a lynch mob, and members of lynch mobs rarely pay much attention to due process, even when they are judges. But that three appellate court judges could have affirmed on a record so full of error was appalling. As much as anything that happened in that dark period of American history, this case is illustrative of the fury of the cold war.

An appeal to the Pennsylvania Supreme Court was possible only by leave of that court. In February the supreme court accepted the appeal and released Nelson on twenty thousand dollars' bail.

In the Pennsylvania Supreme Court, I thought we would get a better shake. We were out of the terrible reactionary ambiance of Pittsburgh, and I hoped that the relatively rarefied atmosphere of Harrisburg would result in a more reasonable consideration of our argument. I had a bit of difficulty in deciding on priorities in writing the brief on appeal. The federal government, in enacting the Smith Act, had made sedition a federal offense and, in legal terms, that act "preempted the field of sedition" so as to oust any state court of jurisdiction to try someone under a state statute punishing the same crime. Pennsylvania argued that the Smith Act punished only sedition against the United States; the state statute punished sedition against Pennsylvania. This was absurd—how could anyone conceive of overthrowing the government of Pennsylvania alone?

Logically this question of the jurisdiction of Pennsylvania to try Steve for sedition was a threshold argument and should be argued first. If we were right in that contention, the court would never have to pass on the outrageous procedures that characterized Steve's trial.

But preemption of the field of sedition by the Smith Act was essentially a dull subject, and besides, I thought that the Smith Act was unconstitutional, too. It would be hard to make an interesting speech to the court on the dry legal issue of preemption, but I could make a swell speech on the outrageous trial of Steve Nelson. And so I played around with the idea of arguing the free speech and due process issues first, and relegating jurisdiction to the end of the brief.

Belle Seligman, who had coauthored the brief in *ACA v. Douds*, was working with me on this brief also, and she thought my idea was ridiculous. She pointed out that the purpose of the proceeding was to reverse the conviction of Steve, not to throw mud at a couple of Pennsylvania judges or even to provide me with an opportunity to make a speech. Fortunately, her good sense prevailed, and jurisdiction came first in the brief we wrote. It was a very long brief, because even if we weren't going to rely primarily on the trial errors, we had to cover them, and we did so. It was a good brief, but I'm not at all sure anybody except Belle and I ever read it beyond the first point.

The argument before the Pennsylvania Supreme Court was what an appellate argument ought to be: quiet and dignified—and partial to my point of view. Musmanno disqualified himself, as did another of the judges. Most of the questioning from the bench came from Chief Judge Stern and Judge Jones, and they were interested only in the preemption argument. They listened politely to my discussion of the other issues but didn't seem to care much.

In January 1954, the Pennsylvania court reversed Nelson's conviction by a vote of four to one. The opinion of Justice Jones, speaking for the court, was quite short. The court alluded to the many issues raised by us that related to the unfairness of the trial, but said that it was not concerned with these issues because the Pennsylvania Sedition Act was superseded upon the enactment of the Smith Act. The Pennsylvania act presumed to punish sedition against the United States, and that is a function reserved to the federal government. The court pointed out: "Out of all the voluminous testimony, we have not found, nor has anyone pointed to, a single word indicating a seditious act or even utterance directed against the government of Pennsylvania. Indeed, it is difficult to conceive of an act of sedition against the state in our federated system that is not at once an act of sedition against the government of the United States—the union of the 48 component states."

There was a long dissent by Justice Bell, also confined to the issue of preemption.

The state of Pennsylvania promptly filed a petition for review in the United States Supreme Court, and that court just as promptly granted the petition.

At this point, a bad thing happened—at least, I felt it to be a bad thing. Someone from the Party called me—probably Bill Patterson, head of the Civil Rights Congress, then the principal defense arm of the Party—and told me that the Party wished to retain another lawyer to argue the case before the Supreme Court—a more "respectable" lawyer and one who would have, I was told, more standing before the Court. I was not being replaced; someone was merely being substituted to argue the case. It was explained to me that no one thought I wasn't good enough; it was just that the Party felt that an establishment-type lawyer—what we on the left called a "broad" lawyer—would better get the attention of the Court.

I was angry for many reasons. I had won, not lost, in the Pennsylvania court. Moreover, I have never believed that the political views of a lawyer affected a court's decision—the views of a client, certainly, but, in my experience, not the views of a lawyer. I was sure that this new lawyer would be paid well and in proportion to his place in the hierarchy of the legal establishment. Mostly, I thought I was as good as, and probably better, than any other lawyer the Party could come up with. The whole thing struck me as disgraceful.

The lawyer the Party fixed on was Herb Thatcher, who was then general counsel to the AFL and had had considerable experience in arguing cases before the Supreme Court. I knew Herb well. He was anti-Communist, but quietly so. We had often been on opposite sides of cases, but I had gotten along with him as well as I had to. He was average—perhaps a bit above average—in competence. I thought he would argue the case adequately. I was confident that we would win. I couldn't see the United States Supreme Court overruling the Pennsylvania Supreme Court on the latter's ruling as to the application of a Pennsylvania statute to a Pennsylvania indictment and record.

I swallowed my anger. The important thing was to win the case, not my self-esteem. It should be noted, however, that the Nelson case was not the only one in which the Party pulled this stunt. Dave Rein had been pulled out of an important case involving Junius Scales and replaced by another "broad" lawyer, Telford Taylor. This was one of the less lovable characteristics of the Party, at least in the treatment of its lawyers, and it did very little to improve our morale.

The pendency of the case had aroused great interest among all the red-hunters of the nation. Forty-two states had sedition laws similar in purpose, and some almost identical in language, to the Pennsylvania statute. Attorney General Wyman of New Hampshire, preeminent among the state red-hunters, took it upon himself to call the pendency of the case to the attention of every state attorney general who otherwise might have overlooked it. Furthermore, there were some twenty-seven persons living in Massachusetts, New Hampshire, Florida, and Kentucky who had either been indicted under state sedition laws or subjected to interrogation pursuant to such laws, and Frank Donner, preeminent among the lawyer-scholars who were resisting application of state sedition laws, took it upon himself to call the pendency of the *Nelson* case to their attention.

And so, when the Court came to consider the *Nelson* case, it had before it not only the briefs of the parties, but an unusual number of *amicus curiae* briefs (those filed as a stranger to a lawsuit). The Court had invited the Justice Department of the United States to submit such a brief, and it did so, supporting the state of Pennsylvania. Given the issue in the case, this was an astonishing position and another illustration of cold war madness. Wyman submitted an *amicus* brief on behalf of himself and twenty-four other attorneys general. Massachusetts and Illinois submitted their own *amicus* briefs. The American Legion also made its views known in a brief also supporting Pennsylvania. On the other side were briefs submitted by Donner on behalf of his twenty-seven clients, by the American Civil Liberties Union, and by the Philadelphia Yearly Meeting of the Religious Society of Friends. The Court always allows the Justice Department to make oral argument if it wants to (as it did in this case), but it also allowed Wyman to speak for a few minutes.

I was only a front-row spectator at the argument, and I didn't enjoy that much, but Herb was quite good. He fielded questions well and spoke with assurance and confidence. Many establishment lawyers representing Communists in those days were prone to go on at some length about how much they despised their clients while defending their legal rights, a process that always infuriated me, although it did have echoes of Voltaire. But Herb was a gentleman. He did not apologize for his client but stuck close to the job. A good job, I thought—almost as good as I could have done.

The United States Supreme Court, by a vote of six to three, affirmed the Pennsylvania decision, and the *Nelson* Pennsylvania sedition case was over. The principal opinion by the Court was by Chief Justice Warren, who pointed out that the whole concept of sedition against a state was inconceivable in our present form of government and that the federal government had taken action sufficient to protect its citizens against sedition. He also pointed out that the state laws were themselves a mess. Many of them were unconstitutionally vague and hardly of any great value in their purported purpose.

The conclusion of Steve's state sedition prosecution was not the end of his troubles. While the state proceedings were pending, Steve was being tried on a Smith Act indictment in the federal court. He had been convicted; his conviction had been affirmed in the Court of Appeals, and further appeal was pending in the Supreme Court when the state conviction was reversed. Shortly thereafter, his federal court conviction was also thrown out by the Supreme Court on motion by the government when facts came to light proving that the principal witness against him was a pathological liar—a man whose credibility was so low that even the government felt required to disown him and to ask for a new trial. The government never proceeded with the new trial.

I had nothing to do with the federal case but continued a close relationship with Steve. He was being harassed incessantly by FBI agents who constantly sought to interview him. I wrote to the FBI advising it that I represented Nelson and stating that agents of the bureau had visited Nelson's home, had interviewed his neighbors, had accosted him on the street, and had attempted to speak to him. I stated that Nelson had no desire to discuss his affairs with representatives of the bureau, but if there was anything that the bureau wanted to talk to him about, they could communicate with me. I concluded with the observation, "In any event, your harassment of Mr. Nelson has continued now over a period of many years and it is time for it to stop."

It was a rather weak letter, but I couldn't think of much else to say. I never got an answer to the letter, but references to it are prominent in my own FBI file. For example, a memorandum to Director J. Edgar Hoover dated August 25, 1960 reads: "Enclosed is a copy of a letter from Victor Rabinowitz (BUFILE 100-336105; New York file 100-68229) to Bureau dated 8/22/60. The contents indicate a copy was furnished you directly by Rabinowitz. Rabinowitz' letter is an obvious effort to intimidate the Bureau. Although such a tactic will not deter us from fulfilling our responsibilities it should be borne in mind in any considerations regarding future contacts with Nelson or Rabinowitz. The letter is not being acknowledged."

I suppose we should all feel more secure in the knowledge that the FBI is not easily intimidated. Thereafter, I am frequently referred to in the FBI files as the man who tried to intimidate the FBI.

Steve wrote an autobiography entitled *Steve Nelson: American Radical* in 1981, and to those who want to know more about this wonderful man, I unhesitatingly recommend it. Particularly engrossing is the story of why he left the Party, to which he had devoted almost fifty years of his life.

The Bail Fund

On the evening of July 4, 1951, Harold Cammer, a fellow member of the National Lawyers Guild and a neighbor living in nearby Larchmont, called me and asked if I could help him out by representing Fred Field at a hearing in the federal court the next morning. Harold had a conflicting engagement, and the Field appearance could not be adjourned. He said he'd pick me up at my house and drive me to the courthouse in the morning and tell me all about it.

I had a good idea about what he was asking me to do. Two days earlier eleven national officers of the Communist party, who had been convicted for violation of the Smith Act in the *Dennis* case, had been scheduled to surrender. Only seven showed up. The media had been discussing almost nothing else for the previous forty-eight hours, and I was aware that the United States government took a very serious view of the flight of Gus Hall, Robert Thompson, Gilbert Green, and Henry Winston, four leading members of the Party.

Harold went over the situation with me on the drive into New York the next morning. Judge Sylvester Ryan had presided at the surrender of the Party members earlier that week. He was a former prosecutor, an able and energetic man, even when he wasn't angry, and now he was very angry indeed. Upon the failure of four of the defendants to appear on Monday, he had directed the trustees of the Bail Fund of the Civil Rights Congress, which had put up the bail for the missing defendants, to appear in court. Fred Field was the secretary-treasurer of the fund. The others were Dashiell Hammett, Alpheus Hunton, and Abner Green. Fred had appeared on Tuesday and had been questioned at some length by Ryan about the bail fund. He answered most of the questions as to the fund and his connection with it, and he produced most of the books, but he refused to submit the names of the contributors to the fund, relying on his Fifth Amendment privilege. Ryan gave him until July 5 to consult a lawyer; in fact Mary Kaufman, another guild member, had been in court and had attempted to represent Fred, but Ryan rode roughshod over her, giving her no time to consult in any meaningful way.

As things stood at that moment, Mary was trying to represent not only Fred, but Hammett, Hunton, and Green as well—and she was also a lawyer for the bail fund. Harold Cammer had been Fred's lawyer for some time, and he asked me to help out by taking part of the burden from Mary.

I had met Fred Field a few years before, when a party was held at his house to raise funds for the Seamen's Defense Committee, which I then represented. He was a member of the very wealthy Field and Vanderbilt families, and his early life at the most affluent levels of New York society is amusingly recounted in his autobiography, aptly entitled *From Right to Left*. He had "become" a member of the Communist party in the late 1930s, though he says he never formally joined. He had been an officer of the Institute for Pacific Relations, one of Senator McCarthy's earliest targets. He had been indicted for contempt of a congressional investigating committee in 1950 and was acquitted. He had become treasurer of the bail fund when it was organized.

Dash Hammett, chair of the bail fund, was a well-known writer, some of whose detective thrillers had been made into successful movies, notably *The Thin Man* and *The Maltese Falcon.* He was a tall, thin, taciturn man who had for years generously supported many left-wing causes. Alpheus Hunton was the president of the left-wing Council on African Affairs; Abner Green was chair of the American Committee for the Protection of the Foreign Born.

The bail fund had been organized by the Civil Rights Congress, the successor to the International Labor Defense of the thirties. In 1946 the congress established the bail fund for the purpose of making bail available to persons charged with political crimes. The fund was made up of deposits by sympathetic members of the public, in sums ranging from $50 to $1,000, certificates of deposit being issued to the depositors. On July 1, 1951, there was about $770,000 in the fund, contributed by about four thousand depositors.

I appeared for Fred Field and Dash Hammett on Thursday morning. Ryan moved in on Field with speed; as soon as I walked into the courtroom, he called on Fred to take the stand. I asked for a recess of a half hour so I could talk to my new client, but Ryan would have none of that.

I objected to the jurisdiction of the court to conduct any investigation into the bail fund, but Ryan brusquely overruled my objections, stating that he wanted the names and addresses of the bail fund depositors so that "law enforcement agencies might go to these . . . addresses to see if the defendants were there." This threat of a mass interrogation of thousands of people was, indeed, frightening. Fred again refused to hand over the names of depositors, pleading once again the Fifth Amendment. Ryan promptly sentenced Fred to ninety days for contempt of court. He denied my application for bail pending appeal, and Fred went to jail. Over the next few days, Hammett, Hunton, and Green were likewise held in contempt for their refusal to supply the names of bail fund contributors. I represented Hammett; Mary represented Hunton and Green. All three joined Fred in jail after all efforts to get bail from the Court of Appeals were exhausted.

In the course of those efforts, I traveled to Maysville, Kentucky, to make an application for bail before Justice Stanley Reed of the Supreme Court; he denied my application a few days later. While I was in Kentucky, Fred was testifying again, this time before a grand jury. Again he relied on the Fifth Amendment in response to almost every question—almost, but not quite. At one point during his testimony, he asked for an adjournment of one day, pointing out that I was not available for consultation. United States Attorney Saypol, who was conducting the investigation, refused any adjournment, and the examination proceeded.

The next few questions turned out to be critical. Fred was asked whether he was one of those who participated in the conduct of the bail fund. He pleaded the Fifth Amendment privilege on that question. He was then asked, "Who is the attorney for the bail fund." He answered, "Mrs. Mary Kaufman." He further testified that she was retained "as a result of a discussion among the trustees." As to other questions he again relied on his Fifth Amendment privilege. Two days later, he was sentenced to six more months for contempt of the grand jury. Immediately after he was sentenced, he was taken from the jail in New York to the jail in the District of Columbia to testify before the Senate Judiciary Committee the next day. I went to Washington to represent him. Fred spent the night in a jail cell; I spent the night in a comfortable hotel.

The next day, Field testified. The subject of the investigation was his relationship to the Institute for Pacific Relations (which had been discussed before a congressional committee fully a year before), with the usual inquiries as to the names of other persons connected with that organization. Fred again took the Fifth Amendment with respect to most of the questions. He was then taken back to the Washington jail, where he spent another sleepless night, and was brought back to New York the next day, still in custody.

In September, two cases were argued before the Court of Appeals in New Haven, one on behalf of Field, Hammett, and Hunton, relating to the sentences for contempt imposed on them by Judge Ryan, and the second on behalf of Field alone, appealing from his six-month sentence for contempt of the grand jury. Roy Cohn argued for the government—it was the first time I had met him. The bench was as good as one could hope for—Jerome Frank and Charles Clark were better than average, and the third judge, Harrie B. Chase, was not too bad. But these were not ordinary circumstances, and there was still great excitement over the missing defendants in the *Dennis* case. I didn't leave the courtroom with high hopes. On October 30, the orders of the district court were affirmed in both cases. In affirming Fred's conviction for contempt of the grand jury, the court held that the two or three answers he gave about Mary

Kaufman were a waiver of his Fifth Amendment privilege. The Supreme Court, as was to have been expected, denied review.

Fred served his sentence at Ashland, Tennessee, and I went down to visit him there a few times. Actually it was a very low-security prison, its population consisting mostly of bootleggers who had been arrested for operating illegal stills in the mountains of Kentucky, Tennessee, and Virginia. Dash Hammett was also assigned to Ashland. Fred's autobiography describes his prison stay in much detail.

The bail fund was ultimately liquidated after several years of litigation, and over 72 percent of the deposits made by the contributors were repaid, which was remarkably good, in view of the high expenses of liquidation (the liquidator, lawyers for the liquidator, a trustee, and other court-appointed officials grabbed chunks of the assets of the fund in accordance with the usual division of patronage in the New York judicial system).

The fight to keep the fund contributors' names secret was successful only for a short time. In mid-1952, Attorney General Nathaniel Goldstein of New York, who had seized the fund records, handed over to the FBI the names of over four thousand depositors in the fund, despite repeated promises that this would not be done.

All of the litigation was the result of the trustees' efforts to avoid making public the names of the contributors and the efforts of the United States government to get those names. The trustees were not acting frivolously, nor was the government—each had an interest in those names.

The trustees' interest was easily understood. In the climate of the times they and others feared that a deposit with the bail fund would be considered a sign of disloyalty in the eyes of the red-hunters—national, state, and local. Membership in the ALP, in the National Lawyers Guild, in the United Electrical Radio and Machine Workers, in ACA, or in a host of other organizations had in many cases been cited as a ground for sanctions to be applied against government employees, and there was good reason to believe that the same would be true of bail fund contributors. Indeed, so it turned out to be after the names of the contributors were in fact disclosed to the FBI.

The interest of the government was the flip side of the coin, though it was never publicly avowed. All government agencies at that time—congressional committees, state investigating committees, the FBI, grand juries—were busily engaged in collecting names to be added to the ever growing blacklist.

Alger Hiss

Four great political cases characterized the years of political repression between 1946 and 1960. *ACA v. Douds* approved legislation that penalized members of the Communist party and those who were "affiliated" with it or supported it. The decision in *Dennis v. United States* was widely perceived as holding the Communist party a conspiracy to overthrow the government of the United States. The execution of Julius and Ethel Rosenberg for espionage struck terror in the hearts of millions of progressives throughout the United States and caused many of us to think, "There, but for the grace of God, go I." The prosecution of Alger Hiss and his conviction for perjury enabled the right wing to attack, as Communist dominated, not only all aspects of the New Deal program of Franklin Delano Roosevelt, but also, by extension, the United Nations.

Alger Hiss had a distinguished career of government service, beginning in 1929 when he served as secretary to Justice Oliver Wendell Holmes of the United States Supreme Court. He had several positions in the State Department from 1936 to 1947, when he resigned to accept the post of president of the Carnegie Endowment for International Peace. As a State Department representative, he had accompanied President Roosevelt to the Yalta Conference in 1944 and participated in the drafting of the Yalta agreement. He likewise had taken part in drafting the United Nations Charter and served as general secretary of the United Nations General Assembly at its organization meeting in San Francisco in 1945.

In 1948, Hiss was subpoenaed to appear before the House Committee on Un-American Activities. He was asked a series of questions concerning his association with Whittaker Chambers and with the Communist party from 1934 to 1937. As a result of his answers, he was indicted for perjury and was tried in May 1949. The jury failed to agree, and a mistrial was declared. The second trial resulted in a conviction. The conviction was affirmed by the Court of Appeals, and a petition for review was denied by the Supreme Court. While Hiss was serving his term he moved for a new trial on grounds of newly discovered evidence. The motion was denied, and appeals again were unsuccessful. He was finally released in late 1954.

The political importance of the Hiss case can hardly be overstated. Richard Nixon was a member of the House committee that examined Hiss, and he took full credit for the resulting conviction. To Nixon and his supporters, Hiss was on trial as a surrogate for the New Deal, the

Yalta Conference, and the United Nations. Although Hiss was tried for perjury, the real offense behind the charge was espionage, but such a prosecution was barred by the statute of limitations. The verdict against him was, to the cold warriors, a verdict against the entire Roosevelt administration, so that in 1953, Senator McCarthy could charge, "twenty years of treason" in his attack on the Democratic party.

The media treated the proceedings as one of the great political sensations of the time. Hiss had been high in public esteem; Nixon, HUAC, and the press took malicious pleasure in tearing him down.

I cannot even begin to discuss the merits of the Hiss case. The subject has been treated extensively in a number of book-length volumes, some written by Hiss himself. I did not know Hiss personally at the time of his trials. I may have met him casually in 1948, and I think I met him briefly at about the time of his release from prison, but my close association with him began in 1975, when the National Emergency Civil Liberties Committee (NECLC) undertook to pry open the FBI files on his case, to seek out evidence establishing his innocence. As counsel to NECLC, I took on the task of collecting the evidence from the government under the Freedom of Information Act (FOIA).

From the beginning, I had perceived the case as a cold war frame-up. Nothing that has happened in the last twenty years of my close association with Alger has changed that perception. I do not believe he was guilty of espionage or perjury; those crimes are totally inconsistent with Alger's persona as I have come to know it. That his trial was unfair I have no doubt.

The first request for documents from the FBI relating to the Hiss case was made in 1975, and subsequent requests were made several times over the next three years. There is no aspect of the practice of the law quite so dull as an effort to get an administrative agency to disgorge documents it regards as confidential, and the FBI is the most adamant in protecting its files. The securing and processing of the files on Alger were undertaken by Jeff Kisseloff and Jim Pruitt, two young, talented, and devoted men who did the footwork in examining the Hiss file.

The procedure is a lengthy one. First we filed applications, and after long delays and repeated requests received thousands of documents. About half were duplicates of other documents produced. Most of the rest were routine and uninformative. A few may have been relevant but the key passages were redacted, leaving us with about a thousand pieces of paper with a tantalizing word or two, but with the important language blacked out. The reasons given for the redactions were variations of the contention that the disclosure of the redacted material would be either harmful to national security or an invasion of someone's privacy, or material for pending or contemplated litigation, or all of the above.

Extended intra-agency appeals followed for about eighteen months, at the end of which we brought an action in the district court seeking a court order directing more complete disclosure. Such litigation is not only tiresome, it is also likely to be fruitless and frustrating. To challenge the FBI resistance to full disclosure we were required to argue that the redacted material was not really confidential. But to do so without knowing the content of the redacted material was an almost impossible task. The solution contemplated by the statute was to have the judge examine the classified material *in camera* (a private examination closed to press, public, and the parties) and to decide whether the claim of confidentiality was justified. Judges have no way of judging the merits of such a classification, to say nothing of the fact that just as the process is dull and uninteresting to a lawyer, so it is to a judge. The result was that courts almost always decide for the government on the theory that the government knows best what ought to be kept secret, and besides, who has the time to read and analyze hundreds or even thousands of documents.

In our appeal to the court in Hiss's case, we weren't arguing to an average judge (which is bad enough), but to an unusually dull and obtuse one. There is nothing so exasperating as arguing a case before a judge who doesn't ask questions, make comments, or give other evidence that he or she is alive. Judge Richard Owen, who heard our FOIA case, was such a judge. He was a Nixon appointee, a person who had been an attorney in the antitrust division of the United States Attorney's Office. In manner he was neither friendly nor hostile. He just sat quietly and ruled against me on substantially every issue raised.

Some small credit must be given to the FBI. At one point in the proceeding, we were supplied with vast quantities of material—thousands and thousands of pieces of paper—which was perhaps an effort to drown us in documents. We (or rather Jeff and Jim) did read and analyze those thousands of documents and did secure as a result some material that made it possible for us to take the next step, despite the adverse rulings of the court.

And so, after much preparation, a petition for a writ of error *coram nobis* (an application to the court to correct serious error in a criminal case in which there is no other remedy) was filed in July 1980, seeking review of the Hiss conviction on the ground that the prosecution had wrongfully withheld exculpatory documents from the defendant; that it had employed an informer who had infiltrated the meetings of the Hiss lawyers; and that it presented evidence to the grand jury that it knew to be false. The petition was supported by hundreds of documents from the FBI files. We asked that the conviction be reversed, or, in the alternative, that a hearing be held to determine facts in dispute.

Judges are assigned randomly by the spinning of a wheel in the clerk's office, but like all practicing lawyers, I was afflicted with a considerable dose of paranoia and was more than half convinced that the draw is generally, in some way, "fixed" when a politically important case was filed. This time, Judge Whitman Knapp was chosen—not the best we could get, but not too bad. We needed a courageous, bold, and learned judge who was prepared to say that the United States had erred in sending Alger Hiss to prison. This was a big assignment, and Knapp was not the worst judge who might have been appointed. Knapp, however, declined the assignment for some frivolous reason, and resort was had to the wheel again. This time it really came up bad. We drew Owen again. My heart sank, and I started immediately to think about a brief on appeal.

In due course, the government's motion to dismiss the petition was argued before Owen. He said not a word during my presentation but participated fully in the argument once Mary Daly, representing the United States Attorney, got up to speak. He helped her to develop her arguments, although she was very good even without his help.

In July 1982, Owen's decision came down, and he denied the writ. He wrote a long opinion, replete with errors of fact and inadequate discussion of the law. We were disappointed but not surprised and immediately took an appeal—and again, intensive preparation was required. The record on appeal was almost five thousand pages long, and this brief, like the one in the district court, involved months of preparation.

We had many grounds for appeal. The information we had been able to uncover in the FBI files had disclosed many areas in which government misconduct seemed clear, especially in its failure to disclose exculpatory facts in its files. At the very least, we were entitled to a hearing at which we could develop further the government's lack of the required candor and its outright concealment of facts favorable to the defense.

The case was heard in the Court of Appeals in the spring of 1983. While I am prepared to concede that perhaps the choice of Owen to hear Alger's case twice in the district court was an unfortunate coincidence, I cannot feel the same way about what happened in the Court of Appeals. There were, at the time, thirteen judges on that court, and they heard appeals before panels of three. The three to whom the *Hiss* case was assigned were Ellsworth Van Graafeiland, William Timbers, and Thomas Meskill. It would have been impossible to choose three judges who were more hostile to Hiss, and who were not even interested in hearing what I had to say on his behalf. They listened to my argument without saying a word; and when my time was up, Van Graafeiland cut me off in the middle of a sentence. (I've never been treated quite as rudely.) The panel listened to my opponent without saying a word, and forty-eight hours later affirmed the decision of the court below, with a few words: "Decision of District Court affirmed."

I may have been wrong in my petition on behalf of Hiss, but it wasn't that bad. Any one of the other judges on the bench would have at least considered the case seriously.

How were those three judges picked to hear this case? I tried hard to find out what the procedure was but, of course, got nowhere.

My paranoia? This time I think not.

The Teachers Union

In 1954, Harry Adler was an electronics teacher in a New York vocational high school. He had at that time about sixteen years of seniority.

In the same year, Minerva Feinstein was a clerk at P.S. 186 in Brooklyn. She had about sixteen years of seniority.

At the same time, Julius Nash was a high school teacher of biology with about fifteen years of seniority.

Also in 1954, Irving Mauer was a science teacher in an elementary school. He was a disabled war veteran with about six years of seniority.

Their story is one of blind cruelty. Supposedly cultured and intelligent human beings set out to destroy the lives of good people who did no wrong and whose only offense was an adherence to deeply felt principles of decency and honesty. For this these victims paid a great price. The Board of Education of the City of New York in the 1950s, the superintendent of schools, the corporation counsel and his staff are all guilty, and there can be no excuse for what they did. I don't know whether Board Chairman Charles Silver, one of the Very Important People in New York at the time, or William Jansen, superintendent of the schools, or Peter Campbell Brown, corporation counsel of the city, ever had any sleepless nights over the plight of the teachers they were persecuting; I know that I did.

The story of Adler, Feinstein, Nash, and Mauer is not unique; it was repeated, in its essence, over and over again in the decade of the fifties.

Most of those under attack were members of the Teachers Union, a courageous and militant organization effectively led by Rose Russell, one of the most greathearted and unselfish persons I have known. My affection for her and for the union was deep, and I was saddened and depressed by the decade-long persecution of the union's members and its ultimate destruction. It was not only that union members were victimized. Among those who suffered most were the schoolchildren whose highly qualified teachers were being driven from the profession.

Adler, Feinstein, Nash, and Mauer were all summoned before Saul Moskoff, who was a representative of the corporation counsel's office and the local one-man embodiment of HUAC. All of them admitted membership in the Communist party in the past and testified that they had in good faith left the Party, although all of them said that such departure from the Party was not the result of any deep disagreement with its policies. They were asked the names of other members but refused to inform.

In March 1955, the board of education passed a resolution requiring past members of the Party to inform on others or face dismissal. Adler, Feinstein, Nash, and Mauer were all called before Moskoff once again and advised of the "inform or else" resolution. They persistently refused to answer the questions concerning others, and early in September the superintendent of schools suspended them. The only charges were that they had refused to name other members of the Communist party.

My firm was retained by the Teachers Union to apply to the state commissioner of education for an order staying the suspension. Commissioner James Allen issued a preliminary stay two days before the suspensions became effective. One would have thought that, the commissioner having spoken, the suspended teachers would have been reinstated at least until a final decision by Allen. But no, the board, ever vigilant to protect innocent twelve-year-olds from the subversive thoughts that might be stimulated by a public school clerk and a physics teacher, immediately filed new charges, this time alleging that the four were guilty of insubordination in refusing to answer questions, and that they had engaged in conduct unbecoming a teacher. This was indeed an astonishing feat of hair splitting, but in the era of the cold war anything went. In addition, Nash and Mauer were charged with having made false statements on application blanks filed many years earlier, in that they had, at that time, denied ever having been Party members. The suspension of the four continued in effect.

I immediately asked Allen for an order to direct the board to reinstate the four suspended members but he refused, apparently having concluded that the temporary stay he had issued was all that could be expected of him, even though it had no effect. I argued the full case before Allen a few months later, and it took him a full eleven months to decide on our petition. The decision was, given the circumstances, a good one. He held that the board of education had no right to suspend a teacher for refusal to inform. He pointed out that this decision was based, not on the law, but on his judgment as to what was the proper educational policy. He threw in the usual obligatory language about how Communists ought to be eliminated from the school system but held that this wasn't the right way to do it.

Still, the suspended employees were not reinstated. Instead, the corporation counsel instituted proceedings in the state supreme court to set aside the decision of the commissioner. That motion was not argued until October 1956. The court decided that the commissioner's decision was proper and the board's suspensions illegal. The corporation counsel took a further appeal to the Appellate Division. The decision of that court was not handed down until May 1958; the result was the same—the board's "inform or else" resolution was invalid. The corporation counsel then made a motion for leave to appeal to the Court of Appeals. That application was granted, but the decision from the Court of Appeals, affirming the decisions of the lower courts, did not come down until May 1959.

During all of those five years the four board employees remained suspended, although every judicial decision had been in their favor. It was not that the issue involved was a difficult one; as a matter of fact, the issue before the courts was very simple. The relevant statute provided that the decision of the commissioner of education should be final unless it was arbitrary or capricious, and no one could reasonably argue that Allen's decision was arbitrary or capricious. The only purpose of the appeals taken by the corporation counsel was to delay a final decision by the Court of Appeals, and so punish the recalcitrant witnesses.

Despite the decision of the court, Feinstein and Adler were not reinstated until June 1960, almost six years after their suspension, and four years after the commissioner had held that the board had no authority to ask them to inform on other teachers. Nash and Mauer, however, were not reinstated, because as to them there was still an open charge pending, namely their having made false statements on their applications.

A hearing followed on those charges against Nash and Mauer before Louis Goldstein, a former judge in New York and a political hack. The decision was a foregone conclusion, although I did my best to make a record that might be successful on a subsequent court appeal. I called Superintendent Jansen as a witness to establish the fact that there were many teachers who had been called in the course of the investigation and who had made false statements on their applications, but they had not been discharged or suspended, because they had also informed. I argued that although on their face, the charges were that Nash and Mauer were being discharged because of their having made false statements, the fact was that they were being discharged for refusal to inform. I made no headway with the trial examiner, who upheld the dismissals. We went back to Commissioner Allen and asked him to direct reinstatement of Nash and Mauer. He refused. Evidently his store of courage had been exhausted by his 1955 decision. We sought review in the state supreme court, to no avail, and the litigation ended.

While all of this was going on, efforts were made to collect back pay for Adler and Feinstein. A long period of time was spent in that, with the city fighting tooth and nail to save every dollar it could, for example, by refusing to pay interest on the back pay due to the victims of the board's unlawful action. It was not until 1963, almost ten years after the original action by the board, that checks were forthcoming.

As noted, the cases of Adler, Feinstein, Nash, and Mauer were not unique. Scores of other teachers were discharged in a variety of circumstances as part of the effort to eliminate dangerous thoughts from the educational system.

Take, for example, the case of Dudley Straus. He was a professor of English at Queens College when, in 1955, he was suspended because he refused to answer questions posed by the board of higher education as to his membership in the Communist party. The board was acting pursuant to the state Feinberg law, which disqualified from employment in the educational system any person who advocated the overthrow of the government by force or violence or who joined any group of persons advocating such doctrine. The law, passed in 1939, had been declared constitutional by the Supreme Court in 1951.

Exact numbers of persecuted teachers are hard to come by. It has been estimated that in New York alone, 334 school teachers and 58 college teachers lost their jobs as a result of the political purges of the public schools. Countless others teaching in private schools suffered similar fates, although it must be said that the private schools, by and large, were much more tolerant of dissenting political views.

The 1951 decision of the Supreme Court stood in the way of any legal remedy at the time, but in 1967 the Court reversed that ruling, holding the Feinberg law unconstitutional. On Dudley Straus's behalf, I began the legal process of seeking to get back pay and restoration of his pension rights. A recitation of the details of those proceedings would be tedious; let it be sufficient to note that it was not until fifteen years later, in 1982, that back pay and pension awards were made to the college professors involved. Checks were distributed at a city hall ceremony on April 29 of that year, and we were all treated to self-congratulatory speeches by city officials. Comptroller Harrison J. Goldin said, "This is a day on which we right a wrong." City council president Carol Bellamy said, "It's nice in government when something finally works out the way it's supposed to." I doubt whether any of the teachers involved agreed that their wrongs had been righted or that things had turned out the way they were supposed to. City officials said the delay in making the payments had been caused by, among other things, the problems of moving unusual problems through the bureaucracy.

The Armed Forces

The army, needless to say, plunged into the cold war with that mixture of extraordinary bureaucracy and stupidity with which it does most anything. A variety of cases were undertaken by me in the mid-1950s, all involving attempts to offset efforts by the army to give less than honorable discharges to men in the armed forces because of their preinduction political activities.

Howard Abramowitz served in the Korean War and was honorably separated from active service and transferred to the enlisted reserves in 1953. Two years later, he received an undesirable discharge from the army because of alleged subversive activities *prior* to his induction. The usual charges were made: he was alleged to have been a member of the Communist party and the Labor Youth League and to have been a subscriber to the *Daily Worker,* the Communist newspaper.

This was shocking. The government plucked a young man out of civilian life, inducted him into the army, sent him abroad where he risked his life in military service, returned him to civilian life with an honorable discharge, and then, years later, sought to stigmatize him for life, for lawful activities he had engaged in four years before his induction. But somehow, the army considered this to be entirely justifiable conduct on its part, and perhaps it was, given the premises of the cold war.

I started an action on his behalf, naively assuming that the mere statement of the facts would be enough to shock the conscience of any court;

of course, that did not turn out to be quite true, although we were ulti-mately successful. But, as in the case of almost all litigation, it took a long time.

Much the same thing happened to Eugene Becker, who got an hon-orable discharge from the army in 1953 and then, because of charges of preinduction subversive activity, found his discharge reduced to a gen-eral discharge in April 1956. The charges against him were much the same as those against Abramowitz, except that Becker committed the additional offense of having registered as a member of the American Labor party.

Teddy Bernstein was one of a group of enlisted men at Fort Dix who, dubbed by the press as the "Fort Dix Eight," were the subject of loyal-ty proceedings in 1955. He got an undesirable discharge, not only for alleged preinduction Communist party and ALP affiliation, but also because he was a member of the National Lawyers Guild and maintained a close relationship with his father, who was equally subversive, and with his half-sister.

I undertook a lawsuit for Bernstein. Becker's case raised much the same issues, and so it was put on ice until the law was settled. In the Bernstein case, Judge Edelstein in New York wrote a good decision at a preliminary stage in the case. He said: "It would seem basic, therefore, that a soldier has a right to an honorable discharge if his military service merits it and that he cannot be held to answer, in the consideration of his discharge, for matters extraneous to that record. . . . A procedure which postulates pre-induction civilian conduct as the basis for a less than honorable discharge could not be countenanced."

However, the court did countenance it, and the Bernstein action was dismissed on technical grounds. It took years before Bernstein's unde-sirable discharge and those of his seven associates at Fort Dix could be corrected. It was not until the *Abramowitz* case reached the Supreme Court that a clear decision on the point was made. The Court agreed to hear the *Abramowitz* case, but I missed a chance to argue the case because along with it on the court calendar was a similar case raising the same issue, and the Court was satisfied with argument on that case alone. So the Court missed an opportunity to hear me, and I missed an opportu-nity to talk to it.

Even in these cases, the Supreme Court did not face the constitutional issue, nor did it indicate that the procedure of the army was an outra-geous and indecent one. It decided the cases on statutory grounds. Un-der the applicable statute a discharge was to be based on the soldier's "record," and, said the Court, "record" meant military record. It took the army another three or four months before its bureaucracy was able to change the discharges given to Becker, Abramowitz, and the Fort Dix Eight to honorable discharges, but ultimately it was done.

Space does not permit a full description of the screening operations undertaken by the Coast Guard to stamp as "disloyal" scores of merchant seamen on charges no more than their membership in ACA or in a dissident faction of the National Maritime Union or other maritime union. The story of that litigation, in which the embattled seamen fought the Coast Guard on both coasts, will have to be told some other time. It's a good story, but too long to be included here.

FBI Surveillance

I was under active surveillance by the FBI from the early fifties until the late sixties. The earliest report on me I've found in my FBI files stated that on June 23, 1943, I was believed to be a member of the Communist party, and it further described me as an "agile-minded labor attorney" [Thanks]. The report stated that I was a candidate on the American Labor party ticket for city court judge and polled 134,000 votes, and then commented: "Subject [that's me] residence, 1080 E. 8th St., Brooklyn, is a private home located in a predominantly Jewish neighborhood and it was deemed inadvisable to conduct a neighborhood investigation."

My file seems to have been closed at about that time, to be reopened in June 1951. From then until the late sixties, reports on my activities were frequent, thorough, and reasonably accurate. My bank accounts were all examined meticulously and notice taken of my contributions to scores of organizations considered by the FBI to be subversive.

Meetings I went to, trips I took, and articles I wrote are recorded. Fundraising parties were held at our house in New Rochelle quite frequently between 1950 and 1963—parties for a variety of causes. The FBI doesn't seem to have attended, or at least there was no report of the substance of any of these meetings, but the license plates of the persons attending were dutifully recorded and, no doubt, entered into the security files of our guests. On September 22, 1951, for example, fifty-eight cars were noticed at my house and, I must assume, were parked on the street for blocks around. The party was for the benefit of the Civil Rights Congress and admission was two dollars per person. I hope that a collection was also taken, since the amount of money taken for admissions was hardly worth the trouble.

Of course, meetings of the Lawyers Guild were recorded, including my attendance at executive committee meetings, conventions, and similar gatherings, and substantially every trip to Cuba, including my first trip with Marcia in 1960.

On at least one occasion, in October 1951, the trash at my New Rochelle residence was searched, with, apparently, no significant findings. I cannot imagine why that day was picked. On March 5, 1960, an agent stationed himself at my house at 7:42 A.M. and logged all persons entering or leaving my house until 12:02 P.M., when he went off duty. Among other interesting events, he reported, at 9:32, "three teenage girls and two teenage boys, all unidentified [were] observed entering 7 Serpentine Drive."

It was not only in New York that I was watched. My dinners with Vito Marcantonio in Washington were recorded, and at least one of the other guests is also named and a picture of the guests was taken. I still have that picture. My trips to Mexico, Paris, British Guiana, Brazil, Spain, Prague, and other places were also noted, and in some places (as in the case of Brazil and Spain) local police were asked by the FBI to keep an eye on me. In the case of Brazil, a full report was made of my activities.

One trip resulted in the creation of quite a few pages in my FBI file. I don't remember the incident, but the FBI says that I was representing a man named Walder and that I visited a United States Attorney in Miami named Gong to discuss Walder's problem. While I was there, it seems that I took from my pocket a baggage check from a Pan American flight to Miami, tore the check in half, and dropped it into Mr. Gong's wastepaper basket. After I left, this careful guardian of the public welfare retrieved it from the wastebasket and sent it to FBI headquarters where it was duly filed for future reference. I have a photograph of that baggage check; for the record, it bears number B-30-41-30.

Another amusing bit turned up in my FBI files. There was, living in Brooklyn at that time, another Victor Rabinowitz. I had spoken to him once or twice when his mail was delivered to me, or vice versa. Also, by coincidence, he worked as a supervisory employee at RCA Communications, and I heard about him from time to time from my ACA client, which represented the nonsupervisory employees at that company. As might be expected, the FBI sometimes got us mixed up, and developed a file on him. I don't know whether he was bothered much by the FBI.

The FBI also monitored the activities of the Rabinowitz Foundation (a family foundation I discuss in chapter 9), and duly recorded many of the grants it had made. I don't know where it got its information, but the grants were not regarded as confidential, and they might have been picked up by snoops on any college campus.

As of May 10, 1955, the FBI admitted its failure to prove my membership in the Communist party, and there appears some indication that a few years later the FBI was interested in the deterioration of my relationship with the Party. Thus in 1962, the file indicates that the Communist party continued to deal with me "in regard to certain items and it is known that he was treated as a Party member," although, "Gus Hall, General Secretary of the Communist Party, and others in the Party leadership complained about Rabinowitz because of information indicating that he had been donating money and listening to the 'left faction' which included a number of persons who had already been expelled from the CPUSA."

Other versions of Gus Hall's alleged displeasure with me appear in my file. At one point (date blacked out), Hall was "severely critical" of me; I tried, he said, to remain in the good graces of the Party while being active with the Trotskyites in the Fair Play for Cuba Committee. Sometime later, it was reported, Hall had no use for me, because I was "sympathetic to Fidel Castro and Communist China." Another report announces that although I was reportedly out of the Party in August 1962, in December of that year I continued to be an officer of the National Lawyers Guild and contributed to Communist party causes.

I have no way of knowing whether the FBI was reporting accurately on Hall's regard for me or lack of it; I do know that neither he nor anyone else in the Party ever discussed the matter with me, and I remained on good personal terms with my friends in the Party throughout all the time in question and, indeed, up to this writing. I never had anything to do with Hall; I doubt whether I came in contact with him more than once or twice.

During all of the time after 1950, I assumed that the FBI was watching me; in fact, I probably overestimated the extent of the surveillance. Although I doubt whether there was any tap put on my own personal wire or on my office phone, there is no doubt that there was a tap on the phones of many of my clients, and perhaps out of an excess of caution, I assumed that my residence wire and business wires likewise were subject to surveillance and that my mail was subject to being opened. Because of that assumption I took some precautions. For example, I stopped keeping a personal diary at the end of 1947, a decision that I made because I saw the gathering storm clouds and I felt that what I was writing in the diary would be embarrassing to me and probably to a lot of other people if it ever fell into the wrong hands. That was a decision that may have been prudent at the time but just now I wish that I had continued to keep the diary. It was an invaluable aid to me in recalling what happened in the few years prior to 1947 and would have been very helpful for later years.

By and large, knowledge of FBI surveillance didn't frighten me. Once or twice in more recent times, younger friends asked me how I felt about the whole thing. The answer is that I didn't care much. I wasn't breaking any law or committing any serious indiscretion, and I didn't think I was subject to sanctions that might be imposed by the FBI, or for that matter, by anyone else.

There was, to be sure, a bit of bravado in my reaction. The fact is that all about me, people were being arrested, tried, imprisoned, and even, in two cases, executed, for conduct that, so far as I understood the facts, wasn't very much different from the conduct I engaged in, or if different, was so in degree only. But I was in a sense taunting the FBI and the security apparatus of the government—"C'mon boys, do your worst"—foolish, perhaps, but I enjoyed it in the same sense that a toreador enjoys taunting a bull.

9

We Survive

I view with wonder those who describe Harry Truman as a great president and who view the period between the end of the war and the election of John F. Kennedy as a time of domestic peace and tranquility. I did not and do not share those opinions. It was a period of domestic repression required by an attempt to establish a worldwide *Pax Americana*. The great wealth of our country continued to be diverted to the building of a powerful war machine, which, even now, stands in the way of the creation of a prosperous nation. Opposition to any significant aspect of U.S. foreign policy was suppressed with all the force the government (federal, state, and local) could bring to bear.

There was no aspect of my life unaffected by the political repression of those days. This was true not only of my professional life but of my personal life as well. Together with my friends, most of whom were members of or sympathetic to the Communist party, I watched the development of the phenomenon now called the McCarthy era with anxiety and distress. Many in my immediate circle of friends lost their jobs, their careers, their families. Many were threatened with criminal trials and some with jail.

Work at the office, it now seems to me, was entirely devoted to the political events of the day. Paradoxically, the era of repression brought, at least in the beginning, great prosperity to our firm. (Prosperity, to us, was defined as lots of work, a larger law office, and adequate, but not generous, compensation. Substantial legal fees were totally outside our universe. We read about them but never put any of them into our bank account.) We had lots of loyalty security cases, immigration cases, congressional committee hearings, grand jury proceedings, criminal cases, and, for a few years, an expanding trade union practice.

Another circumstance helped in terms of the maintenance of our practice. The American Civil Liberties Union, for many years the stalwart defender of civil liberties in the United States, succumbed to the red scare, as did most other people and organizations. It set out to purge its own house of Communists by removing Elizabeth Gurley Flynn, a member of the national board of the Communist party, from its executive committee, and it dragged its feet notably in defending alleged subversives, especially when they were open members of the Party. In response, the Emergency Civil Liberties Committee (ECLC) was organized in 1951, and Leonard Boudin became its general counsel. He and I litigated many cases sponsored by the ECLC, and after it got well started, it paid a retainer, which helped a great deal in running our office.

The most dramatic and tragic episode of the early fifties was the trial, conviction, and execution of Julius and Ethel Rosenberg for conspiracy to commit espionage—the only peacetime execution for that crime in the history of the United States. I had only peripheral connection with the case, though emotionally it affected the entire progressive community of the country.

At about five o'clock on one afternoon in June 1950, I received a call from Julius Rosenberg. He told me that he was a member of the Federation of Architects, Engineers, Chemists, and Technicians, a union we represented, and that he was at that moment at FBI headquarters, being questioned about his political activities. He had been permitted to call me. I asked whether he had been arrested or was free to leave. The agents who were questioning him said he was free to go, if he wished, and I told him to come to my office immediately.

Rosenberg showed up about twenty minutes later and told me he had spent the whole day with the FBI, answering many questions. I did not go into much detail with him because it quickly became apparent that the questions put by the FBI related to espionage or a related offense. It also became apparent that he had talked more to the FBI than ordinary prudence would have dictated. I told him that our office could not represent him. A few months before, Leonard Boudin and Sam Neuburger had been appointed by the district court in New York to represent Judith Coplon, who had been indicted for espionage in New York and Washington. It seemed to me that for our office to simultaneously represent defendants charged with espionage in two separate cases was not going to be helpful to Rosenberg, Coplon, or the office. I suggested he get other counsel and do so quickly.

He asked if I could recommend anyone to advise him in the present emergency and I gave him about three names, one of which was Manny

Bloch. Rosenberg did see or speak to Bloch that same evening, and Bloch represented him through his trial and appeals. I had nothing else to do with the Rosenberg case except that in the later stages I made many speeches on the subject, as I did on nearly every political subject at hand.

There has been a great deal of criticism about the left wing's handling of the Rosenberg litigation. It has been charged that the Communist party did not recognize it as a high-priority political case, that it gave the case almost no publicity, and that there were many other competent lawyers who could have been called on to handle the case or at least to aid Bloch. It is probably true the Party gave insufficient publicity to the case. When the investigation started, and even after the indictment had been handed down and the trial had begun, there was no appreciation of the seriousness of the charge and certainly no one could foresee the dreadful result. The Party can be faulted for this lack of foresight. And, perhaps, so can I.

However, the charge that other or additional progressive lawyers did not come forward to help in the defense of the case is not justified. There weren't many lawyers around who were readily available to represent the Rosenbergs. The number of left-wing lawyers in the city was not very great. Many were involved in the Smith Act cases then pending in the Supreme Court; others were representing trade unions that were themselves under serious attack as being Communist controlled. Still others were busily representing other victims of the cold war. And, of course, funds were not available to retain skilled Establishment lawyers. Most important, so far as I know, Manny Bloch never asked for assistance and never suggested that additional counsel would be of help. Hindsight makes it clear the case was not well tried; even hindsight, however, does not make it clear that it would have made much difference in the result, however it was tried.

The outcome of the Rosenberg case was one of the tragedies of the cold war, and the trial has taken its place as one of the great political trials of the century, along with the Sacco and Vanzetti case and that of Alger Hiss.

Some years later, in about 1960, I received a telephone call from someone who said that he and his wife and some friends would like to consult with me about a pending grand jury investigation. They were driving down from Syracuse on the weekend and were required to appear before the grand jury on the following Monday. I suggested they meet with me at my home in New Rochelle, and on Sunday two couples showed up. It quickly appeared that they had something to do with the

Rosenberg case. I didn't go into the facts in any detail; I advised them that they could refuse to give any testimony to the grand jury on Fifth Amendment grounds and they agreed to follow that course. The interview lasted about an hour and a half. The next day they appeared before the grand jury in the federal courthouse in New York.

I went down with them because, although I was not permitted in the grand jury room, the grand jury usually permitted witnesses to leave the jury room to consult with counsel. All four witnesses testified briefly, stating, among other things, that they had consulted with me as their counsel on the previous day. I believe they relied on their Fifth Amendment privilege as to most questions. A forthwith subpoena was served on me requiring me to testify before the grand jury.

I did so, and when the assistant United States attorney conducting the investigation asked me whether I had met with the four witnesses, I answered in the affirmative. He then asked me what our discussion was, and I refused to answer, on the ground that communication between a lawyer and his client is privileged. He then stated that the privilege was lost when the communication took place in the presence of a third party, and in this instance I had interviewed all four witnesses simultaneously, so that, as to each one, there were other parties present. I was promptly cited by the grand jury for contempt, and several days later my case was heard before Judge Gregory Noonan.

Leonard represented me and argued that the privilege had not been lost because all four of the persons present at the consultation were united in interest and that interviewing each one separately would have been an unnecessary and pointless exercise. He made his usual effective argument, and the judge dismissed the charges. I was more than a bit uneasy during the proceeding. I didn't relish a conviction for contempt.

In June 1951, a group of twenty-one Communist leaders headed by Elizabeth Gurley Flynn was indicted in New York for violation of the Smith Act, and there was a bit of a flurry about securing counsel to represent them. The lawyers who had represented the defendants in the *Dennis* case had made more than reasonable sacrifices, and it was not easy to find attorneys to handle this new indictment. The United States attorney was applying great pressure for speed in trying the *Flynn* case (for no good reason), and Judge Ryan, who was all steamed up over the flight of the four defendants in the *Dennis* case, helped to exert the pressure. And so he took it upon himself to name six lawyers for the *Flynn* defendants: Leonard (who was then appearing before him in the *Coplon* case) and me (then appearing before him in the *Field* proceedings); Mary Kaufman (who was also involved in the *Field* case); Abe Pomerantz (also involved in the *Coplon* case); Abe Unger; and Carol King, a prominent immigration lawyer who represented many alleged subversives in deportation cases.

Quite properly, we viewed this as a hostile act by Ryan. All of the lawyers were members of the National Lawyers Guild and all except for Pomerantz were prominent in left-wing circles. Ryan knew full well that the defendants in the *Flynn* case were anxious to break out of the circle of left-wing lawyers in securing representation. He also knew that Mary, Leonard, and I were fully occupied with other matters and could hardly undertake the complex *Flynn* case.

A stormy court session followed, in which we flatly refused to accept the assignments, as did the other lawyers appointed by Ryan. There was much shouting, and Ryan finally backed down after the defendants told him they were unwilling to accept any of the lawyers he had named. A few days later, Ryan proposed another panel, this one after consultation with the Establishment bar associations in New York. Ultimately a defense team was assembled without his help.

Whatever little time I had to spare, I spent in writing for left-wing publications and in speaking on the Korean War, the Rosenberg case, and anything else that anyone wanted to read or hear about. The FBI not only read but collected many of the articles I wrote (although I did not) and even attended some of the meetings at which I spoke.

Before long, however, things began to unravel. The attacks on the unions were taking their toll. ACA lost much of its membership and was having trouble keeping what was left. The same was true of the UOPWA locals we represented. New organization by any of the left-wing unions was not even seriously considered. Many of our trade union clients were under attack within the CIO and were ultimately expelled from that organization, making it even more difficult for them to hold onto their membership. To make the situation worse, in all of those years, especially between 1950 and 1963, our nonpaying clientele increased substantially.

Disaster struck in the spring of 1952, when District 65 terminated our retainer. By that time, District 65 had become a sort of minifederation and included the department store unions, the former UOPWA locals, and many other locals scattered throughout the country. It was an exciting client, with a great deal of interesting trade union work, and it paid a substantial retainer. We had enlarged our office staff to enable us to provide service to the union.

There had been, however, problems connected with its representation.

David Livingston was its autocratic president, and he ruled with an iron hand. A man of superior intelligence and ability, he had seemingly unlimited energy and applied his creative imagination to the administration of a large militant and growing union. He was a quick thinker and a profound (but sometimes wrong, like the rest of us) political analyst. He was one of the most competent persons I've ever met in my trade union work.

Livingston also was one of the most unpleasant. He was intolerant of the views of others, arrogant, and without regard for the feelings or dignity of his subordinates—and, in his eyes, his lawyers were his subordinates, as was almost everyone else he worked with. He was delightful company when he tried, but he didn't try very often, except on social occasions, and my contact with him was seldom in a social context. As he has moved through life he has left a long train of enemies behind him, and those who continued to work with him did so, I think, because they admired and respected him, not because they liked him.

In the spring of 1952, District 65 held its convention in Atlantic City. During a recess, while I was walking on the boardwalk with Sam Neuburger, some officer of the union advised us that our retainer had been terminated. No reason was given.

It was a terrible and almost fatal blow to the office. We were left with many clients who were victims of the repression of the era, but a major source of revenue had been cut off and there was little money left with which to maintain an office. Leonard and I survived only at the cost of shedding some of our associates. Belle Seligman left to raise a family. Neuburger quit shortly after, and then Shapiro. Essentially what was left was a small firm called Rabinowitz and Boudin, with a large but barely remunerative practice.

In my opinion, our retainer with District 65 was terminated for political reasons. District 65, normally regarded as one of the red unions, was trying to distance itself from the Party. I, on the other hand, was actively engaged in activities regarded as pro-Communist. I was representing Steve Nelson; I was making speeches to any audience that would listen to me about the issues that concerned me mostly, namely, the Rosenbergs, the Korean War, and the onslaught of the forces of repression in Congress and elsewhere. The office had represented Judy Coplon. I suppose we seemed too close to the Party, and I'm not sure the union enjoyed that association. Many years later—perhaps ten or fifteen years ago—I met Dave Livingston in a restaurant and discussed with him rather casually the circumstances of the termination of our retainer. He assured me that my suspicions were not correct. He had not dismissed us because he was unhappy about what I was doing, but rather because he was unhappy with the representation that Sam Neuburger was offering to the union. I don't believe this for a minute.

■

In 1957, my father died suddenly, leaving two of his projects to be carried on by his children: his very profitable business and the Louis M. Rabinowitz Foundation.

I became, at least in name, president of the corporation he owned, but I did very little in that capacity except for a few ceremonial duties such as attending dinners of the Federation of Jewish Philanthropies and I did that very reluctantly and with distaste. The crowd that attended those dinners was not my crowd. My brother-in-law, Sam Perlman, became executive vice-president of the company and was operating head of it for about eight years, after which it was sold. Except for the first few years, he also took over the ceremonial duties.

The Louis M. Rabinowitz Foundation was a bit more constructive and a more pleasant experience. Pop had organized the foundation in 1944. It was funded by royalties from patents owned by him and had financed many projects in which he was interested, including a modern translation of the Laws of Maimonides, the gift of many rare books to the Yale University Library, a large grant to the social work school at Hunter College, and similar projects.

When Pop died, Lucille, Marcia, and I became trustees of the foundation. However, we weren't much interested in Pop's interests, worthy though they were. There was some overlap: the foundation had financed a couple of books on academic freedom, but by and large we believed that a sharp turn in the direction of the foundation was needed. We created an advisory board, which included some of the leading left-wing intellectuals in the New York area. Among those on the board at one time or another were Hugh Wilson, Carl Marzani, Angus Cameron, Russ Nixon, Harry Magdoff, John Simon, David Haber, Carey McWilliams, Margaret Burnett, Ann Lane, and John Williams—all writers, publishers, academics, high-level intellectuals.

Over the next few years the foundation assisted in the research and publication of a number of books that made some contribution to causes we were interested in and helped many scholars working in the social sciences. Included were Piri Thomas's *Down These Mean Streets;* Susan Brownmiller's *Against Our Will;* Kirkpatrick Sale's *SDS;* Vivian Gornick's *Romance of American Communism;* Eugene Genovese's *Roll, Jordan, Roll;* Cedric Belfrage's *The American Inquisition;* and many others.

The foundation was clearly research oriented rather than action oriented, but early in our administration, in 1963, we gave about forty-two thousand dollars to the Student Nonviolent Coordinating Committee (SNCC) for its voter registration drive when it was sorely in need of funds. The foundation continued to function actively until about 1987 when it substantially ran out of funds. It has been semidormant since.

At some time in the sixties, the Internal Revenue Service (IRS) raised some question as to whether the foundation was engaged in political activity. I asked the IRS to be more specific, and the only answer I could get was that some of the research we had assisted was considered subversive. An IRS agent visited me and asked to see some of the books produced by our grantees. I recall letting him examine a three-volume edition of *The Correspondence of W. E. B. Du Bois,* edited by Herbert Aptheker, Marcuse's *One Dimensional Man,* and a few other weighty tomes. In fact, I was quite cooperative and let him use a room in the office, in which he could read the books—I wouldn't let him take them out. For about a week the agent, a dull, unimaginative fellow, sat in the office and pored over Du Bois and Marcuse, and then quit. I heard nothing further.

I was really disappointed, for I had seen a fine free speech case on the horizon.

■

Slowly the office practice was rebuilt, and in about 1959 we added Michael Standard to our staff. Mike is the son of Bill Standard, one of the most prominent trade union lawyers of the previous decade. Bill had represented the National Maritime Union when it was organized and for years after that, and he had built up a very substantial practice in representing seamen in their civil actions for injuries suffered in the course of their employment—a very busy and lucrative specialty. Mike had just graduated from law school; he was wise enough to avoid a professional association with his father and applied to us for a job. Some years later he became a partner, and for many years the firm was known as Rabinowitz, Boudin, and Standard—and indeed, even to this day, some think of it by the same name, although Boudin is dead and neither Standard nor I are active in the firm's day-to-day functioning.

10

The National Lawyers Guild

A warning of future controversy was sounded, if only faintly, at the 1967 convention of the National Lawyers Guild. I had just been elected president and I presided at the final plenary session, usually devoted to dull organizational matters. But early in the meeting, some young fellow at the back of the hall whom I didn't know and whose name I can't recall, presented a resolution calling for the admission of law students to the guild as voting members. I understood that he was from the Boston area, where we had no chapter but where there are many law schools and many potential student members of the guild.

The presentation of the resolution brought the meeting to life. Under our rules, as under the rules of most organizations of any size, resolutions were not to be introduced at a plenary session without prior presentation to a resolutions committee. This rule was often waived when the subject of the resolution didn't matter much, but this was seen as a highly controversial issue. We were an association of lawyers, and students weren't lawyers. In the past, students had been accepted as non-voting members, which didn't satisfy anyone, but this new proposal was for full-fledged participating membership.

The organization of students into the guild had long been on my mind. There had been one or two law school chapters organized in the late forties, but they disappeared when the cold war made membership in the guild seem a possible obstacle to admission to the bar. Years before, I had spoken to students at Yale (a meeting organized by Tom Emerson and Fowler Harper of the Yale faculty), at NYU, and at Columbia, in an effort to solicit membership in the guild. There was a show of interest—but there were no organizational results. In 1966 a nonvoting student chapter had been organized at Boalt Hall at the University of California Law School at Berkeley, but the guild had not before been confronted with the issue raised at the meeting by our Boston delegate.

The Detroit, Los Angeles, and San Francisco delegates, representing about half of our membership, disapproved the proffered resolution vigorously. Their objections did not address the merits of the proposal, but Michigan and California each have an integrated bar, that is, every lawyer must join the state bar association and in return every local bar association (including the guild) participates in making state bar policy on professional matters as well as issues of general public interest. In those states, the state bar association decides policy affecting admission to the bar, questions of ethics, the disciplining of lawyers and other matters that in most states are regulated by the courts.

The fear expressed by Ernest Goodman of Detroit and Ben Margolis of Los Angeles was that if the guild admitted nonlawyers to its membership, it would lose its status as a "bar association" and would hence lose its membership and influence in the state bar association. The guild, particularly in California, had for many years exercised a much greater influence at the state bar association than the number of its members would suggest and it had a significant voice in making state bar legislative policy.

The student who had raised the question neither knew nor cared about the objections raised by the West Coast and Detroit delegates. He urged that the West Coast lawyers, like those elsewhere, could exert their influence on public affairs even if they didn't belong to the state bar association. However, the matter was of such substantial importance to the California and Michigan members that we postponed the issue for further study, which meant the next convention. We may have lost some potential members; I'm not sure that Boston fellow ever came back.

The incident was an early symptom of a viral disease—the generation gap—from which the guild was suffering, as was almost every progressive organization created in the 1930s and 1940s. The disease was often lethal, and that the guild survived, though by a narrow margin, is a tribute to the good sense and the devotion to principle shown by the large majority of its members. It took us almost five years to cure this virus, but we succeeded in the end.

The political climate in the country had changed significantly in the 1960s. The red-baiting of the Truman administration, McCarthy, Eastland, the House Un-American Activities Committee, and other similar forces were things of the past, and there was a rising sense of rebellion among young people, who were becoming a potent political force. The civil rights movement, spurred by the sit-ins at Greensboro, North Carolina, followed by the formation of Students for a Democratic Society (SDS) and its Port Huron Statement of 1962; the Mississippi Summer of 1964; the free-speech movement, capped by the antiwar movement—all of this action was led by young people, far removed from their elders in their mode of thinking and their style of life.

We in the guild were ill-equipped to meet the challenge and opportunity this new turmoil created. We had participated in the civil rights movement from 1962 to 1966, but we were a rapidly aging organization. I was fifty-seven years old when I became president, and I was one of the younger persons in the leadership. Even worse, we were members of a conservative profession, stubbornly resistant to change, and the leaders of the guild had been trained in that tradition. We were radical in politics but were stuffy in our observance of organizational forms, and even more stuffy in our manner of speech and our attitude toward nonprofessionals. Although we despised the political views of the Establishment bar associations, we mimicked them in many ways—in the way we dressed, the way we behaved, the language we used.

There were very few guild members between the ages of twenty-five and forty-five, and there was probably no one under forty in the top levels of leadership. The cold war effectively kept younger lawyers out of the guild, mostly because those who might have joined were concerned, with reason, that membership in the guild would adversely affect their admission to or status at the bar. It was these younger lawyers who should have been moving into power (if that is the right word) in the guild, but they weren't there. A twenty-year gap is hard to close.

The Beginning

"The National Lawyers Guild was born in revolt—a revolt that embraced the entire intellectual life of the times," Tom Emerson wrote in "The Role of the Guild in the Coming Years," in the *Lawyers Guild Review* in 1950, giving an overview of the first fifteen years of the guild's existence. The guild was no stranger to internal struggles. From its origin in 1936 to 1940, the guild was almost torn apart by controversy between political opponents; after 1967, the controversy was among political allies.

The NLG was formally organized at a convention held in Washington in 1937. For some years, Maurice Sugar, active in the organization of the United Auto Workers and later its general counsel, had been urging his friends in New York and elsewhere to create an organization of lawyers that could act as a clearinghouse for the many progressive and radical lawyers who were coming into the legal profession throughout the country in the wake of the New Deal and the formation of the CIO, but who had very little contact with each other.

Also in the picture was Morris Ernst, a leader of what passed for the liberal elements of the bar in New York, who was urged by President Roosevelt to organize a new bar association in aid of the president's program, to counter the anti–New Deal corporation-controlled American Bar Association (ABA), which at that time did not admit black lawyers or Communists to membership. Ernst was a friend of Roosevelt and had contact with many of the lawyers and other political leaders who made up the president's entourage. He invited a group of lawyers to meet with him on December 1, 1936, to consider the organization of a new bar association. His friends came, but some of Sugar's friends came as well.

Ernst was an anti-Communist par excellence, and he found himself in strange company at the December meeting. Among those who showed up were Harry Sacher, Joe Brodsky, Carol King, Nat Witt, and others who supported Roosevelt, but whose eyes were fixed on a new socialist-oriented bar association interested in pushing the Roosevelt program far to the left. Some of this group were members of or close to the Communist party, and some represented the new and militant trade union movement. To them was added a group of lawyers whose political views centered on civil liberties, headed by Osmond Fraenkel, then counsel for the American Civil Liberties Union. They too were prepared to support Roosevelt in his battle against the ABA, but in their view, Communists, like everyone else, were entitled to the full protection of the Bill of Rights. Ernst regarded all these people as enemies. To him they were all Communists.

The twenty-five lawyers who met at the City Club in New York in December 1936 sent out a call for a meeting in Washington on the following February 22 for the formation of a national association of progressive lawyers, dedicated to support of the New Deal.

The call was greeted with unexpected enthusiasm by lawyers all over the country, and even before the formal founding of the National Lawyers Guild in February, chapters had sprung up in New York, Newark, Detroit, Boston, Philadelphia, Washington, Chicago, and New Orleans, all of which held local meetings to organize their own sections of the guild. Perhaps the largest attendance was in New York, where five hundred lawyers gathered to form a chapter; almost as many rallied in Washington. In both of those cities, there were spirited contests for chapter office; in both the Ernst-backed candidates were defeated. In New York, Paul Kern, a close friend of Mayor La Guardia who was supported by the more radical lawyers, was elected chair, and in Washington, Tom Emerson, then assistant general counsel to the Social Security Board, was elected chair.

Thus even before the founding convention met, internal struggles over the policy of the organization arose. This was inevitable, given the make-up of the leadership. Sacher represented many of the left-wing unions in the city and was widely regarded as an influential Party member. He, Witt, Brodsky, and King, all of whom frequently represented Communists, had little in common with Ernst except that none represented large corporate interests and all were to the left of the American Bar Association. The Ernst group would brook no criticism of FDR, but the New Deal program fell far short of the expectations and hopes of Sugar, Sacher, and their friends. The precise issues that divided the guild are not particularly important now, although they were sharp in 1936. For example, the Sacher group opposed the Roosevelt policy of neutrality toward the civil war in Spain, an issue at the top of my personal agenda. Completion of a system of social security was also high on the program of the "radicals," as was defense of the National Labor Relations Act.

The founding convention of the National Lawyers Guild went off smoothly enough, but the split within the guild surfaced publicly during the next two years. Ernst and a few others sought to have the guild denounce communism and fascism, and in 1940, Ernst proposed an amendment to the guild constitution to bar Communists and Fascists from office. All such moves were readily defeated by a combination of the radicals and the free-speech contingents. Ernst and many of his friends resigned from the guild in 1940 when it became clear that their views did not have the support of the organization they had helped to create, and they promptly attacked the guild as a Communist-front organization.

I had not been present at the 1936 meeting (I was very junior), but I did attend the early New York chapter meetings and the national conventions. I took no active part in either. I was a member of the labor law committees of the chapter and the national organization, but a quiet member. To tell the truth, I was quite unsure of myself, and those to whom I looked for leadership seemed much more learned and sophisticated than I. But I voted almost instinctively against the Ernst forces—they were on the wrong side on Spain, and that was a touchstone for me.

In those early years, I had little time for the guild. I had become deeply involved in the American Labor party in 1937, and after 1938 my new job at the Boudin office occupied the rest of my energy. The guild had low priority.

Many years later, at the guild convention in 1989, a discussion developed relating to those early battles in the guild. The younger members, who had not even been born in 1940, were totally unfamiliar with this history, but many were curious about it. By that time only a handful of us ancients were still around, and I tried to explain what those early issues had been and how they had been fought. One of the younger members asked what, in my opinion, would have happened if the Ernst position had prevailed, or if a compromise offered at one time by Ernst—that he and his friends would remain in the guild if the persons he regarded as Communist were to withdraw from leadership—had been accepted. Had such a purge been successful, I said, the guild might have done better for a few years, but soon its program would have been watered down to the point where the organization would have been a pale imitation of the American Bar Association. Indeed, the ABA, in the course of the past forty years, has changed a great deal and on many issues has a program that is relatively liberal, though it is still the voice of the legal Establishment.

Robert Kenny, who had been attorney general of California, became president and Martin Popper executive secretary of the National Lawyers Guild during the war years and both membership and activity increased substantially. We had over twenty-five hundred lawyer members and more than five hundred nonvoting student members in 1946, but the cold war, beginning in 1946 and 1947, reversed this trend sharply. Membership plummeted as we came under increasing attacks from the Department of Justice, the congressional investigating committees, the FBI, and other repressive forces in the political world. The more intense the attacks on radicals and progressives throughout the country, the smaller our membership became, even as need for the guild grew greater.

So a handful of remaining members of the guild led the legal battles in defending the victims of the cold war, either in their own names or in the name of the guild. Together we represented the Smith Act defendants all over the country; we defended witnesses summoned before the congressional committees, beginning with the Hollywood Ten; we defended Harry Bridges, president of the West Coast longshoremen's union and others whom the government sought to deport; we fought the Taft-Hartley Act and represented the radical unions when they were in the CIO and after they had been expelled from that organization. Above all, we came to the defense of thousands of men and women whose names we may not remember but who were victims of the red-hunt sweeping the country in virtually every city and state.

The government attacked us with fury. In 1950, HUAC issued an extensive report entitled, "The National Lawyers Guild: Legal Bulwark of the Communist Party." We responded with a report written by Tom

Emerson: "The National Lawyers Guild: Legal Bulwark of Democracy." In June 1953, Attorney General Herbert Brownell announced in a speech before the American Bar Association that he intended to place the guild on his list of subversive organizations. We responded with a legal action to enjoin him from so proceeding—a countermeasure that was ultimately successful, but only after five years of intensive litigation that drained our finances and energies to an alarming extent.

The winter soldiers on whom the political events made more and more demands stuck to the guild, but the guild itself, as an organization, was in terrible condition throughout the fifties, and our survival was one of the wonders of our time. Ironically, the pendency of the Brownell litigation was a factor in holding the guild together; Brownell's effort to declare us subversive was regarded by all as an attack on the independence of the bar, and much of our energy went to meet that attack. An appeal for funds to beat back Brownell was generally more successful than an appeal for funds to carry out a substantive program.

I was not very active in the guild in the early fifties. ACA was struggling to stay alive, and the demands on our office arising out of the cold war left me with little time for extracurricular work. I dragged along to membership and committee meetings and did a minimum of committee work because, to quote from an anecdote told by Vivian Gornick in *The Romance of American Communism*, "If I don't go, who will?" I attended some of the conventions, too, where I enjoyed long bull sessions with out-of-town friends, but I held no office, either nationally or in the chapter, and I took little responsibility for the welfare of the guild except to write an occasional check when the pressure was put on me to do so. But I was eventually hooked into more active guild work.

Sometime around 1954, while attending a dispirited meeting of the New York chapter of the guild, Ann Ginger, who had just begun working full-time at the guild office, and Robert Silberstein, who was then executive secretary of the national office of the guild, cornered me in a hallway to convince me that it was my political duty to devote all of my spare time to the guild. I found the proposal most uninviting; I had no spare time. But they insisted that my talents were just what the guild needed. I knew that they were lying; I have no administrative or organizational talents but was merely a warm body who might at least appear to be filling a hole in the leadership of the guild. But I've always been susceptible to flattery, and their flattery came in overwhelming degree. After half an hour of discussion, I was snared. I don't exactly remember what my official position was in the chapter, if any; perhaps I only agreed to come to meetings more regularly and joined a committee or two, but I did agree.

The Years of the Cold War

Earl Dickerson, a black Chicago lawyer and a member of the Fair Employment Practices Commission, Professor Malcolm Sharp of the University of Chicago Law School, and John Coe of Pensacola were presidents of the guild between 1951 and 1960. All three did what they could, but there was, for most of that time, no functioning chapter in Chicago, and of course, none at all in Pensacola or anywhere else in Florida. The result was that all three presidents were isolated, and consultation with other members of the guild was difficult. We could not finance regular meetings of the top leadership of the national office, and to provide some sort of collective leadership, a program and administration committee was organized in New York to meet, if I remember correctly, once or twice a month. I was a member, and so were Ginger, Emerson, Royal France—who became executive secretary of the guild at about that time—Osmond Fraenkel, and, on and off, Silberstein and Popper. We were supposed to plan program and administration, and we did some of that. But the meetings of the committee were indescribably dull. Thomas Mann once said that when life is uneventful, every day seems to stretch on endlessly, so that every hour seems to last a month; but in retrospect, all of those uneventful days collapse into each other, and every month seems to have been an hour. So seemed those years between 1954 and 1961 for me in my guild work.

This is not to say that we did nothing during those bleak years. On the contrary, considering the state of our organization and, I must confess, the low state of our morale—or at least my morale—we did wonders. Ann Ginger's energy seemed inexhaustible. Some of it was directed to keeping me and a handful of others to our appointed tasks—appointed most of the time by her. She had enough stamina left over to conceive and bring into life the *Civil Liberties Docket*, a publication of the national office, which reported on civil liberties cases throughout the country, many of them—perhaps most—not otherwise reported. The *Docket* had a wide circulation among lawyers handling civil liberties cases. It put us in contact with hundreds of lawyers, many in the South, who had no other contact with the guild and little chance to find out about the cases reported in the *Docket*. Leo Linder of the New York chapter formulated a set of social security laws far in advance of anything ever conceived by the federal government and far in advance even of anything that has since been enacted. His reports on the subject were circulated in Congress in support of proposed legislation on the subject.

But for all of this, the question arose as to whether we were carrying on a losing battle. How could a handful of lawyers (at a generous count, five hundred) scattered all over the country hope to beat back the tide of repression that threatened to overcome all of us? To make the situation worse, we were not only fighting the House and Senate investigating committees, the Department of Justice, the FBI, and some state bar admissions committees, but, even more inexorable, we were fighting the mortality tables. Every year the membership grew a year older. Members died; almost no one joined.

The aging of our membership almost become my obsession. A guild program had not only to be politically sound; it also had to be one that would attract membership. A sound political program was not hard to formulate, but in the atmosphere of the times, it was counterproductive of our effort to get new members. In 1956 and 1957 it was hard to see any light at the end of the tunnel.

In 1958, we were successful in defeating the government's proposal to list the guild as a "subversive organization," and the Justice Department withdrew its action. This was an impressive victory over the forces of evil. But there was a flip side to the coin. What else did we have to live for? We had established our legitimacy, but now what?

A low point was reached at the 1960 guild convention, where serious consideration was given to dissolving the organization, now that the Justice Department had been vanquished. This suggestion was quickly put down, but it was a disturbing moment. The very thought of dissolution shocked and depressed me. Brownell was gone, McCarthy was gone, and our enemies, while not in retreat, were being held at bay. We had fought for over a decade, and it was disgraceful to quit now. Personal considerations also weighed heavily with me. These men and women in the guild were my closest friends. We were bound together by common professional, political, and social goals, and the guild was the structure through which we could talk to each other and meet with each other, even if only once or twice a year.

We didn't dissolve then. The idea of dissolution arose, in totally different circumstances and in more virulent form, in 1971.

The Guild Goes South

In the early sixties, things began to pick up. The 1962 guild convention was held in Detroit, then the most active—and certainly the most optimistic—chapter in the guild. Under the inspiring leadership of Ernie Goodman, who never seemed to lose his vigor, the convention devoted much of its attention to the need for developing a cadre of lawyers to provide legal protection for the many civil rights workers who were confronted by the united opposition of the white social and legal structure throughout the deep South. We had few members in the South. Clifford Durr and John Coe, both past presidents of the guild, were practicing, respectively, in Montgomery, Alabama, and Pensacola, Florida; and Ben Smith and Bruce Waltzer had an office in New Orleans. Len Holt and Ed Dawley, two young black lawyers, were doing yeoman work in Virginia, and there was a scattering of established black lawyers in the larger cities of the south, notably C. B. King, of Albany, George. But the need for lawyers was overwhelming.

Ernie was a remarkable man among the many in the leadership of the guild. He surely grabbed onto this issue. The convention ran through the usual resolutions, but the issue of guild concentration on the South dominated. Ernie had set up the convention program with skill, and anyone who was there will remember the emotional and eloquent speech that Len Holt gave at the guild banquet. Len is a great orator. He had been engaged in many legal struggles in the South in the previous two years, and his description of the work he was doing was vivid and effective. At the close of the banquet he led the convention in singing "We Shall Overcome," with the traditional ring of usually dignified lawyers holding hands and lifting their voices in the theme song of the civil rights movement.

The result was the formation of the Committee for the Assistance of Southern Lawyers (CASL). Its stated program was to meet the need caused by the failure of the bar in the southern states to provide adequate and effective legal representation for those engaged in the active struggle for civil rights. The committee was headed by Ernie and his partner, George Crockett, as cochairs (or "chairmen," as we then said), and by Len Holt and Ben Smith as cosecretaries.

Like everyone else, I was stirred by Holt's speech and by the emotional atmosphere that pervaded the convention, and I shared in the understanding that there were critical needs that had to be met in the South. I was, I must admit, not quite as enthusiastic about the project as were

Ernie and most of the others. I had some reservations about the whole tone of the convention, but I expressed those reservations only in informal conversation in the lobbies. My hesitancy grew out of the fear that the guild would turn into a one-issue organization, and that the rest of its program would be set aside while we became the legal arm of the civil rights movement. My doubts about this whole project continued for the next two years. I was a socialist, and there were many issues of importance to me other than the work in the South. But I certainly didn't want to raise the sterile argument that we were disregarding our (or at least my) longtime objectives for immediate goals, and maybe this new program would get us some younger members. And so I swallowed my (purely theoretical) reservations.

Goodman and Crockett were energetic in carrying out their assignment as officers of CASL. In November 1962, the guild hosted the first interracial legal conference ever held in the deep South, in Atlanta. The program was designed mostly by the lawyers in Goodman's firm, who felt that we lawyers in the North had skill and experience in fee-generating work, which we could share with southern lawyers (that is, share the experience, not the fees). Most of the southern lawyers attending the conference were black. A stated purpose of the conference was, and I quote from the conference call, "to make it possible for more attorneys to accept civil rights cases by making their practice in other areas of the law more lucrative."

The conference was highly successful, both in terms of attendance and content. I spoke on trade union law and defenses to injunctions. Ann Ginger spoke on "omnibus lawsuits," an innovative concept of extraordinary complexity. Dean Robb of Detroit spoke on personal injury suits. George Crockett spoke on enforcing the federal civil rights laws. Dr. Martin Luther King Jr. spoke at the banquet along with Goodman and Crockett. The enthusiasm aroused by the enterprise was overwhelming.

I kept my doubts to myself. I doubted whether our conference helped southern black lawyers to earn the kind of fees a Detroit or New York lawyer can earn in handling negligence cases. Lack of skill was not the only, or even the principal, reason it was difficult for a black lawyer in Georgia to earn larger fees; there were other reasons the guild conference could not—or did not—address.

But the conference was a great organizational success. My dissatisfaction with its lack of any political approach—of any theoretical basis—was, so far as I knew, shared by no one.

A later conference, having a somewhat different outcome, was held in

New Orleans in October 1963. Again, I was scheduled to speak, although I don't remember the subject. Even as we were meeting, we received word that the offices and homes of Ben Smith and Bruce Waltzer had been broken into by state police officers. The police also raided the office of the Southern Conference Educational Fund (SCEF), an interracial organization in New Orleans, and arrested Jim Dombrowski, its chair. Smith, Waltzer, and Dombrowski were threatened with indictment for violation of the Louisiana Subversive Activities and Communist Control Act. The arrests disrupted the conference; no one could devote much attention to mundane questions of practice and procedure when a real live problem intruded on our deliberations.

Arthur Kinoy, Smith, and William Kunstler immediately instituted an action in the federal court to enjoin the state agency from proceeding with the prosecution against Dombrowski, Smith, and Waltzer. This was an unusual and characteristically imaginative lawsuit. Successful federal proceedings to enjoin state prosecution of unconstitutional criminal laws were virtually unknown. The established practice was that a person threatened with unlawful state prosecution must first go through a state trial and, if convicted, appeal through the state courts, to the Supreme Court—always after years of delay. But this time, though the plaintiffs lost their applications in the district court, they won by a vote of five to two in the United States Supreme Court. The decision, entitled *Dombrowski v. Pfister,* is one of the landmarks in constitutional law, though its holding has been somewhat diluted by later decisions. Judge Brennan, in his opinion, first used the expression "chilling effect" (now a well-accepted phrase in our lexicon) to describe the indirect influence of an unlawful attempt to limit freedom of speech.

In 1963, I was elected president of the New York City chapter and was reelected the next year. The chapter began to develop a program as the pressure of the red-hunt diminished and we could turn our attention to other matters. As always, I tended to emphasize the need for attracting new and young members, and we had a little success.

The doubts (at least my doubts) arising out of the 1962 guild convention and the creation of CASL grew in the next two years. A confrontation of sorts developed between the New York chapter and Ernie Goodman, leading the Detroit chapter. Ernie had eyes only for the civil rights movement and its needs. I feared that the guild was forgetting other critical issues, such as the Smith Act, social legislation, violations of the First and Fourth Amendments, racial discrimination in the North, our foreign policy with respect to Cuba, and the overwhelming fear of nuclear war, which was made even more intense by the nuclear crisis over Cuba in 1962. These problems had been the subject of formal resolutions at the 1962 convention but had since been ignored.

Ernie was supported by the Detroit chapter and by Holt, Ed Dawley, and other black lawyers who were increasingly engaged in litigation in Danville, Virginia, and other points in the South and who were prepared to scuttle the rest of the guild program for work in the South. We in New York, on the other hand, had developed a full program ranging from social security legislation to concern about nuclear war and the growing East-West tensions on the international front. No one wanted to drop civil rights issues, but we were not prepared to give up everything else.

The debate reached a peak in the fall of 1963. The Detroit chapter was relentless in pushing its program, and after some ill-tempered debate, the 1964 convention, scheduled for New York, was transferred to Detroit.

The convention was well attended, not only by members of the guild, but also by an FBI representative, whose full, almost verbatim, report of the meeting, disclosed in the subsequent litigation with the FBI, is quite helpful. Thank you, Agent Winchester.

The first (and almost the only) subject of discussion was guild work in the South. Ernie led the debate for the Detroit chapter, which seemed to be united in defending his view, and I presented the views of the New York chapter, which was not so united. The Detroit contingent wanted to devote the entire budget of the organization to southern activities and to move the national office to Detroit. It advocated the establishment of an office in the South and the issuance of a call to volunteer lawyers throughout the country, who would spend two weeks or more in the South during the coming summer in order to provide legal assistance to the embattled civil rights workers.

All of this was accepted by the convention over my not-very-effective opposition. The debate was never a close one. Everyone remembered the stirring speech by Holt at the last convention—it had been the first time in years that a guild convention had been moved to cheers. Given the politics of the day, Ernie was probably right, and there is no doubt that our work in the South gave a boost to the morale of the guild. The legal representation of civil rights workers in the South presented a challenge our members were anxious to meet. We adopted the proposal, and it worked—perhaps not perfectly, but it worked. I should add that the New York chapter participated fully in the southern project; my doubts were never manifested in any effort to discourage the project, and besides, many of the New York members disagreed with me.

One lasting result of the guild summer project of 1964 was its effect on the lawyers who participated in it. Most had never been south of Washington before (except, maybe, to Florida), and Mississippi, Georgia, Alabama, and the Carolinas were more foreign to them than the European continent. The customs of the deep South were strange and terrifying. To some the experience was a turning point in their lives; none have forgotten it.

The most militant of the organizations working in the South in the early 1960s was the Student Nonviolent Coordinating Committee (SNCC), which had been in the forefront of the southern struggle for civil rights since the student sit-ins in 1960.

A strong fundraising apparatus had been established by SNCC in New York in about 1960. Joanne Grant played a key role in that effort. Marcia and I and, especially, Lucille, together with many of my friends, were also a part of that operation. Until it acquired offices of its own, the New York Friends of SNCC had met at my office. I had become a close friend of many in the SNCC leadership. My daughter Joni had worked for SNCC on voter registration in Albany, Georgia, in 1963, and had been indicted as a result. And so, when the guild offered its services to SNCC in the summer of 1964, I was quick to help to get these two organizations together.

Pursuant to the decision of the guild convention, a guild office run by George Crockett was opened in Jackson, Mississippi, the center of SNCC activity. George was one of the few black lawyers who had joined the guild early in its existence and stuck with it throughout the bad years. He had participated in the defense in the first Smith Act prosecutions in New York in 1948 and had, like the other defense lawyers in that case, served a jail term for contempt. The experience didn't visibly affect his political career. Similarly his legal work as head of the guild office in Jackson didn't injure his legal career. In fact all of those activities may have helped. He went on to become a judge in the recorder's court in Detroit (the court of original jurisdiction in criminal cases), and then served in Congress from 1980 until his retirement in 1990.

George was the perfect man for the job. He walked into a tense situation in Jackson and kept his cool throughout. It was a long, hot summer, but every time I saw George, he was impeccably dressed in a white suit; he was probably the only man in Jackson who wore his white Panama hat every day, whatever the temperature. His job was to administer the office by supervising the white (and a handful of black) northern lawyers who came down that summer and the next under guild auspices without upsetting the Mississippi establishment more than necessary. The state establishment was unnerved by the invasion of so many outside lawyers coming down from up North to challenge well-established Mississippi customs; this was destabilizing, but George managed to stabilize it as much as possible.

Working with him at the office was Claudia Shropshire Morcom, a younger black lawyer. She had originally come from Mississippi and knew the territory well, though she was living in Detroit in 1964. She was breaking southern taboos even more than George was—women lawyers were not part of the Mississippi landscape in 1964 and black women lawyers were almost inconceivable. Miraculously, she was able to earn the respect, if not the affection, of the local legal Establishment.

In all, there were about seventy lawyers who came down from the North under guild auspices in 1964 and again in 1965. There is no question that the contribution they made was substantial. There was endless work to be done, and though responsibility in Mississippi was divided between SNCC and other civil rights groups, SNCC, working out of Jackson, carried the larger part of the burden. The National Lawyers Guild primarily served the SNCC workers.

Let it not be thought for a minute that the only enemies the guild had to face in Mississippi were the governor, the attorney general, the county sheriffs, the local police force, the combined local, state, and federal judiciary, and nineteen out of every twenty whites in Mississippi. That would have been easy. But the progressive forces in this country (and perhaps everywhere) show great facility in fighting each other, and many of those carrying on the battle for racial equality found it necessary to devote a good part of their energy to fighting the guild as well. After all, we were being red-baited by the congressional committees and labeled as Communist by the FBI. Crockett had been a defense lawyer in the Smith Act cases. SNCC's militancy had been pushing Martin Luther King's program toward more and more militancy. Even an unsophisticated red-baiter could put these facts together.

It seems that (in the fervid imagination of the red-baiting contingent) I was one of the links between SNCC and the Communist party. The chain of command was supplied by the FBI. I was president of the Louis M. Rabinowitz Foundation. In December 1963, the foundation made a grant of over forty thousand dollars to SNCC for its voter registration drive. I was a member of the National Lawyers Guild and reported to be a Communist. Someone thought (said the FBI) that my daughter Joni was also a Communist party member, and she had worked for SNCC in 1963. Put all of these facts together and the answer is easy for any red-hunter.

As a matter of fact, Ralph McGill, editor of the *Atlanta Constitution* and a well-known "liberal," went a step further. He pointed out that I was "registered in Washington as an agent for the Castro government," and that fact, when added to the other evidence, raised in his mind the question, Is SNCC supported by Cuba? Havana money?

All of this was a clear signal to those perpetually on the lookout for reds. Fancying themselves latter-day Paul Reveres, Allard Lowenstein, Joe Rauh, and other vigilant patriots galloped down the roads of Mississippi shouting, "The Lawyers Guild is coming, the Lawyers Guild is coming." They were joined by Jack Greenberg, counsel for the Inc. Fund (shorthand for the NAACP Legal Defense and Educational Fund, Inc., to be distinguished from the NAACP—the National Association for the Advancement of Colored People—a different and sometimes rival organization).*

Bob Moses, Jim Forman, Stokely Carmichael, and Chuck McDew, leading officers of SNCC, were not impressed. In vain did Lowenstein point out the appearance of well-known guild (to him, Communist) lawyers in Jackson. Crockett was not subject to much abuse from that quarter, because he was black and acquired some immunity from that fact. But Kinoy, Rabinowitz, and Smith looked to Lowenstein like an invasion by the Red Army. Lowenstein, it was said, was disturbed by the appearance of Marxist slogans in the SNCC headquarters, but he was a bit paranoid on this subject and I'm not sure what he regarded as a "Marxist slogan."

But SNCC never hesitated in its reliance on the guild or on the principled position that it would accept help from any source. SNCC's structure was well accepted by the guild lawyers who went South and who

---

*Jack Greenberg, in his autobiography, *Crusaders in the Courts*, discusses the historical relationship between the Inc. Fund and the guild in some detail. Among other things, he tells of a lunch meeting with me, at my invitation, at which I suggested that the guild and the Inc. Fund work together. Greenberg refused because of the record of the guild as the "legal mouthpiece of the Communist party." Also, I was "a leading left-wing lawyer" who represented "Castro's Cuba." The result was that the Inc. Fund wouldn't work with us. But, says Greenberg, "SNCC went to any lawyer who would help it."

I have only the faintest recollection of that luncheon meeting with Greenberg, but I have no doubt that it happened as he describes. The date must have been late in 1961.

understood that SNCC was a highly decentralized organization that ruled by consensus and whose leaders kept a low profile. Certainly no lawyer, Communist or otherwise, could move into a position of leadership or even of much influence.

In the summer of 1964, I visited the South fairly frequently, for the most part to meet with Crockett, Moses, Forman, and other SNCC personnel to counteract the Lowenstein-Rauh propaganda, which I thought might have an adverse effect on relationships between SNCC and the guild. I don't think my visits were necessary. I doubt that there was ever any doubt in the minds of any of the SNCC organizers about the advisability of accepting gladly the help that the guild was offering.

I was arrested only once in the South, which was pretty good for a northern-looking white in western Mississippi in 1964. On the urgent advice of my friends, when I drove a car in Mississippi I drove very carefully, always ten miles below the posted speed limit, but I was pulled up in Greenwood, where SNCC had its principal headquarters, for allegedly running a red light. The cops were big and unfriendly, and I was scared but militantly stood on my asserted rights as a lawyer engaged in representing actual clients, who I pointed out had a Sixth Amendment right to the aid of counsel. The officers were not impressed by my constitutional arguments, but they decided, I suppose, that it would be less trouble to let me go than to hold me, and after a twenty-minute lecture on the sanctity of the Mississippi traffic code, and on the topic that people from the North should leave Mississippi alone to solve its own problems, I was let go with a warning.

The 1967 guild convention met in February in New York. By that time our work in the South was over and a new interest took its place. The massive deployment of U.S. troops in Vietnam had begun, and the guild had a major role to play in supplying legal aid to those opposing the war and resisting the draft. Our membership, however, had not grown much as a result of the southern campaign, and that I found profoundly depressing. In fact, it seemed that much of the energy of our small membership had been used up in the 1964–65 summers, and although the usual resolutions were passed, and some chapters began to carry on activity in response to the war, the level of activity did not increase noticeably. We were still savoring the results of the work our members had done in the South. We had received a good deal of publicity in the civil rights movement and among other bar associations. But by that time, many other lawyers' associations had joined in the task of representing the civil rights organizations, and our leadership role had diminished substantially.

Much of the confidence that had characterized the past three years had evaporated. Among other things, the removal of the national office of the guild to Detroit had turned out to be organizationally disastrous. Detroit was militant enough in the 1964–66 period, but the national office had given substantially no leadership on any issue other than civil rights, finances were in terrible shape, and there had been little follow-up on the work in the South. There was general agreement that the office should be brought back to New York, which had had far more experience in administering the affairs of the guild on a nationwide basis. (Here my East Coast chauvinism appears again, but I was right.) And so New York again became the home of the national office.

On a slow day during the 1967 convention, Ernie Goodman strolled over to me and asked if I would be interested in succeeding him as president. He spoke as though he had authority to offer the job, from whoever it was who made kings in those days. I was a bit surprised and not at all enthusiastic. As I've said, I've never been good at nor have I enjoyed administrative work, and I couldn't see where I was going to get much help. I had experienced much frustration as president of the New York chapter a few years before. "But," said Ernie, making the inevitable and unanswerable appeal, "who else can you suggest?" I couldn't suggest anyone else, but being elected by default was not a moment of glory. I thought about it for about an hour and accepted. I'm not at all sure I would have acceded to Ernie's request if I had been able to foresee the next few years. It turned out that I wasn't part of the solution of the guild's problems—I was part of the problem.

Revolution in the Guild

In the next four and a half years, the National Lawyer's Guild was completely transformed in its leadership, its organizational structure, its membership, and almost every other characteristic except its long-term, radically oriented, antiestablishment ideology. At least twice during these years, we came within a hair's breadth of breaking up altogether. The turbulence within the guild was a reflection of what was happening in left-wing politics throughout the country in the late sixties and seventies. However, unlike many other progressive organizations, the guild not only survived but did so without significant deviation in its political direction. Furthermore, it accomplished this without the degree of personal acrimony and mean-spiritedness that characterized the breakup of so many other segments of the left. Compare, if you will, any of the guild conventions of 1968, 1970, and 1971 with the convention of Students for a Democratic Society in 1969, or with the history of the Communist party after 1956.

I presided over the guild as its president for the first three of those four and a half years and was actively involved in guild affairs until the Boulder convention in 1971, and I claim some credit for the fact that the guild is still a thriving organization. More credit is due to the younger members who, in 1971, took over its leadership.

It was clear in 1967 that if the guild were to survive, we had to increase our membership, and we had to formulate a program to meet the needs of the time. That new membership had to come from young lawyers and students, and hence the program had to come primarily from them. Immediately after the beginning of my term of office, the national office hired Kenneth Cloke, a young West Coast lawyer, as executive secretary. Bernardine Dohrn, who had just graduated from the University of Chicago Law School, was put on staff as a student organizer, and Alicia Kaplow was pressed into service to join Ken and Bernardine as an additional organizer. All three were full of the energy and vitality of the generation we were addressing.

The new program wasn't hard to find. By 1967, the war in Vietnam was escalating, and it had already became the center of interest among our potential constituency. Many of the chapters had provided draft counseling services even earlier, and our members rapidly became experts in such work. Members of the guild all over the country were litigating issues related to the Vietnam War. Concurrently, mass demonstrations were the order of the day from one coast to the other. Every active chapter had a corps of lawyers prepared to defend those arrested. The national office coordinated the work of the chapters and sought to supply experienced lawyers to many areas of the country in which guild chapters did not exist.

During 1967, the guild sponsored a dozen conferences on draft and military law, taught courses at a few law schools, advised over 2,000 selective service registrants, and distributed 20,000 copies of NLG pamphlets on the law, including detailed advice to lawyers on "How to Try a Draft Case." Every chapter was engaged in this activity, and the national office spurred on the weaker chapters to more activity. And, notably, 9,000 copies of a publication by the national office, *The New Draft Law: A Manual for Lawyers and Counsellors*, were distributed throughout the country. Never in the history of the guild had we, as an organization, been so busy and so successful.

Ken and Bernardine traveled all over the country concentrating on recruitment at the law schools and among recent graduates. Hundreds of new members joined in 1967 and 1968, and dozens of new chapters were organized, many in law schools. The average age of guild members dropped precipitously and the tensions between the older and younger generations in the guild correspondingly increased.

Bernardine represented a firm link between the guild and SDS, then the most influential of the New Left organizations. She was a brilliant organizer with inexhaustible energy and dedication to both the guild and SDS. It seemed to me that in her travels about the country she spent half her time organizing antiwar demonstrations and the other half organizing guild chapters to defend the demonstrators. Many of the Old Left members felt that she was irresponsible and "ultraleftist." I didn't agree, and we kept her on payroll until the February 1970 convention. She was recruiting lawyers and students into the guild, and that was enough for me. I could easily foresee a crisis ahead, but it was a crisis of growth. If the guild couldn't survive the coming storm—well, it wouldn't survive.

I'm not sure that I can find an appropriate label for my own political views at the time. The Communist party was not providing any leadership, and the more radical segments of SDS seemed irrational and self-destructive. I was a Marxist, a Leninist, and a socialist, and I believed that an organized movement was required to overthrow capitalism, which then, as now, was my ultimate purpose. The NLG in general terms provided some correspondence with my views, within the limited framework of its jurisdiction. But how to keep the guild alive?

The 1968 guild convention met in Santa Monica in August. There was an air of excitement at the Hotel Miramar and also a note of apprehension. The guild seemed unstable and off balance. Ken Cloke, in his report to the convention, discussed the result of the youth movement that was sweeping the country and the effect of the work that he and Bernardine had carried on. In his report, he wrote, "We had to deemphasize tradition, not scrap it. We had to jostle the Guild and not try to break it. We had to convince people of the necessity of change and prepare them for the slowness of it." Ken was obviously trying to strike a balance between the New Left, which was raising demands that were far beyond the current guild program, and the older members, who supplied most of the funds and were in control of the machinery of the guild and had in fact had that control since they themselves constituted a part of the New Left of 1937.

Clearly, there were forces out there to which I couldn't relate. For one thing, I couldn't tell one faction from another. Subtleties in political position passed me by, although some of the young members seemed ready to take to the barricades to defend their differing views. The trouble was that they seemed to confuse mounting the barricade with smoking pot. In a broad sense I identified with all of these "kids"; they were all anticapitalist, all for The Revolution.* They were all my comrades; but were we all marching to the same drum? We certainly didn't hear the beat of the drum in the same way.

All of this is, of course, an oversimplification, and I knew it at the time. But there was in reality an incipient revolt against my generation, which viewed all of this turmoil with considerable distrust. I came to the realization rather early, even before the convention opened, that all of this activity was a good thing and could indeed save the guild. It also might destroy the guild. For the first time since 1937 and 1938, young lawyers and students were fighting for power in the guild and were clamoring for the right to bring to the guild their views of the world they lived in. They were, in my view, undisciplined, unlawyerlike and disorderly, but that was very much better than the frustration, apathy, and hopelessness of the 1950s.

Reluctantly, I recognized that I was part of the structure that was under attack. Bernardine had induced a large number of students to come to the convention—perhaps as many as fifty. For the first time in my twenty years, most of the people at the convention were strangers to me, and this was a good thing, albeit threatening. For years I had worked hard to get students into the guild. Now they were fighting to get in, and we— the old guard—were trying to control them. For much of the convention, the students and other younger lawyers, all part of the New Left, met on the Santa Monica beach in caucus, "plotting" ways of carrying out their program, a program, incidentally, which was pretty murky and expressed itself chiefly in slogans: "The Guild is the legal arm of the Movement" was the most popular. Some of us, reacting like lawyers, would have liked a definition of the "Movement," but it turned out to be one of those indefinable concepts (like obscenity or poetry) that we were all supposed to recognize when we met it.

More than the program and more than the "ultraleftism" of some of the newer members, there was a matter of style, and style was an impor-

---

*Kirkpatrick Sale, in his fine history, *SDS*, lists Leonard and me as "other-generation supporters," and the Rabinowitz Foundation had made a number of grants to SDS and other similar groups.

tant component of the reaction of the Old Left to the new generation. These new guild members had none of the perceived characteristics of "professionalism." They were sloppy in their dress, and their language would have been unprintable in the family newspapers of 1968. They were boisterous and lacked the flannel-suit solemnity many of us saw as typifying a lawyer. We also had doubts as to whether they knew or cared much about the law; certainly they didn't act the way we expected lawyers to act. I had heard more serious consideration of legal issues at trade union conventions than I did at that meeting of the guild.

Indeed, the students, or at least a good number of them, seemed to despise the law and everything it stood for. They wore buttons, often scatological in phrasing, ridiculing the legal system and all it represented. I had no quarrel with the expression of these sentiments—they expressed ideas that were not extraordinary or even new. But why on earth did these kids want to be lawyers?

Where were those thirty- to forty-five-year-old lawyers needed to bridge the gap?

Another issue added tension to the convention, and that was the role of black lawyers in the guild. The matter of the racial composition of the guild had long been a matter of much concern. Except for the first few years, when Thurgood Marshall, William Hastie, and others had joined, there were few black lawyers in the guild membership. The pool of potential black members wasn't very large, as the number of blacks who were both radicals and lawyers wasn't great; further, we were sometimes criticized by the black lawyers' National Bar Association for raiding it. There were always some black lawyers in the guild—in fact, Ed Cambridge succeeded me as president of the New York chapter, and Judge Hubert Delaney had been president of the chapter at an earlier date. Earl Dickerson of Chicago had been national president from 1951 to 1954, and Detroit had been successful in recruiting blacks, due in large part to the influence of George Crockett.

But with all of this we were aware of a political weakness in this respect, and sometimes we made errors in attempting to correct it. We not only sought to recruit black lawyers but sometimes moved them up to leadership much too quickly.

One such incident had arisen in 1951 when I met Paul Zuber, a black lawyer whom I first ran into during the New Rochelle school desegregation case. He had had some connection with similar school desegregation litigation in Englewood, New Jersey, and came to New Rochelle in 1952, where he played an active role in preparing the desegregation case. In accordance with the practice of the day, we decided that he ought to become a member of the guild and quickly be put on an officer track. I urged him to become a member.

Long afterward, we discovered an FBI memorandum reporting that Zuber

> was in receipt of a letter from VICTOR RABINOWITZ, asking him to serve as a member of the Executive Board of the NLG. RABINOWITZ explained in his letter that the Executive Board of the NLG is the top policy making body in that organization, and that meetings will be held in NY, Detroit, and in the future in the South.
>
> ZUBER advised that his first reaction was to refuse this appointment, but after reflection, thought that he might be able to help the FBI if he served in this capacity by furnishing any information which might come to his attention. He was advised that the FBI would receive any information he would be able to offer. No attempt was made to direct or control his activities in any matter.

This was a bit of puffing by Zuber; I had no authority to make anyone a member of the executive board of the guild and could not have done so. I held no national office and in fact was not then even an officer of the New York City chapter. I remember that Zuber joined the guild and that shortly thereafter he attended a meeting of the national executive board—meetings of the board were open to members who wished to attend—and made an extraordinarily vituperative and disruptive speech. He then disappeared and was not heard from again. I don't know whether his conduct was instigated by the FBI; it certainly was consistent with FBI policy at the time.

The result of all of this was that the white leadership of the guild was self-conscious about this issue and faced it with considerable feelings of guilt.

Now, at the 1968 Santa Monica convention, the issue was raised sharply. It was a time of the rise of substantial black nationalist sentiment. Many black nationalists did not want to belong to the guild, which they considered a white, middle-class, elitist organization; they also wanted to come to the guild convention and make their views known. And so they did.

One of the black spokespersons was Milton Henry, a guild lawyer from Flint, whom I had never seen before the convention and whom I have not seen since. He was vice-president of the Republic of New Afrika (RNA), a black nationalist group, which urged the guild to support the struggle of black people in the United States to establish a separate nation in the black belt in the South. It was a call for segregation, and was strongly anti-integration.

Henry's speech to the convention, presenting this program, was not only objectionable in content; it was offensive in style—it was demagogic and racist. Holt and Dawley supported Henry and, indeed, nominated him to be vice-president of the guild. Len and Ed are both honest and sincere, hardworking lawyers who performed great service in the South during the civil rights struggle, but Len in particular was too quick to hop on any passing bandwagon that gave him an opportunity to exercise his charismatic skills as a speaker. He had done that to good effect in 1962, but his influence at Santa Monica was harmful. Henry was elected, as was not surprising, since large numbers of members assuaged their guilt by supporting any radical black doctrine.

Dawley (or Holt) then moved that the guild endorse the RNA and, even more, that it write a brief in support of that group's legal arguments, which were pretty tenuous, to say the least. The motion was carried. I understand that a brief was produced, but I don't think I ever saw it, nor do I know how it was used, if at all.

As president of the guild, I presided at the session at which all of this was going on, and I did so impartially and without expressing my views on the proceedings, which I found disgraceful. My silence was not prompted by my parliamentary duty to be neutral, but rather by my unwillingness to confront the militant Henry-Holt-Dawley forces—or to be more blunt, my lack of courage. I could, and should, have asked someone else to preside for a few minutes while I expressed my views on Henry's bid for office (his prior record of guild activity, if any, certainly didn't call for his election as a national officer) and on the resolution supporting the RNA (which I thought was wrong in principle and counterproductive for the guild). My conscience has bothered me since.

George Crockett was so outraged by the incident that he (temporarily) resigned from the guild. Ernie Goodman and a few other senior members were livid with anger. The incident did no permanent harm to the organization, and to the best of my knowledge, Henry never showed up at any of the national guild meetings again. But it was not our proudest moment.

I was reelected president, although it was not as automatic as it had been in the past. I had the substantial advantages of incumbency and tradition, since every president since 1949 had served two terms. I felt that the job of integrating the new members into the guild had only begun, and I was concerned lest a new president might not be as successful as I thought I would be in accomplishing this purpose. Particularly was this so when it appeared that the only suggested alternative candidate for president was Sam Rosenwein, a lawyer from New York who had moved to Los Angeles years before. Sam was a fine lawyer who had made valuable contributions to the radical program of the guild for decades, but I thought he represented the most stuffy traditions of the Old Left. He was repelled by the kind of radicalism evident in the work of Bernardine and Ken—radicalism he perceived to be anti-intellectual—and I felt that he would be unsympathetic to a continuation of their program. The issue never reached the floor of the convention. Nor did anyone even talk about it in a very loud tone of voice, because I think that although I represented the Old Left to the younger members, they saw me as friendly, and Sam as hostile.

As a matter of fact, even before the convention, there had been some dissatisfaction expressed concerning my administration. In June, Ernie had written me stating that Ben Margolis of the Los Angeles chapter had suggested that he would like to run for the office, and to move the national office again, this time to Los Angeles. I was horrified at the idea of moving the office again. I told Ernie I intended to run for reelection because I thought some progress had been made in rebuilding the guild, but that the job was incomplete and I wanted to do my best to carry it forward. I also said that I thought a contest for president would be good for the guild if Ben wanted to run. It is quite possible that if there had been a contest, we would both have been defeated—the convention was certainly not in a mood to exchange one of the Old Guard for another.

The antiwar work of the guild continued in 1968 and 1969 and the membership of the guild increased. Those eighteen months included some of the most momentous struggles, legal and otherwise, in the recent history of the country. The tumultuous riots in Chicago around the Democratic National Convention; the rise of the Black Panthers in San Francisco; the trials of the Chicago Seven—all occupied guild members, who, as always, were in the forefront of the legal fights of the day.

The next convention of the guild, which met in Washington in 1970, was even more turbulent than the 1968 meeting. This time the primary issue, which dominated every aspect of convention discussion, was the role of women in society and in the guild. The challenges that women were making in many aspects of American life all surfaced at the guild convention. The issue had been raised in the guild years before by Ann

Ginger; now it was front and center. The panel presentation on the rights of women was attended by almost every delegate.

It was clear that the guild would elect a woman as president. It was also clear that the only woman with sufficient standing and sufficient experience in the guild who might fill that role was Doris (Dobby) Walker of San Francisco. Dobby had been a pillar of strength not only of the guild but for me personally. She is highly principled and fights tenaciously and with great skill for those principles. Along with this comes some difficulty in compromising. Politics has been called the art of compromise, and in treating of intraguild politics (and every organization has some internal politics) she was not at her best. But in terms of the program of the guild, she represented integrity, and all of us who knew her respected her.

However, there were many at that convention who did not know her. She represented the Old Left if anyone did. She was a devoted member of the Communist party and carried with her a bit of the resistance the Party showed to changes it didn't lead. And it was not leading the changes taking place at the 1970 convention.

Dobby's election was complicated by a second issue that was raised on the floor of the convention—an issue that had been swept under the rug in 1967—namely, the right of students to vote. In 1967 the question was largely a theoretical one. The number of students was minuscule, and their right to vote was almost an abstract question. This was far from true in 1970, when the student vote might well be decisive on any question.

Debate on this issue was interminable, and ultimately the student vote was approved. But unfortunately Dobby felt it necessary to take a position in opposition to student voting. She has deep feelings about questions of professionalism and is justly proud of her legal skills. She was also repelled by the evident hostility toward the law shown by many of the younger delegates, and like Ben Margolis three years before, she was concerned that the California chapter might lose its status in the state bar association. Her speech raised, in the minds of many, serious questions as to whether she should be elected president.

This was the closest the guild had ever come to a real contest for the office of president, and to avoid a floor fight on the issue, a women's caucus met for several hours. The caucus supported Dobby and a floor fight was avoided. Dobby felt rather uneasy about her ability to control the increasingly raucous and disruptive younger members, particularly the students. Many of the younger members would be on the new national executive committee, and she extracted a promise from me that I wouldn't drop out of activity but would attend executive board meetings to provide her with some degree of support.

That was not the end of the turmoil at the convention. The guild had always featured a closing banquet to which prominent members of the bar and sympathetic public officials were invited. The banquet, although traditional, was also something of a burden. With inflation, the price of banquet tickets increased; and with the accretion of large numbers of students as members, it quickly developed that many of the members could not afford to attend the dinner, which, as usual, was held at a large hotel. And so a somewhat ill-advised compromise was reached: convention delegates who could not afford the ticket price could sit in the balcony and listen to the sometimes inspiring but usually dull speeches delivered on such occasions. On paper, this may have seemed a satisfactory conclusion, but in reality it was not; the delegates in the balcony felt they had been shut out of an important function of the guild and made their views well known.

In the midst of all of this, Bill Kunstler, who was one of the great lawyers of our time but who never missed an opportunity to make a rousing public appearance, burned his banquet ticket in the lobby of the hotel in emulation of the draft resisters who were burning their draft cards. Bill, of course, wasn't risking arrest, but it was otherwise a dramatic gesture. He was later carried into the hall on the shoulders of the cheering students. Years later the New York chapter of the guild, in accordance with its practice, gave a dinner to honor Bill. This dinner likewise involved the expenditure of substantial sums of money for banquet tickets. However, this time Bill did not burn his banquet ticket, but instead made his customary amusing and inspiring speech.*

No discernible change in guild program emerged from the convention; we were all too busy focusing on nonprogrammatic problems. No new ideas emerged, except that the work of the guild should be decen-

---

*There is a story about Bill that's too good to skip, though it involves neither the guild nor me. Some years ago, Bill and Leonard Boudin were invited to address a student meeting at Harvard on some subject of current interest. Bill was late, when his plane was grounded, and Leonard opened the program. He explained Bill's absence and then said: "Sometime in the next half hour, Bill will burst through the door and, with his long hair streaming behind him, he'll jump onto the platform, throw his arms around me, and kiss me—a wet kiss—on the forehead."

A few minutes later the door opened and Bill dashed in and embraced and kissed Leonard, exactly as predicted. Bill always expected to get a good hand when he entered a meeting, but he was puzzled by the laughter that greeted him this time.

tralized and regional offices were to be set up; the guild was to continue to be the "legal arm of the Movement." There was in fact plenty of "Movement" work for its legal arm to do; mass demonstrations continued throughout the period, and the chapters were kept busy with their antiwar work, which dominated not only the thoughts of the members of the guild but the thoughts of increasing numbers of Americans.

However, the sharp divisions in the guild gave rise to legitimate doubts as to its survival. A nonlawyer friend who attended most of the sessions remarked to me, "You are the Louis XVI of the guild; Dobby may be the Marie Antoinette."

The youngest person in attendance at the convention was my son Mark, who was seven months old at the time. Since then, the number of children attending guild conventions has increased rapidly and the minimum age has decreased. At the 1995 convention there were about twenty to twenty-five children, one of them five weeks old. A well-organized child care system for the four-to-twelve-year-olds has been available at every recent convention. A far cry indeed from the staid affairs of fifty years ago.

Dobby had a hard time as president of the guild. The national executive committee meetings, most of which I attended, were nightmares and were carried on in an atmosphere of bitterness and anger marked not only by clashes between the Old Guard and the New Left, but also between representatives of various factions in the younger group. The 1969 convention of SDS had fractured the New Left, and its vibrations were felt in the guild. The few older members of the board were rarely given the luxury of finishing a sentence, and the predominant sentiment of many members of the board, as expressed on T-shirts and buttons, was a variant of the philosophical slogan, "Lawyers are shitheads." The idea that a lawyer might be required to do legal research was foreign to them. I've recently checked up on one or two of the 1970 rebels, and they do their research now.

It was a miserable eighteen months for Dobby. Like all good Party members she had a sense of discipline and she expected a disciplined response from people she was working with. The very word "discipline" was anathema to the members of the New Left who made up a good share of the membership of the guild after 1970, and Dobby's efforts to work with guild members whose behavior differed so sharply from hers resulted in a constant struggle. Despite all this, the growth of the guild, both in activity and membership, continued at an accelerated pace as the intensification of the war in Vietnam made greater demands on the services of our members.

All of the tensions that had been building up since 1967 escalated to earthquake proportions at the 1971 convention, held at the University of Colorado at Boulder. By this time, the younger generation represented a clear voting majority, and they rapidly took things into their own hands.

Just as the issue of votes for students and the role of women had dominated the Washington convention, so Boulder was mostly concerned with the question of whether "legal workers" and "jail-house lawyers" were to be admitted into the guild. If the question of voting rights for students had alarmed the Michigan and California delegates in 1967, this proposal shocked them even more profoundly—and not only the Michigan and California delegates.

I had accepted the substance of most of the decisions reached at Washington, although I was deeply disturbed about the way in which the issues were presented. But this convention was much more extreme. I supposed that the term "legal workers" was intended to include legal secretaries and paralegals, but I had difficulty in getting any clear expression of the outer limits of that category. The inclusion of "jail-house lawyers" was typical of the temper of the times, but it seemed to me nonsense. I was wrong on both counts and the inclusion of the two new categories has added strength and purpose to the guild. Discussion of the issues was both highly emotional and highly repetitious. The members of the younger faction carried the day on every vote.

Overhanging all of this was the question of the election of president. As I have said above, I did not feel a contested election for president was unhealthy or that unanimity was necessarily desirable. As a matter of fact, there was a hotly contested election for president much later, in 1992, with no hard feelings left behind.

But this was different. Every guild president had been elected for a second term for the past twenty years, and I assumed that Dobby would want a second term if only as an endorsement of her tireless efforts to hold the guild together in her first term. Further, I feared that a contest for the presidency in the context of that convention would be wholly destructive, and that the opposition to Dobby would be personal and nasty. I also knew that she would lose. Aside from the adverse organizational effect, Dobby was a good friend of mine, and I felt that she would be deeply hurt at the prospect of rejection after twenty years of devoted service to the guild.

But the convention presented a revolutionary situation, and none of the older members was likely to have significant influence. Dobby withdrew her candidacy after a day or two and the convention in a brief moment of sanity elected Catherine Roraback as president, a post she accepted with reluctance, on the understanding no one would ask her to serve a second term. She was a member of the older generation but was respected and admired by everyone. Her office was in New Haven, and like many members not affiliated with a chapter, she was somewhat isolated and was not identified with any of the issues that had been tearing the guild apart in the past few years. Her political credentials were unquestioned, and she was acceptable to everyone.

The convention ended on a note that was for me most depressing. Quite regardless of the substantive program, it seemed to me that disorder and chaos had taken over and that the guild was wasting its resources on fighting issues that were of no real concern either to lawyers or anyone else.

I recognized that this was the generation of the seventies, and many concepts that had been built into my method of thinking were foreign to that generation. Though I had been out of the Communist party for over ten years, I still believed in certain rules for political action, influenced by my years in the Party and the trade union movement. I believed in organization and personal discipline, concepts that, so far as I could see, were unknown to these young people. I did not think anything could be accomplished without some sort of hierarchical structure. I thought that there ought to be some connection between action taken and an end to be achieved—an end that went beyond the day after tomorrow.

The organizational structure of the guild became more and more decentralized, with duties scattered among so many people that responsibility for success or failure was hard to fix. I never could understand the new structure, if any, that evolved.

Survival of the guild was a miracle. A few of my comrades believed that the guild was no longer a bar association but a motley collection of radicals somehow associated with the practice of law. They even projected, at Boulder, the thought of organizing a new progressive bar association that would perform some of the functions they understood such a bar association should perform. The very thought of such a step made my blood run cold. I saw no chance of creating a viable new organization, and I certainly was not prepared to abandon the old. But I wasn't happy.

Some of the older generation of guild members resigned after the 1971 convention; others, including me, went into hibernation. A few hardy souls carried on as before, as well as they could. Prominent among them were Dobby Walker and Ann Ginger, who, like good Communists, continued to work in the chapter and managed to overcome the difficulties they faced in 1971. They were tougher than I was. I went to an occasional New York chapter meeting, where I witnessed bitter ideological battles between Prairie Fire, Progressive Labor, the October 10 Movement, the Weathermen, RYM II, and other sects with equally colorful names— battles over esoteric, revolutionary doctrine in which I had no interest. There was an anti–Communist party undercurrent to all of this, but no overt red-baiting.

I skipped the 1973 convention altogether and stopped in for a day or two in Minneapolis in 1974, where I made a very bad speech on an obscure and unimportant problem at a panel on labor law. The most memorable event of the time was that on the third day of the convention, President Gerald Ford pardoned Richard Nixon.

After a few years, however, things tended to settle down. The New York chapter, in 1977, gave a dinner to honor the "founding members," or at least those of us still around—a gesture that did much to heal the wounds left open by the struggles of the preceding years. In 1980, the convention at Boston honored the past presidents of the guild. I attended, of course, but found fewer and fewer members I knew.

I was stirred out of my lethargy in 1977–78 when the guild faced another internal crisis, this time over the Israeli-Palestinian issue. In 1977, a guild delegation visited Israel and returned with an extensive report charging serious violations by the Israeli government of the civil rights of the Palestinians, especially in the Occupied Territories. Resolutions supporting the report resulted in bitter debate at a meeting of the guild's national executive board in Washington* and in the New York chapter. I was merely an observer at the meeting in Washington but participated in the debate in New York in support of the adoption of the resolution. Feelings on the subject ran high and the guild lost a few of its affluent Jewish members as a result. A few scars are still left, but today the debate over Israel's relationship to the Occupied Territories is such that the

---

*In those days the guild, in its continuing effort to avoid fixing responsibility on anyone, not only held its regular conventions and executive committee meetings in between but also held meetings of a national executive board, which was really a miniconvention attended by hundreds of members, and which, like the convention and the national executive committee, considered and decided policy. Fortunately that practice was abandoned because it was very costly. A better reason for abandoning the idea was that it dispersed rather than centralized responsibility.

1978 report of the guild would probably be accepted without much difference of opinion. The issue of the guild's attitude toward Israel, however, is still a matter of occasional fierce debate.

My activity in the guild continued sporadically over the next few years. As the 1987 convention approached, a decision was made to celebrate the fiftieth anniversary of the guild with a convention in Washington, where the whole thing had started. Several months before the convention, Marty Popper asked me to serve on the organizing committee for the gathering—a few of the "founding members" were needed, he said, to make the necessary connections between 1937 and 1987. I agreed, and also agreed to edit a short history of the guild. Joe Popper (Marty's son), Tim Ledwith, and others undertook to work on various sections of the history, and we turned out a reasonably good fifty-page booklet in time for the convention. The celebration in Washington was pleasant, and I felt that I should end my self-imposed exile.

Since then, I've been attending conventions and an occasional city chapter meeting, assuming a sort of grandfatherly role toward my favorite organization.

11

The Cuban Revolution

In February 1960, a year after Castro's rebel army entered Havana, Marcia and I flew to Cuba to see the socialist revolution. Havana bustled like a crowded street fair: walls and sidewalks were plastered with posters proclaiming high hopes for the revolution, and the intent of Cuba to build its own economy without reliance on the United States. Street-corner meetings were everywhere. On one corner we watched Castro urging his audience to buy lottery tickets (long a feature of Havana street life, as in most Latin American cities) and announcing that the funds realized would be used to build badly needed housing.

We knew no one in the country, but it wasn't hard to make friends. Everyone wanted to take us to a party and once or twice we went. When I walked into the Western Union office in Havana and introduced myself as the lawyer for the Western Union workers in New York, Marcia and I were at once adopted and shown the revolutionary sights of the capital city. Then we were passed on to the Western Union employees in Santiago, and invited to tour Oriente province.

Our airplane to Santiago was crowded with young men and women in army uniforms dancing in the aisles; the pilot could quiet them only by announcing that seatbelts had to be fastened. As we motored to a newly organized collective farm at Dos Rios, near Santiago, we heard radio reports of a plane that had taken off from Miami and crashed while attempting to set Cuban cane fields on fire.

At Dos Rios we were shown the site at which José Martí—a good poet but a poor soldier—had been killed leading the struggle against Spain in 1898. That night on television, we watched Castro report on fires in the cane fields and other counterrevolutionary activities seemingly directed from the United States. He held up, as an exhibit, the U.S. passport of the pilot of one of the marauding planes.

I saw on that first trip and on other visits to Cuba over the next few years what a socialist government could bring to an underdeveloped semi-colonial society, and it was perhaps the most exhilarating experience of my life. I attended, with a lump in my throat and tears in my eyes, a touching meeting at Camp Libertad, a former air force base, at which reading primers for adults were distributed to fifty- and sixty-year-old workers, who pored over books they were not accustomed to handle. We visited new hospitals in Havana and in the Sierra Maestra built to provide up-to-date medical services to all Cubans, many of whom had never enjoyed even indoor plumbing or paved roads. We drove along country roads and saw many new small buildings with a bust of José Martí in front of the door—the universally recognized sign of a school. We witnessed the explosive development of recreational facilities all over the country available to everyone. We saw the development of an agricultural program designed to provide year-round work for all farmers. All over the island, our new Cuban friends were bursting with excitement and enthusiasm—enthusiasm we shared.

I saw lots of mistakes, too—many wasteful projects, some of them quite large, that were started and never finished; extraordinary inefficiency by untrained government employees; some conduct that seemed to be deliberate sabotage. I saw a cargo of fish delivered by Soviet fishing vessels to the docks of Havana rotting on the streets because there were no refrigeration facilities available. In about 1963, a decision was made to devote Cuba's agricultural resources principally to the production of sugar, instead of diversifying—a decision I thought at the time was a serious error, for which Cuba is still paying.

But utopia doesn't come easily. In this case, all of the internal problems might have been solved within a decade, were they not hindered by an external force—the United States, whose hostility made the normal development of a socialist society in Cuba impossible. A paranoia sometimes seems to affect policy of Cuba: the ill-afforded expenditure for armaments, the dependence on the socialist countries of Eastern Europe, the failure to provide a greater degree of civil liberty, and the distortion of the Cuban economic system caused by all of these factors. None of this was necessary, and all of it was the result of the enmity of the United States and its determination, from the very beginning, to prevent a showcase socialist state in Latin America.

But enough of that. The full story of the relations between the United States and Cuba will someday be written and, I'm sorry to say, it will not be a story of which my country can be proud.

The Cuban Retainer

I returned to New York from that first trip feeling that the revolution, if left alone, might indeed develop into a true socialist government, but that efforts by the United States government to prevent such a development were inevitable. My enthusiasm was unbounded; so was my apprehension. I could talk and think of nothing but Cuba.

I went back to Cuba two months later with my son Peter, then fifteen years old. This time I was armed with a few letters of introduction from friends in the United States to persons in Cuba who were moving into politically important positions.

Before I left, I had told the New York radio station WBAI that I planned to make the trip and asked whether it would be interested in anything I could bring back by way of interviews with revolutionary leaders or with rank-and-file farmers, doctors, soldiers, or the like. Of course, the station managers were delighted with the idea, and so was I—they weren't spending a penny and I was able to tell the Cubans that I represented a leading radio station and could claim press privileges. Miraculously this eventuated in an automobile trip from Havana to Manzanillo, on the east coast. I was armed with a 35mm camera, a lot of color film, and a tape recorder. We also picked up a ten-year-old Packard, an interpreter, a driver, and Philip Foner, who was writing a book on the history of Cuba.

It was a swell trip. We stopped overnight at houses of Communist party members, took hundreds of slides, and interviewed about half a dozen people, including a young doctor, a very young army officer (Peter observed that the captain wasn't old enough to get a driver's license in New York), a Catholic priest who had left the church and joined the revolutionary forces, and a sugar worker. They spoke Spanish, and I only English, but our interpreter was good and we got along well.

I had never done anything like this before, or since, and I made many mistakes. I remember a voluble twenty-three-year-old doctor who spoke at length about the need for public health and how he and his comrades would bring better health services both to the people of Cuba and to their farm animals. He spoke very rapid Spanish, and the interpreter had trouble keeping up with him. When we finally finished, after an hour in a hot field in Matanzas, he asked, in perfect English: "Do you think the people in the United States will be interested?" I was, to say the least, astonished, and I asked why he hadn't told me he that could speak English. "No one asked me," he said.

On my return from Havana in April, I had no trouble in persuading Leonard that we ought to represent Cuba in its legal affairs in the United States. We were confident that we could handle whatever legal problems might arise and that we could survive—indeed, flourish—on the political problems that might be presented. We had spent our professional lives fighting the Establishment in the United States, and we had enough political savvy to know that there would be many similar problems in the coming years. We were somewhat arrogant, feeling that we could cope with whatever might come up, even if it were in a field of law in which we had little experience. To this professional outlook there was added, at least for me, a large element of romanticism. How could I resist the lure of a socialist state (maybe) in the Western Hemisphere?

So Leonard and I easily convinced ourselves that we could do the job, and indeed, that no one else could. Neither of us knew anything about international law, but we were quick studies. There remained the task of convincing Cuba. We decided to call in all of our chips and to enlist our friends in the project. We had a lot of chips out there. For twenty years or more, we had been representing progressives and radicals in the United States, and we had a reputation as competent, honest, and courageous lawyers in such representation. Leonard had represented Waldo Frank, who knew Castro well, and who had recently published a book on Cuba. I had represented many members of the Communist party in the United States and knew most of the Party leadership. Leo Huberman and Paul Sweezy, editors of *Monthly Review*, had just written a book on Cuba, and they were glad to help.

From these sources and a few others, we were able to scrape up a dozen or so letters addressed to people with some degree of influence in Cuba, and armed with them, I returned to Cuba several times in May and June, sometimes with Leonard. It was not easy to get through to the people we wanted to see. They were all very busy, and meeting with United States lawyers didn't seem to rate very high priority.

I don't remember how many trips we made before I met the deputy minister of foreign affairs, Carlos Olivares, a tall, handsome, black army officer. We quickly found a subject of common concern since he was interested in getting legal representation in the United States and I was interested in providing such representation. Rabinowitz and Boudin came with excellent credentials, both political and professional. Olivares, with good reason, distrusted the large "downtown" law firms, with large corporate clienteles, who were not likely to be politically sympathetic. As it turned out, many of these firms were later involved in the ensuing Cuban litigation, but on the other side. Olivares and I agreed, in principle, on a retainer, and Leonard and I made several more visits to Havana. We finally signed a retainer agreement, to serve as attorneys for the government of Cuba and all of its agencies, early in the summer of 1960.

On one of these trips I visited La Floridita, a legendary bar in Havana. Standing at the bar a very fat and very drunk elderly, gray-haired man was holding court, handing out peso notes to dozens of admirers who gathered around him to laugh at his jokes. After ten or fifteen minutes of watching the scene, which I found rather disagreeable, I realized that the center of attraction was Ernest Hemingway. A year later he was dead.

The Early Days

It is amusing to recall that in July 1960 a primary interest of Cuba in signing a retainer with us was the establishment of an official Cuban travel agency in New York, to solicit tourists interested in seeing a revolution in the making. Travel to and from Havana was easy in those remote days; there were several daily flights between New York and Havana and many more between Miami, Tampa, and Havana. Leonard and I traveled down almost weekly to discuss the many legal questions that soon developed in New York and Miami. That happy situation continued only for a few months; by January 1961 the United States imposed restrictions on travel by U.S. citizens to Cuba, and regularly scheduled air flights between the United States and Cuba ceased. We quickly forgot about the storefront travel agency on Fifth Avenue.

There were many other problems, both legal and administrative, requiring our attention. A revolution cannot operate smoothly in its early days. Many of the persons charged with administrative responsibility in Cuba were very young, and inexperienced. A bartender in New York once refused to serve the president of Compania Cubana de Aviacion, the Cuban airline, without proof that he was eighteen years old. Those of the older generation who had joined the revolutionary government (such as Carlos Rafael Rodriguez and Dr. Raul Roa, the foreign minister) were overwhelmed by myriad details that should have been handled by subordinates. Most of those charged with running the prerevolution government left the country—some with Batista, and others over the next few years as they found themselves out of sympathy with the political and economic course of events. The result often approached chaos. This was costly to all aspects of the government, but, from our point of view, especially costly to Cuba's legal affairs in the United States. Courts in the States, hostile to the new government, were not tolerant of our inability to find the documents required to establish our claims or to respond to discovery demands by our opposition. They were not tolerant of our inability to make quick decisions on policy in pending cases, and they were not tolerant of our inability even to find local lawyers willing to represent Cuba in cases pending outside of New York and Washington.

In New York there were, in mid-1960, two lawsuits pending that had been started either before or shortly after the revolution. We were substituted as counsel in those cases and proceeded to dispose of them. In Washington there was one lawsuit pending, which Cuba had won in the lower court. Cuba won that case on appeal, too, with Judge Warren Burger, later Chief Justice of the United States, dissenting—a foreboding of things to come.

The situation in Florida was more difficult. There had long been a symbiotic relationship between Havana and Miami. Miami was heavily populated by thousands of Cubans, many of them still nationals of Cuba. They had families and friends in Havana, with whom close ties had never been broken. The two cities were only a few miles apart, and transportation by air took only forty-five minutes. No visas or passports were required for travel between the two countries. Fares were not high and telephone rates reasonable. Communication between Miami and Havana was no more difficult than between New York and Philadelphia, or San Francisco and Los Angeles. Thousands of Miamians, and residents of Tampa and Key West as well, worked in Cuba, vacationed in Cuba, had investments in Cuba, and considered it a second home. Organized crime had a strong foothold in Havana, and middle-class Miami residents often went to Cuba for a weekend of gambling and whoring.

The Cuban revolution changed all of this and caused a profound shock to this community. Both the Cubans and the Floridians concerned were moderately affluent, and as the revolution developed, their hostility to it grew to the point of fanaticism. Beginning almost immediately there was a stream of middle- and upper-class Cubans fleeing to Miami. By July 1960, Miami was a hotbed of Cuban counterrevolution. Every newspaper in town became passionately anti-Castro and a resident of the city who publicly expressed pro-Castro sentiments faced ostracism and sometimes even physical harm. Many legal battles involving the Cuban government had started, and some had even finished before we were retained. Most of the remaining ones, some quite important, were cleared up in the next year. Cuba didn't do well in those cases; it was hard to get competent local lawyers to represent Cuba in that environment, and the Florida state courts were unremittingly hostile.

More litigation in New York was not slow in coming. On September 15, 1960, a Cuban airliner was seized and held at Idlewild (now Kennedy) Airport in connection with a lawsuit filed in the federal court in New York against Compania Cubana de Aviacion. Aside from the merits, the litigation was politically significant. The seizure of the plane received front-page publicity. The airline grounded its Havana–New York commercial flights, to avoid attachment of other planes.

A coincidence of timing heightened the political effect of the suit and added to the publicity generated by the attachment of the plane. The September 1960 meeting of the United Nations General Assembly was the most sensational of the sessions of that body up to that time, stimulated in part by the Cuban revolution and in part by a debate over a Soviet Union demand for disarmament and a ban on nuclear testing. The spotlight was focused on Nikita Khrushchev and Fidel Castro, both of whom attended the meeting. Apart from the excitement of having our most important client in town, the visit of Cuba's prime minister gave us two logistical problems: where the Cuban delegation was going to live while here and how it was to get back to Cuba.

The Cuban delegation numbered fifty-one, headed by Castro and Roa. They came to the United States on September 18, on a Cuban airliner that, like the one involved in the pending litigation, was immediately attached. Castro spoke at the United Nations General Assembly on September 26; two days later he and most of the Cuban delegation planned to return to Havana, but no plane was available because of the court attachment. Leonard, acting for the Cuban government, asked the State Department to declare that the attached plane had diplomatic immunity under international law and to take appropriate action to vacate the attachment. The court, acting in response to a request made by an embarrassed State Department, directed that the plane on which the diplomats were traveling be released. A second order granting immunity was required when the plane returned in October for the rest of the delegation.

Even more sensational was "the Battle of the Shelburne." Prior to the arrival of the Cuban delegation in New York, arrangements had been made with the Shelburne Hotel, a smallish residential hotel on Lexington Avenue, to house the Cuban delegates. For the hotel, it looked like a good deal—it had lots of vacant rooms, and the delegation was large enough to occupy two full floors. But trouble arose almost as soon as the delegates arrived.

Most delegations to the United Nations are composed of quiet, sedate, and middle-aged diplomats who speak softly and wear clothes appropriate to their calling. Not so the Cuban delegation. The average age of the delegates was well under thirty, and the exuberance of their youth was substantially increased by the feeling that they had just pulled off a successful revolution—successful, moreover, in the teeth of "Yanqui imperialismo." Most of them wore beards and were dressed in the army fatigues that were a hallmark of their days in the Sierra Maestra mountains, where the most intense part of the revolutionary struggle had taken place. It had been assumed by the Cubans, and probably by the management as well, that they would be fed, like all other hotel residents, in the hotel dining room.

With the usual keen hindsight, it is evident that these assumptions were unfounded. The other residents of the Shelburne were typical of those who live in midtown residential hotels: elderly ladies and gentlemen, conservative in political outlook and impatient at interruptions of routine. The attendance in the dining room of fifty Cuban youths, dressed in army khaki, speaking loudly in Spanish and representing the (by now) hated Cuban regime, was a serious interruption of that routine, and the regulars complained to the owner of the hotel, Edward Spatz, an excitable man whose blood pressure, he told me, was dangerously high even without this crisis. And so he advised the Cubans that they could not eat in the dining room because they disturbed the other guests.

Spatz claimed that the Cubans, barred from the hotel dining facilities, started to cook in their own rooms, and, he said, the odor of frying chicken soon pervaded the premises, bringing him measurably close to a heart attack. He ordered the Cubans out of the hotel.

The Cubans were inexperienced in diplomacy but well versed in guerrilla action. Moreover, they were furious at the insult, and the most furious of all was Fidel Castro. Someone called the lawyer for Cuba—me—but by the time I could travel the four blocks from my office to the hotel, the problem was far beyond anything I could rectify. When I arrived at the hotel I made my way through crowds of emotional Cuban delegates to the third floor, where I found Fidel buttoning up his army fatigues. He was speaking quite rapidly and energetically in loud Spanish. I can understand Spanish when it uses English-sounding words, and the part of Fidel's remarks I understood was "Parque Central." I couldn't get his attention, and didn't try very hard. He wasn't listening to lawyers—this was, he understood quite well, a political and public relations matter. After a few minutes, I realized that he was threatening to move the delegation to an encampment in Central Park, where his countrymen, just come from the mountains of Oriente, would, he explained, be much more comfortable. But the United Nations Secretariat wasn't comfortable with the idea, and neither was the State Department—nor for that matter, the Parks Department of New York City. Instead, arrangements were made to house the delegates at the Hotel Theresa in Harlem, where they were made very welcome indeed. Sympathizers from all over the northeast headed for Harlem, and Castro held receptions at the hotel over the next few days. It was a public relations coup of the first order.

In the months that followed, Leonard and I spent almost as much time in Havana as we did in New York. Every time we went down, more Cuban government agencies gave us files for cases we were to undertake in the United States. Most originated with Banco Nacional de Cuba, but there were many others involving the Ministry of Foreign Relations, the Ministry of Foreign Commerce, the merchant marine, the aviation company, the insurance industry, and others. On a personal level, I suppose the government official with whom we spent most of our time was Luis Martinez, a young, energetic, and very enthusiastic revolutionary who, for a time, was president of Compania Cubana de Aviacion. He was, he boasted, fluent in Russian, as well as English and Spanish. The only Russian he needed to know, he explained, was "Cuba, Da; Yanqui, Nyet."

I had little contact with the people on the highest level of the revolutionary government. I met Fidel Castro on several formal social occasions and had one extended person-to-person meeting with him. I had more contact with Dr. Raul Roa, the foreign minister, with whom I met occasionally on legal questions relating to foreign policy. I also met several times with Carlos Rafael Rodriguez, who might well be considered the intellectual father of the Cuban revolution. Older than Castro and the others who had carried the brunt of the military activity, he provided a degree of intellectual discipline and political sophistication lacking in many of his younger associates. He was a leading member of the Communist Party of Cuba and an impressive figure indeed. His influence extended far beyond whatever governmental office he held at any moment. Years later, when I met him at his office on the top floor of a Havana skyscraper at midnight (the only hour he had available to see me), I apologized for bothering him about a problem that did not directly affect his department. He gently chided me, saying that any problem relating to the welfare of Cuba was worthy of his consideration, and we spent about an hour discussing issues raised in my firm's litigation, none of which immediately involved him.

I also had a few meetings with Ché Guevara, the most memorable of which was in Geneva, where we played three games of chess, all of which he won. I tried my best, too, notwithstanding the temptation to take a diplomatic defeat. He was then president of Banco Nacional and was in Geneva for a meeting of the United Nations Conference on Trade and Development, where he astonished his fellow bankers by dressing in army fatigues. Leonard, a much better chess player than I, beat Ché once or twice when they met in Havana. I thought that was ill-advised.

I met Raul Castro for the first time in about 1965. I was having a drink with some friends at La Torre, a restaurant on the roof of the Focsa building, which is, in terms of Havana's architecture, a skyscraper. My companions were Lou and Lenna Jones and Jeanne Curtis, all United States nationals working in Cuba. After we had been there about forty-five minutes, Raul, easily recognized by any Cuban, walked through the bar, saw us, and greeted Lou with the customary Cuban embrace. Lou introduced all of us to Raul, who, after the usual social chitchat, continued past the bar to the restaurant. Lenna was astonished; she had never heard Lou mention that he was on such cordial terms with Raul—in fact, she did not even know that Lou had met him. There was some slight tension at the table as Lou tried in vain to explain when and under what circumstances he had met such a high-ranking member of the government, and why he hadn't mentioned it to his wife. After a few moments, he confessed that ten minutes earlier he had met Raul in the men's room and had asked him to go through the act we had just witnessed.

Throughout this period I had (and I continue to have) close contacts with Cuban ambassadors to the United Nations, who were stationed in New York, notably Ricardo Alarcon, who is, at this writing, president of the National Assembly, Cuba's legislative body.

Not only were the Cuban clients intelligent, good lawyers, and excellent hosts, they were ideal clients in other respects. Within the broad framework of carrying on the policies of the government, they readily accepted our decisions as to how to litigate the cases, the issues we were to raise, and the arguments we were to make. We had the usual mild disagreements over the payment of fees and they were impatient with the slow progress of the litigation, but so were we.

By early 1961, there were about thirty-five cases pending in the federal and state courts of New York, in most of which Cuba or its national bank (Banco Nacional de Cuba) was the moving party. We also had a few cases in Florida, and other litigation in San Francisco, Puerto Rico, New Orleans, Washington, D.C., and elsewhere.

Ranged against Cuba in all this litigation was the full strength of the legal and political Establishment in the United States, in which lawyers, judges, and government officials alike come from a common background, share similar social and business interests, and hold similar, if not identical, political views. The Cuban litigation was not unique in this respect, but its political aspects were unusually pronounced. The uncertainty in the state of the law provided a wide range in which the political and ideological views of the participants could be presented.

All of this was a challenge that Leonard and I viewed with exultation. We had represented small unions against Metropolitan Life, Prudential, Western Union, Pacific Telephone and Telegraph, and the New York Hotel Association, and in the preceding decade we had taken on Senators Joseph McCarthy and James Eastland, Congressman Francis Walters, and the entire force of the Senate and House investigating committees (to say nothing of the army and navy security apparatus) on behalf of impecunious, powerless, and often frightened victims of the cold war. Representation of Cuba was right down our alley. The Goliath was the one we had been battling for years.

Adding to our professional interest and personal excitement was our recognition that important issues were being raised by the political and economic warfare between the United States and Cuba, and they were being raised in a rapidly changing international context, as other third world nations sought to assert their national identities against the colonial powers.

The Embargo against Cuba

In the years after the revolution, the United States initiated and carried on political and economic warfare against Cuba with a ferocity unparalleled in our peacetime history.

On October 19, 1960, the Commerce Department put in place an embargo on substantially all exports to Cuba, except for a few commodities such as medicines and medical supplies. Travel was banned in January 1961. Effective on February 7, 1962, there was an embargo on all trade with Cuba. In July of the following year, the Treasury Department issued its Cuban Assets Control regulations, enforced through the Office for Foreign Assets Control (OFAC). All financial and commercial transactions between Cuba and the United States, and between Cuba and U.S. nationals, were prohibited unless licensed by OFAC. All currency and other property in the United States in which Cuba or a Cuban national had an interest was frozen. Those regulations have been amended from time to time, but at the present writing they are, in their essence, still in effect and, indeed, have been strengthened and extended.

Our contacts with OFAC were frequent during the following years, almost on a biweekly basis. We easily secured licenses to permit us to receive funds from Cuba for counsel fees and expenses, to spend money in traveling to Cuba, and to carry on other activities incident to our practice of the law, but in other respects, almost all applications for licenses were denied.

Early on, we sought an opportunity to challenge the constitutionality of the regulations and found such a case on behalf of Juan Rigores Sardino, a Cuban national living in Havana. His son had died in the United States while owning a savings account of about seven thousand dollars in a New York bank. Rigores Sardino sought to collect the money as heir to his son, but the bank refused to pay it, the payment of money to a Cuban national being a violation of the currency regulations. We brought an action challenging the regulations on the ground that they deprived Rigores Sardino of his property without due process of law, in violation of the Fifth Amendment. We lost in the district court and the Court of Appeals; the latter agreed that Rigores Sardino had been deprived of his property without due process of law, but held such deprivation to be justified, because: "Hard currency is a weapon in the struggle between the free and the Communist worlds; it would be a strange reading of the Constitution to regard it as demanding depletion of dollar resources for the benefit of a government seeking to create a base for activities inimical to our national welfare."

The Supreme Court refused to review the case.

In the summer of 1961, the Justice Department demanded that our firm register as a foreign agent, pursuant to the 1938 Foreign Agent's Registration Act, which required agents of foreign principals to register. Cuba was clearly a foreign principal, and the statutory definition of "agent" was not helpful, either. The term was defined as anyone who "acts . . . as . . . a public relations counsel, publicity agent, information-service employee, servant, agent, representative or attorney for a foreign principal." There was an exemption from the registration requirement for persons engaging "only in private and non-political financial and mercantile activities." We recognized some difficulty in squeezing into that exemption, but the lawyers for other foreign countries had never been required to register, and we felt the move against us was part of the war against our client.

Whatever the statute meant, the consequences of registration were serious. The registration form would require us to disclose all of the "businesses, occupations and public activities" in which we were personally engaged, without regard to any relationship of those activities to our representation of Cuba. We would be required to list all "speeches, lectures, talks, and radio broadcasts" that we or any of our employees may have made or any articles or publications we may have prepared. We would be required to list all of our stock holdings or other pecuniary interests in any corporation or other organization, whether or not such enterprises had any relation to Cuba. If we found it necessary to retain counsel in other states in connection with Cuban litigation (a frequent occurrence), a more limited registration form would have to be filed by such associate counsel—limited but still intrusive and burdensome. We had enough trouble finding out-of-state counsel to represent Cuba; if they had had to register as foreign agents, it would have been impossible.

We therefore decided to resist the demand. We first tried to talk the Justice Department out of its demand, arguing that the forms we would have to file were never intended to apply to lawyers. We pointed out that other lawyers for foreign governments had not been required to file. We got nowhere. The Justice Department suggested that we refuse to register, get indicted, and test the law that way. We found that idea not very helpful.

We managed to stall the Justice Department for a year, but when we could get no further extensions of time, we filed an action, in November 1962, asking for a declaratory judgment as to our obligation to file. The case moved quickly to the Supreme Court, where we lost. Justice Arthur Goldberg wrote a short opinion for the unanimous Court, holding that the statute by its express terms required attorneys to register. And so we registered, in 1965 and 1966.

The result was another burden in our representation of a client that was increasingly unpopular. The task of filling out the forms was troublesome, but largely clerical. The side effects were more serious. For years after, when I appeared before a congressional committee either as counsel or witness, I was asked whether I was a "registered foreign agent." In public debate, in television programs, at law schools and lawyers' meetings, the question was asked over and over again. Cuba-baiting was a species of red-baiting, and Rabinowitz-baiting turned out to be a subspecies of Cuba-baiting.

However, the decision in the case, entitled *Rabinowitz v. Kennedy*, resulted in a panic among the "respectable" lawyers who represented more popular governments, and legislation was soon introduced to amend the law to excuse them (and incidentally, us) from registering. The Committee on International Law of the Bar Association of the City of New York, composed of the very cream of the international law bar, in its brief supporting the proposed amendment, said that

> until the *Rabinowitz* case it had been the general policy of the Department of Justice (and of the Bar) to interpret the . . . [law] to exclude from the requirements of registration lawyers engaging in litigation activities for foreign principals. . . .
>
>   The opinion in the *Rabinowitz* decision, however, apparently holds that any litigation activities on behalf of a foreign government . . . are by that nature political and not financial and mercantile and hence require registration. The opinion can also be read to mean that any representation of a foreign government, whether in litigation or otherwise, cannot be deemed "private and non-political."

Arthur H. Dean, senior partner of the firm of Sullivan and Cromwell, made the same point; he added that compliance with the *Rabinowitz* decision would not only be burdensome, but "it is a term of opprobrium to be designated a foreign agent"!

It was the only time during our fifty years of practice that the elite of our profession came up on our side—but, of course, not without an effort to distinguish themselves from Rabinowitz and Boudin. And so Mr. Dean said: "Since the people in that case [Leonard and I] were probably doing something more than representing even commercial activities, even under the things that I propose they might have to register." Congressman Willis, a member of the House Judiciary Committee and also a member of HUAC, wondered whether it might be possible to treat "honorable law firms" differently from others. The law was amended in 1966, and we did not register thereafter, although the provocative name-calling persisted for a few years and still occurs now and then.

■

Toward the end of November 1963, Leonard and I had scheduled a trip to Cuba, traveling through Mexico since direct flights were not available. I intended to leave New York on Friday evening, visit my daughter Joni at Antioch College in Yellow Springs, Ohio, and then meet Leonard in Mexico on Sunday night to catch the Monday flight to Havana. On Friday afternoon, Leonard and I walked over to a local optometrist at lunchtime to pick up a pair of glasses for Leonard. While waiting at the counter, we were stunned by the radio report of the assassination of President Kennedy. Along with the factual report, there were many rumors, one of which was that Cuba might have been responsible.

I had visions of newspaper headlines reading, "Cuba's Lawyers Flee to Mexico as Inquiry in Kennedy Assassination Continues." We decided to postpone our trip for two weeks, but I proceeded to Antioch to see Joni. On the way home the following Sunday, as I waited in the Dayton airport for my plane to leave, I watched a live television news broadcast and saw Jack Ruby murder Lee Harvey Oswald.

Throughout this period, Cuba had been struggling to establish air routes to Western Europe that would not be subject to United States restrictions. Cuba had no planes capable of making a nonstop transatlantic flight. Kindley Field, in Bermuda, was a natural refueling point, and for a short time, Cubana de Aviacion did in fact stop to refuel there. The commercial airport in Bermuda is, however, adjacent to a military base that had been leased to the United States, and the United States, ever ready to tighten its embargo, protested Cuba's use of Kindley Field, making vague claims of possible sabotage and espionage. The British government caved in under U.S. pressure, and Kindley Field was closed to Cuban planes.

Luis Martinez, then president of the Cuban airline, asked us to intervene, first with U.S. authorities and then with the British. We had made no headway with the State Department. We then turned to Great Britain. There were treaties involved, to say nothing of the whole structure of international air traffic, which would be disrupted if refueling points could be cut off for no credible reason.

Martinez was a most energetic and persistent client. He called or telexed almost every day to inquire what was happening. It is difficult to respond to such inquiries when nothing is happening, but Leonard and I did our best to assuage him, and to promise action tomorrow and tomorrow and tomorrow.

On April 17, 1961, the Bay of Pigs invasion started when over two thousand Cuban refugees attempted to invade Cuba in a military operation sponsored by the CIA. New York newspapers carried banner headlines on Monday and Tuesday. "Invasion of Cuba Reported Begun by Rebel Force"; "Anti-Castro Units Land in Cuba; Report Fighting at Beachhead"; and "Cuba Rebels Drive Ahead." Complete disruption of communications (not too good even before the invasion) was reported. All of Cuba's friends in the United States were shocked, disturbed, and depressed. This sort of thing had happened repeatedly in U.S. history, when marines were sent in to quell revolutionary uprisings in Nicaragua, Mexico, and elsewhere, and the fate of the Cuban revolution truly hung in the balance.

Like everyone else, I tuned in to the news broadcasts every waking hour, and while reports were not always precise, the rumors were devastating. Late Tuesday night, I went to bed late and slept fitfully. At 4:00 A.M. the telephone rang. I answered it, and a voice said, "Hello, Victor. How are you? This is Luis." I was amazed. My worst fears were being realized. The government was disbanding and its officials fleeing to some land with which we had telephone communication.

"Luis, where are you?" I asked. He replied, "I'm in Havana, of course; where would I be?" But, I explained, all telephone and telegraph lines were cut off. "Where did you get that news from?" he asked. "The *New York Times*," I responded. Luis snorted in derision. "That's nonsense—I'm calling you, ain't I?"

I stuttered a bit, trying to get my sleepy senses in order. "What's happening down there?" "What do you mean?" he asked. "My God, Havana's being bombed; an invading army has landed; the government is falling," I said.

"Oh, that," he said, "forget it. Everything's well in hand; Havana hasn't been bombed, and there's no trouble at all."

I listened in amazement. With barely a pause, Luis delivered his daily greeting: "What's happening with Kindley Field?"

Nothing was happening with Kindley Field, and nothing ever did.

The Nationalizations of U.S. Property

Our principal work for Cuba over the next two decades involved issues arising out of Cuba's nationalization of property belonging to U.S. nationals. A widespread program of land reform, essential to any revolution in an underdeveloped country, had been initiated in mid-1959. A year later, the government of Cuba nationalized all large-scale commercial, industrial, and agricultural enterprises in the country, both foreign and domestically owned. Since, for more than half a century, Cuba had been in fact, if not in name, a colony of the United States, these nationalizations fell heavily on the extensive property in Cuba owned by U.S. investors. The largest banks, the principal sugar producers, the railroads, the telephone and telegraph companies, the hotels, the valuable nickel mines, the largest manufacturing companies—all owned by nationals of the United States—had been seized by the end of 1960.

These nationalizations of foreign-owned property represented by far the largest such action in history. The foreign-owned banks and insurance companies nationalized by the Soviet Union and the oil installations nationalized in Mexico, Indonesia, and Iran were valued at tens and perhaps hundreds of millions of dollars; the Cuban nationalizations, according to the U.S. owners of the properties, were valued at billions.

The Cuban decrees offered payment for the U.S.–owned property nationalized through the issuance of bonds, but only a tenuous argument could be made that the bonds would have any value, and in the litigation that followed, the courts uniformly held that the offer of compensation was illusory.

At the same time, similar Cuban-owned establishments—banks, factories, retail stores, sugar plantations, farms, hotels—were nationalized. No compensation was made for such seizures.

The State Department had, as early as June 1959, protested to the Cuban government against its land reform program, which threatened to take U.S.–owned property without compensation, and had charged that Cuba was in violation of international law in its nationalization program. As the nationalization proceeded, the protests of the State Department grew more strident.

It was clear that lots of litigation lay ahead. It was equally clear that the attorneys charged with representing Cuba in this litigation would have a tough job. The underlying issue would be the legality of the Cuban nationalization decrees. Trailing behind would be a great many peripheral but serious problems inevitably arising out of the resultant hostility between the United States and Cuba. I don't think either Leonard or I, in 1960, ever dreamt of the extent or duration of these controversies.

There was no question, as a matter of international law, that Cuba could nationalize property within its own borders and that it could decide for itself what kind of economic system it wished to adopt. There was a large question as to Cuba's right to nationalize property without compensation.

To argue in the United States courts that Cuba could legally seize private property without paying for it was contrary to the most basic principles of our domestic law. Everyone who believes in a capitalist economic system built on private property will accept as a fundamental truth that such property cannot be taken without compensation. This principle is enshrined in our Constitution and in the English Common Law. Where would we find the court prepared to rule that Cuba had the right to take two billion dollars' worth of property belonging to American citizens without paying for it?

Nor was this all. Even before we were retained, the executive branch of the U.S. government had made its views known and had denounced the Cuban decrees as a violation of international law. Before a single case had been decided, even on a lower court level, the United States had broken diplomatic relations with Cuba and had imposed a partial embargo on trade with Cuba. Before the Supreme Court even heard argument in the first case raising the issue of the legality of the Cuban decrees, the U.S. government had sponsored the Bay of Pigs invasion, a CIA operation in which a thousand Cuban counterrevolutionaries had attempted to invade Cuba and upset the Castro regime. Thus if a court were to conclude that the nationalizations were legal, it would be condemning the State Department's Cuban policy from the very beginning as being based on a mistaken view of the law. No court is equipped to confront such a political problem, and no court should be put in a position where it would have to face such a dilemma. Certainly in the United States, where the doctrine of separation of powers is inherent in our system of government, it is improper that a court should take upon itself a decision that would so influence the conduct of foreign affairs.

The issue was a thorny one. No matter what the U.S. Constitution may say on the subject, we were to argue that the Cuban decrees were valid under international law, and that this controversy was to be decided under international, not United States, law.

Except for a few well-recognized principles, international law is an amorphous concept. Unlike our domestic law, there is no legislative body to make the law or court to enforce it. The answers are thus often sought in the writings of learned scholars who in turn rely heavily on historical practice as leavened by a concept of what the law, in their view, ought to be. Historically, the right to compensation for nationalized property was by no means generally recognized. When Henry VIII expropriated the foreign-owned abbeys in England four hundred years ago, no compensation was paid or considered. The French confiscated the property of English owners in France without compensation in 1792, and the infant United States did the same with respect to Tory-owned property after our own revolution. And in our own century, Russia nationalized without compensation the property of aliens in the years following the 1917 revolution, as did the Chinese in 1948. There were in fact no court decisions in the United States holding that compensation was required in such circumstances, and while there were many instances in which compensation had been paid, it was not as a result of a legal obligation, but rather by diplomatic negotiations. So it could hardly be said that the law was settled.

There were other considerations, too—political rather than legal—in which both my client and I were much interested. Not only were non-compensated nationalizations legally permissible—they were, I argued, politically necessary if socialism were ever to be established to replace an economic system in which private property was the general rule. Socialism, by definition, meant the public ownership of the means of production; it also meant, in every third world country, the redistribution of land. And no semicolonial country could ever be prosperous enough to pay for the nationalization of private property required to establish socialism. Where in the world could that much money come from?

This problem is not a new one. The classic statement of the respective positions of the industrial and semicolonial nations can be found in the exchange of diplomatic notes between Secretary of State Cordell Hull of the United States and the Foreign Office of Mexico relating to the land reform laws of Mexico that in 1938 resulted in the nationalization of foreign-owned land holdings. Said Secretary Hull: "The Government of the United States merely adverts to a self-evident fact when it notes that the applicable precedents and recognized authorities on international law support its declaration that, under every rule of law and equity, no government is entitled to expropriate private property, for whatever purpose, without provision for prompt, adequate and effective payment therefor. . . ." This pronouncement is known in international law as "the Hull doctrine" and is still the official policy of the State Department.

To this, the foreign minister of Mexico responded:

> My government maintains that there is in international law no rule universally accepted in theory nor carried out in practice, which makes obligatory payment of immediate compensation nor even of deferred compensation, for expropriations of a general and impersonal character like those which Mexico has carried out for the purpose of redistributing the land. . . . The political, social, and economic stability and the peace of Mexico depend on the land being placed anew in the hands of the country people who work it; therefore its distribution which implies the transformation of the country, that is to say, the future of the nation, could not be halted by the impossibility of paying immediately the value of the property belonging to a small number of foreigners who seek only a lucrative end.

I, as legal representative of Cuba, would therefore argue that noncompensated nationalization was legal under international law and was indeed a necessary corollary to the accepted principle that every sovereign state could establish whatever kind of economic system it wished. This meant that I would, inferentially, be asking the court to hold that U.S. policy toward Cuba, over a period of years, had been based on a mistaken premise. Is there a court anywhere in the United States that could make such a holding, whatever it may think about the legal issues involved?

This kind of situation had arisen before, and the courts had devised a solution. That solution was the act of state doctrine.

The act of state doctrine dates at least from the end of the nineteenth century in United States law and has ancient antecedents in English jurisprudence. The simplest statement of the doctrine can be found in *Underhill v. Hernandez*, decided in 1897, in which the Supreme Court said: "Every sovereign state is bound to respect the independence of every other sovereign state, and the courts of one country will not sit in judgment on the acts of the government of another, done within its own territory. Redress of grievances by reason of such acts must be obtained through the means open to be availed of by sovereign powers as between themselves."

If this principle held, the courts of the United States could not pass on the legality of the Cuban nationalization decrees, and they would be given full effect in our courts.

In 1909, and again in 1913 and 1914, the Supreme Court applied the act of state doctrine to action taken by the governments of Costa Rica and Mexico. Major cases arising out of the nationalization decrees of the Soviet Union in 1917 came before the highest court of New York, which also applied the act of state doctrine. The 1960 Cuban nationalization decrees fit squarely within these decisions.

As we shall see, the twenty-year litigation that followed was concerned mostly with the act of state doctrine and issues arising as to its proper application to the Cuban nationalization decrees. The doctrine, expressed in two sentences in the *Underhill* case, was developed at length in the Cuba cases and was the principal subject of three United States Supreme Court decisions. In the first of those, *Banco Nacional de Cuba v. Sabbatino*, Cuba prevailed, when the Court by an eight-to-one vote held that the act of state doctrine governed and that the courts of the United States would not "sit in judgment on the acts of [Cuba] done within its own territory." Ten years later, the personnel of the Court had changed, as had the personnel of the executive branch, and the Court held, by a five-to-four vote, that the act of state doctrine would not apply to the Cuban nationalization involved in *Banco Nacional v. First National City Bank*. And again in *Alfred Dunhill of London v. The Republic of Cuba*, the Court held, once more by a five-to-four vote, that the act of state doctrine did not apply to the facts in that case either. In 1974, we turned to the issue of how compensation was to be calculated if it were to be paid at all—an intricate and legally difficult problem.

How all this came about will be described in some detail in the next chapter. The story illustrates the interplay of a number of legal principles. The discussion will show how the idiosyncratic decision of a single judge contributed decisively to the result. Some readers may find the legal discussion a bit tedious, but I think it will repay careful reading. I find all of this fascinating, not merely as an illustration of how legal decisions are made but also because it's a good tale.

We filed a complaint on behalf of Cuba in *Banco Nacional v. Sabbatino* in the United States District Court in New York on October 10, 1960. For the next two decades this and related successor cases occupied a major share of my time. I wrote several law review and other articles on the Cuban cases; I spoke on the litigation at many law schools and professional meetings, both in the United States and England; I taught a law school course on the subject; I made four highly enjoyable arguments before the Supreme Court. I had a wonderful time. The legal and political issues in the *Sabbatino* case were not only intriguing to me but were important to the development of international law. Above all, those issues are relevant every time a third world state, with a colonial background, seeks to free itself from the domination of a megacapitalist power. In every such case, the nationalization by the developing nation of foreign-owned property is likely to occur, and the rights of the respective parties often lead to a crisis in international affairs. This was an aspect of the struggle against international capitalism in which I hoped I could make some contribution.

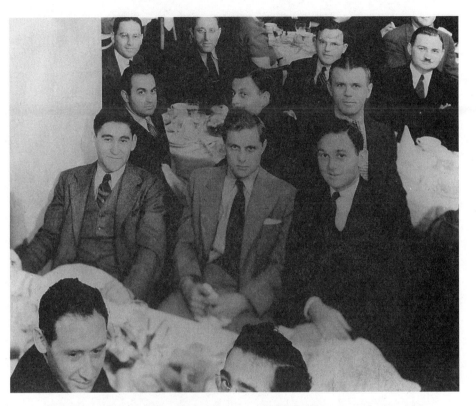

Victor Rabinowitz (right) and his partner Leonard Boudin (center) with Arthur Cowen (left) at the 1939 annual banquet of the New York chapter of the National Lawyers Guild at the Hotel Woodstock in Manhattan.

A Friday night family dinner circa 1941 at the Brooklyn home of Victor Rabinowitz's parents. Menu: chicken, apple pie, and political discussion. Left to right: Victor; his father, Louis, smoking a Melachrino Turkish cigarette; his mother, Rose; his sister, Lucille Perlman, and her husband, Sam; and Victor's wife, Marcia.

Dinner at the Mayflower Hotel, Washington, D.C., 1944. Left to right: Eva Lapin, Victor's former legal secretary; unknown; Eleanor Dreisen, the widow of an American Communications Association (ACA) organizer; Victor; Art Shields, a reporter for the *Daily Worker;* Geraldine Shandross, the legislative representative of ACA; Congressman Vito Marcantonio; Virginia Gardner, a correspondent for the *Daily Worker.*

The American Communications Association, represented by Victor Rabinowitz, called a strike of Western Union workers at 60 Hudson Street, New York, on January 8, 1946. Photo: UPI/Bettmann Archive.

May Day parade in New York, May 1, 1946. Photo: UPI/Bettmann Archive.

Victor Rabinowitz addresses a meeting of the Emergency Civil Liberties Union, 1954.

Victor Rabinowitz represented his future wife, Joanne Grant, in February 1963 at a trial in an injunction proceeding in Talladega, Alabama. The state of Alabama sought to prohibit Joanne, a reporter for the *National Guardian,* from entering the state. Left to right, foreground: Dorothy Vails, a student at Talladega College; Victor; Joanne; right background: another defendant, Carl Braden.

Joni Rabinowitz leaving the courthouse in Macon, Georgia, during her trial for perjury, November 1963. Photo: AP/Wide World Photos.

In 1968, Victor Rabinowitz (left) and Leonard Boudin (right) talked legal strategy with Dr. Benjamin Spock outside Federal Court in Boston, during a noon recess of Dr. Spock's trial for conspiracy to counsel young men to evade the draft. Photo: AP/Wide World Photos.

Mark Rabinowitz, age three, with his father at the beach, 1972.

Victor Rabinowitz met with Fidel Castro during his January 1996 trip to Havana. Shown with them are an interpreter (center) and Ricardo Alarcon (rear), president of the National Assembly of Cuba.

12

The *Sabbatino* Case and Its Progeny

On August 6, 1960, the stevedores employed in the port of Santa Maria on the southern coast of Cuba were loading sugar on the SS *Hornsfels,* a German freighter. They had started work at six in the morning to avoid as much of the midday heat as possible. August 6 was a Saturday, and the workday was over by 10:00 A.M.; on weekdays the workers finished their eight-hour stint at four in the afternoon. The sugar being loaded on the *Hornsfels* on August 6 was produced by the sixth-largest sugar producer in Cuba, Compania Azucarera Vertientes Camaguey de Cuba ("Vertientes," for short), at its two nearby mills. Like most of the other large sugar producers in Cuba, it was owned by U.S. nationals and had a bank account and offices in New York, though it was incorporated in Cuba. The shipment being loaded consisted of fourteen thousand tons of sugar, which Farr Whitlock and Company, New York sugar brokers, had contracted to buy from Vertientes several months before, at a price of about $175,000, for resale to its customers in Morocco. In accordance with customary commercial practice, Vertientes was to be paid for the sugar in New York after shipment, upon presentation to Farr Whitlock of the usual bill of lading and other shipping documents.

By quitting time on Saturday, the five gangs working the ship had loaded about four thousand bags. Loading was finished on the following Wednesday. It was a routine operation, except for one intervening event.

On the afternoon of August 6, by resolution of the "President of the Republic and the Prime Minister of the Revolutionary Government," Cuba nationalized twenty-six enterprises in its territory owned by nationals of the United States, as part of its program to convert its economy to socialism. One of those companies was Vertientes.

The *Sabbatino* Case Begins

Cuba claimed ownership of the sugar on board the *Hornsfels* by virtue of the nationalization decree, and it refused to permit the vessel to leave Cuban waters unless someone paid for it. Farr Whitlock had to get the sugar released to meet its obligation to its customers, and so it signed a second contract to buy the sugar, this time from Cuba, again to be paid for upon presentation of proper papers to Farr Whitlock. The *Hornsfels* was then allowed to leave with its cargo.

Complex legal maneuvers ensued over the next two months, with the result that Farr Whitlock got the sugar but refused to pay for it, claiming it didn't know whether to pay Cuba or Vertientes. Cuba, acting through Banco Nacional de Cuba, claimed payment from Vertientes or Farr Whitlock. Vertientes, acting through Peter L. F. Sabbatino, a lawyer who had been appointed by the New York Supreme Court as receiver over its New York property, argued that the nationalization was illegal and hence it was entitled to the proceeds of the sale, being the true owner of the sugar.

And so started *Banco Nacional de Cuba v. Sabbatino*, a case heard before Judge Edward Dimock in December 1960. Arguing for Banco Nacional, I relied on the standard act of state cases, arguing that the court could not inquire into the validity of the nationalization decree. At the end of March 1961, Dimock dismissed our complaint, holding, first, that the act of state doctrine did not apply when the act in question was a violation of international law; and, second, that the nationalization decree here was in violation of such law. He cited no authority at all for the first proposition and only a few ambiguous decisions in foreign courts in support of his second.

The result of the decision was to stand the act of state doctrine on its head. The very purpose of the doctrine, we argued, was to make it unnecessary for the court to judge the validity of the act of a foreign sovereign; to hold that it was not applicable when such act was found by a United States court to be illegal made the doctrine meaningless. The decision was a disappointment—no one ever likes to lose cases—but the case seemed to be on a Supreme Court track and it didn't matter a great deal what a district court held.

An appeal from the district court decision was taken at once. I filed Banco Nacional's brief in August 1961. I again argued that the court had no right to inquire into the validity of the Cuban decree under the act of state doctrine. In view of Dimock's decision, I further argued that if the court were going to make such inquiry, it should find the Cuban decree valid under international law. This latter argument was developed in considerable detail in this and in the subsequent Cuban cases, not only because I thought the decree valid, but also because the stronger the case for legality, the more likely the court would be impelled to avoid the issue by resort to the act of state doctrine.

The briefs submitted by Sabbatino and Farr Whitlock were superficial in the extreme, making no substantive case for their position other than by reference to Dimock's opinion.

A new dimension, however, was added to the case by a petition of Covington and Burling as counsel for Cuban-American Sugar, Inc., for leave to file a brief in the Court of Appeals as *amicus curiae.* Cuban-American Sugar had been treated precisely as had Vertientes in Cuba; it was also a defendant in a suit brought by Banco Nacional in the district court, in which the issues raised were the same as those in the *Sabbatino* case. Cuban-American's petition to file an *amicus* brief was granted as a matter of course.

Rarely does an *amicus* brief contribute much to a case where counsel for each party is competent. In this case, however, participation by the *amicus* made a major difference. Covington and Burling is one of the best firms in Washington, and John Laylin, the partner in charge of this litigation, a topnotch advocate. He was articulate, deft, experienced, and learned, and he exemplified the very best of this country's corporate lawyers. He filed a splendid *amicus curiae* brief at the end of September. It made a thorough and detailed discussion of the applicable international law in much more depth than had Dimock in his opinion, coming to the same conclusion. He disposed of the act of state doctrine as Dimock had done.

The *Bahia de Nipe* Litigation

While all these appellate briefs were being written and shortly before any of them were filed, a situation arose, unexpectedly and coincidentally, to complicate United States–Cuba relations and the *Sabbatino* case. On July 24, 1961, an Eastern Airlines plane was hijacked to Cuba. The incident caused great excitement. The press and the State Department loudly and urgently demanded the immediate return of the plane and its passengers. Cuba sent the passengers back at once but held the plane. In a letter to the United Nations Security Council, Cuba called attention to the fact that since the revolution, anti-Castro Cubans had been hijacking small boats and airplanes from Cuba and running them to Miami and Tampa, frequently with passengers seeking to leave Cuba. The State Department responded by agreeing to return all hijacked property in the future if application were made to the State Department, and so advised the United Nations. Cuba released the Eastern plane on August 16.

The very next day, the captain of the *Bahia de Nipe,* a vessel owned by the Cuban government, diverted the ship from its course and took it into United States territorial waters at Hampton Roads, Virginia, where he and ten members of the crew sought political asylum. The *Bahia* was taken to anchorage where it remained in the custody of the coast guard. Within a few days, United Fruit Sugar Company sued out a writ of attachment in the district court in Virginia against the ship and its cargo of sugar. (This case was litigated under the name of *Rich v. Naviera Vacuba.*) The company claimed that the sugar belonged to it because it came from its plantation, and that the plantation had been taken by a Cuban nationalization decree that, it argued, was contrary to international law and hence invalid. The Cuban decree was the very decree involved in the *Sabbatino* case.

In fact, in every respect the claim of United Fruit was identical with that of Vertientes in the *Sabbatino* case. If Vertientes was entitled to the purchase price of the sugar on board the *Hornsfels,* as Dimock had held, then United Fruit was entitled to the sugar on board the *Bahia de Nipe.* On the other hand, return of the ship and sugar to Cuba was required by the public representations made by the State Department to the United Nations only a few days earlier.

Diplomatic relations between the United States and Cuba had been broken in January 1961, and the Czechoslovak government, acting on behalf of Cuba, immediately advised the State Department that the ship was owned by the Cuban government and was entitled to sovereign immunity. Immediate return of the ship was demanded.

The doctrine of sovereign immunity is one of the oldest and most widely recognized principles of international law. It declares that a sovereign state may not be sued without its consent. As a corollary, ships owned by a sovereign cannot be seized in the course of a lawsuit. But rare is the legal principle that can be seen as permanent. Changing world conditions have forced changes in the law of sovereign immunity, and there are now two exceptions to the rule as applied by the United States courts.

The first is that immunity will be recognized only when the act of the foreign state giving rise to the litigation was "governmental" in its nature but not when the transaction was "commercial." This commercial exception to the rule of sovereign immunity was important in the *Bahia de Nipe* litigation.

The second exception to the general rule is that immunity will not be granted to defeat a counterclaim. This "counterclaim exception" means that if a sovereign state, for example, China, sues a privately owned bank, such as the National City Bank, and the bank makes a counterclaim against China, China cannot rely on its sovereign immunity to defeat the bank's claim. This counterclaim exception to the sovereign immunity rule became (unexpectedly) very important to the Cuba cases ten years later. We'll come back to it.

The problem presented to the State Department by Cuba's claim of sovereign immunity was an embarrassing one. Under the commercial exception, sovereign immunity should have been denied. The *Bahia de Nipe* was transporting sugar—clearly a commercial venture—and should have been subject to seizure in the lawsuit. On the other hand, it had been hijacked and the United States had, shortly before, given its word that it would return hijacked ships. The good faith of the United States was at issue.

So the government of the United States appeared in the Virginia action, and Secretary of State Rusk advised the court (by telephone) on the very day that Cuba filed its claim of sovereign immunity that "[t]he release of this vessel would avoid further disturbance to our international relations in the premises." In argument before the district court shortly after, U.S. government counsel stated that even the short delay of two weeks already caused by the litigation was proving to be a matter of serious embarrassment to the United States and urged immediate release of the ship and its cargo.

When the case was to be argued in the district court, the Cuban government asked us to intervene on its behalf, but the Justice Department urged me very strongly to stay out. The government attorneys assured me they had everything under control (as, indeed, they had), and that my intervention would only be provocative. So I confined my participation to that of a spectator at the hearings, inconspicuous, in the last row of the courtroom. The court agreed with the government and held that the ship and cargo should be released and returned to Cuba, citing the standard sovereign immunity cases. The argument by United Fruit that this was a commercial enterprise and hence not subject to a plea of immunity was disposed of by the court in a few words: "[T]he Judiciary should avoid any conflict with the Executive in the field of international relations."

The ship was the property of Cuba and, therefore, if the commercial exception was to be ignored it was entitled to immunity. But the same would not be true of the cargo of sugar, *unless it, too, was the property of Cuba*. And it belonged to Cuba *only* if the nationalization decree, involved in *Sabbatino,* was to be given effect as an act of state and hence not to be questioned in our courts. United Fruit argued, as had Dimock, that the act of state doctrine was not applicable because the nationalization decree was a violation of international law and hence invalid. Therefore, it maintained, while sovereign immunity might be applicable so far as the vessel is concerned, it could not be applicable to the cargo, which belonged to it and not to Cuba. Dimock's opinion in *Sabbatino* fully supported United Fruit's position, but the attorneys for United Fruit did not cite that decision and seemed to be unaware of it.

The Court of Appeals heard the *Bahia de Nipe* case in an emergency special session on September 5 and it affirmed with a short opinion two days later. No one mentioned the *Sabbatino* case. United Fruit immediately applied to the Supreme Court for an order to prevent the ship from leaving until it had an opportunity to file a petition asking the Court to review the case.

But the State Department knew all about *Sabbatino.* If the district court in *Sabbatino* was wrong, the sugar belonged to Cuba, the plea of sovereign immunity was sufficient, and the sugar could be returned to Cuba, as the United States had promised to the United Nations. On the other hand, if the district court in *Sabbatino* was right, the sugar belonged to United Fruit, sovereign immunity was inapplicable, and the sugar should be returned to its owner.

The State Department opted for the view that Dimock was wrong and that the sugar belonged to Cuba. And so in a memorandum opposing United Fruit, the solicitor general, quoting *Underhill v. Hernandez* and the other act of state cases mentioned above, argued that even if the Cuban nationalization decrees were contrary to international law, the act of state doctrine directed that they could not be challenged in United States courts. Again the *Sabbatino* case was not mentioned.

Chief Justice Warren, before whom this application was made, quickly denied the applications for a stay, citing the usual sovereign immunity cases but also *Underhill v. Hernandez.*

I had followed the progress of the *Bahia de Nipe* case closely; I lived and breathed *Sabbatino* in the fall of 1961 and could not understand why the lawyers for United Fruit had not relied heavily on it. I remember how delighted I was when I saw Warren's reference to the *Underhill* case. This was an act of state case and had nothing to do with sovereign immunity. To me it meant that someone on the Supreme Court understood that United Fruit's claim would fail by virtue of the act of state doctrine. If United Fruit's claim would fail, so would the claim of Vertientes, and we would win the *Sabbatino* case.

Realistically, Warren's reference to an act of state case hardly justified much confidence. *Sabbatino* had not been briefed or even mentioned in the *Bahia de Nipe* papers; Warren's ruling was his own and not that of the Court. There had been little time to consider a difficult question of law. Finally, the ruling by Warren might have been suggested by a clerk six months out of law school who had a smattering of international law.

Still, it was good to think that someone up there seemed to think Dimock was wrong.

Sabbatino in the Court of Appeals

The ruling in the *Bahia de Nipe* case came after the principal briefs in the Court of Appeals had been filed in the *Sabbatino* case, but I relied on it in my reply brief. The *Bahia de Nipe* litigation was not mentioned by the lawyers for the defendants. It was not helpful to them, and besides, they may not have known about it. The application for a stay in that case had consisted of typewritten papers buried deep in the files of the Court, and aside from brief newspaper items, it received no public attention. Furthermore, it required some degree of sophistication to understand the connection between the unreported *Bahia de Nipe* documents and the *Sabbatino* case, and the representatives of the defendants were not all that sophisticated.

But John Laylin was. Ten weeks after he filed his *amicus* brief in the *Sabbatino* case, he filed a slim appendix to the brief with the Court of Appeals. Eight pages long, it contained copies of three letters. The earliest was from Laylin to Secretary of State Rusk, copies of which were sent to Fischer (attorney for Sabbatino) and to Abram Chayes, legal adviser to the State Department, but not to me. It was a complaint about the position taken by the United States in the *Bahia de Nipe* case and viewed with misgiving its possible effect on the pending *Sabbatino* case and the litigation against his client, Cuban-American Sugar.

The second letter was from George Ball, undersecretary of state, to Laylin, with copies to no one. It responded to Laylin's letter to Rusk, stating only that he and Rusk agreed that the department should not comment on matters pending before the courts. The third letter was from

Laylin to Ball. It quoted a single paragraph of still a fourth letter, evidently written by Chayes to Laylin, saying, "Whether or not these nationalizations will in the future be given effect in the United States is, of course, for the courts to determine. Since the *Sabbatino* case and other similar cases are at present before the courts, any comments on this question by the Department of State would be out of place at this time."

Laylin's petition for leave to file the appendix merely stated that the documents contained therein would explain otherwise damaging statements made by the executive branch in the *Bahia de Nipe* litigation. I must confess that I couldn't quite understand what point Laylin was trying to make.

The Court of Appeals heard the appeal in *Sabbatino* in January 1962. The bench consisted of Judges Sterry Waterman, Irving Kaufman, and Thurgood Marshall. The argument, while spirited, was uneventful except that Laylin had received permission to argue on behalf of the *amicus*. It is my recollection that he urged that the correspondence contained in his appendix was a "Bernstein letter." He has since denied that. However, whether or not he intended the court to regard the correspondence recited in the appendix as a Bernstein letter, the court did so.

A "Bernstein letter" is an interesting bit of legal esoterica, an exception to the act of state doctrine, and of paramount importance in the *Sabbatino* and other Cuban cases. It is another piece of the mosaic going to make up the complete picture of the Cuban litigation.

In 1945 and 1946, Arnold Bernstein, a Jewish ship-owner then living in the United States, brought two suits in the Federal court in New York against the Holland-America Line. He alleged that in 1937, he had been a resident of Germany and had owned the Arnold Bernstein Line. In that year, he was arrested by the Gestapo and was told by German officials that unless he surrendered his shipping interests to the Nazis, he would be imprisoned indefinitely. He acceded to those demands and transferred his stock in the line to one Boerger, who, in turn, sold some of the assets of the line to the Holland-America Line. By his suits, Bernstein hoped to recover those assets.

The defendant pleaded the act of state doctrine. The district court, while recognizing the grave injustice done to Bernstein, held that the confiscation of his property was an act of state not to be reviewed by our courts. Bernstein appealed and the Court of Appeals affirmed.

After the decision, the State Department wrote a letter to Bernstein's lawyer (now known as the "Bernstein letter"), stating that it was the policy of the United States government "to undo the forced transfers of property and restitute identifiable property to the victims of Nazi prosecution." In effect the executive branch of the government seemed to be indirectly advising the judicial branch that in considering the acts of Nazi Germany, the act of state doctrine should not apply. In view of this "supervening expression of Executive Policy," the Court of Appeals, on Bernstein's application, amended its decision, held the act of state doctrine inapplicable in those circumstances, and remanded the case to the district court to proceed with a trial on the issues alleged in the complaint.

The case was ultimately settled, and the Supreme Court never passed on the effect of a "Bernstein letter."

There was at the time much difference of opinion in the legal community as to whether the final decision of the Court of Appeals was legally sound. Everyone was emotionally sympathetic to Bernstein; however, the act of state doctrine was an important legal principle, and every time it is applied, someone gets hurt, usually some innocent party. The critics of the action of the Court of Appeals argued that principles of law could not be ignored because in a specific case it resulted in a seeming injustice. Even more important was the feeling that this was an interference by the executive branch with the functioning of the judicial branch of the government.

The Court of Appeals handed down its decision in the *Sabbatino* case in July 1962. The court, speaking through Judge Waterman, recited the standard act of state cases and then referred to the *Bernstein* case. "[The Bernstein] exception [to the act of state doctrine] is applicable to the case before us," the court said. "While this case was pending we have been enlightened as the court was in the *Bernstein* case . . . as to the attitude of the State Department." The court then quoted from the documents contained in Laylin's appendix. These documents were characterized by the court as "somewhat ambiguous, perhaps intentionally so," but they were held to be a release from the act of state doctrine.

Having held that the act of state doctrine was not applicable, Waterman was free to address the question of the validity of the Cuban decree under international law, just as Dimock had done. As was inevitable under the circumstances, he concluded, like Dimock, that the Cuban decrees were in violation of international law, though for slightly different reasons. The Dimock decision was affirmed.

The case was the most widely discussed international law litigation in a generation, and everyone knew that the issue of the effect of the Cuban decrees in U.S. courts was on its way to the Supreme Court. It was not only investors in Cuba who were vitally concerned. Social unrest was endemic to most of Latin America and indeed to most of the Southern Hemisphere, and similar nationalizations might occur almost anywhere.

But the reliance of the Court of Appeals on Laylin's correspondence with the State Department as a Bernstein letter, to avoid the act of state doctrine, was startling. It is difficult even now to see how three experienced judges could have committed such gross error. Quite aside from the ambiguous nature of those letters, it is elementary that a case on appeal must be decided on the record in the lower court and that new evidence cannot be introduced at the appellate level. It is also elementary that evidence cannot be introduced by the unilateral act of any of the parties, without giving the other parties an opportunity to examine the evidence and to inquire into its authenticity, its competency, its meaning, its reliability. It would be a violation of due process of law for an appellate court to consider evidence not before the lower court except for rare cases where intervening events are unambiguous matters of public record (as when a party to litigation dies).

The evidence on which the Court of Appeals relied in finding a Bernstein letter here was not only outside the record; it was submitted by an *amicus curiae,* by means of a written brief on the appeal. No opportunity was afforded to any party to challenge the letters, to question their authenticity, or even to get their complete text.

I considered a motion for reargument, but I made a tactical decision to apply at once to the Supreme Court for review. The error was central to Waterman's opinion, it was of constitutional dimensions, and it was so far reaching in its implications that it seemed impossible that the Supreme Court could refuse to hear the case.

Moreover, I felt that the Court of Appeals had made clear its ultimate intention and that a motion to reargue would merely give it an opportunity to clean up gross error. Better an appeal from a decision that is palpably bad than one that is only arguably bad. And so we filed a petition for review in September. That petition contained all of the arguments on the merits that had been argued in the court below, in addition to which we pointed out the impropriety of reliance on the letters submitted by Laylin.

Sabbatino in the Supreme Court

As anticipated, the Supreme Court requested the solicitor general to express his views. Solicitor General Archibald Cox agreed that the petition for review should be granted, pointing out, in a very few pages, that the issue was an important one and that there were thirty-six other Cuban cases pending in New York alone, in many of which similar issues were raised. He then addressed himself to the "Bernstein letter" aspect of the decision below, and told an interesting story of high-level lobbying in a litigation context.

Cox first noted that it was not altogether clear that a "Bernstein letter" was a permissible or desirable limitation on the act of state doctrine, pointing out that the Supreme Court had never considered the matter. He went on to discuss the correspondence allegedly constituting the Bernstein letter, stating that "a full account of the correspondence and surrounding circumstances (which counsel did not lay before the court [of appeals])" makes it plain "that the court's assumption that the State Department had written a Bernstein letter was erroneous."

Cox pointed out that in the ten weeks after the termination of the *Bahia de Nipe* litigation, after briefs in *Sabbatino* had been filed in the Court of Appeals, Laylin had directed eleven letters to high-ranking members of the State and Justice Departments. Cox said: "While the letters differed in detail, the purpose of all of them was to obtain . . . from the Executive Branch and particularly from the Department of State, a clear declaration that would serve to lift any restraint upon the judiciary's examination of acts of nationalization by the Government of Cuba."

Cox then set forth the full correspondence from which Laylin had selected the excerpts presented to the Court of Appeals. There was, he said, no Bernstein letter but only "a statement of 'no comment.'"

The Supreme Court agreed to hear the case.

By the time the *Sabbatino* case was heard in the Supreme Court, three *amicus* briefs had been submitted by Establishment bar associations, all three opposing the position of Banco Nacional. Laylin wrote another fine *amicus* brief for Cuban American Sugar (now rechristened North American Sugar Industries). He disavowed any intention of arguing that his correspondence with members of the executive branch constituted a Bernstein letter but argued, somewhat obscurely, that the correspondence was submitted to the Court of Appeals for some other reason that I still do not understand. The solicitor general filed a brief on behalf of the United States, in support of the act of state doctrine.

When the case was called for argument before the Supreme Court on the afternoon of October 22, 1962, Vertientes was represented by the suave and somewhat pontifical Whitney North Seymour, one of the senior members of the corporate bar in New York. Farr Whitlock was rep-

resented by F. Dickerman Williams. The Justice Department participated
in the argument and was represented by Deputy Attorney General
Nicholas de B. Katzenbach. I represented Banco Nacional.

The courtroom was crowded when the *Sabbatino* case was called, although, I must confess, not altogether because of the pendency of that
case. Actually the court had just heard argument in an important political case, namely contempt proceedings against Governor Ross Barnett,
of Mississippi. But the international law establishment was quite well
represented when the *Sabbatino* argument proceeded, shortly after noon.
An hour and a half was allotted each side, an unusually long time in these
days of crowded calendars. (The case of *McCullough v. Maryland* had
been argued by Daniel Webster and others for six days, but that was in
another century and it is doubtful whether we will ever see a return to
those leisurely times.)

This argument, unlike that in *ACA v. Douds*, was pure joy. All nine
of the justices were there and all seemed to be listening intently to the
argument. The issues were clear and important; counsel were experienced and knew the record; enough time had been allowed for the development of arguments, and the argument was exhilarating.

All of us have a style in making oral arguments, and mine has always
been to avoid excessive formality and to try to turn oral arguments into
a conversation between myself and the court—a conversation that, when
I am successful, might have taken place between equals in a living room.
I'm not always successful—it depends a great deal on the personality of
the court, but at least I try. And so I opened my argument in the *Sabbatino* case with an attempt at a witticism—one that I thought up at the
moment I arose to address the court.

Legal jokes at their best are seldom very funny and this one was so
subtle that I now doubt if anyone other than myself understood it. It
concerned an inkwell, an object far removed from the sugar on board the
Hornsfels.

In the case preceding ours, the issue presented to the court was whether Barnett was entitled to a jury trial on charges that he had been guilty
of contempt of court in refusing to permit James Meredith, an African
American, to enroll in the University of Mississippi Law School—an
issue of great importance because no Mississippi jury in 1963 was likely
to convict the governor of the state of such a charge.

It has always been clear that contempt committed in the presence of
a judge could be punished by the court summarily, without the necessity of a trial, but there was an open question as to whether other forms

of contempt required trial by jury. An English case in the mid-eighteenth century had been referred to in the course of the *Barnett* argument—a case I remembered well from law school—in which the contempt alleged was that "a Yankee threw an inkwell at the judge"—an offense clearly not calling for a jury trial.

The desks at which counsel sit at a Supreme Court argument are decorated with a pair of quill pens, intended, I suppose, to emphasize the antiquity of the court. I opened my argument by saying, "I note that the Court supplies pens for counsel but not inkwells." I thought that was a good, informal way to get the argument going, but the Court evidently didn't appreciate my sense of humor. Brennan, with some sharpness, said, "Does that have anything to do with this case?" I apologized and went ahead with the argument.*

I thought it went well. The Justices were all interested and their questions were (mostly) relevant. I was in high spirits and gloried in the occasion. I was, I felt, making some kind of history.

On March 23, 1964, the Supreme Court reversed the Court of Appeals by an eight-to-one vote. It was a splendid surprise, not only in the result, but also in the totality of the victory for Banco Nacional. Speaking for eight members of the Court, Justice John Harlan held that the act of state doctrine was a vital part of our law and that our courts could not examine the validity of the Cuban decrees.

Harlan rapidly sketched the history of the act of state doctrine, pointing out that its roots can be found in English cases as early as 1674. The Court cited the usual act of state cases such as *Underhill v. Hernandez*. It quickly disposed of the so-called "Bernstein" exception to the act of state doctrine; it was an exception upon which the Supreme Court had never passed, and further, it was clear that there was no Bernstein letter here.

Harlan then addressed the principal issues in the case—"the foundations on which we deem the act of state to rest" and its application to a situation in which it is claimed that the act was in violation of international law.

The act of state doctrine, said Harlan, has "constitutional underpinnings" and "arises out of the basic relationship between branches of

---

*Years later, I argued one of the Cuban cases in the Court of Appeals in New York, at which the usual sprinkling of international law aficionados attended. My wife Joanne sat next to one dignified gentleman who, as I rose to make my argument, whispered to his companion, "That's the fellow who made the terrible gaffe before the Supreme Court in the *Sabbatino* case."

government in a system of separation of powers." It expresses the "strong sense of the Judicial Branch that its engagement in the task of passing on the validity of foreign acts of state" was undesirable. That was particularly true in the case at hand because, the Court went on, "there are few if any issues in international law today on which opinion seems to be so divided as the limitations on a state's power to expropriate the property of aliens." It is difficult, said the Court, "to imagine the courts of this country embarking on an adjudication in an area which touches more sensitively the practical and ideological goals of the various members of the community of nations."

The Court then turned to a consideration of the dangers of submitting such issues to a court. Following a nationalization of any significance, the executive will usually engage in diplomatic activity to protect the rights of affected United States citizens and is likely to take a position as to the legality of such nationalization. When a court is called upon to pass on the validity of such nationalization, its action is certain to come at a later time. If the court then agrees with the views expressed by the State Department, it is likely to give affront to the nationalizing state. But, the Court said, "Considerably more serious and far-reaching consequences would flow from a judicial finding that international law standards had been met if that determination flew in the face of a State Department proclamation to the contrary."

Harlan was one of the most conservative judges on the bench during his seventeen-year tenure. An excellent lawyer, a man of integrity and honesty, he came out of a corporate background in New York and generally expressed the views of the right wing of the Court. He was a capable spokesman for the commercial and banking interests of the country, and the fact that he upheld the act of state doctrine gave the result great weight, and the near unanimity of the Court came as a shock to the opposition. Harlan's vote arose out of his respect for the integrity of the Court and for the doctrine of the separation of powers manifested in many of his other opinions. It was not the executive branch he was protecting, but the integrity of the judicial branch. As we shall see, when the personnel of the Court changed in later years, only a minority of its members shared or seemed to understand his concern.

The lone dissenter in *Sabbatino* was Justice Byron White. A Kennedy appointee, he had one of the sharpest minds on the bench. Originally regarded as something of a swing man between the liberal and conservative members of the Court, of recent years he had come down most often on the conservative side.

The case was remanded to the district court "for proceedings consistent with this opinion," a ritualistic phrase that would normally mean merely the entry of final judgment in favor of Banco Nacional. This was not, however, the end of the *Sabbatino* case.

The act of state doctrine was the battleground on which the Cuban litigation raged for the next fifteen years. The ink was hardly dry on Harlan's signature to the *Sabbatino* decision when the opposition moved in. Even before final judgment was entered, the international law Establishment began its counterattack. A bill, sponsored by an *ad hoc* committee calling itself the Rule of Law Committee, was introduced by Senator Hickenlooper as an amendment to the annual Foreign Aid Bill. The members of the committee stated that they were "deeply disturbed" by the decision in the *Sabbatino* case and feared that the impact of that decision would have an adverse effect on overseas investments, "particularly in the less developed countries." And so the committee felt that action by Congress was necessary in order to avoid this "practical threat to U.S. foreign investment."

The bill was adopted by a voice vote, without debate and without public notice. There was a strong lobby in its favor, and not a single member of either house of Congress raised any question about the bill. Cuba had no representatives watching for such unobtrusive legislation, and we knew nothing about the bill until it was passed, although we couldn't have done anything to prevent its passage in any event. The law became effective in October, by which time the district court still had not entered a judgment in the *Sabbatino* case.

The language of the bill was confusing and the syntax unclear. Its precise meaning was the subject of a good deal of litigation in subsequent cases. It appeared from congressional hearings,* however, that it was intended to bar the use of the act of state doctrine in *Sabbatino*-type cases, namely, cases in which property that had been nationalized by the Cuban government was later brought to the United States and sought to be introduced into normal stream of commerce in this country. At least, that was the interpretation that the courts finally fastened upon, although it was argued by the opposition to Cuba in the ensuing litigation that it was intended to have a much broader effect.

*By its terms, the bill was to be effective for only a year, but in 1965 it was extended after extensive hearings before congressional committees at which Katzenbach and a number of law school professors opposed the bill. There was, however, no dissent in Congress in 1965.

And so we were confronted with a new law obviously intended to change *the law* applied by the Court in its *Sabbatino* decision. Whether it intended to change *the decision* in *Sabbatino* itself was not so clear, and so when the defendants moved for judgment in their favor, relying on the Hickenlooper amendment, I argued that if the statute was to be applied retroactively to reverse the decision of the Supreme Court, it was unconstitutional.

We were unsuccessful before Judge Frederick Van Pelt Bryan* when he got around to considering the *Sabbatino* case (now entitled *Banco Nacional v. Farr Whitlock*) on remand. I argued that the law, if applied retroactively, would be unconstitutional. I was supported by Bruno Ristau, one of the highest ranking lawyers in the Justice Department, who appeared in the district court and argued in support of my position. But Bryan would have none of that; he was not the man to defy the clearly expressed wishes of Congress. He found the statute retroactively effective and granted judgment against the plaintiffs. At the end of July, the Court of Appeals affirmed by unanimous vote. The Supreme Court refused to hear our appeal—it had reviewed the case once and was not disposed to do it again. So the *Sabbatino* case was over. We had won on an important matter of principal, but we never enjoyed the tangible fruits of that victory.

By 1961, most of the cases on our calendar of Cuban cases had been settled or otherwise disposed of, but a sizable number of important matters were left. Early in 1961, it became clear that if the pending cases were assigned randomly to the many judges sitting in the Southern District, as the court rules then provided, our work and that of the court would be made much more difficult. International law was not a subject familiar to many of the judges, and the task of educating each successive judge into the mysteries of such law seemed overwhelming. Moreover, many of the cases were interrelated, and we saw a mess ahead if each judge handled his own case at his own speed in accord with his personal temperament and calendar requirements.

The court rules provided that related cases could be assigned to a single judge, and so, in the spring of 1961, Leonard and I paid a visit to Judge Sylvester Ryan, then Chief Judge, to ask him to make such an order. The judge had it in his power to do us serious injury by appointing a radical right-wing judge (of whom we have had our share) who could make life miserable for us for years. We were old acquaintances,

---

*Judge Bryan had replaced Dimock when the latter retired. See below.

Ryan and our office, and relations between us had been at times quite stormy. He had been the judge in *United States v. Coplon,* and had appointed Leonard and Sam Neuburger to represent Judy Coplon when she and her earlier lawyer had parted company in the midst of her trial for espionage. He had been the judge in litigation arising out of the flight of four Communist party leaders after their conviction in the first Smith Act case and he had given me a hard time in that case. Then, over our loud protests, he had sought to appoint Leonard and me as counsel in the second Smith Act case. Further, Ryan was politically quite conservative—even reactionary. His attitude toward Cuba wasn't likely to be friendly.

But he was an experienced judge, a competent lawyer, and he had a sense of humor, which was his saving grace. He quickly agreed that all cases should be sent to a single judge. (Judge Dimock, who had by that date decided the *Sabbatino* case, had retired a few weeks earlier.)

I suggested, somewhat tentatively, that, "Your Honor will, of course, keep in mind the fact that the issues are very complex, and that the judge appointed ought to be one of the more competent judges in the district."

"All judges in the district are equally competent," was the inevitable reply, not without the trace of a smile. "Let us say, rather, that some judges like complicated and difficult cases, and some do not. Let us see who we have available who likes complicated cases."

His eye ran down a list of judges. "Here's the man—Freddie Bryan. A judge who loves complicated cases." And so it was. On August 7, 1961, all Cuban cases were assigned to Freddie Bryan.

Frederick Van Pelt Bryan had been appointed to the bench by President Eisenhower in 1956. He had run unsuccessfully for Congress against Vito Marcantonio in 1946. A more unlikely opponent to Marc would be hard to imagine. Marc was radical, fiery, and eloquent—a vibrant orator schooled in the streets of East Harlem. Bryan was dignified, soft spoken, and aristocratic in appearance and bearing. With his benign and paternalistic smile, and his white walrus-type mustache, he looked the prototype of the conservative judge. He did not fit at all in the rough politics of the Eighteenth Congressional District.

But he did fit on the federal court, and his reputation was a pretty good one—conscientious, a good lawyer though not brilliant, a nice fellow. He had a good record in First Amendment cases and, a few years earlier, had set aside a post office ban on the importation of an unexpurgated edition of *Lady Chatterley's Lover,* holding that the postmaster general had no special competence to judge obscenity. On the whole, he was a good enough choice for our cases considering the alternatives, although hardly the judge one would choose for breaking new ground or for an imaginative and innovative approach to the law in a case with political implications. Besides, most of the issues would be going on to the appellate courts anyhow, and it was sufficient if we had a good-natured judge to help us make the necessary record.

Bryan turned out to have another characteristic, too. He was not only thorough and careful—he was very, very slow. The fact that the issues in the cases were interlocking exacerbated a situation that would have been difficult in any event, but, as we shall see, the extraordinary deliberation with which he acted dragged the litigation out beyond all reason.

One other aspect of the appointment was distressing but inevitable, and it related not only to Bryan but to most other public officials with whom we had to deal. The old boy network was firmly in place. Early in the spring of 1965, Bryan had occasion to call a conference in chambers between me, representing Banco Nacional, and Henry Harfield, a pleasant, witty, very upper-class lawyer and a senior partner at Sherman and Sterling, representing First National City Bank. After the business of our meeting was over and we were collecting our papers and coats, Harfield said to Bryan: "Well, Judge, it's about time for our regular fishing trip, isn't it? The trout must be running pretty well." Bryan responded: "Yes, the weather is getting warmer. I'll be in touch with you to see when we can both get free for a couple of days." Bryan and Harfield then noted that I was standing alongside, and both were considerably embarrassed. Harfield made the recovery first, with the best comment he could think of on short notice: "Oh, Victor," he said, "why don't you join us this year?" I declined politely.

Years later, when four major Cuban cases that had been tried before Bryan were still undecided, the judge died, and it became necessary to choose a successor. Harfield and I met with Judge David Edelstein, then the chief judge of the district court. After we concluded our business and were leaving, Harfield said to Edelstein, "Judge, remember that fish we caught in Shinnecock Bay, that we couldn't recognize—well, it was a shad, although I don't know what a shad was doing in Shinnecock Bay." Edelstein chuckled, while I considered the advisability of taking up fishing as a hobby to supplement my legal practice.

It was not only the judges with whom we dealt who were on first-name terms with our opposition. The same was almost routinely true of State and Treasury Department officials with whom we met. The standard form of greeting was "Hello, John; Hello, David; Hello, Mr. Rabinowitz." Disquieting, but not surprising.

The *Citibank* Case

During the long saga of the *Sabbatino/Farr Whitlock* case, the many Cuban cases still pending before Bryan had marked time. But with *Sabbatino* out of the way, he turned to the rest of his Cuban calendar. *Banco Nacional v. First National City Bank of New York* ("Citibank") and *Banco Nacional v. Chase Manhattan Bank* came first. These important cases both raised act of state issues and in both, millions of dollars were involved. There were at least six other Cuban cases on Bryan's calendar.

The *Citibank* case arose under the following circumstances. In 1958, a Cuban state bank had borrowed $15,000,000 from Citibank and deposited as security United States government bonds having a face value well in excess of that figure. After the revolution, when the United States–owned banks in Cuba were nationalized, Citibank promptly declared its loan to Cuba to be in default and sold the security. It realized almost $2,000,000 in excess of the amount of the loan and when, in November 1960, Banco Nacional sued for that sum, Citibank conceded its liability on the $2,000,000 excess but counterclaimed for the value of its nationalized property, claiming that the nationalization decree was in violation of international law. Banco Nacional conceded that Citibank's property in Cuba was worth more than $2,000,000 but moved to dismiss the counterclaim, arguing, as it had in *Sabbatino:* (1) the act of state doctrine barred the court from examining the validity of the nationalization decree; (2) if the act of state doctrine was not applicable, Cuba had not violated international law. Judgment for the $2,000,000 excess was demanded.

The facts in the *Chase* case were substantially identical, except that the excess realized by Chase in its sale of the securities deposited with it by Cuba was about $9,000,000, and judgment in that sum was demanded.

Citibank came first on Bryan's calendar. Immediately after passage of the Hickenlooper amendment, Citibank moved to dismiss our claim, arguing that the amendment had made the act of state doctrine inapplicable to any nationalization case. After a lapse of three years, Bryan held the amendment applicable, and the act of state doctrine therefore inapplicable. He then proceeded to find, as had Dimock and Waterman before him, that the nationalization decrees of Cuba were in violation of international law.

The *Citibank* case was briefed for the Court of Appeals in 1969. We made a detailed analysis of the Hickenlooper amendment. Citibank, in its brief, was flippant about the whole matter. It merely referred to the Hickenlooper amendment as a "statutory affirmation of those principles which are embodied in the Constitution of the United States and in the United States' construction and interpretation of international law."

The case was argued before Judges J. Edward Lumbard, Paul Hays, and Joseph Blumenthal. I couldn't tell, during the argument, whether Hays was listening or even awake, but the other two certainly were, and they participated actively in the argument. Despite the argument, which I thought went well, despite the good brief we had written, despite what I thought was a rather poor presentation by counsel for Citibank, I never really expected to win. Thus, I was startled to receive a call from Lumbard's clerk on a sunny morning in July, advising me that we had a unanimous decision in our favor. Lumbard made a thorough review of the legislative history of the Hickenlooper amendment, taking most of his analysis from our brief, and held that it did not apply. The *Sabbatino* decision, applying the act of state doctrine, was therefore applicable to strike Citibank's counterclaim, and Cuba was entitled to judgment.

The decision seemed to offer a break in the gloom that followed our failure to collect our judgment in *Sabbatino*. Joanne and I memorialized the occasion by having dinner at Lutèce, then a four-star French restaurant, not one we often frequented. But under the circumstances, we felt that nothing was too good for us, and we had a very pleasant, very expensive evening. Delicious rack of lamb (pink), a tasteful goat cheese salad, and, for dessert, crêpes Suzette, a delicacy that has disappeared from the menu of restaurants I patronize these days. This was all topped off with a rich Margaux. We returned to Lutèce about ten years later to celebrate the nationwide telecast of her fine documentary film, *Fundi: The Story of Ella Baker*.

My euphoria was short lived. I was very apprehensive by the time Citibank filed its petition for review in the Supreme Court. The personnel of the executive branch had changed materially since the *Sabbatino* decision. Lyndon Johnson had been succeeded as president by Richard Nixon, and Robert Kennedy had been succeeded as attorney general by John Mitchell (whose firm had represented Farr Whitlock in the early days of the *Sabbatino* litigation). Cox was no longer solicitor general, and Katzenbach was no longer deputy attorney general. John Stevenson (a long-standing outspoken opponent of the act of state doctrine) had replaced Chayes as legal adviser to the State Department. While the petition for review was pending, Stevenson wrote a letter to the Supreme Court. Referring to the Bernstein letter as a precedent for his intervention, he stated, in part, that the State Department "believes that the act of state doctrine should not be applied to bar consideration of a defendant's counterclaim or set-off against the Government of Cuba in this or like cases." He cited, as authority, a case entitled *National City Bank v. Republic of China.**

The Supreme Court sent the case back to the Court of Appeals "for reconsideration in light of the views of the Department of State expressed in its letter." Back we went to the same Court of Appeals panel for a second argument. We won again, but Hays dissented this time. The majority opinion was once again written by Lumbard, who held that the Stevenson letter was a modern "Bernstein letter," and that the Bernstein exception was not applicable.

Again, Citibank filed a petition for review, and the Supreme Court again granted the petition.

By this time, I had little ground for optimism, despite the double victory in the Court of Appeals. Major changes in the personnel of the Supreme Court had sharply eroded the eight-to-one majority in the *Sabbatino* case. Warren, Clark, and Goldberg had retired; Harlan and Black had died. White, the dissenter in *Sabbatino,* was still on the bench. Of the replacements since 1964, only Marshall, who was not likely to be affected by the views of the Nixon administration, seemed to offer hope of support. The others seemed likely to be hostile. Chief Justice Warren Burger, while on the Court of Appeals of the District of Columbia, had dissented from a decision of that court applying the act of state doctrine in the first of the Cuba nationalization cases, back in 1960. Justice William Rehnquist was the spokesman for the most conservative elements in the Nixon administration. Justices Powell and Blackmun were unknown quantities but were generally regarded as being administration men, and the open hostility of the administration in this case did not bode well for Banco Nacional.

The remaining judges seemed pretty safe votes, but they would make up only a minority. Douglas, of course, was a sure vote for us. Aside from the fact that he had joined in the *Sabbatino* decision and had been, with

*The Republic of China case involved not the act of state doctrine but sovereign immunity. In that case, an agency of the prerevolutionary Chinese government sued the National City Bank to recover a deposit made by it in 1948. The bank counterclaimed on defaulted Treasury notes issued by the Chinese government, and China pleaded sovereign immunity as a defense to the counterclaim. The court held that China could not, on the one hand, invoke our law and, at the same time, resist a claim against it on sovereign immunity grounds. This was the origin of the "counterclaim exception" to the doctrine of sovereign immunity to which I referred on page 223.

Black, the foremost spokesman for progressive views during his long career on the bench, he had written extensively on the problems of underdeveloped countries and could be counted on to understand the problems of Cuba in attempting to build a new society. He was not likely to be politically moved or shocked by the fact that the property of Citibank had been taken without compensation. Nor was he going to be overly impressed by the Stevenson letter.

Just as safe were Justices Brennan and Stewart, both independent judges who had been on the *Sabbatino* bench and were not likely to be swayed by State Department pressure. Marshall, I assumed, would vote with his liberal brethren.

Douglas, Brennan, Stewart, and Marshall: that made four votes. For the life of me I couldn't see where that fifth vote would come from. It looked like trouble ahead. I was right—but the trouble that arose wasn't what we anticipated.

The argument was vigorous since I knew I had a hostile bench and I felt the only chance I had was to be aggressive. I was particularly anxious to emphasize what I considered the primary concern of the act of state doctrine as developed by Harlan in *Sabbatino*. And so in the course of the argument I said:

> Suppose this Court, after consideration of the law, should be impelled, as I would urge it to do, to hold that [the nationalization of Citibank] was not a violation of international law at all. This Court would then be placed in a position of having to disagree with the State Department on a question on which the State Department had expressed itself, not once but many times.
>
> And I submit that this Court should not be placed in that position. This Court should not be placed in a position where it may be called upon to express opinion on questions of international law which are contrary to the opinions expressed by the Executive Branch in pursuit of . . . the Executive Branch's foreign policy, because that's its responsibility.

At this point, Stewart nodded, closed his notebook, and sat back, apparently satisfied. I knew I had his vote.

The decision came down in June. As we had feared, we lost by a five-to-four vote, but it was not the five-to-four vote I had foreseen. We won the support of Blackmun and lost the vote of Douglas.

Four separate opinions were written, none representing a majority view. Rehnquist, writing for himself and for Burger and White, had gone down the line with the administration's wishes as expressed by Stevenson. He held that *Sabbatino* was not applicable here because the act of state doctrine is justified "primarily on the basis that judicial review of acts of state of a foreign power could embarrass the conduct of foreign relations by the political branches of the government." Since in this case the executive branch through the Stevenson/Bernstein letter had stated that its interests did not require the application of the doctrine, it should not be applied. Therefore, the case should be remanded to the Court of Appeals for further proceedings on the issue that had not yet been decided, that is, what was the applicable international law. This was the point that the Court of Appeals had held adversely to us in the *Sabbatino* and *Farr Whitlock* cases. Not much hope on remand.

Powell wrote a decision in which he spoke for himself alone. He said he didn't like the act of state doctrine much and that he would consider application of the doctrine on a case-by-case basis. This was one of the cases in which he would not apply the doctrine. He did make clear that he was not at all influenced by the Stevenson letter because he considered it irrelevant; similarly irrelevant was the fact that the act of state doctrine was being pleaded as a defense to a counterclaim. Just what he did consider relevant he didn't say.

The surprising opinion of Douglas made up the fifth vote needed to reverse. He agreed with five other members of the bench that the Stevenson/Bernstein letter was irrelevant, but in fact he bought all of Stevenson's arguments.

Like Stevenson, he relied on the Supreme Court decision in the *Republic of China* case decided fifteen years before, which established a "counterclaim exception" to the sovereign immunity doctrine, and urged a similar exception to the act of state doctrine. It was unfair, he said, for Cuba to invoke our law and at the same time resist a claim against it on act of state grounds. He was the only justice relying on this argument alone; five justices expressly disagreed.

Douglas, never noted for his careful reasoning, should have been able to distinguish between sovereign immunity and act of state. It is true that sovereign immunity and act of state have an element in common. In both instances, a court abstains from deciding an issue because a foreign sovereign is charged with having done something that results in litigation. But there the similarity ends. The two doctrines have different historical roots and different justifications.

Sovereign immunity is dictated by respect for international comity and the "power and dignity" of the foreign sovereign. It is applicable only when the sovereign (or its agent) is being sued. It is a doctrine recognized, at least in principle, by most countries, and derives from the ancient maxim that the king can do no wrong. It is a right of the sovereign and hence may be waived by it. Under the modern doctrine, a sovereign waives that immunity when it engages in a commercial transaction. The *Republic of China* case held that it also waives its immunity when it institutes an action in the courts of this country and then seeks to plead its sovereign immunity as a defense to a counterclaim against it.

The act of state doctrine is quite different, and this difference lies at the core of much of the Cuban litigation. As Harlan pointed out, in *Sabbatino*, the doctrine has "constitutional underpinnings." Its purpose is not to avoid embarrassment to the executive but to protect the independence of the judiciary. A court ought not to be put in a position where it might be impelled to make a finding that "flew in the face of a State Department proclamation to the contrary." Brennan, writing for four dissenting justices in *Citibank*, likewise expressed concern that the Rehnquist view might result in the Court's becoming "embroiled" in a question that was basically political.

Hence, the executive cannot "waive" application of the act of state doctrine, nor can a foreign state by its action make the doctrine inapplicable. Neither does the act of state doctrine have anything to do with considerations of "fairness." The rule is concerned with the structure of the government and the role of the judiciary in it, considerations that are more important than the rights of an individual in a specific case.

The decision in the *Citibank* case was an anomalous one. Only three judges (Burger, Rehnquist and White) decided on the basis of the Stevenson letter; the other six specifically said that the letter was irrelevant. Only one judge (Douglas) based his opinion on the fact that Cuba was pleading the act of state as a defense to a counterclaim; five others specifically disavowed that argument. No one expressly disagreed with *Sabbatino*, though probably four would have overruled it if necessary. On every issue before the Court a majority of the justices agreed with Banco Nacional; yet a combination of minority views was sufficient to result in a reversal. And so ended the Citibank case.

I've lost many cases in my legal career, but never one that made me as angry as this. When a reactionary court makes a reactionary decision (as in *ACA v. Douds*), I can take it in stride. I was frightened by the probable consequences of that decision, but given the political ambiance of the case, the result was to be expected. However, there was no excuse for the decision of the court in the *Citibank* case, and especially for the opinion and vote of Douglas. I've never thought highly of him. Compared to great modern jurists like Brennan and Black, he doesn't stand up well despite his long series of fine opinions in cases involving the First Amendment. I can respect White's views in the Cuban cases, and even Rehnquist's—they are intelligent conservatives voting the conservative line. But Douglas's vote was stupid; it was possible only because he was too careless to think rigorously.*

The Tobacco Cases

One other Supreme Court case considered the act of state doctrine, once again resulting in a five-to-four vote against Cuba. On its facts, this case was the most complicated of all the Cuban cases. It commenced in 1961 and was not decided by the Supreme Court until 1976, after two arguments in that court. A detailed analysis of the facts would serve no purpose—they are neither interesting nor important. However, the case does have a bearing on the act of state doctrine, and the two arguments in the Supreme Court were, as always, exciting events. The facts, somewhat oversimplified, were as follows:

In September 1960, Cuba "intervened"† the properties of Garcia Menendez and Company, Palicio and Company, Cienfuegos and Company, and Por Larranaga and Company, names that will be familiar to all cigar smokers over the age of fifty. For years before that date, and for several months thereafter, those Cuban-owned companies had been manufacturing and shipping cigars to United States importers, one of which was Alfred Dunhill of London. The importers paid for those cigars on normal commercial credit terms, for the most part sixty or ninety days after delivery. Prior to intervention, payment for the cigars had been made by the importers to the Havana cigar factories through ordinary bank drafts; after intervention, payment was made to the interventor—the Cuban government representative—on the same terms.

---

*Douglas wasn't paying very close attention to the case. He voted to remand the case to the district court for determination of an issue that had been stipulated out of the case from the beginning. This appeared not only from the record, but from several briefs of the parties, from the opinions of the Court of Appeals, and from the opinion of Rehnquist.

†Intervention is a Latin American procedure which does not deprive the owner of title to his property but gives to a government agent, the "interventor," the power to manage it for a time. It is roughly analogous to a receivership in our law. Intervention, when it lasts for a long time, is much the same as nationalization, and in the Cuba cases, the United States courts have refused to recognize a difference.

Trading in cigars continued until after the Christmas season in 1960, when it was brought to a halt by the institution of litigation in the United States by the former Cuban owners of the companies. Extensive litigation followed, involving seven different parties and innumerable claims, counterclaims and crossclaims. The only result that need concern us here is a finding by the district court that the intervenor owed Dunhill about fifty thousand dollars on a counterclaim by the latter, which the intervenor refused to pay. I argued that such refusal was an act of state, the intervenor being an agent of the Cuban government. Dunhill argued that there was no act of state; that if there was, it was not applicable on a defense to a counterclaim (as Douglas had held in *Citibank*) and that the *Sabbatino* decision ought to be overruled in any event.

The district court held that the only evidence of an act of state was my statement during the course of trial, and that such a statement was not sufficient. The Court of Appeals reversed, holding that the mere refusal to pay a debt was, in itself, an act of state.

The Supreme Court agreed to review the case and instructed the parties to brief two questions: Can counsel's statement that the intervenor would not honor Dunhill's counterclaim constitute an act of state? Was the counterclaim exception created by the *Citibank* case applicable here? (At least I think that's what the Court meant, although its language was not clear.)

An attorney does not lightly refuse to brief issues framed by the Supreme Court, and I deliberated for a long time before declining to brief the two issues posed by the Court in this case. But I did so anyhow, because I thought neither question was a proper one for the Court's consideration. As to the first issue, I pointed out that I had never argued that my statement in court was an act of state; as to the second, there was no counterclaim exception created by the *Citibank* case. Otherwise, I argued, as I had successfully in the Court of Appeals, that the intervenor's refusal to pay the debt was itself an act of state.

I came back in the midst of a year's sabbatical in England to argue the case in December 1974. It was an enjoyable argument. By this time everyone on the Court was pretty well up on the Cuban cases, and its personnel had not changed since the *Citibank* case. All I had to do, I thought, was to recapture Douglas.

Many members of the bench greeted me as an old friend. White was particularly cordial, a circumstance I recognized as a bad sign. Burger, with a pleasant smile, even allowed me to speak about seven minutes beyond my allotted time—very ominous indeed. Everyone was quite pleasant.

Except for Douglas. In the course of my argument I addressed him directly, in a polite effort to convince him that his position in the *Citibank* case was wrong (as we lawyers say, "It should be reexamined"). All I got in return was an angry snarl.

To my surprise, the Court ordered reargument and heard the case again in January 1976, by which time Justice Douglas had retired, to be succeeded by Justice Stevens, an unknown quantity. This time, in ordering reargument, the Court asked counsel to brief the question of whether *Sabbatino* should be overruled. In addition, the Justice Department submitted an *amicus* brief suggesting that the Court should create a commercial exception to the act of state doctrine, as Dunhill had requested. This really scared me. Clearly, the *Sabbatino* decision was under serious attack, and most of my argument before the Court was devoted to a defense of that decision. "*Sabbatino* is as good law today as it was when Justice Harlan wrote his opinion in 1964," I said. White, smiling broadly, responded, "At last, Mr. Rabinowitz, you have said something with which I can agree."

The Court held for Dunhill, by the usual five-to-four vote, with White writing the majority opinion and Marshall the dissent for himself, Brennan, Stewart, and Blackmun. The majority held that the mere refusal to pay was not an act of state. To be an act of state, said White, there must be a "public act of those with authority to exercise sovereign powers and . . . entitled to respect in our court." The intervenor had no such authority, held the court. Marshall, like Judge Mansfield in the Court of Appeals, disagreed.

White also argued, as Douglas had argued in *Citibank*, that there should be a commercial exception to the act of state doctrine (as there is to the doctrine of sovereign immunity), but he failed to secure the approval of a majority of the Court when Stevens refused to go along.

The result was that Dunhill got an affirmative judgment against the government of Cuba, which could not be collected because of the currency regulations.*

---

*In two cases—*French v. Banco Nacional* in the New York Court of Appeals and *Bank of Boston v. Banco Nacional* in the United States Court of Appeals—Cuba successfully defended claims against it through reliance on the act of state doctrine. Those cases are both important and interesting, but space does not permit their consideration here.

The *Chase* Case

Bryan didn't get to *Banco Nacional v. Chase* until 1974. Our contention that Cuba did not have to pay for the bank property that had been nationalized had been decided against us in the *Citibank* litigation and we were left with a question, not passed upon or even considered in any decided case in the United States or elsewhere: How is the compensation owed by Cuba to Chase to be calculated?

Had this been ordinary civil litigation, governed by conventional domestic law, it would have been only passably difficult to determine the value of Chase's property even in the rather unusual circumstances present here. Our federal courts handle much more complicated questions every week, and the rules of domestic law governing the valuation of property are well developed.

But this was not ordinary civil litigation. If anything was clear from the decisions—those of both the Supreme Court and the Court of Appeals—it was that the applicable law was not the law of the United States; it was "international law." As the Supreme Court had pointed out in *Sabbatino*, there were no cases holding that *any* compensation should be paid for nationalized property; *a fortiori* there could be no international law as to *how much* compensation should be paid.

And so both we and the court were engaged in making new law where there was no legal precedent. I argued that in evaluating Chase's property, only the physical property (such as cash, real estate, and personal property) should be considered; I further argued that after the property had been evaluated, compensation should be paid at only a fraction of the full value, because, historically speaking, similar claims against the Soviet Union, China, Mexico, and many other countries had been settled, by diplomatic means, at a sum far less than full value. In fact, in almost no case had payment been made for the full value of the property seized.

The bank, of course, disagreed. To the physical value of its property, Chase added a large item representing "going concern value," an estimate based on the likely future profits of the bank. It also argued that compensation should be paid at the full value of the property nationalized.

The trial was over by July 1, 1974; briefs were all submitted by September 1. Bryan took all of the arguments under advisement. It was to be about six years before the case was decided in the district court. The case was not decided in the Court of Appeals until 1981.

On April 17, 1978, Bryan died, leaving the *Chase* case and three other Cuban cases on his calendar undecided. One of them, *First National Bank of Boston v. Banco Nacional,* had been pending for six years after trial, *Chase* for four years. Such delays between the trial of a case and its decision are extraordinary. Although the issues were important and complex, the records were not extensive, and the trials short. The other two cases, *Banco Para Exterior de Cuba (BANCEC) v. First National City Bank* and *Banco Nacional v. Chemical Bank, Manufacturers Trust Co. and Irving Trust Co.* (the *Three Banks* case), had been pending almost as long. All of them are interesting to the specialist in international law, but they had no immediate relationship to the act of state doctrine, which had become my primary interest.

I had seen Bryan frequently after he was assigned to handle the Cuban cases. Aside from several trials and motions, there were many pretrial conferences relating to discovery, trial calendar, and related matters. I tried at least one non-Cuba case before him during this period and had argued another, and I visited him in chambers on a quasisocial basis, especially after the 1974 trial in *Chase.* He had been ill for a part of this period, and I dropped in to see him occasionally when I happened to be in the courthouse, for polite inquiry as to his health. I visited at about Christmastime each year to wish him a happy holiday; I stopped in when he or I were about to go on a vacation, or when we returned from vacation. I once brought my son Mark, then seven years old, in to meet him.

Bryan was a gentle and considerate man, and I liked him. We differed sharply in our political views, but we never discussed politics. He was a bit stuffy and formal and inclined to be paternal, especially in the early days of the litigation, but I was sincerely interested in his health, and I really wished him a Merry Christmas and a Happy New Year.

But my primary reason for all those visits was to try to get decisions from him, particularly in the *Chase* and *Boston* cases. He understood that as well as I did. When I would walk into his office, before I could say a word, he would apologize for the delay. Without much variation, he promised decisions in a few months—promises I duly conveyed to my client.

My last such conversation with him was early in 1978. In a rare moment of candor, he said, with evident distress: "Victor, I'm very sorry about all these delays. The fact is that I can't seem to concentrate on these cases. I sit down at my desk, with the records and briefs, and I find my mind wandering from the job I'm trying to do."

I mumbled some words of sympathy, but I had no helpful suggestions. He promised to take the papers, at least in the *Chase* and *Boston* cases, to his home in Connecticut and to get the decisions out.

I left his office with little expectation. He fell ill shortly after and died in April. Henry Harfield, a close friend of Bryan, told me that he spoke to the judge several times in March, and that his inability to complete his task was in the forefront of his mind and was causing him a considerable amount of anxiety.

In June 1978, Chief Judge Edelstein appointed Judge Charles Briant as Bryan's successor, to decide the Cuban cases. Briant is, like most of the judges in the district, conservative in his political views and hostile to Cuba. He never hesitates to express his deep-rooted cynicism about the law and about other judges, and especially about the judges "upstairs" in the Court of Appeals. In fact, he is quite cynical about everything and seems to consider the law a big chess game in which he is a grand master, grudgingly inferior only to the appellate courts. He is an outstanding example of a judicial humorist and runs a very informal courtroom, in which he makes all the jokes.

A conference was held with Briant on the *Chase* and *Boston* cases in June, and in July, oral argument was held before him on all four undecided cases. I wrote him about six months later, pointing to the fact that the cases had been pending for many years, and requested that they be given priority over other civil cases on his calendar. Briant replied that he was not responsible for the delay, that he did not intend to give priority to the cases as I had suggested, and that "caution and respect for the appellate courts dictate that quality be not sacrificed for speed."

I didn't care much about the quality, since I didn't expect much. The cases were going to be appealed anyhow, but I did want speed. After waiting what I considered to be a reasonable time, in late 1979 I filed with the Court of Appeals a petition for a writ of *mandamus*. *Mandamus* is an order by which an appellate court can direct a lower court to decide a case pending before it, without, of course, directing how the case should be decided. I noted the long delay and asked the Court of Appeals to order Briant to hand down his decisions in the *Chase* and *Boston* cases before January 31, 1980, and in the *BANCEC* and *Three Banks* cases before April 30. The Court of Appeals directed Briant to respond to my petition; instead he filed his decisions in April 1980.

We didn't get much speed, and we certainly didn't get any quality. Every case was decided against Cuba on every issue submitted.

The appeals in all four cases were argued in the Court of Appeals before a panel of Judges Lumbard, Amanda Kearse, and Ellsworth Van Graafeiland on two days in January 1981. Lumbard had sat on three arguments in *Citibank* and was familiar with the Cuban scene. Van

Graafeiland was conservative—one might even say politically reactionary—and a thoroughly incompetent lawyer. Kearse came from a large downtown law office and was a bit on the conservative side—no friend of the Cuban revolution—but a topnotch lawyer (and, incidentally, a world-class bridge player). Kearse wrote all four opinions, all of them unanimous. That Lumbard went along with her is not surprising; that Van Graafeiland did, was.

Briant was reversed or substantially modified on all four cases. The decisions in the *Boston*, *BANCEC*, and *Three Banks* cases need not detain us here, but the *Chase* case discussed issues of considerable interest.

Beginning in 1958, organs of the United Nations had devoted much attention and study to the subject of the nationalization of foreign-owned property and the General Assembly adopted several relevant resolutions on the subject culminating, in 1974, with the adoption of the "Charter of Economic Rights and Duties of States." Article 2(c) of that charter provides that each state has the right to nationalize the property of aliens, in which case "appropriate" compensation should be paid, taking into account its own laws. In the event the question of compensation gives rise to a controversy, it is to be settled under the law of the nationalizing state and its tribunals.

The charter was passed over the vigorous opposition of the United States, by a vote of 120 to 6, with 10 abstentions. Every Latin American state and every African state voted for the charter.

Judge Kearse started with a review of the holdings of the Supreme Court in the *Sabbatino* and *Citibank* cases, pointing out that in the latter case, "none of the various rationales proffered by members of the majority attracted more than three votes." She concluded (reluctantly, I thought) that "while the divergent views of the majority [in *Citibank*] appear to provide no common ground from which we may articulate a *Citibank I* rationale, we are bound to reach the same result as *Citibank I* where there is no difference in circumstances."

She recognized that the task of the court was to apply principles of international law rather than domestic law in evaluating Chase's property. She reviewed the "orthodox doctrine" requiring "prompt, adequate and effective" compensation, and noted that there was widespread criticism of that rule. For the first time, so far as I know, a court gave consideration to the resolutions passed by the United Nations on the question of compensation. All of this was particularly gratifying to me. Although I had been making all of these arguments since my first brief to the Court of Appeals in *Sabbatino* in 1961, this was the first time any court had paid much attention to them. Kearse concluded that the United Nations' actions presented a "confused and confusing picture as to what the consensus may be as to the responsibilities of an expropriating nation to pay 'appropriate compensation' and just what that term may mean."

Kearse held that there was a range of choices, "including (1) no compensation, (2) partial compensation, (3) appropriate compensation, and (4) full compensation." There being no standards by which to decide which of those choices was to be applied, she took a pragmatic approach, giving Cuba a bit more and Chase a bit less than the district court had done, but establishing no rule of law for future conduct. She concluded that, in this case, full compensation would be appropriate, but also held that Chase was not entitled to any allowance for going concern value. This resulted in a material reduction of Chase's counterclaim and in a judgment for Cuba of over $4,300,000, which, with interest from 1961, resulted in a total recovery of about $11,000,000.

Neither we nor Chase had any interest in appealing the case. Given the composition of the Supreme Court, I could not see how we could do better.

In March 1971, Michael Krinsky became associated with our firm, becoming a partner several years later. He worked with me on the Cuban cases after that date, gradually taking on more and more responsibilities. He argued one of the cases (*Banco Para Exterior de Cuba [BANCEC] v. First National City Bank*) before the United States Supreme Court and the *Three Banks* case before the Court of Appeals. In the years after the *Chase* decision, I gradually withdrew from work for Cuba, and as of this writing, I content myself with watching Mike carry on.

Closeout for Me

In December 1984, Joanne, our son Mark—then fifteen years old—and I were invited to Havana to join in the celebration of the twenty-fifth anniversary of the revolution. Joanne went a week early to attend the Havana International Film Festival. She had a professional interest in documentary films and was curious about the developing Cuban film industry.

After the festival, the three of us took in the sights of Havana. Although I had visited Cuba over seventy-five times in the twenty-five years during which my firm had represented the Cuban government, I had done relatively little sightseeing. The three of us made a few tours of Havana—the museums, the restaurants, and the waterfront. With Luis Martinez we visited La Bodegita del Medio, a prerevolutionary tourist spot that was still a noisy, popular, and crowded restaurant. We spent three or four days at a newly developed resort island off the coast. We traveled to visit a huge tobacco cooperative in Pinar del Rio, at the western end of the island, where we were entertained by the local Communist party officials and treated to a dinner of tender roasted pork, of which we ate too much.

The one hitch in our plans was that the anniversary celebration was scheduled for Santiago, five hundred miles east of Havana, the revolution having begun in the mountains surrounding that ancient city. The town square in Santiago is not very large—no more than 2,000 or 2,500 seats could be supplied for the many thousands who wished to attend. So attendance was strictly limited to residents of Santiago and a handful of high-ranking government officials. Foreigners—even foreign diplomats—were discouraged from attending. Travel from Havana to Santiago was strictly rationed, and it was impossible to get an airplane ticket through usual channels.

Joanne goes to more parties than either Mark or I, and one evening about ten days before the anniversary meeting, she went to a festive gathering of film makers. Fidel showed up, as he often does at such affairs. Joanne introduced herself to him, identified herself as the wife of his United States lawyer, and said she wanted to go to hear him speak in Santiago. "Of course," said Fidel, after the customary Cuban embrace, "I'll have my aide arrange for your trip. He'll be in touch with you at your hotel."

I didn't expect anything to happen as a result of this conversation. In my experience, such promises, in Cuba as well as in the United States, are usually forgotten by the next day. Joanne, however, had faith. On about December 27, we received a telephone call at the hotel. "Be ready at 4:00 A.M. tomorrow morning. We'll pick you up at the hotel." At 4:00 A.M., a car came and whisked us off to an army airport on the outskirts of Havana, where we were put on a small military jet (pilot, copilot, flight attendant, Joanne, Mark, and I) and were flown off to Santiago, which we reached as the sun was rising.

We spent three days at a small government guest house—two bedrooms, sitting room, television set, and full kitchen. The house was somewhat overstaffed, with a chef, a maid, and a translator. A car and driver were assigned to us, and we were taken on several tours by a ranking member of the Communist party. We visited the historical monuments of the area including the Moncada Barracks, where on July 26, 1953, Castro led a memorable raid on an army post, famous in the annals of the revolution. Then on the evening of December 31, we were escorted to the crowded Cathedral Square in the center of the city, where, seated front and center and given earphones that provided a simultaneous translation, we listened to Fidel speak for the customary three hours. It didn't rain hard—just a light drizzle.

Fidel was in fine form and the crowd, as usual, was enthusiastic. Then to a dinner (good) and a nightclub (terrible) and the next day back to Havana, this time on a commercial flight.

And then back to New York.

I returned to Cuba only once or twice in the years immediately following the celebration in Santiago, once to help negotiate a contract between the Cuban communications ministry and American Telephone and Telegraph Company. I enjoyed going to Havana, but I find traveling hard as I grow older. Then, in 1989, the collapse of the Soviet Union and the other socialist economies of Eastern Europe threatened catastrophe for Cuba, which depended on those nations for a supply of oil and other goods vital for a modern economy. The anti-Castro forces, located mostly in Miami, saw this as a chance to overthrow the socialist government and persuaded the administrations in Washington, both Republican and Democratic, to maintain and even tighten the embargo. The very existence of Cuban socialism was clearly in the balance.

In October 1995 I met Ricardo Alarcon at a reception held in connection with Castro's visit to the General Assembly meeting of the United Nations. He urged me to visit Cuba—he pointed out that I hadn't been there for years. So I went to Havana in January 1996 and was impressed by the signs of improvement in the economy and the determination of the people I came into contact with to work out of the desperate situation created by the events in Eastern Europe. I met many old friends, both in and out of the government, and all agreed that 1995 had been a much better year than 1994, and all expected 1996 to be still better.

I also had a forty-five-minute chat with Fidel (at midnight on a Sunday). He was, as always, upbeat, and saw the embargo as a continuing challenge that, he was confident, the Cuban people could meet, as they had for over thirty-five years.

Shortly after my return, Cuban military planes shot down two planes piloted by members of a militant anti-Castro organization based in Florida that had for months been provocatively flying over Havana and dropping leaflets. The pilots were killed. In swift retaliation Congress passed and the president signed the Helms-Burton bill, over the formal protests of Canada, Mexico, England, and other U.S. trading partners. The outcome of all this is hard to predict.

I will not attempt an analysis or even a full description of the state of the Cuban economy today as I understand it. Life is still hard for most, but much better than in recent years. There have been compromises with the socialist concepts that governed the economy in earlier days—foreign capital has been invited to join with the Cuban government in many large-scale enterprises, and free markets have been established in Havana in which farmers can sell produce directly to consumers. Some privately owned enterprises (such as small restaurants set up in the homes of Havana residents) have been encouraged. None of these "departures" from earlier policy seem to me to be serious. The health and education systems established by the government continue to operate, and the major aspects of the economy are still run on socialist systems.

More important is the growth of a successful tourist industry (a good thing) and the accompanying creation of two levels of economic existence—a dollar level and a peso level (a bad thing). Those who live in the dollar economy do well; those in the peso economy, not so well. Not a healthy state of affairs, but one of the effects of the skewed economy the embargo has forced on Cuba. But there are many automobiles on the highways ("they use a lot of gasoline," Castro remarked wryly) and lots of life in the many parks of Havana.

My visit resulted in a renewed belief that Cuba could pull it off, despite United States efforts to kill it. The new legislation will certainly make Cuba's task much more difficult.

I have come to love that country—its cheerful and friendly people, its culture, and even its physical characteristics. Had the United States in 1959 taken a friendly stance toward the Cuban revolution or simply treated it with neutrality, we might now have as our southern neighbor a prosperous, friendly socialist state.

Or so I believe. Absent the hostility of the United States, there would have been no need for reliance for support from the Eastern bloc in Europe, with its consequent cost, both political and financial. There would have been no need for an expensive and crippling defense establishment. There would have been no suppression of civil rights, modest indeed by standards of Latin America, Africa, and Asia. Cuba reacts, perhaps overreacts, to the reasonable fear of an enemy ninety miles from Havana. The United States reacted to the unreasonable fear of an enemy three thousand miles away when it interned the Japanese-American population of the West Coast during World War II.

That the Cuban revolution lasted thirty-five years in this setting is a miracle, wrought by the devotion of the large majority of its people to Castro and his associates.

Under more favorable conditions, would a socialist government in Cuba be "democratic"? Who knows? It certainly couldn't do worse than the democracy supplied by the capitalist governments in Latin America over the past three decades. Democracy has many forms, and how it might work out in a socialist Cuba is sheer speculation.

Cuba was an ideal testing ground for socialism. It is small enough so that it presents relatively few administrative problems. It has an equable climate, fertile soil, and an industrious, well-educated population. It has an intelligent and dynamic leadership with a vision of a better world. Even under the most difficult conditions, it provides educational and health services superior to those of any other Latin American country.

At the very least, it could have provided a test as to whether socialism was a viable economic system. It may still do so.

13

Joni's Case and the Civil Rights Movement

A front-page story in the *New York Times* on August 10, 1963, carried an announcement by Deputy Attorney General Katzenbach that nine civil rights workers had been indicted by a grand jury sitting in Macon, Georgia. Eight were leaders of the black community in Albany, located about 250 miles southwest of Atlanta. The ninth was my daughter, Joni.

The indictments must be considered in the context of the dark history of racist brutality in southwest Georgia. "Bad" Baker County and its neighbor, "Terrible" Terrell County were notorious. The reign of terror against blacks in those counties was unremitting and was equalled in only two or three other locations in the deep South. In the 1940s, Claude Screws, the sheriff of Baker County, had killed a prisoner in his custody. He was convicted of murder in the federal court, but his conviction was set aside by the Supreme Court, which, by a sharply divided vote, held, in effect, that the federal courts had no jurisdiction over a local murder. Screws was then tried by a Georgia court and acquitted.

Echoes of the Screws case reverberated when, at a Fourth of July celebration in 1961, Charles Ware, a black farmworker in Baker County, was shot and severely wounded by Sheriff L. Warren Johnson. As was customary, Ware, not Johnson, was arrested and spent some time in a prison hospital. An application for bail was promptly made, but it was a year and a half before Ware was released.

The shooting of Ware caused a great deal of excitement in the black community, especially in nearby Albany. Albany had been a center of the civil rights struggle since early in the year, when the black community demanded the desegregation of public facilities in the city. A series of mass protests resulted in the organization of the Albany Movement in November, and the Ware case became an item high on its agenda when Ware brought an action in the United States District Court, claiming a violation of his civil rights. There was nothing particularly unusual in a black worker being beaten or shot by a sheriff in Georgia, but it was almost unprecedented for the black to sue, and his case and its consequences were watched with great interest in the months and years that followed.

Ware was represented by C. B. King, the lawyer for the Albany Movement. C. B. was the only black lawyer in Georgia, outside of Atlanta, who seemed willing to take on the white establishment. A trial in Ware's case resulted in a decision for Johnson by an all-white jury, on April 12, 1963.

Carl Smith, a white man who owned a grocery store in the all-black segregated neighborhood in Albany (known as "Harlem"), was a member of that jury. The Albany Movement had for some time been carrying on a boycott against Smith because he would not upgrade blacks, and his vote on the jury added an additional grievance and provoked more militant action. A picket line was established at Smith's store for a few hours on April 20, a little over a week after the jury verdict in the *Ware v. Johnson* case. Smith later claimed that the boycott resulted in driving him out of business, since all of his customers were black, and the boycott was a potent weapon.

The Justice Department viewed the picket line as an obstruction of justice, being intended to intimidate Smith because of his vote on the jury. Evidently, in its view, such conduct required much more resolute action than the murders, assaults, and other instances of violence against blacks that had characterized the civil rights struggle throughout the South. Thirty to forty FBI agents descended upon Albany, and they interviewed several hundred witnesses, producing several thousands of pages of reports in the next few months. At the end of July, a grand jury sitting in the federal court in Macon heard evidence presented by the United States Attorney concerning charges of violation of federal law, which made it a crime to coerce or threaten anyone because of his or her vote on a federal jury. One of the witnesses subpoenaed to appear before that grand jury was Joni, then living in Albany.

Joni had entered Antioch College in 1959. Antioch had a program that called for students to study on campus during alternate quarters and to do relevant off-campus fieldwork during the other quarters. Pursuant to this program, in 1963 Joni went to work for SNCC, which was carrying on a voter registration drive in Albany.

She had arrived in Albany on April 3. The city was a hotbed of civil rights activity, and Joni was characteristically in the thick of it. She was arrested at least twice as part of mass arrests in that city in late April and May. On one of those prison stays she engaged in a nine-day hunger strike. Between imprisonments, she worked on voter registration. She kept a detailed journal and wrote lengthy letters from the Albany jail to the school paper at Antioch. Her letters are vivid, detailed, and dramatic. She wrote:

I might not write for awhile 'cause I'm getting weak from not eating. It's been about 60 hours now since I ate anything, and wasn't eating much of that disgusting food, anyway, so I'm not too strong. But please don't worry—they'll take care of me and I'll call as soon as I get a chance. Trial's Friday and people are talking about a 60-day sentence, but I doubt it, myself. I don't think I could take it—it's rough and we've only been in almost 8 days. Of course, all these hard-core dope addicts and stuff who've been in every jail in the South, say this is the worst one they've been in.

We have a drug addict in here now—came in last nite (along with a drunk) and we had to stay up all nite to keep her from killing herself (she attempted to choke herself with a blanket) and from falling on the floor and breaking her head open. She smuggled pills into the cell and took 6 seconal and passed out.

The jail is filthy, and crowded as hell on the Negro side—10 women in a 6 x 6 cell with 4 bunks—and 9 men. We had 4 in our cell—now only 3—me, Joyce and Faith—the other was a perpetual jail bird, a nice woman who I'm sure will never be the same again. In fact, I don't think any of the white prisoners will ever be the same again, after being with us, hearing us yell back and forth and Rev. Wells preach a few times a day and all of us singing. He sure is making some good sermons. It's hard for us to hear each other too well, since the white side faces a stone wall. They say on the other side (Negro) the men's cells face the women's.

Cops are a peculiar breed. At first, they're nasty and intimidating—especially when they're in groups—but when we respond with "love and kindness" they soften up. When we first came, I think every cop on the force came back to look at us and make some nasty comments, like "Look at the niggers" or "How is it like to sleep with them?" or "Aren't you ashamed of yourselves?" When Faith came in, they put all the boys away and decided to feel up Faith to see if she had concealed anything. Ten big cops and Faith alone, and she was scared. (Don wouldn't get up and they dragged him in.) In the middle of the nite some cops came and waked Faith up to ask her what color she was (she's Semitic-looking and has a tan) and then asked her if she was pregnant and which one of the nigger boys she goes with and if he came in the cell could he have a "little sugar." I've been joking around with them and have gotten into discussions with some of them. Most all are willing to talk—even come around during their time off—by now, and don't growl, like they used to—"I don't want to talk to any niggers." But amiable as they may be, I question this whole philosophy of "changing men's hearts." Was it Stalin who said we have to sacrifice one generation? Well I don't see much hope for the present adult generation, but the kids are possible. Wish I could have some contact with whites especially children.

. . . . . .

We're lucky if we have mattresses, and sometimes the metal frames are better because the mattresses are filthy black, wine-soaked and sticky and god knows what else. The run-around got us wash-clothes (which we use to sleep on and keep the smell of the mattresses out) and they let us sweep out the cell each day.

. . . . . .

So don't worry about me—I'm fine and will try to get home for a few days as soon as I can after I get out—if I ever get out.

But we did worry.

Her work in Albany was over in July, and she came home to New Rochelle.

While Joni was home waiting for the next school session to start, she was served with a subpoena to appear before the grand jury in Macon. Of course, she consulted me. I had by that time advised perhaps a hundred clients who had been subpoenaed to testify before congressional committees, grand juries, and administrative agencies and I considered myself an expert on the subject. I had an invariable rule that witnesses were not to answer any questions at all beyond name and address. Whether they relied on the Fifth Amendment or the First Amendment, they were not to answer substantive questions.

For reasons that I certainly cannot understand now, I did not give Joni that advice. We had only a few hours to discuss the matter, but it should not have taken me more than five minutes to advise her. At the time, she and most of her friends in Albany were of the opinion that the grand jury was a friendly one, and that it was holding an investigation in response to the frequent appeals made by SNCC over the past two years for federal intervention to prevent the violence instigated by the White Citizens Council and similar groups. Albany had been the site of much of that violence.

I should have known better. The idea of a friendly grand jury in Albany in 1963 was absurd on its face. If the investigation had been one friendly to the SNCC workers, the FBI agents whose investigation preceded the grand jury would have interviewed Joni and her coworkers before calling her before the grand jury, and that had not happened. In any event, I should have insisted that Joni at least be prepared for a hostile grand jury. Instead, I let her convince me that she should testify before the grand jury because she had nothing to fear from the truth. I didn't even go to Albany to stand by while she testified. I can't explain this now, except that my marriage was in the process of breaking up; I wasn't living in New Rochelle anymore and I wasn't concentrating on Joni or even talking to her much. She went in and testified before the grand jury, and the result was disastrous, at least in the short run.

Over fifty persons in the black community were also subpoenaed to appear before the grand jury on two or three days' notice. Included were leaders of the Albany Movement, which was represented by C. B. King. But C. B. was out of town, handling a civil rights case in Americus; on hearing that subpoenas had been served, he asked his clerk to check the basic law involving grand juries. The clerk was Elizabeth Holtzman, a first-year law student normally resident in New York. Years later she was elected to Congress, where she served on the judiciary committee and was one of the leaders in the movement to impeach President Nixon. She ran for United States Senate in 1980 and was narrowly defeated. She was then elected district attorney of Kings County and later comptroller of the city of New York. Liz knows a lot about grand juries now but knew nothing about them in 1963. As a matter of fact, I would venture to suggest that C. B. didn't know too much about grand jury proceedings either. A black attorney in Albany in 1963 had little contact with federal courts or with federal grand juries.

Liz, in the few hours available to her, looked up the law respecting proceedings before grand juries, or at least the formal aspects of that law, and she met with the witnesses who had gathered in C. B.'s office, a day or two before they were to testify. So far as she can now recall, she had never met any of them before. She told them that a grand jury had twenty-three members; that its proceedings were secret; that witnesses were sworn to tell the truth; that they had the right to refuse to answer if they feared self-incrimination; and that the grand jury had the right to indict people suspected of having committed a crime. She was not a lawyer, and these people were not her clients but C. B.'s. She gave them no advice as to how to answer. Joni was in New Rochelle and not at the meeting in C. B.'s office.

The grand jury convened on July 29, when Carl Smith testified that a white girl had been at the picket line and seemed to be directing it. During a recess of the grand jury proceeding, he saw Joni standing in the court corridor awaiting her turn to testify, and he identified her as the white girl on the line.

Joni was then called before the grand jury and she testified about what she was doing in Georgia. She denied having been at Smith's store or having even seen the picket line. Her testimony will help to draw a picture of the attitude of the United States Attorney toward her.

Q. Now, where did you say you were presently living?
A. 504 South Madison.
Q. Is that in Albany, Georgia?
A. Yes.
Q. Is that in what they call, refer to in Albany, as the Harlem area, section of town?
A. Harlem?
Q. It is the Negro residential area?
A. Yes, sir.
. . . . . .
Q. Why was it that you decided to go to Albany, that is what I am questioning you about now. Did you go of your own volition or did someone—
A. Of course, I went on my own volition.
Q. Did someone suggest or direct or ask you to go there?
A. No, of course not. I decided that I wanted to work in voter registration, and that is where there was work being done in voter registration, so I went.
. . . . . .
Q. Did you do that type of work in New York State before you came to Georgia?
A. No.
Q. You decided you would come down and help the Georgia people vote?
A. Excuse me, could you restate that question?
Q. I was trying to find out where you got the idea that you wanted to help Georgia people vote; you said you didn't help the New York people vote?
A. Well, I wasn't working in voter registration in New York City. As a matter of fact, I wasn't even living there. I was going to school in Ohio to college.
. . . . . .

Q. You say you are working for SNCC in voter registration: where are you registered to vote?

A. I haven't registered. I was out of the Country on my 21st birthday, I mean at the last election after my 21st birthday.

Q. You are helping other people register to vote, but you are not a registered voter yourself?

A. That's right.

. . . . . .

Q. Miss Rabinowitz, it was reported to me—and if I'm in error you correct me—it is my understanding that after you appeared in this grand jury, Wednesday or Thursday or Friday, that you went out in the hall and someone placed a black arm-band around your arm; is that true?

A. Someone?

Q. I'll ask you if a black arm-band was put on your arm after you testified before this grand jury?

A. Yes sir, I put it on myself.

Q. You put it on yourself?

A. Yes.

Q. Do you have that black arm-band with you?

A. No.

Q. What was it you suggested to the people out there in the hall and what was that symbolic of, that black arm-band?

A. Well, we wear it sometimes in Albany when we feel that an injustice is being committed, and it signifies that justice is dead. And I was rummaging through my hand-bag and I found it there, so I put it on.

Q. Well, you wasn't in Albany, Georgia, when you put it on here last week; this is Macon, Georgia?

A. That's right.

Q. Well, what explanation do you have for putting it on your arm out there in the hall of the United States Courthouse outside this grand jury?

A. I don't have any explanation.

Two or three days after Joni testified, she was indicted for perjury, for falsely stating that she had not been on the picket line.

Five black leaders of the Albany Movement also testified over the next few days. Each was asked the following two questions: "Have you attended any mass meeting or meeting where one or more people were in attendance, where it was being discussed about the fact that certain ones were going to have to appear before the Grand Jury in Macon, Georgia?" and "I would like to ask you if you have attended any type of meeting or any type of get together during the week of July 29, 1963 through August 2, 1963, wherein you or wherein others discussed the fact that this Grand Jury was in session here in Macon, Georgia?"

Some of the witnesses answered that they could not remember. In view of the fact that the grand jury session was held only a few days after the meeting in King's office, the grand jury did not believe that testimony and such witnesses were also indicted for perjury.

It is difficult today to explain this testimony, but one must consider the circumstances in May 1963. By the time the witnesses testified, it was clear that the grand jury was hostile. It was not inquiring into the violation of the civil rights of the black residents of Georgia but into an alleged crime by blacks. Any grand jury investigation is a frightening experience to every witness, and these witnesses had more reason to be frightened than many. It is clear that the testimony was ill-advised, and better tactics could have been devised. The witnesses were reasonably enough afraid of a conspiracy charge against all of them and against their attorney, and they were determined not to give testimony that might harm them or C. B. (to say nothing of Liz Holtzman). Unfortunately, the technique that was used, obviously not well thought out, did not accomplish its purpose.

In any event, had it not been for my unfortunate lapse, and the doubtful tactics of the other witnesses, there might have been no indictments—certainly not for perjury.

The next months of my life were full of Joni. I assumed, as Joni did, that I would handle her case, although many of my brethren at the bar were shocked by the idea. It is received wisdom that lawyers in such circumstances are likely to be emotionally involved and therefore may lose the objectivity required to try a case well. That may be true, and it may have accounted for my failure to advise Joni properly when she was subpoenaed, but both Joni and I thought that I was the best lawyer available, and I enlisted the services of Leonard to check whatever downside there might be to my emotional reactions to the case.

Leonard's help was invaluable. We ultimately tried the case together, but more important, he took charge of a major part of the necessary preparation. He was an imaginative technician, and he guided the research into the jury records in Georgia with his customary skill. He was not much help in the political side of the case. His strength did not lie in handling problems like publicity, finances, public relations, and other nonlegal aspects of the situation to which we had to give a great deal of attention, but we made a very good team.

I met with Dr. Martin Luther King Jr. at some length within a week after the indictments, and he agreed that a good public relations campaign was necessary and that we should apply as much political pressure as possible.

Not only was I going to represent Joni; C. B. and I both assumed that I would join with him and Don Hollowell of Atlanta in representing all of the defendants, a prospect I greeted with enthusiasm. That was also the assumption, for a few weeks, of the other defendants. But they were looking to the NAACP Legal Defense and Educational Fund, Inc. ("the Inc. Fund") for financial and other support. I could not offer such support and did not have the public relations apparatus that the Inc. Fund had. The result was that I represented only Joni, who was tried separately from the others, while C. B. represented the remaining defendants. The situation was succinctly set forth in a letter from Dr. King to Russ Nixon, who was helping out on organizational aspects of the case. Dr. King wrote: "The reason for [Joni and the other defendants] being represented separately is purely for the sake of funds. The Albany Movement does not have the funds for such a case, therefore, we ask the Education, Legal and Defense Fund to handle our case, and we had to use their lawyers."

Dr. King oversimplified the matter a bit. The Inc. Fund was adamantly opposed to my participating in the case and so advised C. B. and the other defendants at a meeting in Albany early in September. The general counsel for the fund was Jack Greenberg, with whom I had clashed on occasion in the past, and neither of us trusted the other. I was regarded as a Communist lawyer, whose contribution to the case in public relations terms would be negative. The Inc. Fund couldn't prevent me from representing Joni, but certainly it wasn't going to consent to my representing anyone else. Legal cases in the South for many years had been the turf of the fund, and interference by a lawyer of my political reputation was resented. My membership in the National Lawyers Guild did not help—to some extent, the fund regarded the NLG as a rival. Hostility between the guild and the fund became much more overt the next year, in connection with the representation of SNCC workers in Mississippi. In any event, Greenberg went his way and I went mine. I don't believe we even spoke to each other during the progress of the cases, except for a cold handshake at the time of the final argument in the Court of Appeals.

Immediately after the indictment, Leonard and I went to work in preparing the case. The trial would be confined to a single issue of fact, namely, Joni's presence at the picket line. We assumed that she would be convicted at the trial; jurors chosen from rural Georgia could be expected to take a hostile view of her activities. Direct challenge to a jury verdict on a simple factual issue is not likely ever to be successful on appeal, and so we turned our attention to an attack on the jury system, which seemed to be our best (and perhaps our only) bet.

We therefore undertook a detailed investigation of the method of choosing jurors in Georgia, and we retained Hal Witt, a young lawyer practicing in New York, to look into the facts. Hal's research was thorough, and we were able to present a dramatic picture of an important aspect of the administration of justice in the South in 1963.

The method used to pick juries throughout the South was known as the "key man" system, and it was then utilized throughout the lower tier of southern states in most state and federal courts. The applicable federal statute provided that juries in federal courts were to be chosen in accordance with the laws of the state in which the federal court was sitting. The method employed in Georgia to pick a jury in Joni's case was typical. In 1953 a list of qualified jurors for the Macon Division had been compiled. It originally contained the names of 1,837 persons, of whom 137 (7 percent) were black. Those on the list who were black were identified with the letter "C." In 1959, in accordance with usual practice, the existing list was pruned to eliminate those who had died or who had moved, and the list was replenished with more names.

To accomplish this, Jury Commissioner William P. Simmons, Court Clerk John P. Cowart, and Deputy Court Clerk Walter F. Doyle compiled a list of names consisting of their acquaintances and persons recommended by their friends, together with "the names of people who are active in . . . civil life, a business way, some of them . . . from lists of church members" (testimony of Simmons). Neither Simmons nor Cowart knew many blacks: "Of course, . . . my contacts were heavier . . . with the white race because my association was greater with that particular group," Simmons testified. The two men had in mind "the statutory qualifications plus our desire here to have jurors of integrity and good character and intelligence. . . . Unfortunate as it may be the Negro community [in Twiggs, Hancock, Crawford, and Jasper Counties] does not qualify on the very grounds that we set up, of intelligence, integrity and ability to serve on those grounds alone."

No effort was made to seek out potential jurors from the small black middle class in the Macon division—black schoolteachers, merchants, doctors, ministers, civil servants, none of whom were canvassed for names. Cowart said that he wrote "a good many letters" to people asking for names, but to only one Negro in Macon. Cowart said this individual was a "good Negro," but the man's name did not get to the jury list. No use was made of automobile registration lists, utility users, tax records, or city directories. Voting registration lists, which might have been of value in other parts of the country, were not consulted either, but that omission made little difference, since few blacks were on those lists.

The result of all this was predictable. About 4,000 questionnaires were sent out to those on the 1953 list and to additional names compiled by the key men. About 2,300 of the questionnaires were returned; a few of these were eliminated for possibly legitimate reasons, and a new list of 1,985 persons resulted, of which 1,428 were holdovers from the 1953 list and 557 were new names. Of the holdovers, 117 were blacks; of the new persons on the list, only 4 were blacks. In other words, the 1953 list, despite its low proportion of blacks, was more integrated than the 1959 list. Blacks made up 7.4 percent of the 1953 list but only 5.8 percent of the 1959 list.

This may be compared to the 1960 census figures. Adult blacks made up 34.55 percent of the population of the Macon division. In every county but one, the black population was over 20 percent, and in ten of the eighteen counties the black population was over 40 percent. In Hancock County, with an adult black population of 3,237, comprising 66.3 percent of the total population, there were only 3 blacks on the list. In Twiggs County, with an adult black population of 1,997, there was only 1 black on the jury list.

We presented all of this information to the court by way of a pretrial motion to quash the indictment on the ground that the grand jury was improperly chosen. A motion was also made to change the venue of the trial to New York. In support of the first motion, the information summarized above was presented to the court. In support of the second motion, about a dozen affidavits were submitted and a number of witnesses testified, including historians, sociologists, lawyers, and journalists who attested to the fact that a white civil rights worker representing SNCC in a voter representation drive could not get a fair jury trial in Georgia. Both motions were quickly denied.

Between the indictment in August and the trial, a great deal of effort was exerted to get publicity on the case, with some slight success. The *New York Times*, the *Washington Post*, and *The Militant* carried stories on the indictment, as did the *National Guardian*. Of course, the *New Rochelle Star* carried extensive publicity on the case, sometimes with pictures of Joni, Marcia, and me. SNCC and the Southern Christian

Leadership Conference (SCLC, the organization headed by Dr. Martin Luther King Jr.) promised to get publicity, and Marcia, on a trip to Georgia in November for Joni's trial, happened to sit next to Dr. King on the plane and made a good pitch to him for help. A National Committee for the Albany Defendants, of which Dr. King was honorary chairman, was organized, and a pamphlet was printed and distributed by the committee and the SCLC. A Bay Area pamphlet produced by Ann Ginger was distributed widely, and Joni was interviewed extensively by the press in various parts of the country. Dr. King issued a strong protest and met with Robert Kennedy, then attorney general, and Assistant Attorney General Burke Marshall.

Joni's case came to trial on November 12, 1963, when an all-white jury was chosen. Ninety-four jurors were summoned from the jury list for jury duty, of whom 3 were black; of those summoned, 42 were questioned before the all-white jury was completed. None of the 42 was black.

The trial took four days and was rather routine, since the only issue was whether Joni was at the picket line, and that quickly resolved itself into a question of identification. Carl Smith, the store owner, and his son-in-law, James Fritz, testified, as did an employee of Smith. All were white. All identified Joni as having been on the picket line. Fritz had taken some very poorly focused motion pictures as well as some still pictures of the picket line, but none showed a white woman at the line.

Joni testified on her own behalf, stating that she had not been on the picket line. Joyce Barrett, another SNCC worker, testified that she herself *had* been. Thirteen witnesses (all black) testified that they had been on the line, that Joni had not been and that Joyce had been there. Except for the fact that both Joni and Joyce were about twenty years old and both were white, they didn't look at all alike. It didn't take long for the jury to come in with a verdict of guilty.

Joni was sentenced under the Federal Youth Corrections Act to confinement from thirty days to four years, at the discretion of the parole board. It could have been worse, but I had lots of confidence that we would win on appeal. Joni was released pending appeal, and we proceeded to prepare for the next step. The case was heard in the first instance by a panel of the Court of Appeals in New Orleans in November 1964. The appeal of the other Albany defendants (who, likewise, had all been convicted) was heard the following April, before a different panel. In May 1965 we made a motion for an *en banc* rehearing of both cases, that is, a hearing before all eight judges on the circuit court. Since the primary issue before the court was the validity of the key man system of picking jurors, and since it affected not only these cases but hundreds of other cases throughout the South, the court granted our motion, thus avoiding the possibility that the two different panels of the court might come up with different results.

Between the arguments before the panels and the *en banc* hearing, the government filed a supplemental brief in which it explained to the court that since the first argument it had discovered "new facts." The new facts were not new at all; they had been presented at pretrial hearings before the district court, on the motion to quash the indictment, and to the Court of Appeals in the briefs we had filed with the first panel. Perhaps the government had not read our briefs carefully, but more likely, the Justice Department in Washington, which was now in charge of the case, supplanting local counsel, decided that its position was an impossible one, and it was anxious to beat a retreat, at least insofar as that was consistent with its dignity and insofar as it did not offend its southern friends.

In its supplemental brief, the government noted the fact that only four blacks had been added to the panel in the 1959 revision. This, on its face, was discriminatory, and the government agreed that the jury verdict should be set aside. However, it argued that the indictment itself should stand, pointing to the fact that there were five blacks on the grand jury.

I have always been suspicious about those five blacks who were picked for the grand jury and who, incidentally, were required to sit in a part of the grand jury room separate from the whites. Out of 1,985 persons on the jury list, 121 were black. Assuming a random choice, the probability that five blacks would be picked out of that list seemed low. It never turned out to be necessary to argue the point, and I suppose we would have lost it, since the issue was only one of probability, but I have always suspected that those five were deliberately selected by the government in an effort to establish a lack of discrimination. I'm very paranoid in this kind of situation.

The government urged a retrial, to be held before a jury selected in some unspecified but presumably proper way. This, of course, was totally unsatisfactory to us. If the trial jury was defective, so was the grand jury, both having been picked from the same list, but we proceeded to the appellate argument with the assurance that the convictions, at least, were concededly invalid, although we still faced the possibility of a new trial if we lost.

The large courtroom of the Court of Appeals in New Orleans was pretty well filled on the day of the argument. Aside from our team, the Department of Justice was well represented, including John Doar, the attorney general's field representative, who had been assigned to handle civil rights questions in Mississippi and elsewhere for several years. He was the man that civil rights workers telephoned when they were in danger of being beaten or arrested, or sometimes after they had been beaten or arrested. His assigned job was to put out the little fires and to prevent big explosions.

Jack Greenberg and his Inc. Fund associates were, of course, also present at the argument. Greenberg was to argue the case of the remaining members of the group that had been indicted in Albany, Greenberg's argument being set after mine. Then there was our crowd: Leonard, myself, both Marcia and Joni, a few friends, and a fair sprinkling of lawyers who were interested in the legal issues raised.

This was one of those exhilarating arguments before a multijudge court. This bench was almost as full as the United States Supreme Court, with eight judges sitting, and the fact that eight high-ranking judges are sitting and listening is good for one's ego. The bench, even more than the Supreme Court, was sharply divided, in those days, over any issue touching on race, and the argument promised to be stimulating. The facade of dignity and solemnity differed sharply from the rather shoddy surroundings in which Joni had been tried in Macon. The local courthouse crowd wasn't hanging out in this courthouse.

In this case, the issue was one that went to the heart of the court's interest. It involved the administration of justice throughout the South. All of the judges were Southerners, and three or four were brilliant lawyers, and they appreciated, perhaps even more than the lawyers, the significance of the case before them. Even the dullest and least intelligent of the members of the court paid attention and asked a good many questions, a fact that made the argument even more enjoyable.

I was at my informal best. The fact that I was representing my daughter—a fact given much publicity in the local press—added an element of spice to the argument. Judges Wisdom, Tuttle, and Rives were outraged at the facts presented as to the composition of the jury and the method of its choice, though there was nothing new about it. The courts had for years been considering the method of picking of juries and had been trying to find rules to make the system result in a constitutionally chosen jury. This time, however, the case was unusually well prepared, and historically it came at a decisive moment in the civil rights struggle. School desegregation had been ordered by the Supreme Court; the right to equal accommodations in public transport had been gained, and here was an important case presenting still another issue whose time had come—the integration of juries.

Judges Tuttle and Rives, both of whom had very good records in terms of civil liberties, were very helpful in their participation in the argument. They recognized at once that the system of choosing jurors in this case was inherently discriminatory and hence unconstitutional. Judge Brown was probably the most active of the judges. He had his own read on the situation, which was illustrated in his ultimate opinion; he was in agreement that the system used was improper and that the conviction should be set aside, and his attention was directed to the question of how juries could be properly chosen. He pointed out that automobile registration records and utility records were all skewed against the economically deprived blacks. He asked me repeatedly where I thought the names of jurors could be secured, if not from key men. I said that I thought that was not a matter for me to decide; it was a matter for the courts to decide, and that all I could do was to be, in a sense, negative and point out that the method used for picking the juries in the *Rabinowitz* case was not lawful. I was copping out, and Brown was impatient with me, as well he should have been, but after a while he and I agreed on other sources of names. Voting records, generally used in the North, would not be of much value in Georgia, but there were other sources of names available— none of them perfect, but much better than the existing system—automobile registration records, utility records, telephone directories, real estate tax records, board of education records, and other resources should be considered. Any such records in the deep South were likely to present a distorted picture for purposes of picking a jury, but even a distorted picture is better than the key man system now in use.

On the other end of the spectrum were Judges Coleman, Gewin, and Bell. They were necessarily faced with the fact that the government had, on the appeal, conceded that the trial itself had been held before an invalid jury. I think that if they had been left to their own devices, they would have been prepared to affirm the conviction. The differences of opinion among the judges were further demonstrated when the time came to write their opinions.

The government argument, made by Nathan Lewin of the Justice Department, agreed that the jury system as applied in the *Rabinowitz* case had been improper. Lewin insisted, however, that the key man system of picking jurors was an appropriate one, the only problem being that the key men in this situation had not acted properly. He insisted that the indictment should be permitted to stand, because there were five blacks on the grand jury. His argument, of course, was faulty; the courts had always held that the composition of the individual jury that indicted or convicted a defendant was not relevant. The relevant factor was how the jury list was composed. If a jury list was properly compiled and it nevertheless turned out that all the jurors in a particular case were white or black, it had always been held that the jury was proper. Even the dissenting judges had some problem with the Lewin argument.

The issues were thoroughly canvassed in the argument. I was given as much time as I needed, the usual time limits being disregarded as they often are when the judges are sufficiently engaged in the discussion. After my argument, Jack Greenberg argued for the Inc. Fund defendants, but his argument was almost *pro forma*.

The decision came down in July 1966. We won, but there was a variety of views expressed in five separate opinions by members of the court.

Rives spoke for himself, Tuttle, Wisdom, and Thornberg. He wrote a long opinion in which he made a thorough analysis not only of the method of picking the jury in the *Rabinowitz* case but also of the many decisions involving jury selection that had been made in the previous two decades. Likewise, he analyzed, at considerable pains, the statutory history of the many efforts on the part of Congress to provide for a proper jury. He pointed out that in 1951 the law had been changed to specify qualifications of federal jurors, to wit: that any citizen of the United States over the age of twenty-one who had resided for a year in the judicial district was competent to serve as a grand or petit juror unless he or she (1) had been convicted of a crime; (2) was unable to read, write, speak and understand the English language, or (3) was incapable by reason of mental or physical infirmities to render efficient jury services. Rives argued that these were the maximum qualifications, and that the jury commissioner and the clerk, in attempting to add other qualifications, such as intelligence and the ability to understand what was going on in a courtroom, were acting contrary to the intention of the statute, with the result that, in the South, large numbers of poorly educated citizens, both black and white, were improperly excluded from jury duty.

Brown differed, writing a concurring opinion. He thought the qualifications set forth in the statute were minimum qualifications and that a jury commissioner had the right to set other qualifications, such as intelligence. He agreed that the jury in the *Rabinowitz* case, with respect to both the petit jury and the grand jury, was improperly chosen, but that was because it discriminated against blacks and not because it added qualifications other than the basic statutory qualifications. Brown felt it was proper to leaven the jury lists by giving some degree of preference in choosing jurors on the basis of factors other than the minimum qualifications set forth in the statute—factors such as intelligence and education. He agreed that the conviction should be set aside; he just disagreed with Rives's opinion about how a jury ought properly to be chosen.

There were dissents by Judges Bell, Gewin, and Coleman. All three thought that a new trial should be ordered, although Coleman did so reluctantly and "solely because the government recommends it." Bell and Gewin agreed that in this case the key man system hadn't worked very well, but they found nothing wrong with the system itself. They were all unhappy that the government had surrendered on this issue, and they argued that in choosing a jury, intelligence and literacy were to be taken into account. They explained the statistical discrepancy between the total population and the percentage of blacks on the jury list by claiming that in the Macon district, few blacks met those requirements. "Time and an improved system of education will cure this ill," said Judge Bell.

The result was that the key man system of picking jurors was held illegal, and in the next year or two many convictions were set aside in Texas, Louisiana, and elsewhere in the southern states as a result of the decision.

In 1968 Congress responded to Joni's case with a statute requiring random selection of jurors from a list made up of registered voters, supplemented by other lists where necessary to avoid racial discrimination.

I had been in the South to represent Joanne Grant, then a correspondent for the *National Guardian,* a progressive weekly, in the fall of 1962. Talladega College, located in the small town of Talladega, Alabama, had been the site of much militant student activity in support of the civil rights movement, and in May of that year a state court had issued, at the suit of the attorney general of Alabama, a temporary injunction against the college, its president, its student body, and a host of other persons. The injunction prohibited sit-ins, mass demonstrations, boycotts, and similar activities carried on by civil rights activists. Joanne was then covering the civil rights movement for the *Guardian,* and she was named as one of the defendants. The injunction on its face forbade her entering the state of Alabama. Other defendants included Carl Braden, editor of the *Southern Patriot;* Bob Zellner, a SNCC field worker; and Norman Jimerson, of the Alabama Council of Human Relations.

No one paid much attention to the injunction, which had been issued *ex parte;* student demonstrations continued, and Joanne continued to cover activities in the South for the *Guardian.* The state was not very diligent in pressing the case, and no one was cited for contempt for activities in violation of the court order.

In October, a hearing was scheduled on the application for a permanent injunction. I represented Joanne at the hearing. John Coe, then president of the National Lawyers Guild, represented Braden, and Charles Morgan represented Jimerson.

Morgan and Coe were among the few white lawyers in the South who had the courage to defend civil rights workers in the early sixties. Morgan's office was in Birmingham, the site of strong segregationist feeling, and it took a great deal of courage for him to take a public position opposing the prevailing white sentiment in that city. He never faltered in his devotion to the rights of blacks and others who were participating in the civil rights movement. At one time during this period, he invited me to his house to talk to some of his friends about Cuba; that in itself was far off the beaten path, especially for a white lawyer in the South. Later he moved to Atlanta, where he became counsel for the American Civil Liberties Union. In more recent years, he has fallen from grace and has represented large corporate interests in cases involving discrimination on account of race or sex, but I suppose that absolute purity is too much to expect.

Joanne and the *Guardian* regarded this action with great concern, especially because we didn't know exactly what the state was trying to prevent Joanne from doing. I will confess at this late date that I never regarded the case as seriously as my clients did, because the injunction sought by the state was so absurd that I couldn't see any court granting it, even in the overheated atmosphere of Alabama in 1963. I relaxed even more when I met Judge William Sullivan, the judge to preside at the hearing. He was a young, calm, and lawyerly fellow, far from the cartoon caricature of the Southern judge. From all appearances, he promised to preside over a fair trial and to apply the law in a reasonable fashion. I will admit to some uneasiness when, on the day the hearing opened, the crowded courtroom included not only a good number of Talladega students but about thirty rough-looking whites, some of whom were frisked by the police as they entered the courtroom. They were, it appears, well-known representatives of the local Ku Klux Klan. After a few days of attendance they left, and there was thereafter little tension in the courtroom.

The hearing consisted for the most part of the state's witnesses, who testified about demonstrations at lunch counters and stores. One minister described a church service at which two black couples, students at

Talladega, had appeared at a Sunday service and sought entry to his church. He refused them entry, and I cross-examined. As I recall our exchange:

> "Were the students well dressed?" I asked.
>
> "Oh, yes, they were very neat in their Sunday best."
>
> "Were they well behaved?"
>
> "Oh, yes, they were very polite and soft-spoken; they just wouldn't leave when I asked them to."
>
> "Do you think Christ would have been willing to preach to them?"
>
> "Perhaps he would have, but Christ didn't have a church to support."

The hearing dragged on for a week or so and then was recessed until February, when the defendants were to present their defense. At that point I filed an amended answer charging that the state of Alabama had engaged in a concerted program to maintain an unlawful pattern of segregation in schools, courts, and other arenas of public conduct, and that the lawsuit against Grant and the others was part of that illegal policy. I announced to the press that, in support of my case, I would subpoena the governor and the attorney general to testify as to state policy. A day of negotiation followed, after which the state moved to dismiss the action against Grant and Braden.

I lost track of the case after Joanne was taken out of it, and she doesn't remember what happened to it. It must have been dismissed as to all defendants shortly after; if an injunction had been granted as to anyone, I certainly would remember.

In addition to Joni's and Joanne's cases, I spent some time in the South in the early 1960s. I visited there in connection with various aspects of the National Lawyers Guild work, and in 1964, I spent some time in Jackson, where I did a bit of legal work, not particularly noteworthy, and visited my son Peter, who was teaching in a freedom school in Meridian, Mississippi. All of the Deep South, but particularly Mississippi, was tense that summer. Three civil rights workers had disappeared early in the summer and their murdered bodies were discovered while Joanne and I were in Jackson. The tragedy heightened the feeling of terror that pervaded the area. No one in the state in July or August is likely to forget the summer of '64.

The civil rights movement of the early sixties wrought great changes in the structure of our society, both north and south. They were brought about by young men and women who risked death in confronting a violence-prone southern social system. That these individuals were able to transform the social mores of the south in just a few years is a great tribute to their will and devotion.

The result, seen thirty years later, is ambiguous. African Americans vote in large numbers, both north and south, and we now have black senators, congress members, governors, and judges in all parts of the country. In social terms, too, the situation has improved markedly. But the same cannot be said in economic terms. The income gap between African Americans and whites is increasing, and, most alarming of all, there is a noticeable increase in racism, perhaps more prevalent in the northern cities than elsewhere. There appears to be a strong anti-integrationist sentiment in many parts of the black community. Much of the sweetness of the progress of the sixties has turned sour in the nineties.

As the old hymn goes: Freedom is a constant struggle.

Travels Abroad

Although world travel has become much easier in recent years, I have found long distance airplane flights uncomfortable and have avoided them whenever possible. I have never been to the Far East or to the Soviet Union. I have taken a few vacations in Mexico, British Guiana (now Guyana), and Western Europe, but otherwise my travels out of this country have been limited to frequent trips to Cuba and a handful of other ventures. A few of them are worth reporting on here.

Brazil

In 1964, a quasifascist coup replaced a moderately liberal government in Brazil. At the time of the coup, nine Chinese, members of a delegation visiting Brazil on a trade mission, were promptly imprisoned. On one of my trips to Cuba, the Chinese ambassador to Cuba sought me out and asked whether I could, on behalf of the Chinese government, go to Brazil with a view to securing the release of the prisoners. I was somewhat daunted by the task, since I knew no one in Brazil and had not the slightest idea as to where to begin, but I agreed. I returned to New York and set about trying to find some contacts in Rio de Janeiro.

I knew that the *Monthly Review* had a good many friends in Latin America and, I was sure, in Brazil, so I spoke to Paul Sweezy and Leo Huberman, its editors. They had a number of correspondents in Brazil and they gave me the names of half a dozen people to see. However, they warned me that many of their friends had fled the country, and others might be in hiding, so my efforts to reach sympathetic persons might be difficult. They knew no lawyers. None of my usual contacts among progressive lawyers in the United States were of any help; only a few had friends in Brazil and those were all in flight.

And so I went to see Henry Harfield, a senior partner at Sherman and Sterling, who had represented Citibank in its litigation with Banco Nacional de Cuba. I had, over the previous years, established a reasonably friendly relationship with Harfield and knew that the bank would have Brazilian lawyers.

I did not go into much detail with Harfield. I told him that I needed a lawyer in Brazil to handle a political problem and that I might run into some difficulty with the newly established government. Harfield is a sophisticated man, and no doubt he was able to make an educated guess as to my purpose in going. He made it clear that he could not recommend anybody who was likely to get involved in anything in which I was interested. He did, however, tell me that Citibank was represented by one of the largest firms in Rio and he would be glad to establish a contact between me and the lawyer who represented Citibank there. A day or two later, he gave me the name of a lawyer I could speak to, and I soon set off for Brazil, armed with letters of introduction from the *Monthly Review* and from Harfield.

In Rio I attempted to reach the persons suggested by Sweezy and Huberman but was totally unsuccessful. Several had left the country, and the one or two I was able to locate were so timid that they refused to talk to me. I then visited Harfield's friend. He was part of the upper levels of Brazilian society and had not been in sympathy with the preceding progressive government, but he was not particularly sympathetic with the new government either. He was, however, quite courteous and suggested that I visit Dr. Heracrito da Fontouba Sobral Pinto, a well-known civil liberties lawyer who might be willing to help.

Two days later I managed to reach Dr. Sobral Pinto and met with him at about 8:00 in the evening. He was quite an old man but very intense and forthright. I explained the situation to him and asked if he could help. His answer was that he thought the arrest of my clients was outrageous and contrary to the laws of Brazil, and he promised to do what he could to secure their release. He made it clear to me that he disapproved of the Communists, and that he thought the Chinese government was even more dictatorial than the new government of Brazil, but he felt the civil liberties issues were sufficiently important for him to accept the case. He did so, however, only on condition—that he get no fee and that he have no contact with the Chinese government, or for that matter even with his clients (or with me), except where absolutely necessary.

I had been given a few hundred dollars by the Chinese to take care of necessary expenses, and I offered to pay at least the costs that Dr. Sobral Pinto might incur, but he refused to accept anything and was in fact quite abrupt and, I thought, hostile. He advised me to return to my hotel and wait until he got in touch with me to see what he could do.

I spent about a week in Rio. I did very little sightseeing, although I did spend some time on the beach, which, although very pleasant, could not compare with the beaches on Long Island. I walked around the city for a while each day. I don't like cities generally, and I found Rio distasteful. The traffic, it seemed to me, was as bad as New York City's at its worst, and there was little I found attractive in the downtown sections. The areas surrounding the city were full of dreadful shanties in which the working population of Rio lived—much like similar sections of Caracas, which Joanne and I visited several years later. Currency exchange rates changed from hour to hour, and it was impossible to keep track of the value of my U.S. currency or of the Brazilian currency I had to purchase for daily use.

I located Tad Szulc, a correspondent for the *New York Times,* who was living in a hotel a few blocks from mine and who was interested in the case, which had attracted considerable attention in the United States and which he was covering. We were, as I recall, about equally skilled at chess, although I confess I tend to block out my defeats. Other than providing companionship for an evening or two, Szulc was of no help to me whatsoever.

After a couple of days, I saw Dr. Sobral Pinto again. He was still hostile and abrupt, but he agreed to take the case and repeated his admonition that he was doing so on the specific understanding that no one was to pay or even to offer to pay for his services. He said he would take care of the matter and that I should go home.

I went back to New York and for several months tried to contact Dr. Sobral Pinto, but I got no answers to my letters. I was generally informed of the progress of the case through press reports.

In December the prisoners were tried before a military court and sentenced to ten years in prison. Dr. Sobral Pinto announced that he would appeal the verdict and evidently convinced the Brazilian government to release the Chinese. In February 1965, the Chinese "Communist agents" were "expelled" from Brazil. A communication from the American embassy in Rio to the director of the FBI dated February 22, 1965, advised Mr. Hoover that no information had been developed that "subject [meaning me] had in any way been involved in the defense" of the Chinese, although, my visit and contacts with Sobral Pinto had been duly recorded.

The Chinese were extremely grateful for the service I had performed, although I must say I thought it took a long time—almost a year—to secure the release of the prisoners. In any event, I received a generous fee for my services and, even more pleasant, several magnificent Chinese meals at the embassy in Havana.

Some years later, the Chinese government invited Sobral Pinto to visit China to receive a decoration for his services. He indignantly refused.

Prague

In the spring of 1961, I was invited to attend a convention of the World Federation of Trade Unions in Prague. The federation was an international association of left-wing trade unions and it held conventions every few years. It was a Communist-led organization, dominated by the trade unions of the Soviet Union and the Eastern European socialist countries, with a scattering of representation from like-minded unions in Western Europe, Latin America, Canada, and the United States. I can't recall who invited me—it may have been the Cubans—or why. But I remember the meeting well.

I had never been to Prague, and I looked forward to the trip. I assumed that the meetings themselves would be dull, as almost all such conventions are. However, I did hope that I would get the chance to meet the delegates from other countries and to get some picture of the current status of the trade union movement in Latin America, Italy, France, and England. I counted on the usual conversations in the lobbies, at meals, and over drinks in the evening, rather than what happened in the formal sessions. Contrary to expectations, the formal meetings themselves were not uninteresting.

China had, up to that time, never sent a delegation to a WFTU convention. The year 1961 marked the height of China's ideological conflict with the Soviet Union, and China evidently felt it needed to confront its enemy at every available opportunity. So it sent a delegation—a very large one—to the Prague meeting, prepared to meet the Eastern European bloc on its own turf.

The contrast between the behavior of the Chinese delegates and that of the Eastern Europeans was startling. I went to Prague with two or three other lawyers from the United States, and as soon as we checked into our hotel rooms, two Chinese visited us to introduce themselves and to supply us with a few pamphlets attacking "social imperialism"—their term for the policies of the Soviet Union. There was no equivalent welcoming committee from any of the Eastern European countries, though we were meeting in Czechoslovakia, and it would have been nice if a few local lawyers had come around.

The dining room for the delegates was set up with large tables for twelve. At each table occupied by representatives of the Western countries, two Chinese delegates stationed themselves and, with enthusiasm, joined in and even sought to guide the mealtime conversation. The tables at which the Eastern bloc delegates sat were occupied by silent and solemn men (no women) who seemed to regard with suspicion any stranger who attempted to join them. They appeared uncomfortable in the face of the tactics of the Chinese but quite unable to cope with them.

The convention broke up into the customary panels. At every panel, a Chinese speaker spoke interminably, rarely addressing the subject of the panel and allowing little time for anyone else to speak. I attended about four panel sessions. The Chinese presentation, which consisted mostly of slogans, was the same at each panel—it consisted of an attack on the "imperialism" of the Soviet Union. The Eastern European representatives stood by helplessly while the convention was, in effect, taken away from them.

"A plague on both your houses" was my reaction to the entire proceeding. The Chinese seemed to be trying to make friends, but the result of their intervention was to alienate those few of us (from the United States, Canada, and Western Europe) who might have been willing to listen. The Soviet bloc, on the other hand, did nothing but sulk in response to the Chinese tactics.

I was glad I went. I got to see Prague, which is a beautiful city. I saw the two socialist giants locked in polemical combat, but nothing happened to increase my respect for either contestant. The anticipated informal chats with delegates from other countries were interesting but confined to the delegates from the West. The Chinese we met talked only in slogans, and the Eastern Europeans were too tense to talk much. I had come with some predisposition in favor of the Soviet bloc, whose members, I thought, knew more about the world trade union movement than did the Chinese. But my respect for the organizational ability of the trade union section of the Eastern European Communists to run a meeting in the face of organized disruption was not increased.

Chile

Late in 1970 our office acquired a new and important client. In October of that year, Salvador Allende had been elected president of Chile, under the banner of the United Popular party, a coalition of left-wing parties including the Socialists, the Communists, the Christian Democrats, the Radicals, and some fringe groups. Allende claimed that Chile was one country in which a revolutionary government could carry out a socialist revolution without the danger of an armed confrontation. I hoped he was right, but I remembered Spain.

In the summer of 1971, the Chilean congress, at the instance of Allende, nationalized the interests of the United States–owned Anaconda Company and Kennecott Copper Company in the large copper mines in Chile.* The law provided a complex scheme of compensation that the companies claimed was a violation of international law, because compensation was neither prompt, nor adequate, nor effective, as the Hull doctrine required. The Chilean government, on its part, justified its action under international law by reference to the same arguments we had used in the Cuban cases, including the resolution of the General Assembly of the United Nations, which provided that the terms of compensation in the event of nationalization were to be governed by the laws of the nationalizing state.

This was Cuba revisited. Copper is to Chile as sugar is to Cuba. The victory of Allende and the nationalization of the copper mines was seen by many as the beginning of a Cuban-style revolution on the continent of South America, and it was greeted with much enthusiasm in Havana. Castro visited Santiago early in 1971 and Mario Garcia Inchaustaguii,[†] one of Cuba's top diplomats, was sent as Cuban ambassador to Santiago. Many economists and others who had gone to Havana in 1959 and 1960 from other New World countries now went to Santiago to participate in what they saw as a potential extension of the Cuban revolution; included were Edward Boorstein, a New York friend of mine, and Jaime Barrios, a top-ranking Chilean economist.

Not only the political and economic issues in Chile, but the legal issues also, were clones of the issues in Cuba. Chile needed a lawyer in the United States with experience in handling nationalization cases, and we were most anxious to represent Chile. In 1960, we had to rely on friends in the United States to recommend us; this time, we could rely on friends in Cuba. Castro, Dr. Roa, and Mario Inchaustaguii all vouched for our

*This is something of an oversimplification, but it will do for present purposes.

†Inchaustaguii, who had been Cuban ambassador to the United States in 1962 and 1963, had become a great friend. His unfortunate death in an airplane crash in Southeast Asia some years later deprived Cuba of one of its finest diplomats.

skill and devotion to the cause of Cuba, and they assured the Chilean foreign office that we would give equal devotion and skill to the Chilean cause. We were retained.

I looked forward to more exciting cases in support of a socialist state— more chances to apply the *Sabbatino* doctrine, more chances to challenge the courts and the international law community with my views of international law. Several trips to Santiago were called for. The first time Leonard and I went down; the second time I went with Mike Krinsky. On both occasions we met with the lawyers for the foreign office in Chile and with officers of the agencies that were operating the nationalized copper mines and the other enterprises in Chile. Mike and I had an opportunity to visit El Teniente, the largest of the underground copper mines, and the principal property owned by Kennecott. The miners were strong supporters of the new government—but shortly after it took office they engaged in a strike against the government that was one of the reasons for its ultimate fall. The trips were interesting but exhausting. We did not find as much revolutionary fervor as we had found in Cuba, and it was clear that the unanimity of the revolutionary forces that had been so clear in Cuba was not duplicated in Chile.

The retainer lasted only until September 1973, when a bloody and brutal military coup overthrew the Allende government. Allende and Barrios were killed; Boorstein and Inchaustaguii narrowly escaped the same fate only by taking refuge in the Swedish embassy. Volumes have been written about what went wrong. The role of the United States and the CIA in sponsoring the counterrevolution has been well documented. For me, this was but further evidence of the impossibility of a peaceful socialist revolution.

In the short time we represented the government, it was party to only two major litigations in the United States, one by Kennecott and the other by Anaconda. Both were actions on promissory notes. The *Kennecott* case was disposed of very quickly, when the government found itself unable to withstand a very broad prejudgment attachment of all of its properties in New York and settled the case. The *Anaconda* case was still pending when the Allende government fell. Neither of the cases ever advanced to the point where important issues of international law were presented, and the only court appearances were those involving our unsuccessful attempts to lift the attachments in the *Kennecott* case. The attachments were in fact outrageous and quite contrary to existing law, but the politics were as hostile to Chile as they had been ten years earlier in the Cuban cases, and we never really had a chance.

There was an additional aspect of the *Kennecott* litigation that entranced me, but it too went away when the Allende government fell. Unlike Anaconda and the Cuban sugar plantation owners, Kennecott fought its battle against the nationalization decrees by attempting to seize copper shipped from the nationalized Kennecott mines to various European ports. In France, Holland, Sweden, and Germany, litigation developed between the government-owned Chilean Copper Company and Kennecott. In 1973, I attended a meeting in London called by Carlos Fortin, who was in charge of marketing Chilean copper in Europe. Also present were lawyers from England, France, Holland, and Germany. An interesting and stimulating and, to me, educational discussion of comparative law took place, in which the representatives of the various legal systems involved explained their procedures with respect to the attachment of properties. In fact, Chile won most of those cases in Europe, but here again the litigation was terminated abruptly in September, with the overthrow of the Allende government.

England

In September 1974, I took a year off, and Joanne and I rented a house in London. Together with Mark, then five years old, we spent most of our time in London, with occasional trips through England and Ireland, a month in Portugal, and brief visits to Prague and Algiers. Cuba had some legal work in London and I took care of that. I also took a trip back to the United States for a few weeks to argue the *Dunhill* case in the Supreme Court.

Some time before I went to Britain, I had the idea of speaking at English law schools. In the spring of 1974 I had written to a number of universities suggesting that I would be available to speak during the 1974–75 school term. The response was enthusiastic; every school I wrote to invited me. During the year I spoke at about a dozen law schools throughout the country, and at the London School of Economics two or three times. Most of the time, I got travel expenses. Once or twice I was able to collect two or three pounds in addition. Not profitable, but enjoyable.

I developed three lectures. The most successful was on the *Ellsberg* case, which is discussed in some detail in chapter 16. In that case, the *New York Times* and other papers had printed highly confidential documents, obtained from the Pentagon by Daniel Ellsberg, a civilian employee of the Defense Department during the Vietnam War. It was shocking to a British audience; even the most militant of the civil libertarians found it hard to believe that Ellsberg could disclose, and a respectable newspaper could print, classified government documents of the nature involved in that case. The Official Secrets Act of England prohibits, in language much broader than anything acceptable under our Constitution, any disclosure of information the government decides to keep secret, and there is no Supreme Court to review convictions for violations of the Secrets Act. My speech uniformly drew capacity audiences, and discussion of both policy and law often ran far into the night. Most of my audiences disapproved of the publication of what came to be known as the Pentagon Papers and thought Ellsberg should have been punished severely—"national security" was a concept that could excuse any government cover-up.

I also spoke on the Cuban nationalizations, arguing, as I had in the United States courts, that a state that nationalizes the property of aliens is under no obligation under international law to compensate the former owners. This was of interest primarily to students of international law, and a number of seminar sessions at Oxford, Cambridge, and elsewhere were devoted to that subject. I was representing a minority view, but the discussion was usually stimulating.

The third speech was uniformly unpopular, and I suppose I was being a bit arrogant. Having observed a number of British trials while in London, I concluded that the quality of representation by counsel provided by the English legal system was vastly inferior to the representation available to a criminal defendant in the United States. The medieval trappings in an English criminal court were repulsive to me—the bowing and scraping, the wigs and gowns, the attitude of counsel toward the court and the attitude of the court toward counsel, and above all, the bifurcation of the English legal system into barristers and solicitors. All of this was part of a system in which a defendant in a criminal case was a spectator at an eighteenth-century drama rather than a participant in a trial that might result in life imprisonment. An Irish revolutionary accused of an act of terrorism was not likely to have much confidence that he could get a fair trial from a court that was so clearly the embodiment of the British Crown. This ambiance was defended by many British lawyers as being merely superficial, having little real meaning, but I don't think that's true. There is no doubt that in the cases I observed, which included the trial of a number of Irish Republican Army members accused of acts of terrorism in London, the gulf between the defendant and the court was enormous. To make it worse, the gulf between the defendant and his barrister was equally wide. The barrister, indeed, seemed almost to be a representative of the court rather than of the defendant. This was not uniformly true, but true most of the time.

I was received coldly by my law school audience, many of whom believed that I didn't know enough about the system to talk about it. In some respects, particularly in connection with the supplying of counsel to indigent defendants, the English system seemed superior to our own, but certainly that was not true so far as the actual criminal trials were concerned.

There were then and are now a few brave souls who are fighting the system. While we were in London, Tony Gifford, a barrister, moved his office (his "chambers," in English usage) south of the Thames River, an act that violated many centuries of practice and that brought down on his head the almost unanimous disapproval of the profession. In fact, there was some mumbling about possible disciplinary proceedings against Gifford, but no one could find any written rule he had violated, so that idea was scrapped. In the past few years other reforms have been made in the system, led by working-class barristers like Helena Kennedy, but the scene certainly shocked me in 1973.

One of the projects I undertook in England was to write an extended analysis of the Cuban litigation—a project that over a considerable number of years was expanded and ultimately resulted in this memoir. In the course of my speaking tours, I met a number of academics who were also interested in the problems arising from the nationalization by third world countries of the property of aliens. Included were Carlos Fortin and Julio Faundez, Chilean lawyers who had taken up residence in England after the Allende government was overthrown and the Pinochet dictatorship was established in Chile. Faundez and Sol Picciotto, an English Marxist lawyer and theorist, were both on the faculty of Warwick University and were interested in publishing a book of essays on the legal problems arising out of such nationalizations. I wrote an essay on the Cuban nationalizations, Faundez and Fortin each wrote on aspects of the Chilean situation, and these essays, together with several others, were published in England in a volume entitled *The Nationalization of Multinationals in Peripheral Economies*.

Another international lawyer friend was Albie Sachs. He had spent some years in a South African prison as a result of his activities on behalf of the African National Congress, and I had met him in London a year or two earlier. In 1975, he was teaching at the University of Southampton and arranged for both Joanne and me to lecture there, Joanne on the civil rights movement in the United States. Some years later he returned to Africa and later was almost killed in Mozambique when a car bomb exploded and blew off one of his arms. More recently, after his recuperation, he returned to the United States, with a grant to study and teach at Columbia University. Sachs then returned to London and is now back in South Africa, giving his not inconsiderable talents to the new government.

Portugal

Shortly before we arrived in London, there had been a left-wing revolution in Portugal. A group of radical army officers overthrew the dictatorship of Marcello Caetano and were trying to consolidate political control. August 1975 was vacation time, and our family, together with Sally Belfrage (an old friend), her husband, and their two children, spent a month at Caparica, a beach outside of Lisbon. Joanne knew Silas Cequieras, a leader of the Communist Party of Portugal in Lisbon, having met him years before in New York, and we got the Party line on the situation from him. I also spent much time with Captain Rosa Coutinho and Major Correlia Jesuino, both high-ranking members of the Movement of the Armed Forces, the army revolutionary organization. Both were quite radical as, indeed, was the movement they led. Other leaders and supporters of the new government were easy to meet and anxious to talk, especially to someone familiar with the Cuban experience. The movement looked to Cuba as a model and offered a program that was, in social and economic terms, far in advance of anything the Portuguese population was ready for.

Joanne wrote to one of her friends:

Lisbon's atmosphere is euphoric and fraught. There are so many problems— economic, social, and political—yet the people seem so pleased with themselves. There are constant parades and demonstrations, large crowds everywhere; some just gathered to talk or read a new poster some[one] has just plastered on a wall. After forty years of fascism they have just had an election; they had gone to the polls and voted! Such excitement in the air. About 60 percent of the economy has been nationalized and one senses that people feel that they own their country. Factory workers suddenly find themselves in possession of the plant when its owners flee to Brazil with their cash. Government officials are more sober, their jubilation mixed with uncertainty. Most are quite cautious about predicting beyond tomorrow.

In the rest of Europe people are saying that the Revolution in Portugal is decidedly different from other revolutions. The coup had been led by army captains, not by a political party. Then, too, it had been a bloodless take-over. And the signal for the coup had been broadcast over the national radio network.

However it had been done it looks to me as if the consolidation of the revolution is being conducted totally with poster paint. Every inch of wall space is covered by posters and painted slogans. There were those who thought that the slogans marred a beautiful city, but from a hilltop Lisbon still looks pink and white. The wall, street, and sidewalk paintings evidence political participation. The political debate is, indeed, taking place on the streets.

I must confess that in the back of my mind there was the thought that, if the revolution was successful, we might represent the Portuguese government in the United States. Alas, these radicals could not hold on, and the Socialist party, reformist and bitterly anti-Communist, soon ousted them from power. Many of the people that I had met ended up facing criminal charges.

I couldn't help but contrast Lisbon in August 1975 with Havana in February 1960. In both, reactionary governments had been overthrown, and socialist-minded revolutionaries had taken control. Both cities were bursting with revolutionary enthusiasm, and revolutionary slogans were shouted from every rooftop. There were mass meetings and parades all over the place. The lamp posts and walls in both Havana and Lisbon were covered with posters. But the posters and slogans in Lisbon were not the same as in Havana. In Havana, the posters proclaimed the unity of the revolutionary forces; in Lisbon, they featured the in-fighting among the left-wing parties supporting the revolution.

Joanne caught the difference between Lisbon and Havana in her letter:

On one of our last nights in Caparica we spent a hilarious evening being instructed by a government official and a political activist on the meaning of the array of initials which stand for various political parties or groupings. These were classified as on the left: FEC-MIL, MRPP, UDP, LUAR, MES, MDP-CDE, PRP-BR, PCP-ML, AOC, FSP, LCL, PCP, PRT, MLM, MDM, ORPMEL, ARA, and on the right: CDS, PPD, PS, FDC.

But we spent all of our time talking politics on the beach, talking politics in restaurants, talking politics in government offices, talking politics at home.

There was no corresponding activity in Havana. In Havana, the Cubans spoke of what the revolution was doing, not which political party was preferable.

The Portuguese revolution had no charismatic leader like Castro, no natural enemy like the United States, and no program acceptable to a major segment of the population. There was nothing to hold the revolution together, and it disintegrated after a year or two.

15

Odds and Ends

In 1965 and 1966 Joanne and I spent the summers in East Hampton, where two momentous events happened. In 1965, I decided not to shave for the summer and so came back to New York sporting a full beard, which I decided to keep. Beards were becoming the style among the younger generation but hadn't hit the legal profession yet. So far as I know, there was only one other practicing lawyer sporting whiskers before that date.

The second and more important event was that at my birthday celebration in 1966 in Amagansett, Leonard Boudin, who was visiting us, had a heart attack on the dance floor in a restaurant in Sag Harbor. The attack was severe, and Leonard survived only because of the prompt attention of a doctor who happened to be in the restaurant, and the ministrations of the staff at the Southampton hospital. It was the first of several such attacks he was to have in the following years.

In the meantime, the practice of the office prospered, and our staff increased substantially in size. As I've said, Mike Krinsky joined the office in 1971; a year later Eric Lieberman also became an associate. Both soon became partners, and as of this writing, they are the senior partners directing the firm's activities. Between 1965 and 1975, the professional personnel at the office numbered about twelve attorneys. While most of my attention was devoted to the Cuban litigation, I did have time for a few unrelated activities.

I met Jimmy Hoffa through Joe Selly, who had become Hoffa's close friend as a result of shared union problems. In 1964, Hoffa, then president of the International Brotherhood of Teamsters, asked me to come to Washington to discuss one of his many legal problems. He had been indicted and tried for accepting payments from an employer, in violation of the Taft-Hartley Act. The jury disagreed, but an indictment for jury tampering grew out of the trial. Hoffa was tried on that indictment in 1964 and was convicted. There followed a series of unsuccessful motions for a new trial, which, together with the appeals, extended over a period of several years. When Hoffa expressed some unhappiness about his prospects in the litigation, Joe, who thought I could work miracles, suggested that Jimmy consult me.

I could not work any miracles; all appeals were lost and Hoffa ultimately spent some years in jail. However, he and I hit if off well, and I spent a lot of time at the union headquarters on the new trial motions, the appeals and a series of miscellaneous matters. Jimmy had good outside counsel, but the in-house advisers were a bunch of grossly incompetent lawyers who stopped bickering among themselves just long enough to gang up on me, a rank outsider, and a Commie at that.

Hoffa was a remarkable man, with some serious flaws. He was a dedicated trade unionist and brought to the members of his union substantial increases in wages, a high measure of job security, and fringe benefits that were the envy of workers all over the country. He had a thorough knowledge of the detail of the hundreds of contracts the Union had signed and was militant in protecting the rights won by those contracts.

Once, while I was chatting with him in his office, he took a telephone call that lasted about five minutes, and which I quickly understood was from a retired member in Green Bay, Wisconsin, inquiring about his pension rights. Jimmy gave advice in some detail. When the conversation was finished, I said, "Jimmy, you're the president of an international union with over a million members; couldn't such phone calls be handled by other people—the member's local or the pension fund office?" His answer: "Any member of the union can talk to me on the phone when he has a problem. Those people are my strength. If I lose contact with them, I'm nothing."

He had a strange set of moral values. He didn't permit drinking or smoking at union headquarters, though many of his staff kept a bottle of rye or bourbon hidden in a desk drawer. He took great joy when his grandchildren broke up a business lunch in the union cafeteria to climb all over him. He was puritanical in some respects and disapproved of the fact that Joanne and I were not then married. But he was surrounded by a bunch of thieves who were busily engaged in looting the treasury of various union adjuncts, particularly the pension fund. I don't think that Jimmy stole money from the union. So far as I could see, he lived modestly, and I don't know that he cared very much about money. His principal motivation appeared to be a desire to get better working conditions for his members and, no doubt, to exercise the power that came with being the president of a union that could accomplish such results. However, he must have known that his associates and employees—lawyers, insurance brokers, pension fund administrators—were stealing money, hand over fist. Some have gone to jail since. He kept large sums of cash on hand in his office safe, which he drew upon whenever necessary, to pay legal fees or expenses.

I don't know whether he bribed the juror involved in the case in which he was indicted, but I'm sure he would have seen nothing wrong with it, if he weren't caught.

He could never understand the demand of black members of the union for equality of treatment. At the time, there was an all-black local in the mid-South that was demanding to be integrated into an existing and larger white local. This was at the height of the civil rights movement in the South, and integration of blacks and whites was much in the air. But Jimmy couldn't fathom it. "Why do they want that?" he questioned. "In their own union they can elect their own officers—their own presidents, their own treasurers, their own business agents. If we merge the locals, there will be a lot of trouble, and they'll never be able to elect anyone." I was totally unable to explain to him the principle of equality of treatment. Such subtleties were far beyond him. Or perhaps he was ahead of his time. It is possible that in 1996, separate locals might be the politically correct solution.

In the fall of 1965 Hoffa asked me to represent one of two local union officers in Puerto Rico accused of mail fraud. The charge was an outrageous one, and I saw it as part of the warfare of the Justice Department against Jimmy. There had been a strike in San Juan by a Teamster local against a number of hotels. The international union, in the usual course of events, had sent substantial sums of money to San Juan to meet strike expenses—money sent, of course, through the mails. The Justice Department claimed that part of the funds had been misappropriated by the strike leaders. The international union had made no complaint and the international secretary-treasurer later testified that there had been no irregularity in the handling of the funds. But the Justice Department secured the indictment of the president and treasurer of the local. It was the Justice Department's contention that the union leaders were unable to account for all of the sums that had been sent to them, and that they must have stolen it. There was no direct evidence that anyone had misappropriated money.

I don't believe any money had been stolen, but union leaders, in the midst of a strike, are not likely to be good bookkeepers, and there were few records around. It was a good trial—that is, we won. The case was tried in Washington. There were eleven black jurors and one white. After half a day of trial, the white juror asked to be excused; he said he was uncomfortable meeting with the other jurors. One of the alternate jurors was appointed in his place—he was also white—and the trial went ahead.

The jury was quite friendly to my clients, especially because there was no visible victim of this alleged crime. We called about a dozen witnesses, most of them Spanish-speaking, to testify as to how the money was spent, including the kind of food the pickets got on the picket line. "*Cochifritos*," explained one of the witnesses. The interpreter, a young woman from the Philippines, had trouble translating the word, so I, calling on my extensive Spanish vocabulary of about fifty words, suggested that "chitlins" might be a good English equivalent. The jury loved this homey touch, but Judge Youngdahl, who came from North Dakota, needed a translation of "chitlins," as well as "cochifritos." The jury thought this even funnier, and from there on it was all clear sailing. The jury was out for about an hour before coming back with a verdict of not guilty.

Jimmy was not so fortunate in his own case. He lost all of his appeals and served his term at Lewisburg Penitentiary in Pennsylvania. He was released from prison when President Nixon commuted his sentence, and he sought to regain his office in the union. He retained our office to litigate his rights under the Taft-Hartley Act. Leonard handled that case and most of it took place during my year in England. I never saw Jimmy after his release.

On one of my trips to visit Hoffa at Lewisburg, he introduced me to James O'Callahan, a young man who had been convicted of attempted rape by a court martial in Hawaii in 1956. It was the army's contention, with considerable support from the court-martial record, that O'Callahan, a sergeant on a weekend pass from an army installation near Honolulu, had wandered into the city, where he had overindulged in beer. Passing the Reef Hotel, he saw, through a window on the fourth floor, a woman preparing for bed. The hotel featured outside balconies, and O'Callahan, a spry fellow even when a bit inebriated, was able to climb up the outside of the hotel to the balcony abutting the room of the woman he had seen. He climbed in the window and found a badly frightened fourteen-year-old girl already in bed. She screamed; help came quickly, and O'Callahan was arrested before he could do any harm and before he could escape the way he came in.

So it was alleged at the court martial. He was charged and found guilty of attempted rape and a few assorted charges and sentenced to ten years in prison. He was later paroled, but some years later his parole was revoked when he was convicted of rape in Massachusetts. Ultimately he landed back in the federal penitentiary to complete his federal sentence, and it was there that I met him.

I didn't find O'Callahan a very attractive fellow, but the legal issues were attractive indeed—they were clearly labeled "For the Supreme Court." Did a court martial have jurisdiction over an offense committed by a person in military service, when the offense had no military significance; the alleged offender was off duty, off post, and out of uniform; and the victim had no relation to the military? The Supreme Court had never passed on this question, an important one in principle. The protection given to a defendant in a court martial is far less than that enjoyed by a person charged with an identical crime in a civilian court. There is no jury trial and comparatively little in the way of rules of evidence. In fact, O'Callahan had been convicted on the basis of a confession that would not have been admitted in a civilian court. It has been suggested that "military justice," like "military intelligence," is an oxymoron.

Of course, O'Callahan had no money for legal fees, but Jimmy, very generous with my time, quickly talked me into taking the case and talked O'Callahan into assigning to me the substantial back pay he would get if he won his case. I didn't think the assignment was worth anything, but I couldn't resist the legal issue and Jimmy's blandishments. I was reminded of an observation by a violinist for the New York Philharmonic Orchestra, when, after a long strike, a contract was signed giving the members of the orchestra a good raise. I asked him whether he was happy about the contract. He said: "Yes, but I've never recovered from surprise at the fact that people will pay me to play the violin." So, when I get paid for arguing an issue at the Supreme Court level, I regard it as gravy. The argument itself is compensation enough.

And an important issue it was. O'Callahan had been litigating the case for some years *pro se* (without counsel), but he had lost in the district court and the Court of Appeals. He had started a second action and had already lost that in the district court. I appeared for him in the Court of Appeals in Philadelphia. That court was nice enough to say "petitioner's counsel has ably briefed a detailed and well documented argument to support the proposition that the military courts lack jurisdiction over such a case when the offense occurs . . . while the accused soldier is on leave," but it denied O'Callahan's plea.

The Supreme Court took the case, as I thought it would.

This brief, like the one in *ACA v. Douds,* excited my latent desire to turn historian. Many years before, I had spent some time, just for fun, doing research into a somewhat obscure aspect of prerevolutionary American history—I produced a paper, long since lost, on "The Regulators of North Carolina." This case called for similar research, first into the British Articles of War of 1765, from which the American Articles of War of 1776 were drawn, and then into English and early American history. Both sets of articles were limited in coverage to a narrow class of military offenses and on their face did not cover the O'Callahan situation. Even earlier, it appeared that Charles I and James II of England had both attempted to try soldiers by court martial for nonmilitary offenses. As we all know, Charles I lost his head, and James II his crown, and in both instances their efforts to extend court-martial jurisdiction was cited by Parliament as a contributing factor. All of this history, I argued, was well known to the framers of the Constitution when they provided for trial by jury in a civil court for all persons charged with crime. No one contested the right of the military to try soldiers by court martial for military crimes, but all precedent seemed to exclude O'Callahan's offense.

The argument was spirited. I had never found in Justice Douglas a sympathetic response, but this time we were in sync. We were army-bashing, and both of us loved it. Douglas pressed the government hard on the limits of its claim, and in oral argument the government lawyer was pushed into arguing that under the government's understanding of the current Articles of War, a person in the military could be tried by court martial even for tax evasion.

Douglas wrote the opinion, speaking for five members of the Court. He accepted my historical analysis, added some of his own, and held for O'Callahan. Justices Harlan, White, and Stewart dissented.

O'Callahan collected quite a tidy sum for back pay and allowances lost— money he had assigned to us for legal fees. However, as I had known from the beginning, an assignment of back pay due from the government is not enforceable. I never saw O'Callahan again—not even a "thank you" did I get for my pains. A year or so later, I did hear from him—he was in trouble in Massachusetts, and he asked me for help. This time I declined.

A few weeks after the decision, I heard from another court-martial victim, who had also been convicted of an offense that was not service connected. I disliked O'Callahan, whom I had met briefly, and I wasn't emotionally involved in his case at all. I never met Selden G. Hooper, but his case still upsets me when I think about it. It presents a typical instance of the mindless cruelty of the military.

Hooper was a captain in the United States Navy when he retired in 1948 after twenty-five years of service. He received a retirement rating of rear admiral, with the right to substantial retirement pay and other benefits. He lived not far from the naval base at San Diego. Early in 1957, nine years after his retirement, four agents of naval intelligence undertook surveillance of his home, and after they had spent some time in peeping through his windows with a pair of binoculars, he was charged with violation of Article 125 of the Articles of War (sodomy), Article 135 (conduct unbecoming an officer and gentleman), and Article 134 (conduct of a nature to bring discredit on the armed forces). Testimony before the court martial was extensive, and some of it, if believed, could have led to the conclusion that Hooper was a homosexual and that he engaged in consensual sexual conduct with other males. This was the classic victimless crime, and I couldn't understand why the military was interested, especially since Hooper was no longer in the active service. It seemed that a neighbor had complained.

Hooper was convicted on all charges and sentenced to be dismissed from the navy and to forfeit all retirement pay and all allowances. The sentence was upheld on appeal within the military system.

Subsequently Hooper attacked the jurisdiction of the court martial collaterally by bringing an action in the United States Court of Claims for his retirement pay. He lost that case as well.

There the matter rested for nine years, until the *O'Callahan* decision. Learning of the *O'Callahan* case, Hooper wrote to me and asked me to take his case. It looked like a good case. Even if Hooper were a homosexual (which he denied), his offense was not service connected, and a military court was without jurisdiction to try him.

I accordingly started an action in the District of Columbia to set aside the court-martial judgment on grounds of lack of jurisdiction. I further argued that Articles 134 and 135 of the Articles of War were impermissibly vague, and that the remaining charge, sodomy, charged only sexual conduct between consenting adults and did not constitute a punishable offense. The district court granted the government's motion to dismiss the case, without an opinion. The case was fully briefed and argued before the Court of Appeals, which held that Articles 134 and 135 were unconstitutionally vague, as I had argued. However, after argument but before decision in the Court of Appeals, the Supreme Court had begun its retreat from the *O'Callahan* decision and held that the

O'Callahan decision would not be given retroactive effect. We accordingly lost in the Court of Appeals, which held that the navy had court-martial jurisdiction over the sodomy count, and that ended the Hooper case.

More recently, in 1987, the Supreme Court, with dissents by Brennan, Marshall and Blackmun, expressly overruled *O'Callahan*.

16

The Vietnam War

The era of the Great Fear was succeeded by the era of Vietnam, beginning in about 1964, and my personal and professional life quickly adapted to it. As the nation geared up to prosecute the war, so our office, like the rest of the progressive community, geared up to impede it.

Several major antiwar litigations were undertaken by the office. Two of them—both carried on principally by Leonard—actually went to trial. The first was the defense of Dr. Spock; the second, the defense of Daniel Ellsberg.

Benjamin Spock, the author of a bestseller book on the care of children—a book that had served as a bible to parents for nearly twenty years—was a vigorous and energetic opponent of the war almost from its beginning. His 6'6" frame was a familiar sight on picket lines, in parades, and in mass demonstrations all over the country. In the course of his antiwar work, he wrote, with others, a document addressed to potential draftees, which, the Justice Department held, constituted a conspiracy to counsel violation of the selective service system. He and his co-authors were indicted in 1968, and Spock retained Leonard to represent him.

Ben's prominence made the case a nationwide sensation. The case was tried in Boston for about ten days. I prepared and examined some of the witnesses and sat at counsel table with Leonard to pluck his sleeve. Otherwise, my participation in the trial is described by Jessica Mitford in her book *The Trial of Dr. Spock:*

> As Boudin was in full swing his moment at center stage was turned briefly into the Case of the Facial Demonstration. During all of the summations there had been a complete hush over the courtroom, none of the usual whispered asides just out of earshot of the marshals that marked the more bor-

ing bits of the trial. Therefore a *frisson* of astonishment ran through the spectators when suddenly the judge roared, "No demonstrations! No facial demonstrations will be indulged in here." The press, round-eyed, gazed apprehensively at one another ("Was it *you?*" "Was it *me?*") and Mr. Coffin half rose to ask, "Do you mean me, your Honor?" "No," said Judge Ford, "that gentleman there," pointing to Victor Rabinowitz, Boudin's law partner and the only beard at counsel table. Rabinowitz: "Who, *me?*" Judge Ford: "Yes. Go along." Boudin, with a courtly swiveling movement, turned back to the jury.

Spock and three of his codefendants were convicted in the district court, but the convictions were reversed by the Court of Appeals.

The other case, of much greater complexity, drama and, in context, of greater importance, was the prosecution of Daniel Ellsberg, for unauthorized disclosure of classified material and related offenses.

On June 13 and 14, 1971, the *New York Times,* to the accompaniment of appropriate banner headlines, began to publish Defense Department documents now known as the Pentagon Papers, many of which were classified top secret. Among other things, the documents indicated that the president and the Defense Department had misled the public concerning the conduct of the war in Vietnam. On June 14, Attorney General Mitchell asked the *Times* to cease publishing any further documents, but the *Times* announced that it intended to publish still other classified material and published a third installment on June 15 while stating that more were to come. On that day, the Justice Department brought an action to enjoin further publication, and Judge Murray Gurfein, sitting in the Southern District of New York, granted a temporary restraining order, over the strenuous objection of the *Times,* setting the case down for hearing two days later.

In the next two days, it became apparent that publication of the documents couldn't be stopped. The *Washington Post* published some of the documents on June 14, and the government quickly moved for injunctive relief in the District of Columbia. But the *New York Post,* the *New York Daily News,* the *Los Angeles Times,* Reuters, the Associated Press, and many others had secured access to at least some of the documents in question and had printed or threatened to print them. Successful suits in dozens of district courts would have been necessary to stop the flood of publication.

In the New York proceeding, I appeared before Judge Gurfein on June 18, representing the Emergency Civil Liberties Committee, and sought to intervene and to file an *amicus* brief. So did several other organizations, including the American Civil Liberties Union and the Center for Constitutional Rights. All briefs were accepted by the court; all motions to intervene were denied.

At a hearing held on that day, the government asked for an *in camera* hearing on the issue of whether the documents, or any of them, affected national security. Such a hearing was opposed by the *Times* but not too vigorously. However, it was objected to vehemently by me and by Norman Dorsen, representing the ACLU, as we would be excluded from such a hearing. In the course of the argument before Judge Gurfein, the judge referred to the British practice of holding *in camera* hearings; I responded by charging that he was emulating the notorious Star Chamber proceedings in England, a bit of hyperbole that was true only in a metaphorical sense. Gurfein exploded—he almost threw his gavel at me. Ultimately, he directed the hearing, from which all of the proposed intervenors were excluded.

The next few days saw a frenzy of litigation in New York and the District of Columbia, and the case reached the Supreme Court in near record time. The Court, by a six-to-three vote, upheld the right of the *Times* to print the documents, and publication continued.

During all of this, there was much speculation as to the source of the leak of the papers. Clearly it was someone with access to top-secret documents; just as clearly, the person or persons involved had knowingly incurred the risk of criminal prosecution on rather serious charges. The secret could not be kept for long, and in a few days it was disclosed that Daniel Ellsberg, a civilian analyst in the Defense Department, had made copies of several thousands of pages containing classified material and had given them to two reporters for the *Times*. Ellsberg had been profoundly shocked by the war in Vietnam and considered it immoral. Further, it was apparent that the facts behind the entire military operation in Southeast Asia had been concealed from the public, and that false information had been fed to the public from the very beginning of the conflict. Dan Ellsberg is a passionate man, of strong convictions, and he seized the chance to tell the truth to the public, despite very substantial risk to him.

He and Anthony Russo, a friend who participated in the action, were promptly indicted in Los Angeles, and Leonard Boudin and Charles Nesson, a professor at Harvard, represented Ellsberg. Leonard Weinglass represented Russo. I supervised the support work for Leonard in New York before and during the trial, and I went out to Los Angeles once or twice at Leonard's suggestion when he thought he needed help.

Early in February 1973, the trial terminated under circumstances as dramatic as those under which the incident had arisen. As the trial approached its close, Leonard moved that the government be required to produce documents that the government claimed were (1) confidential and (2) lost. Judge Matthew Byrne, presiding at the trial, directed the government to find and produce the documents. While the parties and the court were arguing about the matter, two startling events occurred: first, it was disclosed that FBI agents had broken into the office of Ellsberg's psychiatrist and examined Ellsberg's medical records and, second, the *Washington Star* reported that President Nixon had secretly offered to Judge Byrne the position of head of the FBI, to replace J. Edgar Hoover, who had just died. Motions for a mistrial flew all over the place, and finally Judge Byrne granted a motion to dismiss the indictment because of prosecutional misconduct.

Most of our Vietnam-related work had a lower profile. Early in the war, there developed some difference of opinion among the several civil liberties organizations in the country concerning their view of the war. There had been for some time a subdued debate within the National Emergency Civil Liberties Committee as to the proper scope of its activities, with some arguing that the defense of civil liberties should not be confused with other equally worthy causes such as, for example, the community control of schools, an issue that tore the progressive movement in New York apart in 1968. The same question of principle arose in connection with opposition to the war.

We all thought the war was immoral and illegal but there were some differences of opinion as to whether it was a matter for ECLC. Specifically, should we defend young men who were resisting the draft? Should ECLC challenge the legality of the war? Some of us argued that there could be no more violent assault on civil liberties than a government policy that took young men out of civilian life and compelled them to go abroad to fight for an unworthy and evil cause. The discussion in the organization didn't last long, being resolved by early 1966, and our office, representing ECLC, plunged into antiwar legal work. The ACLU was more ambivalent and took a bit longer to resolve this question, but in a year or two it was on board.

Early in the war, questions were raised as to its legality, since the Constitution provides that Congress, not the president, has the power to declare war. Such a declaration had not been made by Congress, although the fighting in Vietnam was clearly a war. The issue had been raised sporadically and unsuccessfully as a defense to draft-evasion cases, but in 1970, ECLC decided to make a broad nationwide legal attack seeking declaratory judgments that the war was illegal. It also sought an injunction against further expenditure of funds to prosecute the activities in Vietnam.

Politically, and in terms of public relations, a challenge to the legality of the war made great sense, though I had difficulty in even imagining that a court would enjoin a war. The legal arguments were certainly respectable—in fact, they were quite sound, and we hoped the pendency of the lawsuits would, at the very least, embarrass the administration. And so under the sponsorship of ECLC, I drafted a complaint that was filed in 14 different district courts on August 24, 1971. The government's answer was that while Congress had not formally declared war, it had done so *sub silentio* by passing the Bay of Tonkin resolution and by approving appropriations for the war on a number of occasions.

Ultimately, all such cases failed. Some of them were dismissed on technical grounds; some of them were withdrawn after the Supreme Court had indicated that it was not prepared to hear them; some of them were abandoned when local lawyers were unwilling or unable to pursue them. The case filed in Philadelphia, entitled *Attlee v. Laird,* was the most successful, as success was measured in those cases.

Under the applicable statute, a three-judge court had to be convened to hear an application to enjoin an act of Congress, and the first (and, in some of these cases, the last) step was to move for the convening of such a three-judge court. I convinced Judge Joseph Lord in Philadelphia that our case was not a frivolous one, and that a three-judge court should be convened. The government then moved to dismiss the case. The argument on the motion was a spirited one; the court appeared to be much more concerned about what would happen should there be a confrontation with the executive branch than it was about the legal issue. One of the judges expressed concern over the fate of the soldiers then in the battlefield, if the court should issue an injunction against continuance of the war. I graciously consented to a delay of a few months before the effective date of any injunction that might be granted, so that our soldiers could be removed in an orderly fashion. The court, however, ultimately avoided that hypothetical problem by denying the injunction on the ground that the issue presented was a "political question." Such a device was frequently used by the courts when hot issues are presented concerning the relationship of the various branches of government to each other.

Judge Lord, however, wrote a long dissenting opinion. Although in form the opinion was addressed to the conclusion that the case should be set down for trial, he made it abundantly clear he thought the war was illegal and that an injunction should issue. He pointed out that the president had a remedy if such a decision was made. He need not stop the war but had only to submit the question to Congress and ask for a declaration of war. That would have been a wonderful result, since it would have meant extensive public debate over the war—a debate that the administration might well have lost in 1970.

The Supreme Court refused to review the case. However, Justices Douglas and Stewart dissented, expressing the opinion that the case ought to be set down for trial so a decision could be made on the merits of the question as to whether the war was in fact legal. In other cases raising the same issue, Justices Brennan and Harlan had also voted to hear the issue of the legality of the war, so that in all, four of the nine justices at one time or another expressed the view that the question was one that the Court ought to consider. However, four votes aren't enough—further, we were never able to get more than three in any one case.*

From the beginning of the war, exemptions from service were granted for students and conscientious objectors. It was these latter exemptions that provided most of the work for our office in the years between 1966 and 1974.

I don't know how many draft clients we represented in those years; it certainly ran into the hundreds. The applicable draft regulations were a mass of administrative detail; the applicable law became more and more complex as the war progressed, and a high degree of expertise was required to advise the clients who flooded our office. Michael Standard handled most of these cases at the administrative level. He was thoroughly familiar with the regulations and kept up with the rapidly developing law on a daily basis. He was able to take advantage of every loophole afforded by the selective service bureaucracy and to create a few new loopholes.

---

*In the summer of 1974, our office, acting for the Emergency Civil Liberties Committee, in conjunction with the ACLU, brought an action to enjoin the bombing of Cambodia. Judge Orrin Judd, who was philosophically opposed to war, granted the injunction; Judge Wilber Feinberg, of the Court of Appeals, stayed his order; Justice Douglas, from his camp in the mountains of Washington, vacated Feinberg's order, thus reinstating Judd's injunction; and the Supreme Court, in a vote taken by telephone, vacated Douglas's order. Eric Lieberman handled this case for our office; I was on my way to London for a sabbatical.

In large part, the work was financially self-supporting, an unusual circumstance in our office. While we never turned down a client because he couldn't pay a fee, most of our draft clients could pay fees, and reasonable fees, at that. The skill Mike was able to utilize in handling these cases and his familiarity with the law frequently meant substantial results for the client, justifying substantial fees. We were overwhelmed with requests from young men from affluent middle-class families whose schooling was in danger of interruption or who developed serious conscientious objections (sincere or otherwise) to fighting in a war that was increasingly unpopular and was considered by large segments of the population to be both illegal and immoral.

Almost all of those we represented got their deferments. Of those who failed, a few entered the army; a few went to Canada. I can recall only five or six who were indicted for refusal to submit to induction and only three or four who were convicted, out of the hundreds of cases we handled.

It became apparent to me very soon that the selective service system was seriously flawed, in a constitutional sense, in that it discriminated against those who were economically disadvantaged. Since only those registrants who could afford a college or graduate school education were able to avoid the draft by claiming a student deferment, I argued that the regulations and the law were class-biased, and in our society, class-biased regulations were almost always race-biased as well, since most of those financially unable to attend college were black.

Just a bit of research was enough to justify this factual conclusion. A commission appointed by President Lyndon Johnson to look into this matter made a finding that could have been made intuitively—that the student deferment favors the wealthier classes in our society. As of October 31, 1967, the commission found, the number of registrants granted student deferments was greater than those classified as available for induction. In practice, the student exemption excused from service about half of those otherwise eligible to serve—the more affluent half.

I decided to bring an action attacking the constitutionality of the selective service system on that theory. I recognized a defect in my argument, however. I sought to have the selective service system held unconstitutional, but a much more likely result of a successful lawsuit would be to invalidate only the student deferment. In that event, the selective service system would continue to supply soldiers for the war, but they would be different people—fewer blacks, more whites; fewer poor people, more middle class. The war would go on. It was just that different people would fight it. What would be gained by such a suit? There would be some negative effects on our office; such a decision would be contrary to the interests of many of our affluent clients. Indeed, it would even make my son Peter, who had a student deferment, eligible for the draft (unless he could convince his selective service board that he was a conscientious objector—always a doubtful matter where CO status is not based on religious training).

But I was convinced that the political arguments in favor of such a lawsuit were substantial. It would result in a considerable increase in middle-class opposition to the war. Most of its men-children would suddenly be at substantial risk. Besides, racial and economic discrimination were inherently evil.

And so I started to search for a few plaintiffs. They had to be classified 1-A and economically unable to attend college, and, most difficult, they had to be sufficiently interested to bring such a suit. Finding such individuals wasn't an easy task.

After a while, I located four young black plaintiffs, and I started an action in the district court entitled *Boyd v. Clark*, attacking the constitutionality of the statute, and argued the case before a three-judge court. The government made no effort to defend the constitutionality of the Selective Service Act or of the student deferment; it merely argued that under the terms of the act, the court had no jurisdiction to hear a challenge to a registrant's classification except as a defense to a criminal case. The court (Judges Hays, McLean, and Edelstein) accepted this argument and added one of its own, not thought of by the United States Attorney, namely, that the court had jurisdiction only of cases in which the amount in controversy amounted to ten thousand dollars and that none of the plaintiffs could prove such a monetary loss.

The decision was not much of a surprise. Hays, it seemed to me, always decided against me. (This wasn't quite true; he cast one vote in our favor in a Cuban case. I don't think he was personally hostile to me; it's just that he didn't believe in much that I believed in, and vice versa.) However, there was a good dissent from Judge Edelstein, who thought the statutory limitation on judicial review of the classification of registrants was not applicable when the plaintiffs were challenging "an integral part of the selective service system." Further, he found the requirement that the case involve the sum of ten thousand dollars to be unconstitutional if it was to be applied to this kind of case. He said: "Although it might be said that human rights are incapable of valuation, and hence valueless, it is better to view them as incapable of valuation but only because they are of infinite value. The latter view is, in my humble opinion, the only view compatible with the commitment of our nation to a belief in the dignity of man and the inherent worth of a free individual in a free society."

We appealed the adverse decision to the Supreme Court, which denied the appeal without opinion. Shortly after, the scope of the student deferment was sharply reduced when the regulations were changed to terminate such classifications at the end of the school year.

The decision in the student deferment case left open the possibility of raising the same constitutional issue as a defense in a criminal case. Following their indictment for refusal to be inducted, Tony Fargas and Tony Hudson presented that case. Both were registered with the same draft board on Manhattan's West Side; neither could afford to go to college; both had claimed deferment as conscientious objectors, and both had been indicted.

Fargas and Hudson not only presented a chance to push the issue I had raised in *Boyd v. Clark;* they also presented a chance to make in New York the challenge to the jury system I had made successfully in *Rabinowitz v. U.S.* ("Joni's case," in my vocabulary), since the New York method of choosing jurors wasn't much better than that in Georgia in its results.

I first moved to dismiss the two indictments on the ground that the grand jury had not been properly chosen. In Joni's case, blacks had been kept off the juries because they were black. In New York, in practical terms, blacks (and Hispanics) were kept off the juries because they were poor. The result was exactly the same: juries were composed almost entirely of whites and, especially in the case of grand juries (which in New York were then chosen from a separate list), almost all jurors were affluent whites.

As in Joni's case, extensive research was undertaken as to the make-up of the grand juries, this time in the Southern District of New York. We used a large street map of Manhattan and stuck white-headed pins into the map to show the addresses of the persons on the grand jury list. The result was a vivid demonstration of the class character of the grand juries. There was a large cluster of pins on the upper East Side; a smaller, but still large, number of pins on Central Park West and adjacent side streets. There were very few pins in Greenwich Village and none at all in Harlem or on the lower East Side.

The visual evidence of the map was supplemented by statistical evidence. The Eleventh, Fourteenth, and Sixteenth Assembly Districts, predominately black and Puerto Rican, had 11.3 percent of the registered voter population in New York and less than 1 percent of the grand jury members. The affluent Eighth and Ninth Assembly Districts, with 15.7 percent of the registered voters, supplied 58 percent of the grand jury panel. Similar contrasts were shown in the Bronx and Westchester (many more grand jurors from Scarsdale and Rye than from Mount Vernon and New Rochelle). Income analysis showed the same pattern. Twenty-five percent of the grand jurors were listed in the *Social Register, Who's Who in New York,* and Poor's *Directory of Directors.*

I argued on the basis of the decision in Joni's case that this was an unconstitutional imbalance, not primarily on the basis of race but on the basis of affluence (another word for "class"), which was reflected in a racial imbalance. There were no more blacks sitting on the grand jury in New York than there were in Macon, Georgia.

We lost the motion, after a hearing before Judge Harold Tyler. He wrote a long and apologetic decision. The imbalance, he found, was unavoidable and was caused by the fact that poor people could not afford to sit on grand juries and were excused from service for that reason. He found the decision in Joni's case not binding on him because it was in the Fifth Circuit and there was, in the Second Circuit, a long line of prior decisions approving the New York method of choosing juries. Finally, he pointed out, Congress, responding to Joni's case, had just passed a new law governing the selection of jurors so that whatever was wrong with the jury system at that moment would be corrected in a few months when the new law came into effect.

There was no right to an appeal from Tyler's decision at this stage of the case. Appellate review would have to await appeal from a conviction, if any. If Fargas and Hudson were to be convicted, they would be the appellants to challenge the jury selection process.

The Fargas case was set down for trial first, before Judge Bryan. A few days before the trial, I advised the court that I intended to challenge the constitutionality of the Selective Service Act on the ground urged in *Boyd v. Clark* and asked for a pretrial hearing on that issue. Judge Bryan directed the issue be presented to him at the time of trial, and so I showed up for trial with voluminous files, most of them relating to the *Boyd v. Clark* issue.

A few minutes before the opening of court, I exchanged trial briefs with the United States Attorney. As I thumbed through the government's brief, I noticed an excerpt from the minutes of a selective service board meeting in June 1966, at which Fargas had presented his CO claim. The excerpt looked somewhat unfamiliar. Long before—in fact, over two years before—I had received from the government a copy of Fargas's selective service file, which included minutes of that same meeting. I checked my file and found that the minutes given to me by the government in 1966 and the minutes now presented by the United States Attorney, though both purporting to be minutes of the same meeting, were in fact materially different.

I pointed this out to the United States Attorney, who seemed as surprised as I was. He said that he'd never before seen the document I had; I certainly had never before seen the document he had. We quickly asked the court to adjourn the case for a few days so that he could look into the apparent alteration of a critical record.

His investigation disclosed that after the local selective service board had met with Fargas in June 1966, the Court of Appeals had decided the case of *United States v. Geary*, which, like the Fargas and Hudson cases, concerned a registrant who hadn't claimed CO status until after he received his notice of induction. In that case, the court specified the kind of findings the draft board had to make, if it was to deny CO status. The original minutes of Fargas's draft board, given to me in 1966, had not been sufficient to meet the *Geary* standard—and so the state headquarters of the selective service system directed the local board to alter the minutes to conform to the *Geary* decision.

When the court reconvened a few days later, the United States Attorney, much embarrassed, moved to dismiss the indictment against Fargas. To my surprise, he threw in a motion to dismiss the case against Hudson, as well. Up to this point, Hudson's case hadn't even been mentioned. It shortly appeared that the alterations made in Fargas's record had likewise been made in Hudson's.

My clients had been successful, in that the indictments against them were about to be dismissed, but I was far from happy. Dismissal of the indictment would leave the notices of induction pending, and both Fargas and Hudson were technically in violation of the law and could theoretically be indicted again. The government quickly agreed to withdraw the notices of induction as well. Fargas and Hudson were both later classified as COs but, strangely, were never required to perform the alternate service required by law of other COs.

That was fine so far as Fargas and Hudson were concerned, but it left me frustrated. (Judge Bryan said he didn't share my frustration. It was a couple of cases off his calendar.) I had spent a great deal of time in preparing the case with respect to the student deferment issue, and I was being deprived once again of a chance to present it in court. Similarly, my clients weren't going to be convicted, and therefore I wasn't going to have an opportunity to present to an appellate court the issue I had raised before Judge Tyler with respect to the selection of a jury.

All of this, I will concede, was somewhat self-centered; I had been retained to represent my clients, not to satisfy my ego or even to push some of my favorite legal theories. Nevertheless, I had a great interest in these theories because they affected not only these clients but many other clients, and opportunities to get rulings on them were not always readily available.

There was another problem that concerned me. The draft board had acted under the instructions of the state headquarters in illegally changing the minutes with respect to the CO status of Fargas and Hudson. The practice of the selective service system was likely to be uniform in all cases, and so I urged Judge Bryan to direct that an investigation be made to find out how often this practice had been followed, and how many other persons had been denied CO status because of this illegal practice.

I got nowhere. Judge Bryan refused. His calendar was heavy (the Cuban cases!) and he was not the crusading type. I then tried to get the United States Attorney to look into the matter. He, too, was not interested. Next I tried the *New York Times*. I did get stories on the Fargas and Hudson cases, but that was all.

As I have said, no more than a handful of our draft clients had been indicted. One of them was David Malament. David was the son of Ed Malament, one of my closest friends, who had died during the 1958 convention of the National Lawyers Guild. David was a tall, dark, and very handsome young man, who, in 1970, refused to submit to induction. He was then twenty-two years old and was a graduate fellow in philosophy, studying at the Rockefeller University in New York. His field of study was astrophysics.

David had originally been classified as a student by the selective service system, while studying at Columbia, Stanford, and Free University in Berlin on a Fulbright scholarship. By April 1970, his student deferment had run out, and he wrote to his draft board saying that he considered the war in Vietnam to be illegal and that he would not participate in the war in any capacity, by reason of his conscientious scruples. He stated that there were some circumstances in which he could conceive of fighting, but not in the Vietnam War. He said that his father had fought in World War II and he was proud of that fact. Were there ever to be a repetition of the political situation present in World War II, there was a possibility that he might fight, but he would not take part in the Vietnam War. He was, in legal terms, a selective conscientious objector.

David's draft board called him to a hearing to discuss his position on his obligation to serve. David did not attend. He was directed to appear at a preinduction physical examination; he did not appear at that, either. He was directed to appear for induction. He reported but refused to fill out a security questionnaire relating to his political beliefs and activities. He told the inducting officers that he would refuse to be inducted, and when, subsequently, he refused to take the ceremonial step forward, symbolic of induction, he was arrested. Later that day he was released on his own recognizance.

David was indicted, and his case was assigned to Judge Irving Ben Cooper. Cooper was an emotionally unstable judge and never should have been on the bench. I knew him fairly well. He had been a New York City magistrate and had risen, largely because of seniority, to the position of chief magistrate. Later he sat as a judge in the court of special sessions. His erratic behavior in those positions had resulted in a great deal of difficulty, and perhaps in order to get rid of him, he was kicked upstairs to the United States District Court. He was very talkative on the bench; at every opportunity he launched into a detailed story about how, when he was a small boy, he was very poor and picked up lumps of coal at a local railroad yard to supply his mother with heat during the cold winter months. He also had a fearful temper and, when crossed burst into a fury that was almost psychotic.

It was, however, quite possible to avoid trouble if one spoke softly and agreed with his philosophical remarks, and I had never had any difficulty with him in the magistrate's court. He was in fact a warm-hearted fellow. As a magistrate, he was generous and as kind as one could be in my cases. In cases involving picket line violence—and those were the cases in which I had occasion to meet him—the picket almost always got a good break, so long as his lawyer was prepared to listen to Cooper's ramblings about his terrible childhood.

In David's case, Cooper was probably a good judge if he were kept in good humor, since conviction was likely and Cooper would probably impose a light sentence. After indictment, I moved for dismissal, on the grounds that the war in Vietnam was illegal, and that good-faith selective conscientious objectors were entitled to exemption from the draft on constitutional grounds (freedom of speech? freedom of religion?). I even argued that the federal government had no constitutional right to conscript citizens, basing such contention on a tendentious historical analysis that flew in the face of a hundred years of history.

A month after we submitted our brief to the district court in support of our motion to dismiss, the Supreme Court, with only Justice Douglas dissenting, ruled that selective conscientious objectors were not exempt from the draft. The ruling came as no surprise. The lower courts had been ruling that way for some time, and it had no significant effect on any pending case except to foreclose one of the defenses that had been urged by those of us who were representing selective CO's. Shortly after, Cooper denied our motion to dismiss.

David's trial took only a few hours. There were no facts in dispute. The government put forth its case in the usual fashion. It put the selective service board representative on the stand; he read from the board files; an officer of the induction center testified that David had refused to step forward and be inducted, and the government's case was closed. We offered to prove that the war was illegal, submitting an affidavit by Professor Richard Falk of Princeton University in support of the argument. The offer of proof was, of course, rejected, and David then took the stand and made an eloquent and moving plea for his selective conscientious objector position.

Cooper was surprisingly tolerant and heard him out, probably because David was a very attractive person, and he permitted David to talk as long as he wanted to. Finally, the case was submitted to the jury, the court having charged that David's arguments were all insufficient defenses. In summing up to the jury, I argued, as much as Cooper would permit, that the selective conscientious objector position should be recognized by the jury, despite the Supreme Court decision, but I wasn't permitted to spend a great deal of time on that argument.

No one expected the jury to be out for long, but no one was prepared for what happened. In about twenty minutes the jury returned and said that it could not agree on a verdict. Cooper was surprised, but he took it pretty well. He pointed out that the jury had been out a very short time and that it should try a bit longer to decide the case. The jury dutifully resumed deliberations. Two hours later it returned. The foreman then told the judge that as soon as the jury had gone out the first time, one of the jurors announced that he didn't care what the law was or what the judge said. "I'll never vote to convict this young man. I don't care if we stay here two weeks," that juror told the others. He then sat down in a corner, pulled a book out of his pocket, and started to read. (One of the court attendants later said to me that it would teach the United States Attorney to challenge any prospective juror who came to court with a book.) Cooper dismissed the jury and set the case down for a new trial, a day or two later. This time, the jury came back in about fifteen minutes with a verdict of guilty.

A few days later, when David came up for sentence, he again spoke of his deep convictions and his conscientious objections to the Vietnam War in particular. Cooper answered, telling of his childhood poverty and agreeing with David at least in tone of voice and appearance of sincerity. He then sentenced David to a year, of which three months were to be spent in jail and nine months in community service. David served the three months, and his probation officer assigned him to work at New York's Judson Memorial Church as a draft counselor. In view of the fact that Judson Memorial Church was a center for young men who were objecting to induction, the result was that David spent the last nine months of his sentence in counseling persons like himself how to avoid selective service.

I ran into Judge Cooper subsequently. During the winter of 1972/73, I spent weekends in East Hampton and rode the Long Island Railroad into New York very early every Monday morning with Joanne and Mark, then three years old. The train, each morning at about 7:00, made a stop at Speonk, and Cooper, who had a home nearby in Remsenberg, got on the train. Mark was quite excited about this, and he watched carefully out the window and exclaimed with great joy, "Here comes the judge," every time he saw Cooper on the platform. Cooper responded by bringing candy to Mark, and quite a friendship grew up between them. I had several conversations with the judge on the ride into New York, and we discussed life in general—conversations that consisted in large part of the judge talking about his childhood. He didn't remember much about the Malament case.

There were other kinds of litigation during the war as well. Street demonstrations were common and they sometimes turned into violent action. Picket lines were established to block entry into the induction center at the Battery, and peaceful parades sometimes broke up into marauding groups of young folks intent on demonstrating their opposition to the war and, in fact, to the government and all it stood for. Such activities brought out the police force, usually on horses, resulting in arrests that dragged me now and then into night court, an institution I hadn't visited much for about twenty years.

But some of the criminal cases were more serious. In November 1968, the FBI staked out a residence on Sumter Street in Brooklyn, in which it believed Reggie Oliver, wanted for draft evasion, lived. After several evenings of surveillance, the agents, who had a warrant, entered the building and knocked on the apartment door. Oliver's wife answered. The agents identified themselves as FBI agents and asked whether Oliver was inside. Ms. Oliver said that she was an orthodox Muslim, as were her sister and her husband. Furthermore, the apartment was a mosque, and if Reggie were there at all, he had taken sanctuary in the mosque. The agents were not prepared to accept this as an excuse, and they forced their way in and found Oliver in the apartment. They attempted to take him into custody, but he resisted. A scuffle resulted: one of the women wielded a hammer; Oliver himself was a big man, and the FBI agents—there were four of them—had a considerable amount of difficulty in getting him under control. The struggle was quite violent, and one of the agents drew his gun. Oliver tried to kick the gun out of his hand, and a shot went through the roof.

Oliver shouted to his wife, "Get the brothers." One of the women ran out of the house. By the time Oliver was handcuffed and taken downstairs, about forty to fifty brothers (and a few sisters) had collected, and a violent fracas resulted, in the course of which Oliver escaped and was last seen walking down the street, still handcuffed, with his wife and sister-in-law.

One of the agents suffered a broken jaw, and the others incurred lesser injuries. The crowd dispersed only when the city police showed up.

Three men were arrested at the scene of the disturbance. All of the others scattered. The next day, fifty to sixty FBI agents (none of whom had been at the scene of the conflict) were sent out into the neighborhood to look for the perpetrators. They were told to make arrests "for failure to have identification." They came back to FBI headquarters with five young men who had been arrested, more or less at random, on charges that they didn't have in their immediate possession their selective service ID cards.

At the FBI headquarters, the five men arrested were taken around and shown to the FBI agents who had been the victims of the assault. Four of them were identified as the persons who had been in the crowd the evening before.

The three men arrested at the scene of the conflict, the four who had been identified the next day by the FBI agents, and the two women were all indicted on charges of assaulting FBI agents, interfering with agents of the FBI in the performance of their duty, and in aiding and assisting in the escape of Oliver. At the trial, I represented four of the nine defendants; Sandy Katz represented two, Neil Fabricant represented one, and Samuel Lee represented the two women.

The defendants were brought to trial before Judge Edward Dooling in the Brooklyn federal court, and a fine trial it was. Dooling was a compassionate man. Rarely have I met a gentler, more considerate judge, totally out of place in a criminal court. He opened the trial by telling the jurors that the defendants were Muslims; that they would not stand up when he entered the room; that they would not take off their turbans, and that they would not take an oath on the Bible, because all these things were against their religion. "We must all respect their religion, because they have as much right to practice it as you have to practice yours." He also noted that all of the defendants had abandoned their Christian names and would refer to each other at the trial by Arabic names; he told the jury that they had a right to do so.

The trial took about eight days. The defendants, all of them black, were dressed in long, white gowns and wore white turbans. Every morning, they marched in an orderly file from the subway to the courthouse, two by two, in size order. At the head of the line was an imposing, 6'3" handsome man, who was not a defendant but seemed to be in charge. The women, being shortest, were last in line; an observer could not help concluding that the women weren't very important in the order of things. At lunch hour, they marched in similar order to a restaurant on Court Street, passing on the way a group of yellow-clad Hari Krishna celebrants who were preaching on the corner of Court Street and Pierrepont. The noontime crowds enjoyed this colorful scene.

Every day at four o'clock, Dooling called a recess so that the defendants could say their afternoon prayers, and the courtroom was cleared for that purpose. Prayer rugs were spread out, and the defendants faced Mecca and performed their daily afternoon ritual. News of this event spread quickly through the courthouse, and spectators came by to peek through the windows of the courtroom doors.

Commenting on Shirley Oliver's refusal to let the FBI agents into the apartment because, she said, it was not only her home but also a mosque, Dooling told the jury that if persons tried to enter his church, the Roman Catholic church, with hostile intent, and for the purpose of profaning the church, he, too, would use force to keep them out. Dooling's remarks conveyed a slightly comic picture, since he was an elderly, rather frail gentleman, and the idea of his trying to keep a burly cop out of a Catholic church would have been laughable, had he not been so indignant about this hypothetical invasion of his hypothetical sanctuary.

The trial was devoted mostly to a full description of what happened on the street, with graphic evidence by the FBI agents as to how they were assaulted by a large crowd of people, and by some of the defendants about how they weren't even at the scene.

Throughout the trial, the defendants referred to each other by their Arabic names; the prosecution referred to them by their Christian names, causing no little confusion. The principle issue in the case was one of identification. The crowd on the street had been dense; there had been lots of people milling around, and the night was dark. Nevertheless, the FBI agents identified the seven male defendants as persons who had participated in the struggle. The issue of identification was not very important as to those arrested at the scene, but it was critical as to the other four. The court accepted the courtroom identification of those defendants even though we contended that such testimony was suspect in view of the fact that the prior identification at FBI headquarters had been made without a lineup and hence improper. Further, we argued, the arrests of the four defendants on the day after the melee had been without just cause and was illegal, and that the identifications were therefore tainted.

Alas, the case was colorful, but the broken jaw plus the identification testimony was sufficient to result in a jury verdict of guilty as to all of the men. One of the women was found not guilty, the other guilty on only one of the counts.

As was to be expected from this judge, the sentences were light, considering the offense. When one of the defendants was asked whether he wanted to say anything before sentence was passed, he said, "I want to point out that Christianity is not a peaceful religion, and that sometimes violence is called for. Your Honor will recall that one of Jesus' followers cut off the ear of a priest." "Yes," said Dooling, who was quite familiar with Scripture, "and what did Jesus do?" "He put the ear back on," said the defendant, "and if Jesus had been on Sumter Street that evening, he might have put the FBI men together again, but he wasn't there."

I took an appeal on behalf of the seven male defendants who had been found guilty. I won a reversal as to four, on the ground that their arrests the day after the fight were illegal, and that their identification at FBI headquarters had resulted from the illegal arrests and hence were tainted. This was particularly true because, said the Court of Appeals, the FBI "deliberately seized the appellants on a mere pretext for the purpose of displaying them to the agents who had been present at the scene of the crime." The court held that the evidence of identification presented at the trial had been secured by the "exploitation" of the illegality of the arrests.

Judge Hays, true to form, dissented. The conviction of the three defendants arrested at the scene of the fracas was affirmed. It was difficult to find an argument for reversal as to them.

■

The Vietnam War didn't allow for many light touches, but one can be found in *Gwathmey v. Town of East Hampton,* one of the enjoyable cases of the time.

In 1968, Joanne and I bought a second home in East Hampton. Over the years, we made many friends there but none were more valued than Bob and Rosalie Gwathmey. Bob, who died in 1988, was an artist who was a product of the WPA days during the Great Depression. Like other artists of the same background—Rafael and Moses Soyer, Jacob Lawrence, William Gropper, Philip Evergood, and Ad Reinhardt—he was not only very successful in later years but radical as well. Rosalie is a successful textile designer. Joanne had met Bob years before, and when we visited Bob and Rosalie in Amagansett, they had just moved into a sensational new house designed by their talented son, Charles, who, in later years, became one of the most successful architects in the country. Bob was very proud of that house and of Charles as well. My admiration of both was later somewhat tempered by the fact that Mark fell down the circular staircase in the house when he was two years old and cut his lip badly. But he has shown no permanent ill effects, and I've long since forgiven both Bob and Charles.

Bob and Rosalie were generous beyond reason. They were ever ready to lend their house and its expansive lawn to "cause parties" and to lend their names and talents to help raise money for the proper political programs. And they were hospitable, too—every weekend found their spacious living room comfortably filled with pleasant people. It was there that we met many who became fast friends, and who remain so. The Gwathmeys and their house were a popular feature of East Hampton.

And so, when Bob was arrested on a citizen's complaint in June 1970, the event aroused widespread interest throughout the east end of Long Island. His offense was the flying of a large peace flag—an American flag except for an inverted trident replacing the stars in the field of blue—outside his house. The flag was widely recognized as a symbol of the movement opposing the Vietnam War. Bob was hauled off to the local police station but released on one hundred dollars bail. The charge was a violation of Chapter 136(a) of the New York General Business Law, which made it a misdemeanor to display a word, figure, mark, picture, design, drawing, or advertisement on the national flag of the United States or on a picture of the flag or on a design that to a casual observer might look like a flag.

This was a silly statute, and I jumped at the opportunity to represent Bob. I promptly brought a federal action to enjoin the prosecution. We ultimately won the case, though it took several years, during which the local prosecuting officials, a bit embarrassed by the original arrest, did nothing to proceed against Bob. We lost the first step when Judge Travia, one of the stupidest men ever to sit on the federal bench, held the statute constitutional. On appeal, we won easily. The case was argued before Judges Lumbard, Waterman, and Anderson. It was a fun argument. I had prepared a large graphic display—a 4' x 4' poster, on which I had mounted a number of illustrations showing common, everyday uses of the design of the American flag in ways that were in violation of the words of the statute: advertising logos and displays, T-shirts, hatbands, cigarette papers, and other similar material. The centerpiece of the poster, and the illustration that most appealed to Judge Lumbard, was a large photo of Raquel Welch in a bikini made up of the American flag. "That," he observed, "is a flag one could wear close to one's heart."

We won, and the state surprisingly took an appeal to the Supreme Court. We filed answering papers, and the case was ready for argument before the end of the court term in June 1971. The case wasn't heard during that term, which was somewhat unusual, as the court normally hears all such cases by the time the term ends. It wasn't heard in the 1972–73 term, either, which was even more unusual, since the court rarely keeps a case on its calendar for so long a period of time. In July 1973, I called Mr. Rodack, then clerk of the court, and asked him what happened to the case.

"Oh," he said with a smile in his voice, "that must be a radiator case." "A radiator case? What's that?" "That's a case in which the file has fallen behind the radiator," he explained. The file was evidently found by the next July, when the court sent the *Gwathmey* case back to the district court for technical reasons. At the same time, the court in another case held the statute unconstitutional, and Bob's prosecution was dropped.

17

Up to the Present

At about 11:00 on the morning of October 20, 1981, a distraught and tense Leonard Boudin burst into my office. "Get your coat," he said, "We're going up to New City. Kathy's been arrested. It's serious."

It took me a few minutes to orient myself enough even to ask questions. By that time, we were down the elevator and into the street, where a car driven by Bill Kunstler was waiting. Leonard's daughter Kathy had disappeared over ten years before, after an explosion in a townhouse on East Eleventh Street in New York. I hadn't heard, seen, or spoken to her since, although her whereabouts and her welfare had been a matter of much concern to me and had been a topic of considerable discussion between myself and Leonard. I had no doubt that Leonard was in touch with her; it seemed to me impossible that he would not have made contact over so many years, but I didn't know what those contacts had been, and to be frank, so long as she was well, I didn't want to know.

Bill drove us up to the jail in New City, and on the way he and Leonard filled me in on the outlines of the story. Kathy had been arrested after a shootout following an attempt to rob a Brinks armored truck in Nanuet. Three men were killed in the encounter—two police officers and a Brinks Company guard. Kathy hadn't done any of the shooting, but she and David Gilbert, the man with whom she was living, were driving a getaway car. It was some days before I heard all the details, but I learned enough on the ride to learn that a grave felony charge—perhaps murder—was likely.

The local police force and the state troopers were out in force by the time we got to the jail. So was the press. Kathy was in a state of shock. Four or five others of her associates on this adventure—including David—had also been arrested, and we had to fight our way through the crowd to get into the jail and then to get out again. Neither Leonard nor

I had had any experience in handling this kind of case. Dealing with street crime—with guns, with jail wardens, and with angry cops—was not our kind of work. But it was Bill Kunstler's. He had been called into the case by someone—I'm not sure by whom—and he was the person, I believe, who had notified Leonard. He handled the press, the police, and the prison authorities with his usual skill. A bail hearing was set for the next day or the day after.

On the way back to New York, I picked up a few more background facts. Kathy had been living in New York with David and their infant son, Chesa, for some time before her arrest. Leonard had seen her on several recent occasions; indeed, he had been visiting her and Chesa just a few days before the arrest. Kathy had just about decided to surface, he said, but, obviously, not soon enough. She had a few unrelated criminal charges, actual or potential, against her, arising out of the 1970 explosion on East Eleventh Street and out of demonstrations against the police in Chicago before that, but none of these seemed very serious, and Leonard thought they could be straightened out without much trouble. This new charge could not be so easily disposed of.

I had known Kathy since she was born and saw her frequently as a child and a young adult. Between my personal contacts with her, Leonard reported regularly on her activities—her attendance at Bryn Mawr, where she played an important role in student politics; her employment in San Francisco and Cleveland, working with the poorest and most deprived in our society. She was a member of Students for a Democratic Society and a leading figure in Weatherman, the militant and confrontational segment of SDS that provided its leadership after its tumultuous convention in Chicago in 1969. Weatherman put "black liberation" at the top of its political agenda, and I remember a discussion with Kathy in Chicago in about 1969 in which she expressed her despair as to the possibility that the democratic process could ever solve the problem of racism in this country. While in Chicago, she had been arrested in connection with demonstrations against the police, and I had represented her in a challenge to the jury system in Illinois, relying on my experience in Joni's case. I wasn't successful, and Kathy was released on bail pending trial of the charges. She had not been tried on these charges when she disappeared.

Weatherman gravitated more and more toward violence as a means of achieving its goals and was evidently responsible for a number of bombings in 1969 and 1970. In March 1970, the townhouse on East Eleventh Street in which Kathy was then living was accidentally blown up, with some fatalities, and Kathy went underground, as did many other members of Weatherman. For the next several years the "Weather Underground" continued its political activities, but it disintegrated in time.

In the months that followed Kathy's arrest, I attended many gatherings of friends of mine and Leonard's to rally support for Kathy, both financial and in terms of public relations. The refrain of most of those attending the meetings was "We love Kathy, and we will do what we can to help her, but what she did was unmitigated evil—it was a terrorist act, and terrorism is evil." I doubted that very many of those persons really loved Kathy. They loved Leonard and were supporting him. I was profoundly annoyed by their reaction. Their quick dismissal of Kathy's cause was offensive to me. At some of these meetings I analogized the raid on the Brinks truck to John Brown's raid on Harpers Ferry in which ten soldiers were killed or Nat Turner's rebellion in Virginia (fifty-one fatalities) or Castro's raid on the Moncada Barracks (nineteen dead). My analogies were my own, and I had no reason to believe that Kathy had given a thought to historical precedent. But her actions were not self-serving. Her life had been devoted to helping the disadvantaged of this earth and I thought that this incident was a tragically wrong way to seek the same end. So much at least could have been said for Kathy, but I didn't hear anyone say it.

But back to those dreadful days in October 1981. A day or two after the arrest, Kathy was arraigned in New City. The scene in the neighborhood of the court was that of an armed camp. The street was lined with state troopers, with guns ready. The roofs of buildings surrounding the courthouse were manned with police armed with machine guns. To get into the courthouse one was searched three or four times by armed guards. It's hard to imagine what the cops were thinking; perhaps a rebel army was expected to appear to rescue Kathy and her friends.

There was no rebel army, and the proceedings were almost routine, except that the courtroom was so jammed with press it was almost impossible for a spectator to get in, and even Kathy's lawyers had trouble getting through the crowd. Everyone involved was held without bail. Not only had there been killings, but those killed had been police officers, and that is indeed murder raised several degrees in public perception.

It was agreed at once that our office, while available for all necessary legal research, was not really equipped to represent Kathy without expert help. We had no experience in handling this kind of felony, and we weren't about to use Kathy to learn how to do it. Early in the process, Leonard asked me to stand in for him in deciding the policy questions that would arise. He said he was too close to Kathy to make such decisions objectively. He was right, and I agreed, on the understanding that Leonard would stay out of the situation. It was a futile agreement, effective for about a day. Leonard interfered with all decisions on all levels at all times, leading to a considerable amount of tension, because disagreements were frequent and substantial. In the circumstances, it really didn't make much difference, because the end result was ordained, but the road to that result was very rocky indeed.

Leonard Weinglass, Martin Garbus, and Linda Bakiel were retained to represent Kathy. Weinglass (known in the office as "Lennie," to distinguish him from Leonard Boudin) has wide experience in trying radical political cases of many kinds in all parts of the country and in many different settings. A free spirit who moves from cause to cause with great agility and mobility, he was quickly able to establish the necessary rapport with Kathy and her codefendants. Marty is a brilliant and courageous lawyer both in the courtroom and as a scholar, with high standing at the bar of New York and a sympathetic understanding, though not agreement, with Kathy's political stance. Linda, a militant young lawyer, was probably the one closest to Kathy. The three worked well together as a team, doing as good a job as could be done in the circumstances.

Much of my time over the next two and a half years was occupied by Kathy's case. My role was to keep Leonard off the backs of the others, to address intraoffice tensions (which were many), to help to decide strategy questions, and to supervise legal research at our office. Lots of preliminary litigation followed—on prison conditions, on change of venue, and on a host of other issues—but by early 1984, the preliminaries were all over and a trial was imminent. It was abundantly clear that Kathy could not be acquitted. She was unwilling to undergo the emotional ordeal of a trial in the remote hope that a dissenting juror or an error by the court might cause a mistrial and necessitate a second trial—the most that we could hope for, and that would hardly be classified as a victory.

After much discussion, Kathy pleaded guilty to murder in the second degree and was sentenced to twenty years to life. That means that after twenty years she will be eligible for parole. That will not be until the next century.

In late November 1994, after Governor Cuomo had been defeated by George Pataki in his bid for a fourth term, we were advised, somewhat indirectly, that Cuomo might be sympathetic to an application by Kathy for gubernatorial clemency, action that would make her eligible for parole at once. And so our team (Lennie, Marty, Linda, and myself) set to work to prepare an application for clemency. Much work was done on this. Letters of recommendation were collected from many; Kathy was interviewed by a member of the parole board and prison officials, and a summary of Kathy's impressive prison accomplishments was prepared. While in prison, she had secured a master's degree in education from Norwich University and had written a highly praised article for the *Harvard Educational Review*, entitled "Participatory Literary Education Behind Bars: AIDS Opens the Door." She also conducted programs within the prison in adult basic education and on AIDS counseling.

The governor turned Kathy down, and I suppose we were wrong to have hoped for favorable action. Cuomo had not been generous in his grants of clemency petitions, and had it not been for the suggestion that an application might be favorably considered, I never would have thought of such an application.

My favorite clients have been Joni and Peter, both of whom have been somewhat litigious. Joni's Georgia adventure has already been told; she had one or two other minor encounters with the law arising out of her political activities. Peter's cases have been confined to the civil side of the law. They all turned out better than I had any reason to expect.

From his earliest days, Peter seemed headed for academia. After compiling an outstanding record in high school, he attended the University of Chicago and got his doctorate at that institution. I don't fully understand his doctoral thesis or his subsequent books, but he tells me his books and articles were not written for me and that he doesn't understand my briefs. I hope he'll understand this book. He also writes a lot of music criticism, which I accept on faith.

Judging from reports, Peter is an extraordinary teacher and popular with his students and (most) other faculty members. That popularity, however, has not always extended to the administrations of the institutions with which he has been connected; rarely can he find an administration whose policies he can accept. This proclivity had manifested itself in 1967, when he was one of the leaders of a student occupation of the administration building of the University of Chicago.

Upon graduation, Peter was employed as a teacher at Southwest College, a public junior college in Chicago. He and two other faculty members were elected to a faculty committee of the college, where they successfully sponsored a series of resolutions opposing administration policies, mostly on personnel matters. Implicit in this activity was criticism of the union that represented the faculty of the college, for its failure to vigorously enforce the collective bargaining agreement. When Peter and his friends were ordered transferred to other colleges, they claimed that the administration regarded them as disruptive rank-and-file members of the union and that the transfers were intended to break up the trio, which was challenging both the administration and the union. Peter called me for legal advice.

This was something of a relief from the international law problems I was facing daily in the Cuba litigation. The matter was important to Peter and his friends, but hardly life threatening. I responded to Peter's summons with enthusiasm. We started an action in the federal court in Chicago, claiming that the transfer was a violation of the free speech rights of the plaintiffs and of their right to a hearing under the due process clause of the Fifth Amendment. Mike Krinsky, then a junior in the office and a friend of Peter's, did much of the preliminary discovery work on the case, and I argued a motion for a preliminary injunction to enjoin the transfer, which was scheduled to be effective the following month.

The hearing, before Judge Hubert L. Will, was a good one. The college officials were hard put to give any reason at all for the transfers and argued only that they had the right to take such action as a matter of administrative convenience. Will granted a preliminary injunction to maintain the status quo until a full trial could be held. I must admit that I was a bit surprised. We don't have many judges that good in New York.

In October, the college amended its contract with the union to prohibit faculty transfers and shortly after, it rescinded the transfer of Peter and his friends. It then moved to dismiss the case as moot, a motion granted by the district court. We appealed. I can't now think of why, except that we were enjoying ourselves, and I habitually appeal whenever I lose. To my continued surprise, the Court of Appeals, by a two-to-one vote, held the case was not moot, because the collective bargaining agreement would expire in two years, and the transfers might then be reactivated. The case was sent back to the district court, where it died a natural death. For years afterward, the case was cited as an authority as to what does or does not constitute a moot cause of action.

Peter left Southwest College shortly after and became a member of the faculty of Kirkland College, which later merged with Hamilton College, in Clinton, New York. In 1986, the student body at Hamilton, or at least a portion of it, was concerned over the fact that much of the college endowment was invested in South Africa and, like students at many other institutions, they demanded that Hamilton divest itself of all South African investments. The administration of the college refused, and student demonstrations followed. The students were joined by a number of faculty members who considered the fight their fight as well, and as I could easily have predicted, up front and center was Peter.

The college applied for an injunction in the state court in Utica to restrain the demonstration, naming Peter and half a dozen students as defendants. Peter called on his lawyer, and Mike Krinsky and I again responded, taking with us Haywood Burns, then the president of the National Lawyers Guild and later dean of CUNY law school. We relied heavily on the college rules, which provided for all sorts of internal steps that had to be taken before application could be made to a court. More important, we served subpoenas on the president of the college, several deans, and a few other administrative officers, seeking the production of a truly imposing number of college records. This promised a big show, to which I looked forward—cross-examination of college presidents and deans, I thought, would be as enjoyable as cross-examination of the president of Western Union had been forty years earlier.

The court denied the injunction without calling any witnesses, and I never had the chance to cross-examine anyone, though I did make a short and successful speech to the court. We had submitted an elaborate set of papers, suitable for the United States Supreme Court, and the court was glad to find some way to get rid of us. "If Hamilton College lacks the courage to enforce its own rules . . . it cannot ask the court to interfere," said Judge Charles H. Tenney.

After a while, the whole dispute wound down, as these things usually do, especially on college campuses, where examinations, vacations, and graduations interfere with long-range student political action.

A year later, the scenario was repeated, with some modification. This time, twelve students sat in at the administration building and refused to leave, to protest college discrimination against blacks, gays, and other minority groups. Peter was not in the occupying forces, but he and other members of the faculty, including Peter's wife, Nancy, stood by to supply tactical advice to the students, as well as moral support, while Peter acted as spokesperson for the students in a number of meetings with the president and the deans. Once again we were called upon for legal representation.

As before, the college moved in the state court for an injunctive order and secured one, but it was somewhat ambiguous and the students ignored it. The president responded by suspending the students for the rest of the academic year; we then took the offensive and brought an action in the federal court on behalf of the students to enjoin the college from suspending them. Mike and I remembered Peter's Southwest College lawsuit and tried to repeat it.

We had a pretty good case in that the president had once again failed to utilize the applicable college rules. The trouble was that the federal court had no jurisdiction unless the action of the college, a private institution, constituted action "under color of state law." (Southwest College had been a public institution, giving the federal courts jurisdiction.) The question is one of those metaphysical concepts that gives rise to endless law review articles and even more legal decisions. We were on thin ice in claiming federal jurisdiction, but Krinsky is a very inventive lawyer, and he worked out an ingenious theory to support our claim. In any event, we thought we had no chance in the state court at Utica where the influence of Hamilton College is great, and therefore we went ahead with the federal action.

Mike's theory required a most elaborate collection of documentation from the state education department relating to the disciplinary rules in effect in many other New York colleges, which resulted in the submission of several hundreds of pages of evidence, all collected within a very few days. Mike's energy was inexhaustible. I was totally unable to keep up with him, and the result was that I stepped aside and let him take care not merely of collecting the evidence but of handling the whole case. I merely hovered in the background to give some sort of vague advice on what ought to be done next.

The result was a hearing in the district court in Albany before Judge Cholakes, who, after a full day of proceeding, dismissed the complaint in an oral opinion from the bench. He found injury to the plaintiffs and improper procedure by the president but, as I had anticipated, could not find the requisite federal jurisdiction. Mike promptly moved to stay the suspension of the students until we could get an appellate court to hear the case. Such relief was likewise denied.

In accordance with office practice, we appealed. A limited stay was granted by the Court of Appeals to allow the students to attend classes pending a decision by that court. Argument was held in the spring, and in July, Judge James L. Oakes reversed the decision of the lower court and issued an injunction against the college, finding the requisite state action in a statute requiring colleges in New York, both public and private, to draft and file procedures for disciplinary action. The fact that the college had violated these procedures was in the court's opinion sufficient to constitute state action, or at least "action under color of state law."

The decision was totally unexpected by me, but more important, it was totally unexpected by Hamilton College and sent shockwaves through the institution. The college immediately moved for reargument *en banc*. The immediate practical effect of the decision on the suspended students wasn't very important since the academic year was over and the suspensions, by their terms, were no longer effective. But the effect was disastrous for the administration of the college. The president resigned, as did several of the deans. An entirely new administration, much more sympathetic to the complaints of the students, was appointed.

A year later, the Court of Appeals in an *en banc* decision reversed the decision of Judge Oakes and held that there had been no state action. This was a full year and a half after the original suspension. The affected students had been protected by a series of injunctions ever since the original suspension. By that time, the students were gone, and so was the president.

From 1947, and in fact even before that at Boudin, Cohn and Glickstein, Leonard and I had worked in the closest harmony. This wasn't always easy, since we differed in many respects. Speaking somewhat abstractly, I saw the law as a tool to accomplish a social and political purpose—to create a better world. Leonard had no such vision—he would say he had no such illusions. He saw the law as an end in itself, as a scholarly pursuit, as an intellectual game. He did not overlook the social and political aspects of the law, just as I did not overlook the intellectual and scholarly elements of it. We both agreed that we were to represent good guys fighting the government, large corporations, and other bad guys. But I'm not sure he wouldn't have represented Chase Manhattan Bank or American Telephone and Telegraph Company if either had wanted to retain him to litigate interesting legal issues. I believe I would have refused. The occasion never arose, so we never found out what our reaction would be.

He was a more accomplished legal scholar than I; I had a much keener appreciation of the political effect of what we were doing. We shared each other's interests and beliefs, but we gave different weight to the elements in those interests.

He was much more of a public figure than I. He enjoyed a high profile; he was essentially a social creature, especially so far as the legal community was concerned. I prefer a low profile. Most social gatherings tend to bore me—the larger, the more boring. His legal arguments were more learned, but, as he recognized, insufficiently focused; I thought mine more effective. He pitched his argument to the most intelligent member of an appellate panel; I aimed primarily at the least intelligent.

Nevertheless, for many years, our association was very close. In the early days, most of the briefs submitted by the office were written jointly, and strategy and policy were the subjects of discussion and agreement between us. We rehearsed each other's arguments before appellate court appearances, and we attended each other's arguments even in the lower courts. In time, this practice tended to diminish as the office grew larger and our responsibilities greater. Throughout the years, we held office meetings with the partners and associates to discuss new cases, to report on old ones, and to decide recurring questions of "good and welfare." I considered such meetings a necessity; Leonard considered them a nuisance. Generally speaking, policy questions, including the taking of new cases, were decided by a vote of the lawyers—both partners and associates.

In 1973, a sharp disagreement arose over a new case that was offered to us. It challenged a somewhat fundamental view I had always had as to my role as a lawyer. I had always adhered to a few basic rules: I would not represent a landlord against a tenant; I would not represent a drug dealer; I would not represent an employer against a union; I would not represent a fascist or right-wing institution. This sounds a bit sanctimonious, and I don't mean to preach, but these were the parameters beyond which I was unwilling to go. The case then being offered was a criminal charge that a union organizer had taken a bribe from an employer to enter into a "sweetheart" contract. I was convinced that the defendant was guilty and that this was an antiunion cause. I urged the office to reject it. Leonard disagreed. After quite a bit of discussion, the office voted not to represent the defendant.

In 1974, I took my year off in England. On my return I discovered that the defendant had been convicted at trial and that in my absence he had retained the office to represent him on appeal. Leonard told me that Ben Gold had put lots of pressure on him to take the case on appeal. He did, and lost. Perhaps, if I'd been here I would have succumbed to the pressure, because I had a high regard for Ben, but I was annoyed anyhow.

Another, more serious, difference arose a few years later when a defendant accused of dealing in drugs sought to retain us. The debate at our office meeting was long, loud, and angry. Leonard wanted to take the case; I was adamant in refusal. The office finally voted five to four against me, but both Mike Standard and Leonard agreed to reject it in view of the closeness of the vote.

Leonard did little Cuba work after the first few years, but we jointly tried Joni's case, and in 1976 we jointly tried a criminal case in Virginia involving three builders charged with defrauding a bank, the only case we ever handled involving a white-collar crime with no political significance at all—just an ordinary criminal case. These enterprises ran smoothly and there was no significant disagreement between us.

In the late seventies the office was retained in litigation involving Bank Markazi, the national bank of Iran. Early in 1979, the Shah of Iran was deposed by a coalition of Islam fundamentalists led by Ayatollah Rhuhollah Khomeini and a young radical group led by Abolhassan Bani-Sadr and others. Some months later we were retained to represent the bank in connection with extensive litigation in the United States involving very large sums of money. The case was handled primarily by Leonard and Eric Lieberman—I had no role except as an interested observer, and, of course, I shared in the substantial fees earned by the office. In June 1981, Eric argued and won in the Supreme Court the case of *Dames and Moore v. Regan*, upholding the validity of the Algerian Declaration, the agreement that ended the hostage crisis of November 1979, when Iran captured and held hostage about fifty American citizens.

In the meantime, an internal coup in Iran led by the fundamentalist faction overthrew Bani-Sadr and his associates as officers of the government and shortly after, the officers of the National Bank as well. A period of extreme repression followed during which Bani-Sadr and some of his group went into exile and others were executed or imprisoned. By October 1981, the *New York Times* estimated that over fifteen hundred persons had been executed by the Khomeini regime.

I was shocked at the thought that we would continue to represent that government or any of its agencies; Mike Krinsky agreed with me. But Eric and Leonard insisted on continuing the representation. There was indeed some ambiguity about the situation, and some of the opponents of Khomeini (including some of those who had retained us in the first place) thought that it would be helpful if we remained in the picture. The government of Iran was a third world country, seeking to preserve its sovereignty, and this was a cause that the office had espoused in its representation of Cuba. One of the principal legal issues raised was the act of state doctrine, in which I felt I had almost a proprietary interest, and the result of the litigation might well affect the Cuban cases.

But I found it hard to agree that we should represent a severely repressive government. Among those executed or in exile were officers of the bank we had represented, and although I had not personally known them, I was, at least vicariously, their friend.

The debate within the firm went on for several months. The fees involved in the litigation were high; the legal and political questions remaining after the *Dames and Moore* case were substantial and interesting. Eric wanted to litigate the legal issues; Leonard, faced with the prospect of great expenses in Kathy's case (she had just been arrested), needed the money. After a lot of ill-tempered argument between Leonard and me, a somewhat awkward compromise was worked out. Leonard and Eric would continue to represent Bank Markazi in their own names, at least until the then-current litigation was completed; Mike and I would waive our share of the fee. Not a very neat solution, but the best that we could fashion.

In a few months, the question was taken out of our hands, when Iran decided it did not want to be represented by Western lawyers and would substitute its own in the proceedings that followed. Those proceedings are still continuing, now before the special U.S.–Iran claims tribunal at The Hague.

During all of this period, I was involved in winding up the Cuba litigation, in working on Kathy's case, and in the Alger Hiss litigation. But further, I was trying hard to rebuild a trade union practice, which was my first love and which had virtually disappeared in the 1950s. In about 1978, we were retained by the union representing the flight attendants employed by Eastern Airlines, largely through the efforts of Kathy Stone, one of the younger office associates who was a friend of some of the union's leaders. Several arbitration cases and two intense federal lawsuits followed, one finally decided by the Court of Appeals. The representation ended when Eastern Airlines filed a petition in bankruptcy.

Of even more interest was our representation of the Hospital Workers Union, Local 1199. I had represented that union in a few strike situations back in the late forties, when both it and I were very young. The union was organized by Leon Davis, one of the great trade union leaders of our time. Davis was intense, autocratic, arrogant, and single minded but he inspired a generation of young union organizers to accomplish miracles. He never lost sight of his goal, which was to improve the working conditions of some of the most exploited workers in our society, and he was prepared to sacrifice himself and all his associates to that end. A handful of drugstore clerks in 1945 grew to a local union of one hundred thousand in 1995, holding contracts covering many of the largest hospitals and other health care facilities in New York and its vicinity. It is the largest local union in New York and perhaps in the country.

My early association with Davis and Local 1199 ended in the early 1950s when our trade union practice disappeared, though Leonard rep-

resented the local briefly in a special situation in 1972. When Davis retired in 1982, a series of bitter disputes broke out over the issue of suc-
cessorship and the future structure of the union. The story is much too
complicated to recite here, but there was a good deal of intraunion litigation, involving not only factions within the local union but also relations with the Retail, Wholesale, and Department Store Employees
Union, the international with which the Local was affiliated. I was asked
to represent some of the warring parties. Associated with us in this litigation was Richard Levy of the firm of Eisner and Levy, and Jim Reif
of Gladstein and Reif. When our clients won in June 1986, it became
necessary to retain new general counsel for the union, and Richard, Jim,
and I all bid for the job.

Eisner and Levy, and Gladstein and Reif were both (relatively speaking) young firms with substantial trade union practices and staffs of lawyers who were expert in the field. While representation of a local as large
as 1199 would require additional personnel, there was no reason to believe that either of those two firms could not have undertaken the task.

Our firm presented a different picture. We were larger than either of
the others and had had much more experience over a much longer span
of time in very difficult and complex litigation. Leonard and I had had
a great deal of experience in the trade union field, but that had been
twenty-five or thirty years ago. I was almost twice as old as the principals in the other firms. Few of my partners were really interested in trade
union work, and the fees that Local 1199 was prepared to pay were very
low compared with what we got from many of our other clients in our
1986 practice. Mike Krinsky was outspoken in his opposition to our getting too deeply involved in Local 1199. He pointed out, quite correctly,
that I was seventy-five years old and couldn't expect to practice law very
much longer. "Who would be prepared to take over at that point?" he
asked. Only Judy Levin, who had just become a partner, and Beth Margolis, the youngest of the associates, were really interested in trade union
work; the others were willing to do the work, but without the passion I
thought necessary.

I had many friends among the officers of the local, particularly among
the older members, with whom I had some sort of political rapport. In
political terms they were comfortable with me, but the issue was not one
of political trust but of competent legal representation.

After some weeks of deliberation, the union decided to retain Richard Levy and his firm. A footnote was graciously added—Richard was
authorized and encouraged to retain our firm and Jim's for overflow work,

which was expected to be necessary and substantial. I was disappointed but not surprised. I recognized the decision as a wise one and was comforted by the knowledge that the union, which I admired and respected, would be well represented. In retrospect I doubt that either I or the office could have handled the client as well as has Richard. Our office was not really attuned to represent such a large, low-paying client.

The result, however, was that my hope of getting back into the trade union field was gone. The 1199 litigation continued for another year or two, and that was great fun.

Ever since I had reached the age of seventy, I had been thinking in terms of retirement or at least partial retirement, but it didn't really work out for some years. In 1983, I announced to my partners that I would work only half time and collect only half of my usual draw, but it turned out I was working full time, and after a few years I rescinded that agreement.

On top of this, a new situation arose in the office. In mid-1987, an attorney practicing in Virginia suggested an association with our firm. He specialized in criminal law, including the representation of persons accused of violation of the drug laws. A sizable portion of the legal profession of New York and elsewhere, including many friends, is engaged in such representation. It is, however, a kind of work in which I would not engage, nor was I was willing to remain a member of a firm that accepted drug cases. The deal was one that was potentially profitable to the firm; the assumption was that the attorney would attract clients charged with violation of the drug laws, and a formula was proposed whereby the fees he earned from such cases would be shared with the firm, while we would supply legal support work. He was to be "of counsel" and to have an office in our suite.

The proposed associate was a pleasant man and seemed to be competent at his work. Like most lawyers engaged in this type of work, he saw nothing wrong in the representation of drug dealers. The usual argument was made: that everyone—even a murderer, terrorist, or drug dealer—is entitled to competent legal representation. Maybe so, but that didn't mean that he was entitled to representation by me. I had no qualms about representing an accused murderer (maybe not a professional killer—I don't know about that) or a terrorist, but drug dealers were off limits.

The matter was debated for weeks within the firm, with Leonard arguing strongly for the proposed association. I represented a minority point of view, but I felt strongly about it. I considered a few alternatives. I had the feeling—perhaps shared by my associates—that I had the power to veto the proposed arrangement, in which case the project would be dropped. Or I could just register my dissent and continue as before. Or I could leave the firm.

I was unwilling to continue in the firm if the firm were to engage in a significant amount of drug-related litigation. I considered my assumed veto power but decided not to exercise it; if my associates wanted to engage in this sort of law practice, I didn't see that I had the right—moral or legal or any other kind—to prevent them from doing so. And so I decided to resign from the firm and become counsel to it. The status of "counsel" to a law firm covers a multitude of relationships. It is less than a partnership but more than an employee. That was me. An agreement was worked out whereby I retained the normal support facilities of the office and engaged in minimal practice of the law when cases came along that seemed to be interesting. In return the firm paid me a stipend, which came in quite handy.

The retirement thus came a bit closer. The Local 1199 litigation was not finished until 1990 and I've worked on a few arbitration cases for that union since. I undertook several cases in East Hampton, one involving a charge against a local merchant for selling obscene pictures and the other relating to a real estate venture of a friend in that town. I've handled two estate matters of modest size and fee. Otherwise, I have little connection with the cases in the office and have spent my time writing these memoirs and giving fatherly or often grandfatherly advice to the younger lawyers in the office.

Leonard died quite suddenly on Thanksgiving Day 1989.

Epilogue

I think I chose correctly sixty-five years ago when I decided to become a lawyer. I doubt whether there is any other occupation in which I could have better used my abilities, such as they are, nor any other vocation in which I could have been happier.

When I graduated from law school in 1934, the legal profession, like the rest of the country, was mired deeply in the Great Depression. But within a very few years I fell into the job at the Boudin office and was immediately engaged in a rapidly growing (though not remunerative) field of law. The explosive growth of the labor movement and the closely related field of constitutional rights meant a lot of work for lawyers—at least for lawyers with my interests. I didn't make much money but I was doing work I enjoyed and that corresponded closely to my political agenda. On the day I stepped into the Boudin office, I met men like Gold, Potash, Albertson, and Selly—men whose names I had been hearing for years and who were in a sense demigods to me. I was a middle-class Jewish boy from Brooklyn who believed in trade unions, but who had never met a trade unionist before. I felt that I was participating in a struggle to make the world, in some small way, a better place. Even as I worked in a law library and especially when I got into court I could, metaphorically but clearly, hear the sound of "you can't scare me / I'm sticking to the Union / till the day I die" in the street outside the walls.

It was indeed a new world. *McCullough v. Maryland,* the *Dartmouth College* case, *Fletcher v. Peck,* the great decisions of the early nineteenth century that created the basic framework of our federal system and which I had studied at length in law school at Michigan, disappeared forever from my mind. To take their place were the cases that transformed the American legal structure with the coming of the New Deal: First came *Schechter Poultry Corp. v. United States,* and *Carter v. Carter Coal Com-*

pany, holding Roosevelt's New Deal legislation a violation of the rights of property, and then (gloriously) *NLRB v. Jones and Laughlin Steel Company,* holding the National Labor Relations Act valid, and *United States v. Darby,* upholding the Wage and Hour Law.

And in the field of First Amendment rights, a host of new concepts suddenly arose: *Thornhill v. Alabama, Thomas v. Collins, West Virginia v. Barnett,* and *Hague v. CIO,* which proclaimed in unmistakable tones the rights of free speech, press, and assembly. All of this was new: new to me and new to the country. And it was new to the legal profession as well. A brief look into some significant statistics will demonstrate how the profession changed.

The *Federal Digest,* used when I worked at the Boudin office, was published between 1938 and 1940. It purported to digest all reported federal cases "from 1754 to date." It had no classification for labor law, and cases relating to labor unions or collective bargaining were to be found digested under the heading of "Master and Servant" or, sometimes, "Conspiracy." The next digest was published in 1970. It was the *Modern Federal Practice Digest* and it covered thirty years of litigation. It had a classification called "Labor Relations" that occupied approximately five thousand pages. The current digest (1992) covers twenty years and needs almost twenty-five hundred pages to cover the subject.

A similar growth can be shown in the development of the First Amendment law over the same period of time. The 1940 *Digest* devoted 7 pages to cases relating to freedom of speech and press. The 1970 index devotes 110 pages to this subject. The 1992 *Digest* has 115 pages listing cases of freedom of speech.

These statistics should not be regarded too literally. Style in digesting cases differs from edition to edition; so do size of type and similar factors; but the figures do provide an index of the changes that have occurred.

My view of the world I moved into in 1938 was somewhat romantic, but it was the way I felt, and this romanticism, if such it was, stuck throughout my legal career. Sometimes I was playing the role of Saint George slaying the Dragon, and sometimes the Dragon was slaying me, but it was always a struggle between social good and antisocial evil. The sense of exhilaration I felt in those first few months at the Boudin office lasted all of my life with only a few lapses. I felt that every case I won was a victory for socialism and every case I lost was a defeat for socialism. Did I get Frank Dutto off on a charge of unlawful picketing? The class struggle gained a small point. Did the Supreme Court decide against ACA in the Taft-Hartley case? The class struggle lost a big point.

Once Leonard and I together with Michael Hertzberg, an office associate, defended three real estate builders in Virginia charged with fraud. Our clients were very pleasant and intelligent men, and I enjoyed their company. One was convicted and two were acquitted. After an appeal and a few days of the customary postmortems the case was forgotten. It had no political implications and when it was over, it was over.

But Steven Nelson, ACA, Joni's case, the *Sabbatino* case are ever in my mind. Those cases are never over.

I cannot remember representing any client whose cause I didn't personally approve, and very few clients whom I personally disliked. I can't recall ever having done anything in my professional career or political career that I'm ashamed of (well, hardly ever). And I've broken very few of the rules I formed for myself. On the whole it has been a good life and if I had an opportunity to live it over again I'd make a few changes but not very many.

Yet it has been a profoundly sad experience as well. The great causes for which I've fought and to which I have devoted myself have almost all gone down to defeat—temporary defeat I like to think, but still defeat. The trade union movement is a shadow of its 1938 self, both in numbers and in spirit. We kept people out of jail during the era of the Great Fear of the fifties but only after thousands had been hurt, some of them very badly. The United States withdrew from the Vietnam War but not until almost sixty thousand Americans, and millions of Vietnamese, had been killed. The civil rights movement made great strides, but when I read the daily newspaper and observe the inner cities of our country, I see the rise of a new and virulent form of racism which in some respects seems worse than that of forty or fifty years ago.

On the world scene, the socialism that I had striven for has been, at least for the present, defeated. The few years after the collapse of socialism in Eastern Europe have presented an interesting paradox. While the rest of the world proclaimed socialism's failures, many of those who had presumably suffered most under communist rule seemed to prefer that rule to the free market alternative offered to them by capitalism. So in Russia, Poland, Hungary, and elsewhere, the CP, or former leaders of the CP, was chosen by large numbers (sometimes a majority) of the people voting in presumably democratic elections. Evidently the failure of socialism, flawed though it was, was not so evident to many who experienced it as it was to its critics.

It is too early to predict how all this will shake down in the next few years. Every month another learned expert predicts the end of history, or the end of the nation-state, or the end of civilization in the early twenty-first century. I would not dare to leap into such a maelstrom.

Of one thing I am sure. As Captain Jack Boyle says, in Sean O'Casey's *Juno and the Paycock,* "The world's in a state of chassis." What will come out of that chaos I cannot know.

I must keep in mind that I am a lawyer, skilled in my trade, but neither king nor prophet.

I have known intuitively since the beginning of my legal career that the law may advance, influence, or impede social change, but it cannot determine its direction. That function is performed by more powerful forces—economic, demographic, ecological, political—which may be influenced by but cannot be controlled by the law and perhaps cannot be controlled at all. This of course raises still another question. Can any structure of society—capitalist, socialist, fascist, or anything else, save civilization as we know it from destructive factors that may be inherent in the civilization mankind has created? Isaiah Berlin has called the twentieth century the most terrible century in Western history. There is no reason to believe that the twenty-first century will be any less self-destructive, and there is a point at which self-destruction becomes absolute.

I've come to the end of this volume and have no intention of taking on any of these questions, but they do trouble me and make it sometimes difficult for me to see the question of capitalism versus socialism as a decisive one when it is not at all clear that either system will save us.

If so, why carry on the struggle? Why not spend our lives in making as much money as we can in an honorable fashion and in spending our spare time lying on the beach, walking in the woods, or reading a good novel?

There is an old folk tale that tells of the frog and the scorpion. The latter, unable to swim but wishing to cross a river, asked a frog to carry him across. The frog at first refused, for fear that the scorpion would sting and kill him. "Why should I do that?" asked the scorpion—"If I kill you, we'll both drown." The frog, convinced, agreed and plunged into the water with the scorpion on its back. Halfway across, the scorpion stung the frog, and as both sank beneath the waters, the frog said, "Why in the world did you do that? Now we'll both drown." To which the scorpion responded, "It's my nature."

Poets write poetry; painters paint; musicians play music; dancers dance, and political activists carry on political activity because it is their nature. As Robert Browning said: "A man's reach must exceed his grasp, / or what's a heaven for?" My reach and that of my comrades is for socialism. We fall far short of grasping it, but we continue to reach for it because it is our nature to do so.

I can't explain why some will give up their lives on the barricades for the revolution and why others will betray their best friends to make a fast buck. We all have a system of values—as the scorpion said, we all have our nature, and we all live by it. I've lived by my values, and I don't think I could have done otherwise. Those values require me to try to achieve a better world, and that's what I've done.

There are a few things I can point to with some pride. The National Lawyers Guild is almost sixty years old, and I played some part in building it. I cannot think of more than a handful of national progressive organizations that have lived so long in this perilous world.

Together with Leonard Boudin, I created and built a law office that has a nationwide and richly deserved reputation for integrity and professional skill. While I cannot claim credit for its accomplishments over the past few years, I know that it is still devoted to my favorite client, Cuba.

Joni, Peter, and Mark have all grown up to be intelligent, honest, and decent human beings with sound political and social views. I can and do claim half credit, along with Marcia and Joanne, for that.

That's not too bad.

Index

Amendment privilege, asserting, 107, 108, 111, 113, 117–30; First Amendment rights, asserting, 114, 117–30; government employees, dismissal of, 100–101; McCarthyism, 109–16; Memphis, Tenn., 103–5, 108; motion picture industry, 100, 102, 117–18. *See also* House Committee on Un-American Activities (HUAC)

Congress of Industrial Organizations (CIO), 22, 23, 25, 47, 52, 99; AFL unions, raids by, 49; smaller unions, organization, 24; Taft-Hartley Act, impact of, 47–53, 99. *See also* American Communications Association (ACA)

Connor, Donald, 103–4
Coolidge, Calvin, 9
Cooper, Irving Ben, 308–20
Coplon, Judith, 159, 235
Cotton, Eugene, 26
Coutinho, Rosa, 285
Covington and Burling, 221
Cowart, John P., 264–65
Cox, Archibald, 228–29, 238
CPUSA (Communist Party of the United States of America). *See* Communist party
Crawford, John, 61
Crockett, George, 175, 176, 179–80, 182, 189
Cuba, 198–254, 286; act of state doctrine, defending claims in U.S. based on, 217–50; air routes to Western Europe, struggle to establish, 212; Bay of Pigs invasion, 212, 215; diplomatic relations with U.S., breaking of, 222; Eastern Airlines plane hijacked to, 221–25; and Helms-Burton bill, 253; litigation in U.S., 200–202, 205, 207–50; Miami, Fl., and, travel between, 203; nationalization of U.S. property, 213–18; socialist revolution, 198–218; Soviet Union, relationship with, 88–89; United Nations, delegation to (1960), 204–6; U.S. embargo against, 208–13; Western Union office in, 198
Cuomo, Mario, 320–21
Curtis, Jeanne, 207
Czechoslovakia, 86; World Federation of Trade Unions, Prague, 278–79

Daily Worker, 152
Daly, Mary, 147
Dames and Moore v. Regan, 326
Darwin, Charles, 5, 7, 8

Davis, John W., 9
Davis, Leon, 327–28
Dawley, Ed, 175, 178, 189
Dean, Arthur H., 211
Debs, Eugene, 8, 12
Delaney, Hubert, 187
Democratic centralism, 81
Democratic National Convention (1924), 8–9
Dennis, Eugene, 82
Dennis case (*U.S. v. Dennis*), 101–2, 144, 161–62
Dewey, Tom, 24, 66
Dickerson, Earl, 173, 187
Dimock, Edward, 220–22, 227, 235, 237
Dmitrov, George, 12–13
Doar, John, 267–68
Dohrn, Bernardine, 184–85, 186
Dolsen, Jim, 132
Dombrowski, Jim, 177
Dombrowski v. Pfister, 177
Donner, Frank, 137–38
Dooling, Edward, 311–13
Dorsen, Norman, 298
Douglas, William, 49, 52, 53, 54, 239, 240, 241, 242–43, 245, 293, 301, 309
Doyle, Walter F., 264
Dubinsky, David, 58, 59, 60, 63
Duclos, Jacques, 82
Durr, Clifford, 34, 175
Durr, Virginia, 36
Dutt, S. Palme, 16
Dutto, Frank, 24, 332

Eastland, James, 104–8
Edelstein, David, 236, 248, 303
Egan, Joseph L., 39–40
Einstein, Albert, 114
Ellsberg, Daniel, 282–83, 298–99
Embree, William Dean, 35
Emergency Civil Liberties Committee (ECLC), 145, 159, 299–300, 301n
Emerson, Thomas, 126, 127, 166, 169, 171–72, 173
Engels, Friedrich, 6
England. *See* Great Britain
Ernst, Morris, 169–71
Espionage, 75

Fabricant, Neil, 311
Falk, Richard, 309
Fargas, Tony, 304, 305–7

VICTOR RABINOWITZ is counsel to the New York law firm of Rabinowitz, Boudin, Standard, Krinsky, and Lieberman. He served as partner of that firm and its predecessors for fifty years. A 1934 graduate of the University of Michigan Law School, he was a member of the American Labor party at the time of its organization and was a founding member of the National Lawyers Guild, of which he was president from 1967 to 1970.